ATAN BURAGOHAIN AND HIS TIMES

ATAN BURAGOHAIN AND HIS TIMES:

A HISTORY OF ASSAM, FROM THE INVASION OF NAWAB MIR JUMLA IN 1662-63, TO THE TERMINATION OF ASSAM-MOGUL CONFLICTS IN 1682 COMPILED CHIEFLY FROM INDIGENOUS ASSAMESE SOURCES

COMPILER

SURYYA KUMAR BHUYAN

GYAN

Published by

GYAN

Gyan Publishing House
5, Ansari Road
Daryaganj, New Delhi-110002
Phone: 011-47034999, 9811692060
E-mail: books@gyanbooks.com

Distribution Network
gyanbooks.com
India, USA, Canada, UK, Australia

ISBN: 978-93-6920-158-7 (HB)

First Published, 1957

2nd Impression 2025

Printed at: Gyan Press, Delhi.

ATAN BURAGOHAIN AND HIS TIMES
Compiler: Suryya Kumar Bhuyan

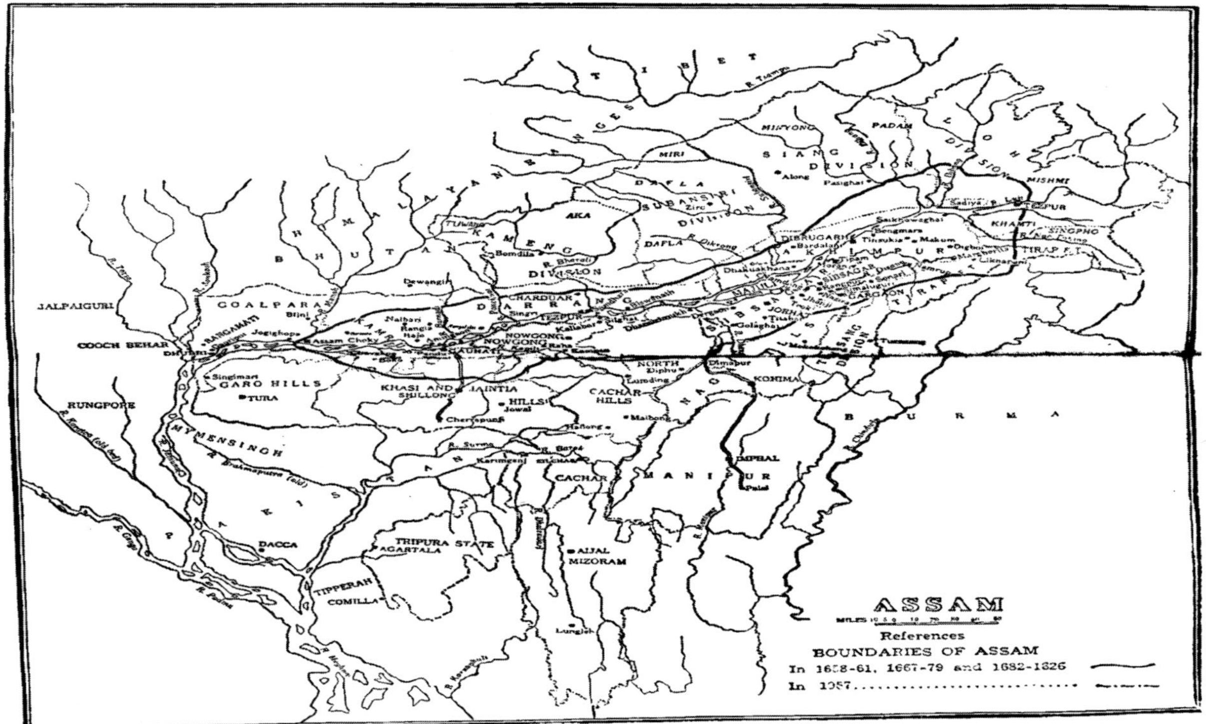

Dr. S. K. Bhuyan: *Atan Buragohain and His Times.*

ATAN BURAGOHAIN
AND HIS TIMES

A History of Assam, from the invasion of Nawab Mir Jumla in 1662-63, to the termination of Assam-Mogul conflicts in 1682. Compiled chiefly from indigenous Assamese sources.

BY

SURYYA KUMAR BHUYAN,

M.A., B.L. (CAL), PH.D. (LOND.), D.LIT. (LOND.),

Vice-Chancellor, Gauhati University.

LAWYER'S BOOK STALL

GAUHATI, ASSAM

TO

MY SECOND SON

SRIMAN BHAVANI KUMAR BHUYAN

WITH

AFFECTION AND LOVE

CONTENTS

APPENDICES

PREFACE

This book is named *Atan Buragohain and His Times* as the pivotal figure is Atan Buragohain who was prime minister of Assam from January 1662 to March 1679. The narrative continues up to the year 1682 when the Moguls were finally expelled from Gauhati, that event being a memorable sequel to the developments of the two preceding decades. Atan Buragohain's appointment as premier synchronised with the entrance of the Mogul forces into Assam early in 1662; and the conflict of 1682 witnessed the termination of the long-drawn hostilities between Assam and Mogul India. The intervening years represent a fateful period in the history of Assam, both on account of its external dangers and its internal disruptions.

To bring the narrative to its logical conclusion, I have inserted a few pages describing the reign of King Gadadhar Singha, 1681-96, which witnessed the restoration of sanity in the counsels of the nobles and firmness in the administration of the country in contrast to the anarchy and confusion of the previous decade.

The book may be regarded as a companion volume and a sequel to my earlier work *Lachit Barphukan and His Times*. Assam's success in the resistance against the imperialistic menace of the Moguls during the years 1667 and 1671 was due to the efficient organisation and leadership of Lachit Barphukan the general and Atan Buragohain the premier, and the details have been narrated in Chapters IV and V of the present volume. The Buragohain played a conspicuous part in the events of the period following the death of Lachit Barphukan in 1671, and they constitute the subject-matter of the remaining portion of this book.

I was first drawn to the personality of Atan Buragohain about the year 1925 when, as the result of a close study of the unpublished Buranjis or chronicles, I realised his greatness as a patriot and a statesman. I then resolved to unravel the story of his uncommon leadership to Assam and the world, so that my brother mortals may draw inspiration from the example of his lofty character and disinterested endeavour. During the winter of 1930, I spoke on Atan Buragohain at a meeting of the Assamese Students' Literary Club at the Cotton College, Gauhati. It was followed by the publication of two articles in *The Cottonian* for March and September 1931. I proceeded with the work during intervals of business; and I could compile the concluding chapters and give the finishing touches only during the last few years. Each chapter has now been revised and enlarged in the light of materials discovered meanwhile. The book has thus been my constant and agreeable companion for the last twenty-five years, and I have turned to it again and again whenever I obtained some relief from my other avocations and preoccupations.

Atan Buragohain's name is now completely blotted out of human memory. This oblivion is primarily due to the sudden break in Assam's historical tradition brought about by political changes and upheavals. Purnananda Buragohain, the last great prime minister of Assam, who died in 1817, is remembered because the sons and grandsons of his contemporaries lived till the other day. His name is associated with the invasion of the Burmese whose oppressions have passed into the common parlance of the Assamese people. Atan Buragohain's name had long ceased to form part of the traditional lore of the Assamese, their normal life being completely shattered by the Moamaria and Burmese disturbances which preceded the British occupation of the country. The catastrophes of the early nineteenth century which produced so much misery and suffering are still remembered and talked about to the comparative forgetfulness of all that had gone before. The chronicles which enshrine the deeds of Atan Buragohain are scarcely read, for their study is no longer a matter of political or social necessity; and even when read, the grandeur of Atan Buragohain's character cannot easily be grasped by the general run of readers. Historical resurrection presupposes an atmosphere of universal awakenment and solicitude, and canonisation takes place centuries after the passing away of a saint.

Besides, no Buranji contains a connected account of Atan Buragohain, and his actions are interspersed in narratives of political events and transactions. The uninitiated reader is hardly capable of weaving out a complete texture with the help of the disjointed patches. The task of bringing together the scattered details, and synthesising them into a coherent whole has been an extremely arduous and laborious one. We have cheerfully undergone this labour being animated by a desire to place before the world the eternal inspiration emanating from the example of a noble and patriotic soul whom posterity should not let willingly die.

A narration of the outer layer of facts was for long the characteristic of history-writing. But our old Assamese Buranjis are profusely rich in intimate revelations. The Persian chroniclers of Mogul India were not generally aware of the reactions and repercussions produced in Assam by the contact of the two powers. But the Buranjis give us accurate glimpses of what the Assamese thought and did, and how the Mogul commanders and officers behaved in this land at a distance from the vigilant gaze of their masters. Plutarch, the prince of biographers, has said,—"Often a man's most brilliant actions prove nothing as to his true character, while some trifling incident, some casual remark or jest, will throw more light upon the manner of man he was than the bloodiest battle, the greatest array of armies, or the most important siege."* Such incidents and utterances, illuminating the inside story of the times, have been reproduced in this book as abundantly as possible.

We have, in the course of the narratives, inserted the original utterances as they first came out of the lips of the

* Life of Alexander, in *Plutarch's Lives,* translated by Aubrey Stewart and George Long. George Bell and Sons, London, 1924, Volume III, p. 300.

speakers, because they possess an archaic and realistic flavour, and because they enable us to obtain an insight into the political ideology of the people of old Assam. We have paid special attention to the observations and reflections of Atan Buragohain as they are found in the description of crucial situations, in his chronicle and in his letters: they are all collected and inserted in a separate chapter in the body of the book and in two Appendices. The Buragohain's utterances speak more about his character and personality than all the narratives put together.

From the description of the events readers will obtain a faithful picture of the inner working of the Assamese mind, showing how it reacted to surrounding circumstances, specially in critical situations both in public and individual affairs. As the Assamese people have been subjected to indelible influences and changes in the modern times, an intimate study of the past is the only way by which we can get at the core of the inherent Assamese spirit and temper. We are confident, as time advances, and as we recede further and further from our original pattern and prototype, the progressive utility of the record as preserved in this book will be appreciated more and more.

As the name and fame of Atan Buragohain is practically unknown to the average reader, I have, for his convenience, inserted a brief introductory sketch in Chapter I, and a fuller sketch in Appendix B of this book. A perusal of these two pieces will be helpful in following the trend of the historical narratives. The background has been set forth in Chapter II; and the abstract of the chronicle of Atan Buragohain, inserted in Chapter XVIII, will provide the nucleus of information about the history of Ahom rule in Assam up to the reign of King Pratap Singha, 1603-41. The last two chapters will serve as a recapitulation of the major events and salient features of the period.

The materials used in the compilation of this volume are drawn from the existing literature on the subject of Assam-Mogul conflicts as far as they could be collected in an out-of-the-way place like Gauhati. The principal sources of information are however the Assamese Buranjis, a complete list of which forms part of the Bibliography.

The events of the period under review represent a series of crises in the national life of the Assamese people. There were crises also in the lives of individuals. What was done in the storm and stress of the times can now be reflected upon with poise and dispassion. The results of such scrutiny constitute the abiding lessons of history; and in this light the actors of past events appear before us as perennial contemporaries, inasmuch as the problems which our predecessors faced and which we are facing day-to-day and which our posterity will face, are the same in spirit and substance. In the delineation of the events I have adhered closely to the principles of humanism and truth by humbly following in the footsteps of master historians who have made their performances an instrument of liberal education and 'a sovereign corrective of human nature'.

"Almost all historians", says Polybius, "have eulogised the lessons of history as the truest education and training for political life, and the study of others' vicissitudes as the most effective, or indeed the only, school in which the right spirit for enduring the changes of fortune can be acquired"† How far I have succeeded in my attempt to follow this ideal is for readers alone to judge.

My thanks are due to Dr. Hariprasanna Das, M.A., Ph.D., for giving a final shape to the map of Assam inserted in the book; to Sriman Purnendu Kumar Medhi, B.Sc., for doing the preliminary work in the matter; and to Dr. Maheswar Neog, M.A., D.Phil. and Sriman Hemrath Barman, for helping me in the revision of the proofs and the compilation of the Index. I am thankful to Shri G. Srinivasachari, Proprietor, G. S. Press, Madras, for his unfailing courtesy,

† Arnold J. Toynbee, *Greek Historical Thought*, Mentor Book, 1952, p. 43.

promptness and neat workmanship in the matter of printing the book.

In conclusion, I take the opportunity of expressing my gratefulness to my old student Sriman Bichitra Narayan Datta-Barua for very kindly undertaking the publication of this book from the Lawyer's Book Stall, Gauhati, of which he is the proprietor. The handicaps and difficulties experienced by authors in Assam with regard to the publication of their books are well known; and Sriman Datta-Barua has earned their blessings by coming to their rescue by his patriotic zeal to bring their works to light.

Company Bagan Road,
Gauhati, Assam.
The 15th September, 1957.

S. K. BHUYAN

CONTEMPORARY APPRECIATION OF ATAN BURAGOHAIN

From a conversation between the Mogul general Raja Ram Singha of Amber and his envoy Punditrai. Venue: Ram Singha's camp at Hajo.

Ram Singha: Well, Punditrai, during your visit to the Barphukan's camp you must have formed some idea of the Ahom ministers and commanders. Please tell me what you have seen and what you think of them.

Punditrai: The Barpatra Gohain, the Bargohain, the Barphukan and the Bargohain-Phukan have all impressed me as wonderfully capable commanders presenting a rare combination of handsomeness, accomplishment, valour and wisdom. As to the Buragohain [Atan], he is young in years, fair and attractive in features, sober and deep in intelligence, dexterous in all matters, and he rivals all others in the soundness of his counsels.

Ram Singha: It is really wonderful that a man can be so intelligent when he is so young.

Punditrai: The Buragohain is also an arch-diplomat.

Ram Singha: Who will be able to cope with such a minister when he comes to years? Pride should be the heritage of the land where such a counsellor has taken his birth.

—*MS. Assam Buranji No. 15.*

ATAN BURAGOHAIN AND HIS TIMES

CHAPTER I

INTRODUCTION

You all did see that on the Lupercal
I thrice presented him a kingly crown,
Which he did thrice refuse: was this ambition?
Yet Brutus says he was ambitious:
And sure, he is an honourable man.

—*Julius Caesar*, III-2.

Atan Buragohain Rajmantri Dangaria was the prime minister of Assam for more than seventeen years, January 1662 to March 1679. During this period Assam passed through a series of crises in the shape of foreign invasions and internal disruptions; and Atan Buragohain conducted the affairs with rare foresight, probity and judgment, and disinterested patriotism. The versatile qualities of the Buragohain and the proofs that he gave of his lofty and noble ideals made him the darling of the people; and kings, potentates and the populace were united in showering tokens of their admiration and respect on this man of their country's destiny. Twice the crown was offered to him which he did twice refuse, saying,—"It does not behove a minister to become a monarch. Kingship should go to the scion of a royal family, and saintship to the descendant of a saint."

The counsels that he gave to his colleagues, whether in the king's chamber or in the war camps, reveal his deep political insight and his courage of conviction. They served as a brake to impetuosity and as an incentive to spirited action; and they afforded a ready solution of the vexed problems of the state, and gave a new turn to the course of events.

His varied attainments included a mastery of the science of military engineering. The forts and ramparts of Gauhati, on both banks of the river Brahmaputra, were constructed under his supervision and direction. The Chintamani rampart, at a little distance from the capital Gargaon, was initiated, planned and constructed by the same Buragohain.

To the qualities of a consummate leader the Buragohain added the equipment of a trained historian as we know from the chronicle compiled by him. His observations interspersed in the narratives, and the eclecticism displayed in his emphasis on particular events illustrate his extensive knowledge of precedents, his political ideology and his human approach to history, while the numerous references to other sources of information bear evidence of his erudition and scholarship.

The unique personality and leadership of Atan Buragohain elicited the admiration of his Mogul adversaries. Punditrai, the envoy of the Mogul general Raja Ram Singha of Amber, after a visit to the Assam camp, thus reported to his master his impression of Atan Buragohain,—"The Buragohain is young in years, fair and handsome in features, sober and deep in intelligence, and dexterous in all matters, and he excels all others in the soundness of his counsels. The Buragohain is also an arch-diplomat." On this the Rajput Raja observed,— "Who will be able to cope with such a minister when he comes to years? Pride should be the heritage of the land where such a counsellor has taken his birth."

Atan Buragohain figures in the contemporary records of Assam under various names and appellations. He is usually called Bahgaria Buragohain on account of the association of his family with the village Bahgara situated in the vicinity of Gargaon. In the diplomatic epistles of the period he is generally styled as Rukma Buragohain, and in some places as Arjun Buragohain, as his gallantry in the battlefield was supposed to have equalled that of Rukma-vir and Arjun, the two great heroes of the Mahabharata war.[1] He was also known as Gidamukali Buragohain, owing probably to some peculiar characteristic of one of his bodily organs. The Ahom title of Chao-phrang Thao-rup-rung, literally, the grand old man of the country, was conferred on him by

1. It was customary to confer a new name upon a noble or official in recognition of his distinguished services to the state. Gendhela Barbarua was known as Kirtichandra; Haranath Bhitarual Phukan as Abhimanyu; and Gendhela Barphukan as Pratap-ballabh.

Dihingia Raja as a reward for his services in placing that prince on the throne of Assam. The grateful monarch observed on this occasion,—"The nobles and the populace recognised the Buragohain as their king, but he refused to accept the honour. On the other hand, in consultation with his colleagues he appointed me as king. In appreciation of his noble sacrifice, and as a token of my esteem and regard for him, I should give him some presents and confer on him some distinctions."[2]

Atan was born in a patrician Ahom family, that of the Buragohains, whose ancestor had accompanied Chao-Sukapha in his conquest of Assam in 1228 A.D. Very little is known about Atan's upbringing and education. The pillars of the government, known collectively as the Patra-Mantri, consisted of the Buragohain, the Bargohain, the Barpatra Gohain, the Barbarua and the Barphukan. These offices and other high appointments were the exclusive monopoly of the ancient Ahom families. Their youths were therefore given the necessary education and training to qualify them for positions of trust and responsibility, both civil and military. Learned Brahman Pundits were attached to the leading families who introduced the youths to the principles of Hindu polity and to the stories of the epics and the Puranas, and the extensive literature of didactic tales and narratives. This education was in addition to that imparted by the orthodox Ahom priests. In his chronicle and in his utterances Atan Buragohain gives evidence of his knowledge of the traditional lore of the Hindus. He brings out the differences in the condition of the people in the Satya-yuga and the Treta-yuga; and in an appeal to the monarch he speaks of the primordial days when Mahadeva swallowed poison to deliver the gods from the clutches of fear.

Atan first makes his appearance as Khanikar Barua, head of the official guild of artisans, sculptors, image-makers and wood-carvers, and other allied professions. This appointment presupposes a great deal of proficiency and skill

2. MS. Assam Buranji No. 5.

in crafts and technical pursuits which provided the foundation of Atan's subsequent employment in the construction of forts and ramparts. He was appointed as Buragohain in January 1662 during the first phase of Nawab Mir Jumla's invasion of Assam, and he continued in that exalted office till his incarceration at the hands of Laluk Barphukan in March 1679. His prime ministership thus spread over the reigns of eight successive sovereigns of Assam,—Jayadhwaj Singha, Chakradhwaj Singha, Udayaditya Singha, Ramadhwaj Singha, Suhung Samaguria Raja, Gobar Tungkhungia Raja, Arjun Dihingia Raja, and Sudoipha Parvatia Raja.

Atan Buragohain's manifold qualities of leadership come out best in the resistance he organised against the army of Nawab Mir Jumla during their occupation of the Ahom capital, and in the adroitness and vigour with which he fulfilled the first instalment of the treaty terms which secured the prompt retirement of the Mogul forces. Atan Buragohain was also responsible for the speedy rehabilitation of the country after the ravages of Mir Jumala's invasion, and for the successful execution of the plans for the recovery of Lower Assam from the Moguls. The latter tried again to take possession of this territory, but the united efforts of the Ahom forces led by Lachit Barphukan and Atan Buragohain resulted in the infliction of a severe defeat upon the Moguls in the ever-memorable naval battle of Saraighat.

The expulsion of the Moguls from Lower Assam was followed by vigilant preparedness on the part of the Ahoms to counteract any eventual renewal of hostilities. The best generals and leaders being absent at Gauhati, the Ahom capital in Upper Assam had to be manned by inferior talents who took advantage of the situation and exploited the opportunity for self-aggrandisement; and intrigues and machinations became the order of the day. Atan Buragohain succeeded in suppressing the disturbances, but the effect was not permanent, and he himself fell a victim to the inordinate lust for power on the part of Laluk Barphukan who had planned to become Raja of Assam with the help of Sultan Azamtara, Subedar of Bengal. During this "era of weak and imbecile princes, and of unscrupulous and ambitious ministers", Atan Buragohain kept his head high above low politics and sordid self-interest, and never allowed himself to be swayed by any consideration except the honour and well-being of his motherland.

No contemporary portrait of Atan Buragohain is available as yet. We have however the following pen-picture in the account of the leading Ahom commanders compiled by an erudite astrologer attached to their camp during the hostilities with Raja Ram Singha,— "The Buragohain is tall in stature, and his strides resemble the steps of a goose. His face is broad, and he has two moles on the forehead. He is ruddy in complexion. He wears a buffalo-coloured *gati*, and carries a big sword in his hand."[3]

3. S. K. Bhuyan, *Lachit Barphukan and His Times*, pp. 39-44, where pen-pictures of the leading Ahom commanders of Saraighat are reproduced as they are recorded in MS. Assam Buranji No. 12. *Gati* is a cloth tightly wrapped round the upper part of the body with the two ends made into a knot round the waist.

CHAPTER II

HISTORICAL BACKGROUND

During the period under review, Assam was governed by the Ahoms who had originally come from the Shan principality of Mogaung in Upper Burma. By the year 1228 A.D., they conquered the regions lying on the banks of the two rivers Dihing and Dikhow, and gradually consolidated their power over the original inhabitants by a policy of appeasement and conciliation, and force and stratagem when necessary. Sukapha, under whose leadership the Ahoms first established their domination in Assam, was a gallant warrior and a farsighted statesman, and the dynasty which he founded continued in power for six hundred years, up to the twenties of the nineteenth century.[4]

The reign of Suhungmung Dihingia Raja, 1497-1539, witnessed a marked expansion of the Ahom territories and also of their sphere of influence. The Chutias living round Sadiya, the Bara-Bhuyans of the north bank of the Brahmaputra, and the Kacharis of the Dhansiri valley were brought under submission, and the territories of the first two were annexed to the Ahom dominions, while the land of the Kacharis was placed under Ahom vassalage. The invading armies of the Padshah of Gaur were repulsed with heavy losses; and Ahom generals overran the territories up to the river Karatoya. The Padshah of Gaur sued for peace by offering two princesses to the Ahom king; the Raja of Kamata who had been ousted by the Gaur Padshah was reinstalled on his ancestral throne which was however on the verge of extinction; and Biswa Singha who had made himself master of a small territory, taking advantage of the decadence of Kamata, sought the support of the Ahom monarch.[5]

4. S. K. Bhuyan, *Anglo-Assamese Relations,* Introduction, for an account of Ahom rule in Assam and of the Ahom system of administration, relations with the hill tribes, etc.

5. A short account of the Ahom kings from Khunlung-Khunlai is embodied in the abstract of Atan Buragohain's chronicle inserted in Chapter XVIII, *poste.*

As occupation of the subdued territories was not the object of the Ahom expedition, the victorious generals returned to their country after having allowed the rulers of Gaur, Kamata and Cooch Behar to continue in the exercise of their power and authority. This expedition of the generals of Dihingia Raja was regarded ever afterwards as a great landmark, and Ahom kings looked upon the Karatoya river as the ultimate western limit of their dominions. This view had also the support of Hindu traditions as embodied in the *Kalika-purana* and *Yoginitantra*. Expediency however dictated the contraction of the Ahom dominions, and the consequent fixation of the western boundary at the Manaha river which falls into the Brahmaputra opposite Goalpara.

Cooch Behar grew into a first-rate power during the reign of King Naranarayan, son of Biswa Singha. The kingdom of Kamata was dismembered in the meantime, and the ruler of Cooch Behar now assumed the title of *Kamata-adhipati*, or the lord of Kamata. In the company of his warrior-brother Sukladhwaj, King Naranarayan proceeded on a career of conquest, and compelled the Ahom king Khora Raja, 1552-1603, and the other neighbouring rulers and chieftains to sue for peace. Several Ahom youths of noble families were sent to the Koch capital as hostages, but they were allowed to return soon afterwards.

To accommodate the demands of his refractory nephew Raghudeb, son of Sukladhwaj, King Naranarayan divided his kingdom into two parts. The western portion, extending from the Mahananda to the Sonkosh river, was retained by Naranarayan for himself and his descendants; while the eastern portion, from the Sonkosh to the Barnadi river, was allotted to Raghudeb on a tributary basis. The western portion came to be known as Cooch Behar, or Bar-dewan, and the eastern part as Koch Hajo, or Saru-dewan. The latter comprised the territory from Dhubri to Gauhati, and was also called Kamrup, Western Assam and Lower Assam. The two divisions underwent occasional changes in their limits and dimensions.

Raghudeb was not satisfied with his uncle's plan; he assumed independence, and entered into hostilities with Lakshminarayan, the son and successor of Naranarayan on the throne of Cooch Behar. Parikshit, the son of Raghudeb, continued the feud with Lakshminarayan who appealed to the Mogul emperor Akbar, and then to Jahangir, for mediation in the disputes. Lakshminarayan was allowed to continue as a vassal ruler under the Moguls, and the territories of Parikshit were annexed to the Mogul dominions. Parikshit's brother Balinarayan, also known as Dharmanarayan, was installed by the Ahoms as the tributary Raja of Darrang which lies on the north bank to the east of the Barnadi river, opposite Gauhati. It also included the strip of country between Kaliabar and Gauhati on the south bank. The territories of the Ahoms and the Moguls thus became contiguous, the meeting point being at a distance of a mile to the east of Gauhati.[6]

The close proximity of the two powerful and expanding states led to inevitable clashes and conflicts, and they continued in an intermittent manner for sixty-eight years, 1614-1682. Resistance of the imperialistic designs of the Moguls, and the repercussions produced in the internal situation of Assam owing to its preoccupation in organising this resistance, became the dominant feature of Assam politics during the eventful years of this period.

The Moguls had their eye on the precious *agar* wood and elephants which abounded in the forests of Darrang. A number of Mogul traders were once collecting *agar* wood for the imperial stores in an unauthorised manner. The Ahoms plundered their boats, killed two merchants, and captured their companions. The Subedar of Bengal despatched a powerful army under Raja Satrajit who instituted retaliatory measures against the Ahoms. This was in 1614.

6. For further information about the early history of Cooch Behar, see S. K. Bhuyan's *Anglo-Assamese Relations*, pp. 259-65; Sir Edward Gait's *Kuch kings of Kamarupa*, J.A.S.B., Part I, No. I, 1893; and Khan Chaudhury Amanatullah Ahmed's *History of Cooch Behar*, in Bengali, Vol. I, 1936.

Two years later, the Mogul forces under Sayid Abu Bakar were defeated in a battle near the Bharari river with heavy losses. It was followed by a protracted warfare for twenty-three years with varying fortunes on both sides. The war was conducted under the guidance of the Ahom monarch Swargadeo Pratap Singha, 1603-1641, the actual command being wielded by Momai-tamuli Barbarua of the Ahom Lukhurakhun clan. The conflicts brought the Assamese in close touch with the Moguls, and they remodelled their war-strategy and diplomacy to fully exploit the weaknesses and peculiarities of their Mogul opponents.

In the year 1639, a treaty was concluded fixing the Barnadi river and the highway Asurar Ali, near Gauhati, as the boundary between Assam and Mogul India. The plenipotentiaries engaged in drawing up the terms were Momai-tamuli Barbarua and Nawab Allah Yar Khan representing the Ahoms and the Moguls respectively. Kamrup was thereafter ruled by Mogul Fauzadars with their headquarters at Gauhati. Momai-tamuli Barbarua remained at the garrison of Kajali, to the east of Gauhati, for twelve years, to protect the frontier from the aggressions of the Moguls. The imperial outpost on the Assam frontier was situated at Rangamati lying on the road between Dhubri and Bilasipara.

The treaty of 1639 became the pivotal point in the subsequent relations of the two states. The Moguls insisted on the maintenance of the stipulated limits, while the Ahoms aimed constantly at repudiating them. Reverses did not unnerve the Ahoms; on the other hand, they served in stimulating them to more spirited and vigorous endeavours. Their foreign policy was thus set forth by Kirtichandra Barbarua, an eminent official of the reign of King Lakshmi Singha,— "When a king becomes subjected to the monarch of another country, diplomatic measures should be adopted so that the conqueror may return to his own kingdom. On his retirement, the subdued prince should remain in preparedness with his army, and when opportunities present themselves for action he should strike promptly and reinstate himself in his lost suzerain power."[7] An Ahom king had declared, —"Even when the sun is once eclipsed, does it not make its appearance again?" Another king had said in the same vein, —"Because the Moguls have discomfited us once, does it follow that we should make no attempt to throw off this position of subordination to them?"[8]

Acting in consonance with this policy of speedy recuperation, King Jayadhwaj Singha took advantage of the fratricidal conflict at Delhi following the illness of Emperor Shah Jahan, expelled the Mogul forces from Gauhati, and recovered possession of Lower Assam. It was followed by Nawab Mir Jumla's invasion of Assam in 1662-63, which resulted in the re-annexation of Kamrup to the Mogul territories. The Ahoms recovered their lost dominion in 1667 which continued in their possession till 1679 when Laluk Barphukhan, the Ahom governor of Gauhati, treacherously surrendered it to the Moguls. It was finally recovered by the Ahoms in 1682, and the Manaha river continued to be the western boundary of Assam till the termination of their rule in 1822.

The northern limits of Assam were the mountains inhabited by the Bhutanese, Akas, Duflas and Abors. The eastern boundaries were the hills peopled by the Mishmis and Singphos, and they extended to the borders of China. On the south were the Garo, Khasi and Naga Hills. The kingdom was protected from the incursions of the tribes by grant of blackmail, and by other conciliatory measures, and by the application of force when occasion demanded. Outposts were established to guard the frontiers at all important strategic points, and wardens were appointed from the families of the three Gohains. The population of the kingdom could be estimated at about two million and a half, and the number of effectives was about the tenth part of that number. During the war with Raja Ram Singha, the infantry

7. MS. Assam Buranji No. 23.

8. MS. Assam Buranji Nos. 3 and 8.

and cavalry under the command of the Ahoms at Gauhati were reported to have totalled about one lac.[9]

The capital of the kingdom was at Gargaon, literally, the city of ramparts. It was situated on the Dikhow river, and lay at a distance of about 235 miles to the east of Gauhati. The splendour and magnificence of Gargaon caused amazement to visitors from Mogul India. The distance from Gauhati to Gargaon could be covered by boat in about seven days, and by swift riders in four days. The capital was shifted to Rangpur, near the town of Sibsagar, in the beginning of the eighteenth century. The importance of Gargaon was however not bedimmed by the ascendancy of Rangpur; and associated as it was with the best days of the Ahoms, Gargaon figured in the imagination of the people and in their unsophisticated parlance as the real metropolis of the country.

The Ahoms ruled the country with justice and firmness, and critical observers have attributed the long continuance of their domination to some intrinsic worth in their system of administration. Achievements in the battlefield or in the sphere of diplomacy were the criterion for the conferment of high offices and honours. Delinquency and treachery were ruthlessly suppressed, and delay in taking appropriate measures was always discountenanced. There was a general practice to preserve the details of all important events,—wars and embassies, appointments and dismissals, rewards and punishments, and even the proceedings of important trials.

9. In a letter to Raja Prananarayan of Cooch Behar, written in September 1663, King Jayadhwaj Singha of Assam defined the boundaries of the kingdom of Swarga-narayanadeva, grandfather of Sukapha, as follows: "Kherh [China] on the east, Gauda [Bengal] on the west, Rukhanga [Arracan] on the south, and Lalung [Bhutan and Tibet] on the north. Landha [Jayantia] was given to the first son, Assam to the second, and Rukhanga to his nephew." Swarganarayanadeva was perhaps Sam-lung-pha who is credited, in the Shan chronicles, as the first Shan conqueror of Assam. He is described in King Jayadhwaj Singha's letter as an elephant-statured emperor, *Gajasambhava raja-adhiraja*. See the chapter on Atan Buragohain as a historian, *poste*, and also S. K. Bhuyan's *Deodhai Asam Buranji*, Introduction, pp. xxxi-xxxv.

Historiographers were appointed by the state for this purpose; and some nobles also compiled chronicles of their own accord to supplement and elucidate the official versions. These chronicles, known in Assam as Buranjis, were periodically revised and brought up to date. The precedents recorded in the Buranjis served as an incentive to patriotic deeds and a deterrent to ignoble acts. All political measures and reforms were aimed at securing the prosperity and happiness of the people, the immunity of the kingdom from foreign domination and the maintenance of the stability of the government. The demands of art and literature, and the encouragement of learning and piety were not ignored by the Ahom rulers. They refrained from interfering with the social and religious life of the people, and discouraged innovations tending to disrupt the harmony and solidarity of the state.

The security of the kingdom being the primary concern of the government, foreigners were admitted with great caution; but those who came to stay here for good with the avowed purpose of serving the country in some capacity were given every facility to do so. All outsiders were called *Bangals,* but this term was generally restricted to those who entertained hostile intentions against Assam and its people, or whose association was detrimental to the interest of the country. Assam was usually described as *sonar saphura*, or a casket of gold, the lustre of which must always be kept shining. In the diplomatic parlance of the seventeenth century Assam was occasionally given the figurative appellation of *Uday-giri*, or the hill of the rising sun, which was in consonance with the older name *Pragjyotishpur,* while the epithet *Asta-giri* was used with reference to Mogul India which lay to the west of Assam. One king had declared that death was preferable to a life of subordination to foreigners. A general exclaimed at the sight of the vast array of hostile forces and equipments,—"It is a tragedy that my country has to face this dire calamity during my Phukanship! How will my king be saved? How will my people be saved? How will my posterity be saved?" This undivided attention to political affairs on the part of the nobles and leaders was the keynote of the efficiency of the administrative system of the Ahoms.

The king was the supreme head of the state, and all efforts were made to create round him a halo of divinity in order to make his person and his commands inviolable and sacred. All honours, offices and war-measures emanated from him. Sentences of death, involving the shedding of blood, had to be passed by the king. He could dismiss the highest officials, and could even order their execution. Misuse of his prerogatives was sure to bring the monarch to obloquy and disgrace resulting in the penalties of deposal or death. The king was regarded as the fountain of all energy and vigour, and victories in the battlefields, diplomatic successes and singular achievements were attributed, by convention, to his inspiration and prowess. The imbecility of a monarch was therefore eternally despised, and his speedy elimination was sought for by all sincere patriots. The epithet of the Ahom kings was *Swargadeo,* or the god of heaven, as their patriarchial ancestor, was believed, in Shan traditions, to have been born of Lengdon or Indra. *Swarga-maharaja* or *Swarga-raja* was the name usually applied by the Moguls to the Ahom monarchs.

The instructions given to an Ahom king, by his customary advisers, at the time of his coronation, as recorded below, gives us an idea of the primary duties and functions which he was expected to discharge: "Cherish and protect your subjects as your own children. Employ secret emissaries to ascertain their condition. Bring capital criminals to condign punishment. Reverence the virtuous. Nourish kine and Brahmans. Prefer four-eared advice to six-eared counsel, that is, do not act upon counsel taken jointly with two other advisers, but rely upon the united deliberations of a single counsellor with yourself. Avoid the evil consequences of delaying the execution of a measure the expediency of which is determined on, by acting promptly upon your decisions at all times. Let not the demands of equity be superseded by the dictates of injustice. The law of the land, the institutions of seats, and the rights and usages of families are to be upheld. All cabals are to be suppressed. The purse-proud worldling is to be humiliated. Old, obedient and faithful servants are to be rewarded. Select from the predecessors of your line a model for imitation; follow his ways, and to that end apportion your time for the discharge of all your functions, as well as the enjoyment of your recreations, bearing in mind that a prince is ruined by trusting to the guidance of his own propensities. Should you observe any one of us swerve from allegiance, let us be punished; even though we should be found to compass your harm were it only in thought. Exterminate traitors root and branch. Let not might prevail over right; and let the strong who oppress the weak be punished. Let thieves and robbers be diligently searched out: thus shall your country be benefited by increased security. Closet the experienced sages of your court, and learn from them lessons of morality, justice and good government. Examine the institutes of law used by the predecessors of your race, and learn thence the punishment awarded to bad kings."[9a]

The highest functionaries of the state constituted themselves into a cabinet, and were known as the Patra-Mantri. It consisted of the Buragohain, the Bargohain, the Barpatra Gohain, the Barbarua and the Barphukan. These offices were conferred only on the descendants of the commanders and followers of Sukapha in his conquest of Assam. The succession to the throne was decided upon by the three Gohains; they could even sanction the deposal and execution of a monarch. The Buragohain usually acted as the prime minister, and conducted the affairs of the government during interregnums. The Barbarua was the head of the executive and the judiciary. It was his duty to secure the proper execution of the orders of the king and the Gohains. The Barbarua adjudicated on the appeals received from the lower courts. Important original cases were tried by himself, and sentences on such occasions were usually passed by him with the con-

9a. Bengal Secret Consultations, July 14, 1826, Nos. 2-5, containing David Scott's Historical Notes, forwarded in his letter of April 15, 1826, addressed to George Swinton, Secretary to the Government of Fort William in Bengal.

currence of the monarch and the three Gohains. The Barphukan was the governor of Lower Assam; his headquarters were at Gauhati, and during its occupation by the Moguls the viceregal capital was shifted to Kaliabar in the upper rapids of the Brahmaputra. The office of the Barphukan was a very important one as he had to conduct the relations with Bengal, Bhutan and the other adjacent territories. The office of Rajmantri was generally held by the Buragohain, and sometimes by the Bargohain; and there were also instances when nobles outside the Patra-Mantri were appointed to this office by virtue of their influence upon the sovereign, manipulated by ingratiation or by coercion.

The Phukans were next in rank to the Patra-Mantri, and each was in charge of a department of the state; *e.g.*, the Naobaicha Phukan was in charge of the boatmen; the Naosalia Phukan looked after the boat-builders and the dockyards; the Paniphukan was the admiral in charge of the Lower Assam flotilla; and the Choladhara Phukan conducted the commercial and foreign affairs of the country. The Rajkhowas were governors of districts; and they administered justice and supervised the working of the *paik* system in their respective areas. The Baruas were the heads of minor departments, or deputies of those departments which had a Phukan at the head. The junior officers were the Hazarikas, or commanders of 1,000 men; Saikias, of 100; and Baras, of 20 men.

These were several families of the kings and nobles, generally named after the places where they lived, or where their lands and establishments were situated. Each such clan was known as a *phoid,* which was different from a *khel,* the latter name being applied to an official guild organised on occupational or territorial lines on the basis of the services it rendered to the state. There were seven princely families,—Charingia, Namrupia, Tipamia, Tungkhungia, Dihingia, Samaguria and Parvatia. In the absence of a regular nomination to the throne, any unmutilated prince from the seven houses could be made a monarch if the three Gohains so decided. There were eight clans of the Buragohain family, and sixteen of the Bargohain family. The family of the Barpatra Gohain was descended from a prince of royal blood, though in the latter period the office was held by several nobles of non-royal origin. The Barbaruas and the Barphukans were generally selected from the four families of the Lahans, Sandikois, Duaras and Dihingias. These two offices were also held by members of the Lanmakharu Chetia and Lukhurakhun clans. The latter came to prominence with the appointment of Momai-tamuli as Barbarua, a great general and statesman of the reign of King Pratap Singha. Several members of the Lukhurakhun *phoid* occupied high offices during the period 1657-81,—Debera Barbarua; and Momai-tamuli's four sons, Lachit Barphukan, Laluk Barphukan, Marangi Barbarua, and Bhatdhara Phukan; and Momai-tamuli's brother Baduli Phukan. Lachit commanded the Ahom forces in the recovery of Gauhati, and in the expulsion of the Moguls from Assam in 1671. The actions of Lachit Barphukan's brothers were however hostile to the interests of the Ahom government. The princes and the nobles were generally known under their toponomous appellations, such as, Dihingia Raja, Parvatia Raja, Samaguria Raja, Tungkhungiya Raja, Kuoigayan Buragohain, Bahgaria Buragohain, Madurial Bargohain, Kenduguria Barpatra Gohain, and Gargayan Sandikoi Barphukan.

All able-bodied adult male subjects were registered as *paiks*, and they had to perform specific services for the state. There were however exceptions to this liability in the case of persons of high status, and those who followed specialised professions. The *paiks* were grouped into *gots* or squads of four men, and one man in a squad had to be engaged in public duties, and sometimes two, and sometimes three; or the number in the *got* was reduced to three. A levy of the first men was known as *mul*, of the second as *dowal*, and of the third as *tewal*. The men or man left behind in the village had to look after the cultivation and other domestic concerns of their comrades of the *got* who were absent from home on state duty. In return for their services, the *paiks* enjoyed about three acres of land on a revenue-free tenure. The *paiks* were grouped together according to the nature of their duties; and each such division was known as a *khel*. The guild of musketeers was known as *Hiloidari Khel;* of gunpowder makers and workers at the arsenals and armouries as *Khargharia Khel;* of arrow-makers as *Dhenu-chocha Khel;* of arrow-shooters as *Dhenu-dharia Khel;* of honey-suppliers as *Mau-jogania Khel;* of the men of Dimaruguri as *Dimaruguria Khel,* and so on. The lands and establishments allotted to the prince, princesses, queens and queen-mothers were known as *mels,* such as, Tipamia Mel, allotted to the Tipam Raja; Charingia Mel, to the Charing Raja; Gabharu Mel, to the unmarried princesses; Parvatia Mel, to the Parvatia queen; and Enaigharia Mel, to the queen-mother. The officers of the *khels* and the *mels* were assigned a certain percentage of the *paiks* under their management as their remuneration and pay, because there was no cash salary attached to any office.

Besides the Phukans, Rajkhowas and Baruas. there were the important functionaries,—the Katakis and the Kakatis. The Katakis served as envoys to foreign courts, and also as intermediaries between the king and his principal nobles and officers. As the duties were of a highly important and responsible character, trained Brahmans were generally appointed at Katakis from amongst a number of selected families. The Kakatis were employed in keeping accounts, in maintaining registers of assessments and *paiks,* and as scribes and reporters. Kakatis were attached to every *khel* and *mel* for carrying out the secretarial work connected with its management. The heads of the *khels,* together with their respective quotas of officers and men were mobilised in times of war. This practice enabled the villagers to pursue their vocations in an undisturbed manner in times of peace, and the government to command the services of a large army in emergencies; it also did away with the expenses of maintaining an enormous standing army at the capital and the strategic centres. But its evil effect was seen when a Kheldar diverted his men's loyalty to promote his own selfish designs, as such an attempt would be usually effective owing to the existence of old obligations and ties between the two parties.

The Assamese *paik* system was like a vast tutorial organisation in an educational institution. The conduct and work of every individual *paik* was watched and checked by his immediate supervisor, the Bara, who had only twenty men in his charge at a time. Delinquency and truancy would be easily detected and punished; and if the Bara could not deal with the matter himself it would be taken up by his master the Saikia. The senior officers could punish a *paik* by slicing off his nose and ears, and cutting his hair. The Ahoms recognised that energy and efficiency on the part of the officers and their men are of greater moment than equipments and provisions, as the utility of such materials lay in their proper management by living men. The Buragohain of the reign of King Rudra Singha once remarked,—"In the reign of Jayadhwaj Singha there was an abundance of provisions and men, and still he acquired the title of 'Bhagania Raja', or the deserting king; arms and ammunitions, materials and supplies are torpid and impotent; the followers and subordinates of the king are symbols of life and animation; they alone can infuse into the immobile war-provisions a dynamic force." This emphasis on an individual's rectitude of public conduct was a marked feature of the administrative system of the Ahoms.

The kings of the period were all disciples of Vaisnava Gosains. Owing to the preachings of the great reformers Srimanta Sankardeva, Madhabdeva and Damodardeva, and the pious exertions of their apostles and followers, Vaisnavism had gained a firm footing in Assam since the beginning of the sixteenth century. The first Ahom monarch to take formal initiation in Vaisnavism was however Jayadhwaj Singha, 1648-63, though Hindu influence had crept into the Ahom court since the reign of Sudangpha Bamuni-kowanr, 1397-1407. The influence of Vaisnavism can be seen from the use of the articles of Vaisnava worship in the oath-taking ceremonies of Ahom nobles and commanders; and there are references to the use of the books *Ratnavali* and *Dasam* on critical occasions, the two classics being venerated by the Vaisnavas of Assam. Co-discipleship of the same Gosain served as a cementing bond of friendship and mutual protection. The Assamese monks were held in very high esteem, and any attempt to tamper with their authority and influence was vehemently opposed. Reports of the devotional spirit of the Vaisnavas of Assam had reached far-off Rajputana; and the mother and consort of Raja Ram Singha of Amber communicated to him their warning that the sanctity of Assam where *Nama-kirtana*, or religious music and recital, was universal should not be violated. The Ahom kings and nobles, in spite of their acceptance of Hinduism, did not ignore their orthodox Ahom priests, the Deodhais. Mohans and Bailungs, who continued to minister to the spiritual needs of the Ahoms according to the traditions of the Shans. The Ahom language was gradually replaced by Assamese, the knowledge of the former being confined to the priests and a number of top-ranking Ahom officials.

The main stay of the people was agriculture; and the products of their fields satisfied the requirements of individuals and the state. All necessaries, including labour and materials, were obtained generally in exchange for paddy, and officers were paid by the services of the state *paiks* allotted to them. The peasants cultivated the lands themselves with the help of their sons and nephews; and as polygamy and joint-family system were in vogue the householder could command the services of a large number of capable hands belonging to his own family. The women assisted in the lighter side of the work, such as transplantation of paddy, weeding and harvesting; they also furnished the family with home-spun and home-woven garments. The gentry and the nobles employed bondsmen and slaves in the work of cultivation, and of the state *paiks* when they were holders of offices. Every Assamese gentleman, except the Brahmans and a few others, knew how to plough, and manual work was never looked upon with any odium or disgrace. Some monarchs, being overwhelmed by the besetting thorns of political intrigues, expressed a longing to return to their pastoral surroundings where they could earn their livelihood by means of ploughing in the field. The versatility of the Assamese caused an amazement to foreign visitors, and the Rajput general Ram Singha had to admit that he had not seen such specimens of versatility in any other part of India.

The practice of compiling Buranjis or chronicles reached its high-water-mark during this period. They are copious and prolific. We have different versions which agree on the basic trend of an event or circumstance, but vary in length regarding the details. The epistles exchanged between the Ahom kings and nobles and the foreign courts are carefully preserved, and inserted in their appropriate contexts. Besides the general chronicles dealing with all the events of a monarch's reign, we have monographs on isolated events and topics. There are monographs dealing with the Assam-Mogul conflicts, the tributes paid to Nawab Mir Jumla, the war with Raja Ram Singha, the fortifications of Assam, and Assam's relations with the frontier chiefs of Cachar and Jayantia. An old historian of Assam, bewildered at the mass of details, thus pointed out the difficulty of tracing and collating the events in a systematic order: "After due salutation at the lotus-feet of Sri-Krishna, which are drunk by the hearts of the righteous like so many honey-sucking bees, the origin and deeds of the monarchs sprung from the line of Indra [Ahom kings] are here described. O, learned ones, in the recital of the history of those kings who are credited with varied and brilliant achievements, one is not to be an object of laughter [if mistakes and discrepancies creep in], as the accounts exist in diverse places, and in their unification whose powers are not strained?".[10]

The Persian chronicles of the Mogul court, throwing light on the Assam-Mogul conflicts of the seventeenth century, are equally prolific. Besides the narration of the political transactions between Assam and Mogul India, the Persian chronicles give us a glimpse of the character of the inhabitants and resources of Assam. Mir Jumla's chronicler Shihabuddin Talish thus described the seclusion of Assam,--"No Indian king in former times ever conquered Assam. Even the intercourse of foreigners and the Assamese was very limited. They allow no stranger to enter their territories, and they prevent their own people from leaving their

10. Sanskrit preamble to MS. Assam Buranji No. 9.

country." Referring to the magnificence and adornment of the houses at the capital Gargaon, Shihabuddin wrote with regret,—Besides the palace, "there are other houses in Ghargaon, beautifully adorned, strong, very long and spacious, full of fine mats, which really must be seen. But alas, unless this kingdom be annexed to His Majesty's dominions, not even an infidel could see all these things without falling into the misfortunes into which we fell."[11]

We have, besides, several accounts of Assam left by European writers—Bernier, Tavernier, Manucci and Glanius, the last having personally visited Assam as a naval officer attached to the expedition of Nawab Mir Jumla.

"Assam", in the words of Manucci, "lies among mountains, and is a very fertile country, most luxuriant in food products and fruit, which are here found of various kinds such as we have in Europe—that is, pear, apples, peaches, grapes. With it as a base they could take Pegu, and through it enter into China."[12]

11. H. Blochmann, *Kuch Behar and Assam*, J.A.S.B., 1872, Part I, No. II, and Jadunath Sarkar, *Assam and the Ahoms in* 1660, J.B.O.R.S., 1915.

12. For sources of information about Assam, see the bibliographies appended to S. K. Bhuyan's *Anglo-Assamese Relations, Early British Relations with Assam. Lachit Barphukan and His Times, Ramani Gabharu*, and *Mir Jumlar Assam Akraman.*

CHAPTER III

MIR JUMLA'S INVASION OF ASSAM

By the treaty enacted in 1639 between the Moguls and the Ahoms, the western limits of Assam were fixed at the river Barnadi, falling into the Brahmaputra at the foot of the Manikarneswar Hill, on the north bank; and Asurar Ali, a road to the east of Gauhati, on the south bank. Thus the whole territory from Gauhati to the Manaha river, which falls into the Brahmaputra opposite Goalpara, passed into the hands of the Moguls. The Sarkar of Kamrup was thenceforward governed by Mogul Fauzadars from their headquarters at Gauhati.

Things went on smoothly up to the year 1657, when a deadly contest broke out among the sons of Emperor Shah Jahan. Sultan Shuja, Subedar of Bengal, left his charge to contest for the throne, having collected the whole Bengal corps and flotilla to oppose his brothers. The garrisons in the frontier districts of Bengal were thus emptied of the imperial detachments.

Taking advantage of this opportunity, Prananarayan, Raja of Cooch Behar under the vassalage of the Mogul emperor, assumed his independence, and his general Bhavanath Karji marched against the Mogul Fauzadar at Gauhati, and encamped at Hajo on the north bank of the Brahmaputra.

The Ahom monarch Jayadhwaj Singha was not slow in seizing the opportunity to regain his lost territory, and extend it to the age-old limits of the Karatoya river. He too despatched a powerful army to capture Gauhati. The Mogul Fauzadar, Mir Lutfulla Shiraji, now hemmed in by the two forces, effected his escape to Jahangirnagar or Dacca without offering any resistance.

After the expulsion of the Moguls, Chengmun Rajasahur Barphukan and Pikchai Chetia remained in charge of Gauhati. The Ahoms also fell upon and defeated the Cooch Behar army in a decisive encounter near Hajo, and gradually removed from Kamrup all vestiges of Mogul and Koch authority. The whole territory from the Barnadi to the Sonkosh river which had once been the dominion of the Koch prince Parikshit now fell into the hands of the Ahoms. As Kamrup was a perpetual source of misunderstanding between the Moguls and the Ahoms, its entire population, excepting the heads of Vaisnava monasteries and temple servitors, were transferred to and settled in Eastern Assam. Kamrup became in consequence a deserted wilderness for a year and a half.

Not content with this success, the Ahom army, under the command of Baduli Phukan, Lapeti Phukan and Phulbarua Phukan, overran the territory up to Hatichola in Karaibari at a distance of five days' march from Dacca, and brought to Assam a large number of Mogul subjects as captives. In the words of the Muslim historian of Bengal, "The Assamese raised the standard of daring and insurrection, and without contest, they conquered the province of Kamrup, swept it with the broom of plunder, carried by force to their own country all and everything, including the movable and immovable effects of the people, pulled down the edifices, left no trace of fertility, and reduced the whole province to one plain level ground."[13]

After Aurangzeb had consolidated his position on the throne of Delhi, he appointed Mir Jumla to the governorship of Bengal with express orders to punish the Raja of Arracan for harbouring the emperor's surviving brother and rival Sultan Shuja. The operations against Arracan had to be postponed for unavoidable reasons, and the veteran general decided to employ his soldiers in an expedition against Cooch Behar and Assam where Mogul prestige had been undermined. Aurangzeb ratified this modification of the original proposal with the hope that an expedition under an able soldier like Mir Jumla could not but culminate in victory; and that in any case for some time at least he would get rid of a powerful and dangerous friend like Mir Jumla who

13. *Riyazu-s-Salatin*, by Ghulan Hussain Salim, translated into English by A. Salam, A.S.B., 1904, p. 223.

could, with his extensive resources, assert his independence as Sultan of Bengal. As Assam was then well-known all over Mogul India as a land of witchcraft and pestilential diseases, the old nerves of Mir Jumla, thought the emperor, were sure to be affected by its climate.

Mir Jumla, on the other hand, had evinced proof of his personal attachment to Aurangzeb by the facilities which he had offered to the prince in the subjugation of the independent state of Golconda of which Mir Jumla was the Vizier, and subsequently by the gift of eighteen maunds of diamond which helped Aurangzeb in successfully conducting the war of succession against his brothers. But the veteran soldier and diplomat had hitherto achieved nothing to perpetuate the obligations of the Mogul state to his family the benefits of which could be enjoyed in perpetuity by his children and descendants. He was all-powerful in Golconda and the Carnatic, and his services were at one time sought simultaneously by the rulers of Persia, Delhi and Bijapur. The pomp and magnificence of his palace and seraglio were rivalled only by those of Agra and Delhi, and they caused the amazement and wonder of the European visitors of those days. He naturally sought this opportunity to utilise his experience and leadership, and wield the imperial arms to crush the enemies on the eastern frontier. Mir Jumla who had risen to power and eminence from the position of an attendant of an oil merchant of Ispahan was by nature an ambitious dreamer, and he hoped, after the subjugation of Assam, to carry his victorious arms to the mountainous steppes of China.

Accordingly, on the first November 1661, Mir Jumla started from Khizirpur near Dacca with an army consisting of 12,000 horse and 30,000 foot, and a fleet of 323 war-boats mostly manned by Portuguese and Dutch sailors. Cooch Behar was occupied on the 18th December without any opposition. The negotiations with Jayadhwaj Singha for the restoration of the territory from Gauhati to Hatichola having failed, the general entered Assam early in January 1662. The fort of Manaha commanded by Baduli Phukan was occupied without striking a blow, and so were the Ahom garrisons at Saraighat, Pandu, Gauhati and Kajali. The king's maternal uncle Lecham Buragohain was then commanded to take the field in person, but he died on reaching the Sonai river. Atan was then appointed Buragohain and despatched against the invaders.

The easy success of the imperialists was mainly due to the defection of the Ahom commanders at the appointment of Manthir Bezdoloi Bharali Barua, a Kayastha store-keeper, as commander of the Lower Assam flotilla, with the rank of Parvatia Phukan. The Ahom general in charge of the war operations was Chengmun Barphukan. Langichang Bargohain and Kenduguria Barpatra Gohain were placed in charge of the northern division. The next stronghold to which the Ahoms now retired was the fort of Samdhara, situated on the Bhomoraguri Hill to the east of Tezpur, beyond which the Moguls had scarcely penetrated on previous occasions.

Atan Buragohain was now placed at the head of a division of the Ahom army, and he concentrated his forces on both banks of the Brahmaputra to offer an effective resistance to the invaders. Fighting went on for some time without any decisive result. The fort of Simalugarh on the south bank opposite Samdhara was an impregnable one made so by nature and by man. It was situated on the top of a high hill with the Brahmaputra on the north, and was surrounded on the other sides by a moat bristling with bamboo *panjies* or spikes. The fort was now besieged by the enemy who had pitched their camp in its immediate vicinity. The Ahoms opened their heavy artillery on the beleaguring force, and the enemy's batteries could not make any impression on the massive walls of the fort. But unfortunately the Ahoms fell short of provisions and men due to an error of judgment on the part of Langichang Bargohain, commander of the northern division, who failed to despatch the reinforcement solicited by the besieged garrison. Diler Khan Daudzai, an Afghan commander of Mir Jumla, marched desperately at the head of his stalwarts, stormed the fort and broke open the entrance. Mir Jumla himself entered the fort on February 26, 1662, and expressed his wonder at the fortifications of the place.[14]

This reverse at the last resort of the Ahoms was looked upon as a dire calamity. The Buragohain retreated to Gargaon, while Mir Jumla now marched to Kaliabar which he easily occupied, though some resistance was offered by the Ahoms at the fort of Potakalang on the Diju river, but without any success. The gallantry displayed by the Ahom commander Lecham Hatibarua caused the amazement of the Moguls. The Moguls then proceeded to Lakhau at the confluence of the Dihing and the Brahmaputra where they left their fleet. The general marched through Gajpur and Tiromani to Gargaon, the Ahom capital, and occupied it on the 17th March. The Ahom king had in the meantime retired to Chorai-khorong in Namrup on the outskirts of the Naga Hills. The Buragohain's father and a few Baruas remained with the king in his retreat. The king and his consorts described their present plight as a retribution for the devastation of Kamrup a few years earlier.

The task of defending the country against the imperialists now fell upon the shoulders of Atan Buragohain. He was assisted by Baghchowal Khamun Rajmantri Naobaicha Phukan, and the latter's brother Chengmun Phukan. The Ahoms inaugurated a campaign of harassing the invaders. The methods which they adopted for this purpose were unprecedented in the history of warfare. The Mogul army stayed for some time at Gargaon, Mathurapur, Gajpur, Dergoan and other outposts which they had established soon after their occupation of the capital. But the two essentials of victory, allegiance and domination, were untasted by the so-called victors. The whole period of the Moguls' stay in Upper Assam, from March 1662 to January 1663, was a terrible chapter of suffering and misery. In the words of Shiha-

14. S. K. Bhuyan, *Mir Jumlar Assam Akraman,* Appendix II, which contains a short life-sketch of the Mogul commander Diler Khan Daudzai.

buddin Talish, the Mogul historian who accompanied the expedition,—"A similar case had never happened before in the history of Delhi. Here were 12,000 horse and numerous infantry locked in for six months, prevented by the rains from continuing operations, yet scarcely attacked by the enemies that surrounded them. Nor did during this time provisions arrive. The Amirs turned that eyes longingly to Delhi and the soldiers yearned for their wives and children."[15]

The formidable weapon in the armoury of the Assamese was surprise attacks, specially made at night. Their army, divided into batches, lay in wait at all possible points covering the paths and retreats of the invaders. At times when the Moguls remained care-free in their camps perfectly satisfied that no enemy was lurking near by, the Ahoms would fall upon them and carry off their men, till it became widely known that no Mogul soldier could stray out of the camp at night without being shot at. The quarters from where the Ahoms came or directed their operations could neither be guessed or spotted. The captives were tortured by a peculiar appliance made of iron and looking like a Turkist padlock, and then made to go back to their camp lamenting and screaming, and ultimately dying in a desperate state.[16]

At the same time the Ahoms organised measures of retaliation by open encounter. They wrested Gajpur back from the invaders after having killed its Thanadar; and the Charing Raja, afterwards Swargadeo Chakradhwaj Singha, almost succeeded in reoccupying the capital where the Moguls had established their emporium and arsenal. The Buragohain personally engaged the Moguls at Murkata. Within a few weeks of the Moguls' occupation of the capital the Ahoms recovered the whole country except Mathurapur and Gargaon. The Ahom king maintained a line of communication with his nobles and issued instructions for the conduct of the war.

15. H. Blochmann, *Kuch Behar and Assam*, J.A.S.B., 1872, p. 88.
16. Manucci, *Storia do Mogor*, tr. Irvine, Vol. II, p. 99.

The second method of harassment was the cutting off of the supplies of the enemy, as a result of which Gargaon, Mathurapur and Lakhau were reduced to the verge of starvation. The Mogul commissariat could not function satisfactorily on account of the interception by the Assamese of their food-stuffs during transit from one place to another. In the words of Manucci,—"The Rajah blocked all supplies, setting fire to everything, and posting soldiers so that no food outside could find its way into the town." The shortage of provisions was aggravated by a famine which broke out at Dacca. The invaders had to pay a fabulous price for the local stuff, specially coarse red *sali* rice. The horses in the stables of the Moguls became emaciated due to underfeeding, and they could not perform the work for which they were maintained. In the words of Mir Jumla's chronicler,—"The soldiers were forced to eat the flesh of horses and camels and anything of that sort they could find."

To add to all this misery the monsoon broke out with torrential showers, submerging under water all those places which had appeared dry and elevated before. The Mogul camps became detached from one another on account of the intervening floods. An epidemic of fever swept over the Mogul headquarters at Mathurapur which carried off a large number of their army. Diler Khan's detachment consisting originally of 1,500 horse was now reduced to less than 500. Mir Jumla's nephew perished by the fever, and his remains were interred at Mathurapur. In August 1662, the Nawab was compelled to shift his headquarters to Gargaon. But the fate of the Mogul army did not improve by this change. Fever and dysentery broke out at Gargaon which were as bad as their precursors at the previous camp. The Moguls were now counting the day when they would be able to go back to the salubrious climate of Northern India.

The position of the Moguls in Assam was a very unenviable one. Mir Jumla had nominally conquered the districts round Gargaon. But he could never dream of establishing a government there. He had issued rupees and pice struck at his mint in the Assam camp with the name of Emperor

Aurangzeb, but this was in the beginning of the campaign. The Assamese resented the idea of foreign domination, and whenever possible, they deserted their homes situated within the Mogul enclosures. The imperialists occasionally manoeuvred demonstrations in their favour by the Assamese, but they were done under compulsion, and they failed to produce the desired moral effect. By the end of 1662, the Moguls were anxious for return if they could do so with some semblance of prestige and honour. "But", as it has been said by Manucci, "if it had been easy to get into, it was very difficult to get out of the country, owing to the floods, also the ambushes laid by the natives. It looked as if Mir Jumla would be quite used up there, and had it not been that by his prudence he was able to manoeuvre so skilfully, his retreat would have been a disaster.[17]

The Ahoms, too, on their part, could not bear the sight of a foreign army occupying the capital. The Moguls were no doubt harassed, but they were not totally crushed and expelled. Had the Assamese waited for a few months more and continued their guerrilla operations as before they would have certainly witnessed the compulsory retirement of the enemy from their land. But a recognised principle of Ahom diplomacy was the adoption of means to secure the withdrawal of a hostile army from the country by promises of indemnity and tribute, to be followed by open defiance of the treaty terms when they could mobilise sufficient power to recover their lost possessions; and thus a treaty, entered into under sufferance and pressure of circumstances, was not unusually considered as a mere scrap of paper when opportunities for repudiation offered themselves, due to some reverses in the enemy's position or to their own increased internal efficiency. As the Assam-Mogul relations stood at the end of the year 1662, no price was, therefore, too exorbitant to the Ahoms if by it they could see their country emptied of the foreigners.

17. Manucci, *Storia do Mogor*, tr. Irvine, Vol. II, p. 101.

Atan Buragohain himself realised that the continuance of hostilities would be disastrous to the Ahoms. He paid a short visit to the king's retreat at Chorai-khorong, and deliberated with the monarch on the grave situation of the country. King Jayadhwaj Singha lamented over his misfortune, saying—"God, the great dispenser, has deprived me of everything." To this Atan Buragohain replied,—"His Majesty should not lose his heart because of what has happened. Success and failure, victory and defeat constitute a normal phenomenon of life. When God becomes propitious, it will be possible to destroy our enemies under the inspiration of His Majesty's prowess." The king then asked the Buragohain to procure the withdrawal of the Mogul forces from Assam by offering them an appropriate indemnity and tribute; otherwise, he declared, he would retire to Nara, the ancient homeland of the Ahoms.

The Ahoms accordingly proposed peace terms to the Mogul general, and offered a daughter of the king to the imperial harem with a dowry worthy of the reputed wealth of the country. They also promised to pay a war-indemnity of three lacs of rupees and ninety elephants, to be delivered in three quarterly instalments within the course of a year. The annual tribute was to consist of twenty elephants. A redistribution of the boundaries was also made, according to which the Moguls were to obtain possession of the country from the Manaha to the Bharari.

The peace offers made by the Ahoms created some surprise in the Mogul camp as coming at a most unexpected juncture, when the invaders were themselves waiting for an opportunity to make an honourable retreat. The terms were readily accepted, and they were incorporated in a formal treaty enacted on the 9th Magh, 1584 *saka*, or the 23rd January 1663, the venue of the agreement being Ghilajharighat, Tipam, and the signatories on behalf of the Ahom government being the Buragohain, the Bargohain, the Barpatra Gohain and the Rajmantri Phukan. When Mir Jumla issued orders for return, the raptures of the Mogul army knew no bounds: and the Mogul chronicler has devoted two full pages to the description of the transport and joy which swept over the camp on the receipt of the long-awaited announcement.

The princess who was offered to the imperial harem was Ramani Gabharu, called also Nangchen Gabharu. She was the daughter of King Jayadhwaj Singha, through his junior consort Pakhari Gabharu who in turn was the daughter of the famous general and statesman Momai-tamuli Barbarua. Ramani was subsequently married to Sultan Mahammad Azam, the third son of Emperor Aurangzeb, on May 2, 1668, with a dowry of 1,80,000 rupees, when her name was changed to Rahmat Banu Begum. Prince Azam is usually styled Ali-jah, and often Azamtara.[18]

The Mogul army left Dergaon on the 25th January 1663. The hostages which the Moguls were to retain till the full payment of the indemnity included Ramrai, the nephew of the Buragohain; Dhala Gohain, son of the Bargohain; Langi Gohain, son of the Barpatra Gohain; and Maupia, son of Rajasahur Rajmantri Phukan. During the progress of the Mogul army from Lakhau to Kajali, "the men lived on water and the animals on grass". The general halted at Gauhati from February 9 to 22, and settled some financial matters. Rashid Khan, after great reluctance, for which he was reprimanded by Emperor Aurangzeb, accepted the Fauzadarship of Gauhati; and Muhammad Beg was appointed Thanadar of Kajali under Rashid Khan. The first few instalments of the war-indemnity were delivered by the Ahoms with promptness and strict conformity to the terms of the treaty for which they received the unstinted admiration of the Moguls.

The general's health had failed in the meantime owing to the privations of the Assam expedition. While in Upper Assam he had suffered several times from pain in the chest and asthmatic paroxysms, and had occasional fainting fits. On reaching Baritola in Karaibari the Nawab's condition became worse. His physicians made contradictory diagnosis of the

18. S. K. Bhuyan, *Ramani Gabharu,* life-sketch of Princess Ramani Gabharu, or Rahmat Banu, consort of Sultan Azamtara, Gauhati, 1951.

disease; and it was commonly believed in the Mogul camp that Mir Jumla's sickness was the result of witchcraft practised upon him by the Raja of Assam. The Nawab passed away on Wednesday, March 30, 1663, on board the barge, four miles above Khizirpur, a fortnight after the anniversary of his occupation of Gargaon. Thus the Assam expedition saw the end of the man, who from a humble station in life had risen to be the most powerful subject in the India of his days, who was a king except in name, the proud possessor of the world-famed Kohinoor, which the owner presented to Emperor Shah Jahan as the only gift befitting the aesthetic eminence of the conceiver and builder of the Taj.

The impression which the Assam expedition of Mir Jumla made upon the Moguls has been very graphically described by the Muhammadan historian, Muhammad Kazim, the author of the *Alamgirnama,*—"The Rajas of Assam have never bowed the head of submission and obedience, nor have they paid tributes or revenue to the most powerful monarch, but they have curbed the ambition and checked the conquests of the most victorious princes of Hindustan. The solution of a war against them has baffled the penetration of heroes who have been styled conquerors of the world".[19]

The minister whose tact and statesmanship practically compelled the Moguls to enter into the terms of peace and obtained their easy retirement from the country was no other than Atan Buragohain. He organised the operations against the enemy, and considering the straits to which the Moguls were subjected we cannot say that the Buragohain did not succeed. "Go on killing your enemy, but do not get yourself killed" was obviously the motto of the Buragohain. The guerrilla methods which the Assamese adopted, combined with the cutting off of the enemy's provisions, were the factors which contributed to the discomfiture and impatience of the Mogul army followed by their withdrawal from the invaded territory.

19. H. Vansittart, *A description of Assam from the Alamgirnama* Asiatick Researches, Vol. II, 1807, pp. 179-80.

There were defections in the Ahom camp. Baduli Phukan and his brother Maupia had gone over to the camp of the Moguls. Baduli had even promised to seize the persons of the Ahom king and his principal nobles, and hand them over to the enemy, in return for which he was made Deka-Raja or governor of the country between Gargaon and Namrup. Maupia, under the direction of Baduli, fought at Mekurikhowa at the head of a Mogul force against his own countrymen, where he lost heavily. Baduli's plans to capture the king were however frustrated by the timely intervention of Atan Buragohain. On the conclusion of peace, Baduli could not be persuaded to remain in Assam. He went with his family to Bengal in the company of the Mogul forces, and was given a perganah near Dacca with an income of three thousand rupees per year. He became the medium of the treasonable correspondence which some recalcitrant Ahom official carried on afterwards with the Nawab of Dacca. Another noble, Manthir Bharali Barua, the Bijdili Phukan of the Persian chronicles, followed the treacherous example of Baduli, but he was executed on the detection of his felony.

CHAPTER IV

GAUHATI WRESTED BACK FROM THE MOGULS

The relations between the Ahoms and the Moguls during the years immediately following the departure of Nawab Mir Jumla constitute a glorious chapter in the annals of Assam, inasmuch as the Assamese brought their diplomacy, martial ardour and sense of prestige to the highest pitch of efficiency and organisation.

By the treaty of Ghilajharighat, the Ahoms ceded to the Moguls the territories extending from the Bharari river on the east to the river Manas on the west, and Darrang, Gauhati and Kamrup thereby became part of the Mogul empire. The Assamese had to pay a war-indemnity of rupees three lacs and ninety elephants, and an annual tribute of twenty elephants. To ensure the fulfilment of the terms of the treaty, the sons of the four principal nobles of Assam had to remain as hostages at the court of the Mogul Fauzadar of Gauhati. Besides, two Ukils and one Barmudoi or merchant had to remain attached to the Fauzadar's establishment to assist him in the conduct of his political and commercial relations with Assam.

But, before the lapse of five years, the Ahoms succeeded in recapturing their lost territories by inflicting on the Moguls a crushing defeat, and expelling them altogether from their strongholds in Gauhati and Kamrup. The Moguls under Nawab Mir Jumla had devastated Assam, and its administration had been dislocated to a great extent. The success achieved by the Assamese so soon after this dire catastrophe bespeaks of their grim determination to restore the honour of their country by marshalling all the resources at their disposal. Where states without stamina would have collapsed under the burden of this mighty calamity, the Assamese raised their head once again and successfully challenged the enormous fighting equipment of the Timurids.

The Assamese conducted their rehabilitatory measures on a very subtle and secret basis. The first requirement was the revival of Assam's man-power, so that the working of the government, and of the economic and social life of the people could be restored to its former equilibrium. The corporate guilds, generally known as Khels, were depleted owing to the flight of the people during Mir Jumla's invasion. The prime minister Atan Buragohain Dangaria himself scoured the country from one end to the other, and persuaded the fugitives who had taken shelter in the outlying hills and forests to return to Assam. Most of these repatriated fugitives were settled in the villages round Kaliabar. Their quick return to normal life required a great deal of vigilance and helpfulness on the part of the Buragohain and his subordinate officials.

The morale of the people had been greatly undermined during Mir Jumla's invasion. Most of them had become panicky, or the opportunists entertained secret sympathy with the powerful invaders. In fact, Assamese reverses were attributed to the delinquency and treachery of a number of top-ranking nobles. For successful implementation of the measures of recuperation, the ultimate object of which was the resumption of hostilities with the Moguls, the king tried to bring all offenders to book, so that the recurrence of remissness in the performance of duties, or any treacherous inclination would be unknown in the Assamese camp.

As regards the payment of the war-indemnity, the Assamese had paid a substantial portion during the last few weeks of Mir Jumla's stay in Assam, and they continued to pay the balance in instalments. They tried to impress upon the Moguls that they were making a serious effort to deliver the remaining portion, and if there was any delay they attributed it to the difficulty of catching elephants during the rains, and of collecting money in a country which had been ravaged by the Moguls themselves. The Ahoms were extremely polite but firm in explaining the delays; and when arguments were weak, they pointed out to the presence of the hostages at the Mogul Fauzadar's court, saying,—"Is it possible on our part to desist from payment wilfully, having our four sons living in your place?"[20]

When the Moguls were engaged in insisting on the prompt delivery of the indemnity, the Assamese were preparing secretly to launch an attack upon the Moguls at Gauhati. Supplies were ensured by conducting the cultivation of crops on an intensive scale. The army was remodelled to attain the highest degree of efficiency. Guns and swords were cast in the smithies established within the palace enclosures; and the king personally supervised the training of the soldiers, and conducted their final manoeuvres and parades.

The Ahoms carried on secret negotiations with the Rajas and chieftains of the neighbouring territories, and made a common cause with them for co-operation in the event of renewed hostilities with the Moguls. The Ahoms even took into consideration the discomfiture of the Moguls at the hands of Shivaji prior to the siege of Purandar in 1665.

But a successful campaign requires an exciting provocation to stir the minds of the combatants with a feeling of the justness of their cause. This provocation was furnished by the extremely indecorous and humiliating requests made by the two successive Mogul Fauzadars, Rashid Khan and Firoz Khan, for being furnished with a number of pretty damsels from Assam. The infuriated monarch Swargadeo Chakradhwaj Singha could no longer tolerate the rising tempo of Mogul effrontery. The Moguls were attacked and expelled from Gauhati with very severe losses both in men and materials. Thirteen days later, Atan Buragohain Dangaria wrote to Nawab Shaista Khan, Subedar of Bengal,—"His Majesty the Swarga-Maharaja of Assam came to know that Syed Piroz Khan was a good man, and we also came to the same conclusion. We were then told that Syed Piroz Nawab had made a request for furnishing him some virgins from this place. Having heard this the Swargadeo was seized with indignation and wrath, and ordered an attack on Gauhati. Now, if you are desirous of establishing friendly relations with us, please

20. MS. Assam Buranji No. 41

send for that purpose Ukils and epistles. If you have no such desire, well, it is your look-out. What shall I say more? You are all-knowing yourself."[21]

Let us now take up the chronological enumeration of the events of the period. Nawab Mir Jumla had left Gauhati towards the end of February 1663. Rashid Khan was appointed Fauzadar of Gauhati, and he accepted the office after a great deal of hesitation for which he was rebuked by Emperor Aurangzeb.

The Ahom monarch Swargadeo Jayadhwaj Singha became impatient at his long stay in the camp at his retreat in Namrup. He now proceeded towards the capital, and fixed his headquarters at Bakata at a distance of some five miles from Gargaon.

The first act after the king's return was the despatch of Atan Buragohain to different parts of the country and gather the fugitive subjects. The king then instructed his father-in-law Khamun Rajmantri Phukan to punish all those who had proved unfaithful during the invasion of Mir Jumla. A number of leading Ahom nobles were punished accordingly; some were chained with iron fetters, some whipped, while others were removed from office. Barukial Langi Bargohain who had failed to send reinforcements to the southern army was beaten by the king himself with the blunt edge of a sword.

The principal offender was of course Chengmun Barphukan, the brother of the Rajmantri Phukan, who had wilfully desisted from fight owing to the appointment of a non-Ahom official, Manthir Bharali Barua, as commander-in-chief of the Lower Assam army. The Barphukan had also helped the Moguls to penetrate into the Potakalang area by placing at their disposal a number of Assamese guides. Chengmun could easily foresee his doom, and he consequently averted it by self-immolation.

King Jayadhwaj Singha's plan to punish the offenders was however checked by the Rajmantri Phukan. The total

21. MS. Assam Buranji No. 41.

collapse of the authority of the Swargadeo, followed by the king's flight to Namrup, and Mir Jumla's occupation of Gargaon, had reduced the morale of the Assamese people to its lowest ebb, and a considerable number, including some leading nobles, had wilfully neglected their duties, or had fraternised with the Moguls with the hope of obtaining preferments from the enemy. Crime no longer smells the odour of an offence if it be general and wide-spread, and Khamun Rajmantri Phukan advised the king as follows,—"When a few hairs of the head are grey it behoves one to pluck them out. But when the whole head is grey, who ever thinks of that painful operation?" The king accordingly suspended the penal measures as he thought that their enforcement would give a new impetus to discontent and discord.[22]

King Jayadhwaj Singha then tried to harness the co-operation of the neighbouring Rajas in an eventual conflict with the Moguls. Prananarayan, Raja of Cooch Behar, had taken shelter with the old king of Bhutan who as a pious Buddhist had refused to make over his royal fugitive to the conquering Moguls. While residing at Namrup, Jayadhwaj Singha had despatched emissaries to Prananarayan enquiring of his present condition. The Raja managed to return to his capital after having heavily bribed its Mogul Fauzadar Nawab Isfandiyar Khan. The Raja sent a letter to King Jayadhwaj Singha to which the latter replied as follows,—"My soldiers had fought at Samdhara for seven days. As in your case, my own men went over to the side of the enemy, and made it possible for them to enter into the fortifications of Samdhara. My army was dispersed in the subsequent engagements, and the Moguls occupied my capital Gargaon. Fighting continued in many places, and the Moguls were on the point of retreat. But our inveterate enemy Baduli went over to the Moguls and induced them to return. Having seen no other way I took shelter in the hills. I then arranged the withdrawal of the Mogul army from Assam in the interest of

22. H. C. Goswami, *Purani Assam Buranji*, K.A.S., p. 129.

the cows and the Brahmans as well as of the people of my country."[23]

To this Raja Prananarayan sent a reassuring reply comparing himself to Arjuna, and the Ahom king to Sri-Krishna, and adding,—"I lost my kingdom, and so you lost yours. As we did not harbour evil intentions towards each other both of us have now regained our kingdom. You should not feel distressed at having temporarily lost your dominion, as Ramchandra, Suratha and Yudhisthira could not escape similar calamities. But their prestige has not been affected as they reacquired their territories by dint of their own exertions. Our prestige will be lowered only if we remain inactive in the matter." Jayadhwaj Singha's reply bore an evidence of his unflagging self-confidence, for wrote he,—"Even when the sun is once eclipsed, does it not make its appearance again? We are making preparations according to our might, and I hope you are also doing the same. When fire and wind act in unison they take no time in burning the trees and the grasses. So we can also defeat and destroy the enemy if we establish an effective alliance between us two."[24]

The Raja of the principality of Jayantia had entertained a grievance against the Moguls for having conferred a tributary status on the contiguous territory of Dimarua on which he had himself claimed an overlordship for a long time. The Jayantia Raja Jasamatta Rai had sent two men to Assam during the invasion of Mir Jumla, but they were captured by the Moguls before they could reach their destination. Jasamatta Rai now wrote to Jayadhwaj Singha,—"Jayantia and Gargaon are not separate and divisible. At your discomfiture at the hands of the Moguls I am feeling as if my own country has been harassed and humiliated by the enemy. What has happened cannot be undone. Henceforward we should attempt to strengthen our bonds of friendship. The Moguls have simply invaded your country; they have not been able to hold it under their domination permanently.

23. MS. Assam Buranji Nos. 3 and 8.
24. MS. Assam Buranji Nos. 3 and 8.

The land and the people are all intact, as well as your august self. Measures should now be concerted to organise a more effective co-operation between ourselves so that we may wreak vengeance upon the Moguls."[25]

The letter of Raja Manik Singha of Nartiang, a vassal state under Jayantia, was cast in a more heroic mould. "The loss of two men", said Manik Singha, "is nothing. We would not have been sorry even if we had lost ten or twenty thousand men for your sake. We are aggrieved that we could not render you any assistance with our men. We have no greater friend than yourself, and we know that your sentiments are not dissimilar. Distance becomes proximity if the hearts of the two parties are pure and sincere, as you know from the saying in Sanskrit, "He who is attached to one does not recognise any distance." Jayantia and Gargaon are not two different places. What pains me most is the fact that I was living in peace and comfort while your country was overrun by the Moguls. It will be my life's regret that I had no opportunity to order ten or twenty thousand of my stalwarts to run to your aid in your emergency. The Moguls have done according to their strength and might. They should get retribution for the devastation they have caused. The humiliation will be blotted out only on the day when we shall be able to extirpate our foe."[26]

The Ahom diplomacy of the post-Mirjumla period was a masterpiece of casuistry and subterfuge, of concealment and make-believe. The Ahoms succeeded in creating confidence in the minds of the Moguls by prompt payment of the first instalment of the indemnity. But after their country was physically rid of the enemy they took recourse to numberless excuses for deferring payment. They delivered the articles only to the extent as would retain the good-will of the Moguls, and lull them into a sense of security with regard to the absence of any hostile intentions. The Ahoms had to continue their policy of superficial friendship owing to the

25. S. K. Bhuyan, *Jayantia Buranji*, 1937, pp. 22-23.
26. S. K. Bhuyan, *Jayantia Buranji*, 1937, pp. 24-25.

unsettled character of the state, and the inadequacy of their military preparations.

King Jayadhwaj Singha had established an intimate personal relationship with Nawab Diler Khan Daudzai, the commander of Mir Jumla's vanguard. The veteran soldier had been instrumental in persuading Mir Jumla to accept the terms of peace offered by Assam. "You had promised to give protection to our land," wrote King Jayadhwaj Singha to Diler Khan, "and having become our surety you have preserved our cows and Brahmans, and our subjects both men and women. You have acquired great merit and fame by this deed."[27] While sending the presents to Diler Khan from the two princes Brajanath Gohain and Chikan Gohain, the Swargadeo referred to them as Diler Khan's nephews, thereby placing himself in the position of a brother to the Mogul commander.

King Jayadhwaj Singha had written a letter to Emperor Aurangzeb admitting his aggression to Mogul territories, and reiterating his acceptance of the terms of the treaty of Ghilajharighat. In reply, the emperor sent an epistle with presents which included a *sirpao* or a robe. Two Ahadis, Dor Beg and Rustom Beg, sent by the emperor, arrived in due course at Gauhati, and proceeded from thence to Dergaon. Having heard the news King Jayadhwaj Singha expressed his regret that he would have to accept and wear an imperial robe sent to him in consideration of his being a virtual tributary of the Moguls. "Death is preferable to this abject humiliation", declared Jayadhwaj Singha.

Untoward circumstances had compelled Jayadhwaj Singha to abandon the capital and flee to the wilds of Namrup. But he was in essence endowed with a high sense of patriotism. Lying on his sick-bed at Bakata he expressed a desire to visit Gargaon where he had lived in pomp and magnificence for fifteen years as the Swarga-Maharaja of Assam. But Gargaon was a deserted city, and it was feared the Moguls might have infested it with mines and traps. Besides, it was

27. MS. Assam Buranji No. 41.

polluted by the slaughter of forbidden animals and the sale of their meat. Atan Buragohain and his colleagues therefore dissuaded the monarch from going to Gargaon, and they were supported by the priests and the astrologers. But King Jayadhwaj Singha would not listen; and, in spite of his illness, he proceeded to Gargaon, and stood near the principal entrance of the city. He peeped through the door, and wept bitterly in remembrance of his disgraceful desertion of Gargaon which was in his own words a Sonapur or a golden city. He fell on the ground in a fainting fit, and was removed in that prostrate condition to his Bakata camp where he died nine days later. Before his death, he enjoined his ministers and nobles to protect the people according to the traditions of the land. "It should be your earnest endeavour", said the dying monarch, "to extract from the nation's bosom the spear of humiliation fixed upon it by our enemy the Moguls."[28]

The death of Jayadhwaj Singha was followed by a scramble for the throne mainly engineered by Khamun Rajmantri Phukan and his kinsmen. Khamun and his two brothers Chengmun and Lechai owed their influence and power to their being the sons of the eminent administrator and soldier Baghchowal Haladhithenga Neog Gohain who had become Barphukan in the reign of King Pratap Singha, and who had died at Amrajuri near Kamakhya while fighting against the Moguls. Neog Gohain's first son Changmun rose to be the Barphukan at Kaliabar; the second, Khamun became Naobaicha Phukan with the rank of Rajmantri; while the third, Lechai held the office of Hatimuria Phukan.

Khamun's two daughters had been married to King Jayadhwaj Singha. The younger one was Kusumi Barkuanri; and her elder sister had first been married to a member of the family of the Buragohains, and the king being infatuated with her beauty took her away from her husband and made her his wife with the title of Parvatia Kuanri. Her son by her first husband was adopted by King Jayadhwaj Singha. His name was Langichang Gohain, but he was generally

28. MS. Assam Buranji No. 8.

known as Kalia Gohain. Khamun Rajmantri Phukan was known as Rajasahur, or the king's father-in-law, and the same title was applied by courtesy to his elder brother Chengmun Barphukan, though a distinction was maintained by designating Khamun as Gargayan Rajasahur as he lived most of the time at Gargaon; and Chengmun as Namanial Rajasahur in view of his Barphukanship of Namani or Lower Assam.

Kusumi and her sister had pressed their dying husband to nominate Kalia Gohain as his successor. But King Jayadhwaj Singha did not accept their recommendation in view of Kalia Gohain's non-royal origin. He nominated his uncle's son Chakara who had shown great bravery during the invasion of Mir Jumla, having once almost succeeded in recovering Gargaon from the enemy. Chakara held the status of Charing Raja, a premier duke of the realm; and was in office a Hengdan-dhara or a sword-bearer to His Majesty.

Immediately after the death of Jayadhwaj Singha, Chikan and Sariah, the two sons of Chengmun, sought to occupy the throne for themselves with the help of their brothers and nephews, Kamala, Langcha, Lokcha, Khamcha, Rangcha and Tolan. There was a great commotion in the country, and it abounded at that time in persons of treacherous disposition. A contemporary chronicler has thus succinctly described the situation,—"Then came Chikan and Sariah, the sons of Rajasahur. There was confusion in the land, and it became unsteady and tottering. The kingdom continued in a state of anarchy for three days; and conspirators and malcontents spread all over the country."[29] To avert further deterioration the Dangarias brought Chakara Charing Raja to the Bakata camp at midnight and declared him to be the king. The new monarch assumed the name Chakradhwaj Singha. The ministers and nobles knelt down before the Swargadeo and offered him their allegiance and respect. Khamun Rajmantri Phukan paid his homage three days after the others had done. The king postponed investigation into the treachery of

29. MS. Assam Buranji No. 13.

Khamun's kinsmen as he was engaged at that time in preparing for the reception of the two envoys deputed to the Ahom court by Emperor Aurangzeb.

The imperial envoys had been ordered to hand over the epistles and presents to the new king Chakradhwaj Singha. They left Gauhati accordingly in the company of Diler Khan's messenger Gadai, and Rashid Khan's Ukils Taj Khan and Sheikh Kamal. Diler Khan, in his letter, advised the Assam king to receive the tokens of imperial good-will with proper respect. According to the custom of the Mogul court, a tributary Raja was to descend from his throne and advance a few steps at the time of receiving the epistles and presents sent by the emperor. He was also expected to wear the garments forming part of the presents. The emperor's ambassadors had to report to their master on the details of the actual ceremony of reception.

King Chakradhwaj Singha was very much upset when he thought of the approaching ordeal of an interview. He asked his nobles to procure the return of the imperial messengers. Atan Buragohain Dangaria characterised the king's decision as an impolitic one as it was bound to precipitate a friction with the Moguls at a time when the Ahoms were not ready to encounter the enemy for lack of preparations. The Buragohain pointed out that in times of emergency one should protect the country and its people by following a line of conduct not sanctioned by ordinary usages. The king then permitted the messengers to be brought to his presence. The nobles decided to arrange the interview in a manner acceptable to the Swargadeo, by plying the envoys with heavy bribes in order to induce them to connive at the shortcomings in the formalities of the occasion, in view of the alleged sickness of the Ahom monarch.

The Mogul envoys Dor Beg and Rustom Beg were then ushered into the presence of the Ahom king, his throne and its immediately surrounding space being heavily curtained to protect it from the gaze of the courtiers. The envoys insisted as usual upon the king's receiving the articles by coming down from the steps of the throne. They had already been tutored to permit the Assam king to act on the occasion according to the practices of the Ahoms, and not according to Mogul usages. They had also been threatened that should they refuse to comply, dire consequences would follow their refusal, and the Assamese would justify their action by saying that the Ahadis had misbehaved in the presence of the Ahom monarch. The two envoys were now given a fresh bribe of two hundred gold mohurs and two thousand silver rupees, and they agreed to allow the Assam king to receive the imperial presents in the way he chose.

A pile of heavy carpets was dumped before the throne in order to give the impression that the king was in a standing posture. The articles being presented to King Chakradhwaj Singha they were kept on the tray before the throne, and were subsequently deposited in the royal stores. The messengers of Diler Khan and Rashid Khan were not admitted to this interview which was meant only for receiving the imperial envoys.

At the end of the interview the king asked the Rajmantri Phukan to communicate to the envoys his regret that though he had parted with his daughter, three lacs of rupees and ninety elephants, he did not get back his old territorial limits. The king's wishes were embodied in a letter addressed to Emperor Aurangzeb. "The presents which you have sent through Dor Beg and Rustom Beg", ran King Chakradhwaj Singha's message, "consisting of a *sirpao* and a jamdar, were received by me by advancing a few steps, and with due salutation. I am remembering the Padshah a great deal. Being pleased with me you should always look upon me as your friend. I have made over my daughter to your *mahal* only because of the friendship subsisting between us. It is desirable that our mutual friendship should ever be on the increase."[30] The Assamese envoys Chandra Kandali Kataki and Sanatan Kataki were asked to accompany Dor Beg and Rustom Beg, and carry with them the epistles and presents to Emperor Aurangzeb.

30. MS. Assam Buranji No. 41.

The treacherous propensities of Khamun Rajmantri Phukan had meanwhile found an outlet in the presence at the capital of the two envoys of Fauzadar Rashid Khan. Having failed to gain the throne for his grandson Kalia Gohain, or for his nephews Chikan and Sariah, he now aimed at seizing it for himself by deposing and killing the reigning monarch Chakradhwaj Singha. He submitted a proposal to this effect to the two envoys for being communicated to Rashid Khan. He offered to capture the Assam king provided the Moguls would support him in the enterprise. He averred that the late monarch Jayadhwaj Singha had promised to deliver four lacs of rupees and one hundred elephants, and that this fact was assiduously concealed from the knowledge of Chakradhwaj Singha. The Phukan regretted that the king gave weight to the advice of the Buragohain and the Barbarua to the exclusion of his own representations and submissions.[31]

On receiving the overtures of Khamun Rajmantri Phukan, and the reports on the developments at Gargaon, Rashid Khan encouraged his views by writing back on December 5, 1663 A.D.,—"Please let me know if any person in your kingdom, either on your right or on your left, is contemplating your downfall and destruction. We shall give whatever aid is needed and we shall despatch immediately our horses, boats, soldiers and other necessary war materials."[32]

As regards the widowed queens Kusumi and her sister, King Chakradhwaj Singha lived with them for some time intending to allow them to continue in their old status of Barkuanri and Parvatia Kuanri. The widows resented this move on the part of the younger brother of their deceased husband. They said,—"The crow which used to be frightened

31. Golapchandra Barua, *Ahom Buranji*, p. 188.
32. MS. Assam Buranji No. 41.

at the mere sight of a bow now stares us in the face and keeps on croaking."[33]

Enquiries were now instituted into the rebellious manoeuvres of Khamun Rajmantri Phukan and his relatives. Formal information had been lodged by Laluk Dolakasharia Barua, Sanatan Kataki, Ganak Barua and Rama Brahman. Khamun's brother Lechai Hatimuria Phukan was also arrested meanwhile and imprisoned. The sentence of death was passed against the accomplices, including Chikan and Sariah.

King Chakradhwaj Singha intended to spare the life of Khamun in view of his wide experience and extensive knowledge as an administrator. But Khamun declined to accept the proffered immunity, saying,—"My sons and nephews have all been killed. I now stand bare like an inauspicious tree bereft of its branches and leaves. No good will come out of me in future. Hence I pray that I should be given an opportunity to depart from this world." Khamun and his brother Lechai were then strangled to death.[34]

Kusumi and her sister were now accused of participation in the revolutionary designs. They pleaded ignorance of the move on the part of their father and uncle, and said,—"We live within an enclosure of seven walls. How is it possible for us to know what has happened? More specially, the offence committed by the right hand does not pollute the left hand, and similarly, the action of the left hand does not contaminate the right." While the two sisters were taken to the place of execution they said,—"We had proposed to accompany our deceased husband. We were not allowed to do so. Our honour has been violated, and we are now going to be killed without any justification. If Dharma be paramount, the consequences will be seen in no time." Kalia Gohain, the adopted son of Jayadhwaj Singha, was also killed with his mother and aunt.[35]

33. S. K. Bhuyan, *Assam Buranji*, recovered from the family of Sukumar Mahanta, pp. 104-5. This chronicle is henceforward referred to as *Assam Buranji, S.M.*

34. MS. Assam Buranji Nos. 10 and 40.

35. MS. Assam Buranji Nos. 10 and 40.

The extermination of the family of the Rajasahurs was completed towards the end of February 1664. Laluk Barua was rewarded with the office of Naobaicha Phukan for his vigorous prosecution resulting in the capital conviction of the accuseds. The office of Rajmantri was conferred as a matter of course on Atan Buragohain Dangaria.

After the liquidation of the family of Khamun, the king turned his attention to the reception of the two envoys of the Gauhati Fauzadar. Their attitude was markedly defiant, as they claimed the privileges enjoyed by the messengers of the Mogul emperor. "We shall adopt the salutation of *tuslim,*" they said, "and offer our courtesies to the Assam Raja by simply raising our hands folded, as we did when we saw him last in the company of Dor Beg and Rustom Beg." The Ahom nobles pointed out that the exception had been allowed because they had come in superior company, but that they were appearing this time as the representatives of the Gauhati Fauzadar. Taj Khan and Sheikh Kamal had first refused to change their proposed mode of salutation, but a few days later they agreed to offer their salutation by *salam.*

Chandra Kandali and Sanatan who had gone to Delhi returned to Assam in September 1664. In their audience with Emperor Aurangzeb, the latter had promised to return the territories which were in possession of the Moguls in excess of the limits legitimately belonging to them. The emperor did not send any Ukil or epistle, but he directed the Assam envoys to meet Nawab Shaista Khan at Dacca who, he said, would hand over a proper reply to the representations of the Assam king. Shaista Khan told the Assam envoys that the territories in question belonged to the Koches, and that Assam's legitimate boundaries were Bharari on the north bank and Kajali on the south. The Ahoms did not send any Ukil this time with the Bengal envoy Punditrai, nor did they send any letter to Dacca.

Whatever might have been the offshoot of King Chakradhwaj Singha's request for equitable adjustment of his claims, his spirited nature could no longer brook his subordinate position. He convened a meeting of the three ministers, Bahgaria Atan Buragohain, Baghchowal Barpatra Gohain, and Barukial Langi Bargohain, and his other nobles and officers. His Majesty broached his proposal to attack the Moguls, saying,—"Death is preferable to a life of subordination to foreigners. I have to surrender my independence for a suit of sewn garments ! My ancestors were never subservient to any other people, and I for myself cannot remain under the vassalage of the Moguls. I am a descendant of the Heavenly King, and how can I pay tribute to the wretched Moguls? You should devise and adopt measures so that I can regain my garrison of Gauhati after expelling therefrom the foreign usurpers."[36]

The king's proposal was accepted by the general body of his counsellors. But the prime minister Atan Buragohain realised its inopportune character specially because the war preparations were still then incomplete, and hostilities might have to be conducted for any length of time. He analysed the situation in a forceful speech which will remain for ever a standing monument of his farsighted statesmanship and patriotism.

"It is the legitimate duty of a king", said Atan Buragohain Dangaria to the king and his colleagues, "to restore the old limits of his dominions by defeating and destroying his enemies. His success in war can alone enhance his glory and renown. So, His Majesty's proposal is just and proper. We have been enjoying absolute and uninterrupted sovereignty from time immemorial, and the high-handed imperiousness of the Moguls has transcended the limits of our forbearance. His Majesty has only voiced the sentiments of his ministers when he declares that we should fall upon the Moguls this very moment. But we must provide the army with sufficient quantity of food provisions and war materials, and must hold in stock a sufficient reserve to enable us to replenish the stores of the expeditionary army as soon as they become empty. This task of supplying reinforcements will become a matter of frequent occurrence.

36. MS. Assam Buranji Nos. 10 and 15.

"The country has become depopulated owing to the flight of the villagers from their homes during the last war with Mir Jumla. His Majesty has recently procured their return to their country and settled them in different places. We shall have to enquire whether these people have been able to obtain their rice and food. Rice is the most indispensable of all the necessaries of life; and if it fails nothing will succeed. The officers who have to supply the allotted quota of boats, sailors and provisions, will now assert, on enquiry being made by Your Majesty, that they have got all the equipments ready, and that they will be able to deliver them whenever they will be required to do so. But it may be they will fail just at the moment when we shall badly need them; and nothing will come out even if we kill or chastise the officers in default. We shall have to face dire disaster in the eventual failure of boats and provisions. Unless we have sufficient surplus in store at present how shall we meet the situation if war has to be prolonged for two or three years? We must take the necessary steps now, and arrange for all future contingencies. In the event of failure of supplies even torture or death will not help us in overcoming an emergency.

"A *kari paik,* or a humble subject of Your Majesty, buys an earthen pot to boil his coarse rice for the trifling sum of two *cowries.* Lest the rice and the pot, the total value of which will not, in any case, exceed twenty *cowries* or one pice, be spoiled, he tests the soundness of the vessel by striking it with the fingers at the bottom and the sides two or three times before making the purchase.

"A bird erects a nest on high where she hatches to life her young ones. She takes them round from one bough to another after they have grown up a bit. They are brought down to the ground when they can fly. If they are let loose before they become full-fledged they are eaten up by dogs and jackals. The mother-bird leaves them only after they can pick up and eat their food themselves.

"Similarly, when the three batches of rowers, posted at the middle and the two extremities of Your Majesty's barge, strike their oars simultaneously the sight becomes beautiful to look at, the oarsmen feel inspirited, the boat moves swiftly, and the helmsman wields the steering with ease and comfort. But, if on the other hand, there is no harmony and synchronism in the strokes of the three batches of rowers, the helmsman is inconvenienced in steering his shaft, the boat does not make any headway, and the spectators are far from being delighted.

"If the king directs his measures on the lines indicated above then only he will be able to vanquish his enemies and extend his territories to the old limits."[37]

The council accepted the suggestions of the Buragohain, and elaborate arrangements were then instituted to expedite the completion of the preparations. Every regiment was split up into two sections, each containing five hundred soldiers, and bearing the full quota of officers and equipments of a full-fledged chiliarchy. The king moved about amongst the recruits, stick in hand, watching and directing their training. He gave rewards to those who appeared to be alert and bold. The villagers were compelled to cultivate their fields on an extensive scale to provide for the normal food provisions of the army as well as for emergency supplies and stores in reserve.

The preparations for war were supplemented by an effort to win the co-operation of the neighbouring chiefs, as was done by King Jayadhwaj Singha during the last few months of his reign. In June 1664, King Chakradhwaj Singha despatched an embassy to Raja Prananarayan when he said,—"You know for yourself all about the manner in which we have dealt heavy blows upon the Moguls. If God has inflicted on us a reverse on this single occasion, does it follow that we shall be subjected to discomfiture again?" To this Raja Prananarayan replied,—"What has happened is through the inevitable ordinance of Fate which alone is to be blamed, and no body can overcome it. When Fortune becomes favourable even a weakling can overcome a giant. If we two combine, the enemy will not obtain any superior advantage;

37. MS. Assam Buranji Nos. 7 and 15.

on the other hand, Fortune will offer a fitting opportunity to both of us for retaliation and revenge."[38]

In a subsequent communication, the Assam king wrote to Raja Prananarayan,—"You have sent the verbal message that war has commenced between Shewa [Shivaji] and the Moguls, and that Shewa, having defeated the Moguls, has pushed them back to a distance of twenty days' march, and that Daud Khan has fallen, and that Dilil [Diler] Khan is wounded, and that the Badshah has come from Delhi to Agra. It cannot be predicted as to who becomes vanquished, and who becomes victorious. You have asked us to strengthen our fortifications and to train our soldiers. It is meet and proper that you should give us such friendly advice and encouragement. Because the Moguls have discomfited us once, does it follow that we should make no attempt to throw off this position of subordination to them? They have discomfited us once, and we have dealt them severe blows on repeated occasions, and of this fact you are fully aware."[39]

The correspondence of the period reveals a state of subdued tension between the Moguls and the Ahoms. The Moguls never failed to impress the Ahom monarch of the necessity to please the emperor, and also the Subedar of Bengal. They of course insisted on the prompt delivery of the stipulated instalments of the indemnity. Failure on this score, they hinted, would result in unfavourable consequences, which in plain language meant the suspension of friendly relations and the resumption of hostilities. The Ahoms in their turn complied with the terms as far as was necessary to avoid an open rupture; they offered plausible excuses for delay which the Moguls could not easily deny. The Ahom replies were evasive but firm, and it appears that in the misunderstanding they saw the existence of grounds which they could in future cite as *causus belli* when the time for strike would arrive.

Diler Khan Daudzai wrote to King Chakradhwaj Singha about the timely payment of the war indemnity. The

38. MS. Assam Buranji Nos. 3 and 8.
39. MS. Assam Buranji Nos. 3 and 8.

Swargadeo mildly protested against it saying that such matters were dealt with by the ministers and officers, and not by the Swargadeo. Fauzadar Rashid Khan advised the Ahom sovereign to correspond with the Mogul Subedar at Dacca. "But", wrote Chakradhwaj Singha in reply, "it was never our practice to write to the governor of Bengal. The Fauzadar of Gauhati writes to my government whenever the occasion arises, and my ministers send replies thereto. It is our desire to follow the same procedure even now." Rashid Khan asked the Assam premier to send him some boats, each forty or forty-five cubits long, for being used in *shikar*. The prime minister wrote back,—"As to your request for boats, I searched for them. But I am sorry I could not get any boat of the requisite measurement. If I get such boats, they will be sent to you; do you think a boat is more precious than yourself?"[40]

Rashid Khan had once asked Atan Buragohain Dangaria to send him a Kakati or accountant to help him in the preparation of an inventory of the elephants and money already delivered and of the balance still to be delivered. The prime minister of Assam evaded compliance with the request by writing back,—"We have maintained here proper accounts of what we have delivered, and you must have done the same with regard to what you have received. What we have given to you in the shape of elephants and money is only due to the reason that we have our four sons with you as hostages. Could you ever doubt that you will not get the balance?"[41]

The Mogul Fauzadar constantly reminded the Ahoms of their obligation to pay the stipulated indemnity in time. The Ahom replies were generally of the following tenor and purpose,—"The extent of the devastation recently undergone by our country is known to you well. It is for this reason that we have not been able to make over to you the full complement of elephants and money. We have already given you a substantial portion, and the delivery of the balance

40. MS. Assam Buranji No. 41.
41. MS. Assam Buranji No. 41.

will be kept by us in view. Do you think that we have deliberately withdrawn payment of the indemnity? We shall send elephants when we catch them in the coming winter, and when the roads become dry for their transport. As regards the balance of the money, we have no money to give now. We have kept our four sons with you, and the Nawab knows the affection which a father bears to his children".[42]

The Gauhati Fauzadar once accused the Assamese of the murder of three Mogul subjects. But the incident had taken place in the territories of the Moguls, and the Assamese could not therefore be held responsible for the crime. "You have made a reference to some murders", wrote Atan Buragohain to Rashid Khan, "but, how is it possible for us to indulge in such wanton slaughter, and to what purpose, having kept our four sons, two Ukils and one Barmudoi in your care and custody? I would ask you to overlook this incident. You have fixed your eastern boundary at the Bharari river, and the incident has thus taken place in your jurisdiction, and how shall we know who is the murderer and who is murdered? It is not proper that you should hold us responsible for murders inside your territory. If it transpires that our subjects have perpetrated the offence we shall hand over the criminals to you, and you can cut off their heads. If the crime cannot be laid at the door of our subjects, then, what shall we do?"[43]

As a punishment for the delay of the Ahoms in the payment of the indemnity, Rashid Khan had once threatened to remove the hostages to Dacca. But Bharmal Dewan, a Rajput official of the Mogul Fauzadar, interceded, and obtained a relaxation of the orders. He kept the sons of the Assam nobles under his own protection and care, and thus informed the Rajmantri Phukan of the circumstances,—"They planned to remove your four sons to Dacca, but I succeeded in keeping them here in my place. They are living here in the enjoyment of the same happiness and comfort

42. MS. Assam Buranji No. 41.
43. MS. Assam Buranji No. 42.

which they used to receive in their own homes. You should not entertain any anxiety on their account."[44]

The atmosphere of tension, in varying degrees of severity, continued for some time. The Moguls complained of the delay; the Ahoms delivered the balance of elephants and money as they considered desirable under the circumstances, while they were strenuously engaged in maturing their plans of revenge and perfecting their preparations for war. But now a new circumstance arose the ignoring of which, thought King Chakradhwaj Singha, would not be commensurate with the dignity of his exalted position, nor of the age-old prestige of his country.

Both the Mogul Fauzadars, Rashid Khan and Firoz Khan, proved to be romantic guys, and they intended to redeem the drudgery of a pro-consul's life by a little diversion in their seraglio. They had seen for themselves the proverbial beauty of Assamese women, and they also knew that flirtations with them were a tabu according to the code of Mogul service in Assam. Nawab Rashid Khan therefore managed to obtain from Assam a number of beautiful virgins, and having passed some time with them in 'the primrose path of dalliance' sent them back to their homes. The puritanical emperor of Delhi, nor his uncle the Subedar of Bengal, would not excuse these undignified indulgences; there was also the fear that these pretty victims of the Fauzadar's lust were bound to do some mischief as 'poison girls' or spies, notorious as they were all over India for their enchantments and cunning.

King Chakradhwaj Singha was seized with fury when he heard of the indecorous intentions of Rashid Khan, and he proposed to launch immediate hostilities. But the nobles lightened the rigour of his determination by pointing out the inadequacy of their preparations.

Rashid Khan was succeeded in the Fauzadarship of Gauhati by Nawab Firoz Khan sometime in March 1667, and he succeeded in impressing upon the Assamese of his good-

44. MS. Assam Buranji No. 41.

ness and accommodation. "I have succeeded to the arduous duties of a Fauzadar in this pestilential territory of Assam", probably thought Firoz Khan, "and why not also to the amiable pleasures of my predecessor?" He accordingly sent a request to the Ahom ministers to furnish him with a number of damsels, debonair and gay.[45]

The correspondence in this matter was initiated on behalf of Nawab Firoz Khan by his revenue agent Bholanath Kanungo. Sometime in June 1667, the Kanungo wrote to the two Assamese ambassadors Madhabcharan Kataki and Purananda Kataki about the intention of his master. "You should come," ran the epistle of Bholanath Kanungo, "with the remaining elephants along with Syed Jafar Ukil, and there should be no delay in the matter. After having informed your Gohains, you should also bring with you two or three handsome girls for our Nawab Saheb. Our Saheb will be very much pleased when you come here with girls, and you will receive proper rewards from our Saheb. Our Saheb has asked us to make this request, and hence we have written to you. There should be no slackness in this matter, and you should bring the girls with you when you come here".[46]

A Mogul underling asks the ministers of Assam, the pillars of the state, to send girls to him for his amusement! Perhaps no such request had ever been made to a Hindu court by any Mogul official. King Chakradhwaj Singha's resentment now transcended the limits of patience. The preparations being brought to the verge of completion, the king ordered the immediate inauguration of offensive measures, and the nobles agreed with his animated decision.

Final arrangements were now made for the despatch of the army to Gauhati. Atan Buragohain advised the holding of an army manoeuvre on a road newly constructed for the purpose between Jhanji and Teliadonga-pukhuri. The soldiers were mustered in their war array, and the king was

45. MS. Assam Buranji No. 41.
46. MS. Assam Buranji No. 41.

satisfied with the mettle and adroitness displayed by the troops on that occasion.

The general selected to command the expedition was Lachit Deka, son of Momai-tamuli Barbarua, the great statesman-warrior of the reign of King Pratap Singha. Lachit had given proofs of his gallantry and leadership in the operations against Mir Jumla's troops and in the various offices he had occupied. When King Chakradhwaj Singha observed that only a commander of unusual stamina and judgment would be able to expel the Moguls from Gauhati, Lachit came forward, and said,—"Could it be that there is no fit man in Your Majesty's realm? What are the enemies? They are after all ordinary mortals. Shall we not find similar men in our country? Your Majesty should only confer the dust of your feet, and the man equal to the occasion will be readily found."[47] The king subjected Lachit to further tests and ordeals from all of which he came out successful. He was forthwith appointed generalissimo of the army, and was also made Barphukan and placed in charge of the civil administration of Lower Assam.

After the performance of the religious rites customary to the initiation of a campaign, the Ahom army sailed down the Brahmaputra in two divisions, under the leadership of Lachit Barphukan, the other commanders being Guimela Bargohain-Phukan, Kaliabaria Bargohain-Phukan, Nimati Laluk Naoboicha Phukan, Charingia Pelan Phukan, Miri-Sandikoi Phukan, Dihingia Sandikoi Phukan, Dauki Bheba Phukan Namdangia Rajkhowa, Kalanchu Sandikoi Dikhowmukhia Rajkhowa, Kalanchu's son Betmela, Haladhia Chenga Abhaypuria Rajkhowa, and Pani-Abhaypuria Rajkhowa. It was Thursday, Bhadra 3, 1589 *saka*, or August 20, 1667 A.D. Before the departure of the army from their rendezvous near the capital, Swargadeo Chakradhwaj Singha delivered the following injunction to the commanders and troops: "I desire that your wives and children and the cows and Brahmans should be duly protected and preserved;

47. S. K. Bhuyan, *Assam Buranji, S. M.*, p. 109.

and that I should also acquire the prestige and reputation of having vanquished the Moguls. If you prove incompetent in the task of defeating the enemy at Itakhuli [Gauhati] you shall not be let off with impunity. And, do you think that there will be paucity of commanders, Phukans and Rajkhowas like yourselves?"[48]

The Ahom army encamped at their base at Kaliabar which was generally the headquarter of the Barphukan when Gauhati was under the Moguls. Early in September 1667, the Ahom commander Dihingia Phukan succeeded in expelling the Moguls from their garrison at Bahbari. Two leading Mogul commanders, Lal Beg and Roshan Beg, were captured together with a quantity of war provisions, and sent up to Gargaon.

Proceeding by land and water, the Ahoms directed their attention to the storming of the Mogul garrisons situated between Kapili and Gauhati; and the forts of Kajali, Sonapur, Panikhaiti and Tatimara soon fell into their hands. Their primary objective being the occupation of Gauhati, the Ahoms posted detachments in the eastern precincts of the city on both banks of the river. The Moguls had strongly fortified the town, and the Ahoms experienced considerable difficulty in their attacks on its several fronts.

The Ahoms threw up a stockade near the mouth of the Barnadi, in the vicinity of the two Mogul outposts at the place. Baduli Phukan, the protegé of the Moguls, came out of the fort at Shahburuz, shield in hand, and spurred his Mogul contingent to action. Two Assamese commanders, Haladhia Chenga Rajkhowa and Kalanchu Dikhowmukhia Rajkhowa perished in the engagement after having displayed conspicuous gallantry, but the result was not favourable to the Ahoms.

The Ahoms then concentrated their efforts on the attack of Gauhati situated on the south bank of the Brahmaputra. They anchored their boats on the bank of the Brahmaputra near the Bonda village. The city commenced from Jaiduar,

48. MS. Assam Buranji No. 10.

its eastern entrance, which is now marked by a narrow passage on the public road at Chanmari. The fort of Itakhuli was situated on the riverside hill on which are now located the Sukreswar temple, the Janardan temple, the Deputy Commissioner's residence, and the District Police Superintendent's quarters and office.

The Ahoms by a stratagem besieged the Mogul garrison at Jaiduar, and Betmela Sandikoi, son of Kalanchu, approached its gate and exclaimed,—"If there be a Mogul sirdar let him come out and give me a fight." A captain issued out of the fort, and fought a duel with Betmela during which the latter tightly gripped his opponent, threw him to the ground, and then decapitated him. Betmela emerged out of the contest with sword-cuts on his thigh and back.

After the occupation of Jaiduar, the Ahoms advanced into the city and threw up stockades keeping the fort of Itakhuli within the range of their guns and arrows. The Moguls succeeded in defending the garrison for a length of time. The Ahom commander Pelan Phukan looked upon Itakhuli as being impregnable, and he was reported to have remarked,—"I shall become the bondsman of the soldier who can storm the Itakhuli fort." This observation was communicated to King Chakradhwaj Singha who instantly despatched a quantity of fetters, axes, *mekhlas* or skirts worn by women, and broomsticks, with the order,—"You are to rip open the heart of Pelan Phukan and send it to me. Should he speak in this way? As regards the other soldiers who entertain similar defeatist views, make them wear the *mekhlas*, and beat them with these broomsticks." When the message was delivered to the Gauhati commanders they exclaimed in one voice,—"No one here has heard Pelan Phukan making any such remark, and we do not know wherefrom the king has heard it." The reply satisfied the monarch.

The Ahom commanders then met to devise means for the successful storming of Itakhuli. Japang Gohain was appointed to lead the attack. Under the orders of the Gohain, a number of commando soldiers put water into the muzzles of the Mogul guns. The Ahoms then attacked Itakhuli towards the end of the night of Thursday, the seventeenth Kartik, 1589 *saka*, or November 4, 1667 A.D. The walls of the fort of Itakhuli were scaled with the help of ladders. Having entered the fort the Ahoms created a havoc in the enemy's camp by slaughtering the inmates. The survivors who managed to escape in boats were chased down beyond Hajo.

As the routed Mogul troops were sailing down towards the river Manas, they were intercepted at the mouth of the river. In the engagement that ensued, Assamese sharpshooters began to mow down the fugitive enemy. A prince of Dimarua, who was sitting on an elephant with Maupia, was killed by a shot from the Assamese side. His companion was then made to alight from the elephant, and transferred to a horse. The Fauzadar Syed Firoz Nawab then sent a message offering his submission to the Ahoms and asking the latter to desist from firing their guns or shooting their arrows. The Ahoms asked the Moguls to lay down their weapons. This was done, and the battle came to an end.

Fauzadar Syed Firoz Khan and his Mirbukshi Syed Sala were captured and brought up as prisoners. The Ahoms also rescued a large number of their countrymen who had been taken by Nawab Mir Jumla. The sons and nephew of the Dangarias,—Dhala, Langi and Ramrai, who had lived at Gauhati as hostages, had died meanwhile, and the Fauzadar had sent up their bodies to Gargaon for the performance of the funeral obsequies. The above-mentioned Maupia, the son of the Rajmantri Phukan, was now the only surviving hostage. The Ahoms also got possession of the Mogul stores consisting of war-provisions, boats, horses, elephants, camels, bullocks, buffalos, asses, and a large quantity of gold and silver, and brass and copper.

As a result of the defeat of the Moguls, Gauhati and Kamrup extending up to the river Manas, became once more a part of the Ahom kingdom. King Chakradhwaj Singha was highly delighted at this happy culmination of his efforts to restore the prestige and honour of his motherland, and he observed, "It is now that I can eat my morsel of food with ease and pleasure. It is a pity that the wretched Moguls exacted tribute from me in exchange of a suit of sewn garments!" He then sent appropriate presents to the commanders at Gauhati, and performed a sacrifice at Biswanath in the way of thanksgiving to God for having conferred upon him the blessing of a victory. The temporary fortifications at Kaliabar were converted into a strong and permanent citadel and fort known as Rangaliburuz.

The Gauhati commanders were then strictly enjoined by the king to remain ever-vigilant and cautious as the resumption of hostilities with the imperialists was a foregone conclusion.

Thirteen days after the expulsion of the Moguls, Atan Buragohain Dangaria, the prime minister of Assam, wrote to Nawab Shaista Khan, Subedar of Bengal, apprising him of the circumstances leading to the conflict. The ultimate triumph of the Assamese was however left unmentioned, though the Buragohain referred indirectly to the reversal of fortune by a mild challenge in the concluding sentences. As the letter contains a vivid picture of the Assam-Mogul relations of the period, it deserves to be reproduced in its entirety: "All the prestige and honour of our country vanished," wrote the Buragohain, "when you devastated our territories. We then promised to give three lacs of rupees and ninety elephants. We made this promise only to preserve our boundaries as well as our integrity and honour. In pursuance of that promise, we have given to you elephants and money, and our sons are with you as surety for the balance of the indemnity. Still we have not got back our territories, nor our subjects who had gone over to your land. Rashid Khan Nawab inflicted severe insults on our envoys during the reception at Umananda; and our Barmudoi was also grossly abused and scolded. Besides, requests are made for the supply of damsels, and when they are sent they are returned back. His Majesty the Swarga-Maharaja of Assam became highly incensed on receiving reports of these affronts, and he commanded us to attack Gauhati; but we interceded at the feet of the monarch, and he condescended to withdraw his orders. After this, Syed Piroz, on assuming charge of his office [as Fauzadar of Gauhati] deputed Syed Jafar Ukil to our place. His Majesty came to know that Syed Piroz Nawab was a good man, and we also came to the same conclusion. We sent nine elephants to Gauhati during the stay of Syed Jafar Ukil at our place. We were then told that Syed Piroz Nawab had made a request for furnishing him some virgins. Having heard this, the Swargadeo was seized with indignation and wrath, and ordered an attack on Gauhati. Now, if you are desirous of establishing friendly relations with us, then please send for that purpose Ukils and epistles. If you have no such desire, well, it is your look-out. What shall I say more? You are all-knowing yourself."[49]

The victory of the Assamese forces was commemorated by a stone pillar set up at Gauhati shortly after the engagement. The inscription which is in Sanskrit can be thus translated: "In the year 1589 *saka,* there flourished the Barphukan of Namjani [Lower Assam], the son of the Barbarua [Momai-tamuli]. He became victorious in the war waged by the Yavanas in the full array of various kinds of weapons and arms, elephants, horses and captains. The body of the Barphukan is adorned by all varieties of ornaments, his heart is illumined by manifold learning, he is endowed with the qualities which are not tainted by the sins of the Kali-yuga, he is effulgent in prowess and enterprise, he is the commander of elephants, horses and soldiers, and he is like an ocean in regard to fortitude, self-respect, heroism and gravity."[50]

49. MS. Assam Buranji No. 41.

50. H. C. Goswami, *Barphukanar Jayastambha,* Alochani, Vol. VII, pp. 480-81.

CHAPTER V

MOGUL FORCES DEFEATED AT SARAIGHAT

After the expulsion of the Moguls, the Ahoms turned their attention to the perfection of measures for the retention of their newly recovered territories. All their best leaders, whether in statesmanship or war, were now stationed at Gauhati. The commanders deliberated frequently on the plan of defence, and they concluded that the first necessary step was the strengthening of the fortifications of Gauhati, taking advantage of the high hills which skirt round the city on both banks of the river Brahmaputra, so that soldiers and war provisions could be safely accommodated in the area inside. The intervening field between one hill and the next was to be linked by a newly constructed earthen rampart. The hills and the ramparts taken together would provide a ring of defence about twenty-five miles in circumference, and the city inside, with the Brahmaputra flowing in the middle, would provide a suitable base from where, to quote the words of Lachit Barphukan, "they could fight as if sitting in their own homes".[51] Some captains suggested Samdhara near Tezpur, but the proposal was rejected in view of its being too much inland, from where, in the event of an Assamese reverse, the enemy could easily march to the Ahom capital, as it happened during the invasion of Mir Jumla. Gauhati was therefore finally selected as Assam's war base in view of its superior strategic advantages.

Urgent priority being attached to the construction of the fortifications of Gauhati, the work was entrusted to the premier Atan Buragohain. The Buragohain employed all the resources at his disposal, and finished the work within an unexpectedly short time. The impregnable character of the fortifications, made so by nature and by man, led the

51. S. K. Bhuyan, *Assam Buranji, S.M.*, p. 117.

Assamese to say ever afterwards that they were made by Viswakarma, the god of engineering, and that they were impenetrable even to the gods. A soldier was posted on the hill-tops, spurs and ridges, at an interval of 13½ feet, and on the ramparts after every 9 feet. A specified area known as *pali,* was allotted to each captain. The remains of the earthen parapets and of the bastions in brick are still to be seen all along the outer fringes of Gauhati.

The civil administration of Kamrup was organised on the lines of the *zemindari* system in vogue in the neighbouring western provinces, as opposed to the *kheldari* system in Eastern Assam; and the revenue was collected by the Chaudharis, Bujarbaruas, Thakurias and Patwaris, and by the vassal chiefs, known as Satrajias and Panchrajias.

Lachit Barphukan used to inspect the strong and vulnerable points in the area on the pretext of hunting on horseback or on foot. Batteries were mounted at specified intervals on the hill-tops, the hill-slopes and the ramparts, and properly trained artillery-men were posted at each point. During this period, the Assamese perfected the art of constructing improviso walls and stockades on river banks and in midstream, and also of constructing bridges of boats across the river Brahmaputra.[52] The whole area was divided into a number of sectors, each being commanded by an officer of distinguished gallantry and proved efficiency. The war zone extended from Pandu to Asurar Ali on the south bank, and from Agiathuri to Kurua on the north. Itakhuli Hill, commanding a view of the entire area, was the headquarter of the general Lachit, while the Buragohain remained in charge of the northern division at his base on the Lathia Parvat. The eastern command on the north was in charge of Baghchowal Barpatra Gohain whose headquarter was at Kurua. The whole arrangement was a masterpiece of strategy and planning, and it appeared no enemy would be able to break into the invulnerable environs of Gauhati. According to a report submitted to Emperor Aurangzeb on December 10,

52. MS. Assam Buranji No. 4.

1669, the total strength of the army at the disposal of the Barphukan at Gauhati came up to one lac, of which the cavalry was very small in number.[53]

In December 1667, Emperor Aurangzeb heard of the recapture of Gauhati by the Ahoms, and the consequent loss of Mogul prestige in Eastern India so soon after it had been restored through the hardships and sufferings of Mir Jumla's expedition. The emperor at once decided to depute the Rajput general Raja Ram Singha, son of Mirza Raja Jai Singha of Amber, to lead an expedition against Assam. Ram Singha had offended the emperor by his instrumentality in the escape of the Mahratta leader Shivaji and the Sikh Guru Teg Bahadur from virtual imprisonment at the Mogul capital. The Raja had been punished by being deprived of his mansab, and being forbidden to appear at court. He was now restored to his former rank and privilege. Assam was then well-known all over India for its pestilential diseases; and Ram Singha, thought the emperor, would share the fate of Nawab Mir Jumla who died on his way back from Assam.

Ram Singha's mother and his consorts were seized with fear having heard of the Raja's deputation to Assam. As advised by them, Ram Singha visited Guru Teg Bahadur in the company of his ministers and a large retinue of soldiers. "My mother and the queens", said Ram Singha to the Guru, "asked me if I desire an untimely death. They represented that there was none so brave as Mir Jumla, and if he perished what hope was there for me? Of all the generals who had been on that errand none except Raja Man Singha had ever returned. Then I too saw the danger of my position. It was certain death to command the invading army, and it would be equally fatal for me to disobey the emperor's orders". Guru Teg Bahadur asked Ram Singha to have faith in God.

53. The defensive arrangements of Gauhati are described on pages 37-44 of S. K. Bhuyan's *Lachit Barphukan and His Times*. For the number of Assamese soldiers under Lachit Barphukan, see Akhbarat-i-darbar-i-Muala, Royal Asiatic Society MS. No. 12-11, quoted by Professor Jadunath Sarkar in J.B.O.R.S., 1915, p. 189.

"Guru Nanak", he said, "will assist thee, and thou shall conquer Kamrup". The Guru offered to accompany Ram Singha to Assam.[54]

Ram Singha's army consisted of 21 Rajput chiefs, 4,000 troopers in his own pay; 1,500 gentlemen-troopers or *ahadis*, and 500 artillery-men; and with reinforcements from Bengal, his total army swelled upto 30,000 infantry, 18,000 Turkish cavalry, and 15,000 Koch archers. His commanders included Raja Indramani, Chadmend Khan commander of 2,500, Alam Khan Dui-Hazari, Bakram Khan Dui-Hazari, Dewan Sayid Gazap Khan Ek-Hazari, Kayam Khan, Zulel Beg, Raja Prithu, Raja Manik, Mir Gazraf Khan Beldari commander of 2,500; Nasiri Khan, Kirat Singh Bhurtiah, Raghunath Singh of Mirthah, and Bairam Deo Sisodia; as well as the following captains of Cooch Behar, — Raja Jainarayan, grandson of Parikshit, Kavisekhar Barua, Sarveswar Barua, Manmath Barua and Ghansyam Bakshi.

Ram Singha was accompanied in his expedition by Nawab Rashid Khan who had been in Assam during Mir Jumla's invasion, and who had served as Fauzadar of Gauhati for four years. It was the practice of Emperor Aurangzeb to depute a Muslim officer as second-in-command when a Hindu was placed in sole charge of an expedition, specially when the enemy himself was a Hindu. It was in pursuance of this policy that Diler Khan Daudzai had been sent with Mirza Raja Jai Singha in the war against Shivaji. Aurangzeb's orders to Rashid Khan ran as follows,—"Rashid Khan, you are to join the expedition against Assam. You had been there before with Mazum Khan [Mir Jumla], and you know the language and customs of the people".[55]

Ram Singha met Nawab Shaista Khan at Dacca. Being a close and intimate friend of Mirza Raja Jai Singha, now deceased, the Nawab received Ram Singha very cordially, and offered to help him in all possible ways. He at once

54. Max Arthur Macauliffe, *Sikh Religion*, Vol. IV, pp. 348-52, and 360.

55. H. C. Goswami, *Purani Assam Buranji*, p. 138.

sanctioned a reinforcement of 2,000 soldiers from the Bengal command. Shaista Khan was however not very optimistic about the Raja's success in the Assam campaign; and the old Assamese chronicles bear evidence of a desire on the part of the Nawab himself for the continuance of Assam as an independent kingdom as it raised the prestige and importance of the Bengal Subedar who had to manage the Mogul relations with that state.

Nawab Shaista Khan's advice to Raja Ram Singha is thus recorded in an old Assamese chronicle,—"You are to act in a way that you may remain in the good graces of the emperor who is a clever politician. I have heard that Assam has constructed huge fortifications. I am also told, the Ahoms are shrewd diplomats. Shujanagar [Hajo] is an unhealthy place; its hills are covered with forests, and poisonous waters flow in the streams during the two months Baisakh and Jaistha. The air that blows there is infected with poison. For this reason, our men die there in large numbers, and you should live there very carefully. Do not drink any water except that of the Lauhitya or Brahmaputra. Do not admit the women of that place into your mahal; they are wicked and treacherous". "Please write to me", added Shaista Khan, "when you fall short of food-stuffs, war provisions or money, and I shall send them to you, looking upon you as one of mine".[56]

In February 1669, Ram Singha arrived at Rangamati, the frontier garrison of Mogul India. The Assamese generals now became more vigilant and circumspect in their preparations for resisting the invading forces led by a commander of Ram Singha's reputation and valour. Fresh ramparts were constructed on both banks of the river and the units, known as *palis*, were reorganised in order to render the Gauhati fortifications an impenetrable wall of defence. Lachit Barphukan's maternal uncle was entrusted with the construction of a rampart on the north bank of the Brahmaputra. Having failed to complete it within the prescribed time he

56. S. K. Bhuyan, *Annals of the Delhi Badshahate*, pp. 165-66.

was executed by Lachit Barphukan who declared on the occasion,—'My maternal uncle is not greater than my country'. The general also issued a command that he would cut off the head of every delinquent without any mercy or favour. This stern warning caused some opposition in the Ahom camp as all executions involving bloodshed could be carried out only under the orders of the king. His Majesty, on the advice of his Barkuanri, approved of Lachit Barphukan's proposal as such spartan strictness, he thought, was imperative in an emergency.

The Assamese forces attempted to oppose the advance of Ram Singha from their strongholds situated near the Manaha frontier. In the few skirmishes that followed the Assamese were discomfited, the main reason being the employment of war hounds by the Rajput general which snatched away Assamese soldiers from their lines. The Assamese pretending to retreat upstream lured the invading forces to follow them to the environs of Gauhati where the Ahoms could fight with convenience and ease.

In April 1669, Raja Ram Singha pitched his camp at Sualkuchi on the north bank and spread his soldiers in the outlying villages situated in the immediate vicinity of the Assamese fortifications. Reports began to reach the Ahom camp about the numerical superiority of the Mogul army, and Lachit Barphukan verified them by surveying the position of the enemy from the top of an Assamese fort. It is recorded by an eye-witness that at the sight of the Mogul army tears rolled down the Barphukan's cheeks, and he was overwhelmed with a consciousness of the grave responsibilities of his situation. 'How will my king be saved?', said Lachit Barphukan, "How will my people be saved? How will my posterity be saved?" But, sentimentalism, however high and noble it might be, would not enable the general to face the grim realities of war. He soon came back to himself, went round the several units, and retired to his camp to devise the best means of counteracting the enemy.[57]

57. MS. Assam Buranji No. 12.

The first object of the Barphukan was to gain time to consolidate and perfect his preparations. He despatched a messenger to Ram Singha to enquire of the reasons for his coming to Assam, adding that if there was any issue or dispute it could be settled by peaceful negotiations, as war was not the only method for such settlement. In return, Ram Singha demanded the restoration of the limits fixed in 1639, in default of which the Barphukan was asked to give the Rajput Raja 'a fight for an hour'. Ram Singha even offered to furnish war materials to the Assamese general if there was a shortage in the latter's camp.[58]

The Barphukan's reply to the demand for the restoration of the 1639 limits was evasive but determined. "Gauhati and Kamarupa", he said, "do not belong to the Moguls. We have taken possession of the place by turning out the Koches. It was through mere chance that they fell into the hands of the Moguls for a few seasons. Now God has been pleased to give them back to us. When He pleases to give them to our brother-sovereign, the Mogul emperor, he will then get Gauhati, and not before that". As to Ram Singha's request to fight for an hour, the Barphukan said that the Assamese were prepared to fight as long as there remained a drop of blood in their veins. The Rajput Raja's offer of war materials was dismissed with the remark that "he has come over a long distance undergoing fatigue in his journey, and the provisions may be inadequate for his own purpose. Our Majesty the Heavenly King has nothing unavailable to him. If the Rajput Raja falls short of materials, let him ask me, and I shall try to oblige him".[59]

Ram Singha then advanced to Hajo and pressed closer to the Assamese fortifications on the north bank. He despatched a messenger named Daivakinandan reiterating his demand for the evacuation of Gauhati. A bag of poppy seeds was sent with Daivakinandan to impress Lachit Barphukan of the numerous character of the Mogul forces. The Barphukan

58. S. K. Bhuyan, *Assam Buranji, S.M.*, p. 96.
59. S. K. Bhuyan, *Assam Buranji, S.M.*, p. 113.

replied through his messengers Nim and Ramcharan that Gauhati would be delivered only if the Swargadeo of Assam and the Padshah of Delhi decided on such an arrangement by mutual agreement. The Barphukan sent a tube filled with sands with the brief remark,—"This is the characteristic of our soldiers", meaning thereby that the Assamese army was as numerous and indissoluble as the sands in the tube.

Lachit Barphukan gathered from the report of a visitor to the Mogul camp that the hostile forces had already been seized with consternation and dismay at the sight of the Assamese fortifications and plans for fighting. Ram Singha was reported to have said to his lieutenant Rashid Khan,—"The enemy is beyond the reach of our heavy artillery; and there is no opportunity for fighting with arrows and guns. Their ministers, commanders and infantry are all to be admired for having constructed such an impregnable wall of defence". On hearing this report the premier Atan Buragohain asked the soldiers "to note carefully that at the sight of our fortifications demoralisation has already crept into our enemy's camp. His enthusiasm is already on the wane". The officers and men responded to this appeal by promising to fight to the last drop of their blood.[60]

The situation in the Mogul camp received a set-back owing to a friction between Ram Singha and Rashid Khan. The latter considered himself entitled to the same privileges as Ram Singha, and blew his Nahbat as many times as the Rajput general. Once when Rashid Khan was attending a musical *soiree* with dancing and high revelry, he received a command to repair to Ram Singha's tent for a conference on the war situation. Rashid Khan refused to go, and this made matters worse. Ram Singha cut off the ropes of Rashid Khan's tent, and the latter marched farther into the interior. It was even suspected that he had entered into a collusion with the Ahoms.

60. S. K. Bhuyan, *Assam Buranji, S.M.*, pp. 114-15; MS. Assam Buranji No. 5.

Ram Singha made an attempt to enter the fort at Sarai or Amingaon on the north bank by digging an underground passage. But it was frustrated by the Assamese who filled the surrounding moat with water. The Moguls succeeded in effecting a breach at Rangaliburuz near Pandu on the south bank, but it was promptly repaired by the Assamese who had kept a number of men with materials ready for such an eventuality.

Sporadic engagements accompanied by proposals of peace continued during 1669 and 1670. The Moguls made an attempt to enter Gauhati through Darrang but it was baffled through the timely warning of the vassal Raja of Rani. In an engagement near the Sesa river in the vicinity of Agiathuri the Ahoms first obtained a victory over the Moguls; but Ram Singha then took the field in person, and inflicted a crushing defeat upon the Ahoms. At Rangmahal on the north bank, the Ahom forces led by Gohain-Phukan, first encountered a reverse. But the commander re-formed the phalanxes, and compelled the Moguls to withdraw their forces from the attack without achieving any tangible result.

The Assamese supplemented these open encounters by guerrilla fighting for which ample facilities were provided by their unobserved camps and garrisons situated in thick woods and lofty hill-tops. They would come out of their forts at midnight and fall upon the enemy unawares: invest them if they could, and in the event of their repulse they would hurry back to their retreats. To Ram Singha's accusation that these attacks amounted to 'Thieves' affairs', the Assamese replied that lions alone fought at night while others fought during daytime. They also made a visible demonstration of the reported presence of Rakshasas or demons in their camp.

Ram Singha fully realised that the conflicts and negotiations were protracted beyond limit without any decisive issue. He enquired of the Assamese envoys Bhakatdah and Dhuli, as to who were the commanders who had thus been toying with him. The envoys gave a formidable list of the Ahom captains, and concluded with the observation,—"Not to speak of yourself, even the Padshah of Delhi will be unable to vanquish them in war".[61]

Ram Singha received confirmation of the report of the Assamese messengers from the lips of his own envoy Punditrai. The latter described the Bargohain, the Barpatra Gohain and the Barphukan as "wonderfully capable commanders presenting a rare combination of beauty, accomplishment, valour and wisdom". "As to Atan Buragohain" said Punditrai,—"He is young in years, fair and handsome in features, sober and deep in intelligence, dexterous in all matters, and he excels all others in the soundness of his counsel. The Buragohain is also an arch-diplomat". Hearing this Ram Singha observed,—"It is really wonderful that a man can be so intelligent and circumspect at this tender age. Who will be able to cope with such a minister when he comes to years? Pride should be the heritage of the land where such a counsellor has taken his birth".[62]

Ram Singha was also informed of Churamani Daivajna, astrologer-in-chief to the Barphukan, whose calculations were reported to be so accurate and infallible that the Assamese army were sure to achieve the desired result when they acted according to his auspicious indications. Ram Singha attempted to entice the astrologer to accept service under him, but he failed. Bhakatdah was punished by the Barphukan for having promoted Ram Singha's designs in this connection.

Atan Buragohain then adopted a new device in the campaign of harassing the enemy. He employed a number of commando soldiers and daring spies who entered into the Mogul tents at night when the captains fell fast asleep and their servants retired to their respective quarters. The spies removed the silver *hookahs* or hubble-bubbles used by the commanders as well as the treasures and belongings on which they could lay their hands.

61. MS. Assam Buranji No. 12.
62. MS. Assam Buranji No. 15.

But these guerrilla tactics did not carry the Assamese very far beyond harassing the enemy. They realised that the enemy must be definitely repulsed and dislodged and expelled from their position, and the prospect of their re-attack completely eliminated. The Assamese avoided open encounters with the enemy, and they dreaded cavalry charges, as they believed that their soldiers who were mostly infantrymen could not stand the dash and fury of attacks by trained troopers on horse-back. The situation was discussed in a war-council when they decided that the Moguls should be lured to a naval fight on the waters of the Brahmaputra.

The postponement of a decisive encounter implied some degree of vacillation on the part of the Ahom commanders. Exaggerated reports of the Barphukan's dilatory methods reached the ears of the Ahom king Chakradhwaj Singha. He threatened the Barphukan and his commanders with dire punishment if they further postponed their offensive operations. The Moguls had then concentrated near Alaboi Hill on the outskirts of a vast plain which touched the Brahmaputra on one side and the Sesa river on the other. The Barphukan knew very well that an attack upon the Moguls at that juncture would spell disaster to his own army. At the same time, he felt that he had no other alternative but to obey the king's command.

Ram Singha despatched at that time a force under Mir Nawab, and the Barphukan sent an army of forty thousand men. A female warrior named Madanavati was posted at the vanguard of the Mogul army. In the engagement that followed the Ahoms first received a terrible repulse, their soldiers being dispersed with heavy casualties. The victors were then confronted by the Assamese fighters who had concealed themselves in the trenches. Madanavati was shot dead by a hostile bullet on the bank of the Brahmaputra: and the detachment under Mir Nawab was routed by the Ahom forces.[63] He was captured alive, and was kept under strict guard in the Ahom fort. Elated by their victory the Assa-

63. MS. Assam Buranji No. 12.

mese soldiers began to return to their camps with spoils and captives. Ram Singha then issued out of his camp and ordered his veteran troopers to fall upon the Assamese forces. The latter could not stand the onset of the Rajput cavalry; and ten thousand soldiers of the Barphukan lay lifeless in the Alaboi plain. Ram Singha, on receiving this first taste of a decisive victory, cried out,—"Look at the rashness of the Assamese! They venture to fight on the plains with Amber horsemen!" He requested the Barphukan to desist from provoking the Rajput cavalry in future. The Barphukan wrote back to Ram Singha describing the Alaboi attack as an unauthorised diversion on the part of some border chieftains who had joined the Assamese forces directly under the orders of the king. "A detachment has been lost", wrote Lachit Barphukan, "and we have many more fully prepared for action".[64]

However unperturbed Lachit Barphukan might try to appear before his adversary, it is a fact that he was greatly upset by the disaster at Alaboi. "Each of our soldiers is a pillar of strength," said the Barphukan, "and we have lost to-day ten thousand such stalwarts." The premier Atan Buragohain consoled the young generalissimo by saying, —"Well, general, such a reverse should never shake your confidence in our ultimate victory. Eventualities of this character are normal in a protracted warfare. When you agitate the waters of a pond for catching large fishes the fish-catchers will be pricked by the thorny scales of the smaller fries. You should judge your success by the number of large catches".[65]

Ram Singha now thought that the disaster at Alaboi must have humbled the spirit of the Assamese, and he repeated his demand for the evacuation of Gauhati with vehemence and vigour. The following reply was formulated in consultation with the premier, and was delivered to Ram Singha in the name of the Barphukan,—"I am only a servant of His Majesty. Any terms into which I may enter with the Raj-

64. S. K. Bhuyan, *Assam Buranji, S.M.*, pp. 116-17.
65. MS. Assam Buranji Nos. 5 and 15.

put Raja may not receive the approbation of our sovereign. Therefore, the Raja should desire for a treaty which will be ratified by all the parties concerned, and its objects enhanced by continued observance. If such a treaty can be concluded the Raja will be praised in all quarters. The Raja has been despatched by the emperor of Delhi for his intelligence and skill in warfare. If he goes from here without the credit of a victory over our arms the expectations made of him will no longer be justified."[66]

Attempts at conciliation having thus failed, the Rajput general now adopted the two other stereotyped methods of overcoming an enemy—rupture and gifts. Ram Singha used to shoot arrow messages to the camps of Ahom commanders alleging secret promises on the part of their colleagues to give the Moguls an easy passage to Gauhati. The hostile hand in these allegations was quickly detected, and the Ahom leaders were not the least disturbed in their mutual confidence and cohesion. Ram Singha attempted to bribe the Phukans and Rajkhowas, but no such corruption could contaminate the patriotic zeal of the Assamese commanders. He sent a necklace studded with gems as a present to the Barphukan: and it failed to produce the result it was calculated to achieve. To Ram Singha's repeated demands for the evacuation of Gauhati, the Barphukan replied as before that it could be done only when it was so decided by the king of Assam and the emperor of Delhi.

No other course was now left to Ram Singha but a definite attack on Gauhati. He had learnt from his envoy Punditrai that there was only one possible venue for attack, afforded by a slight opening in the rampart in the sandbanks between the Barphukan's headquarter at Itakhuli and the foot of the Kamakhya Hill. The sandbank is known as Andharubali and it stretches north of the present Strand Road of Gauhati on the bank of the river Brahmaputra. Amrajuri-ghat is the landing station for boats at the foot of the Kamakhya Hill. Opposite to Kamakhya Hill is the Aswak-

66. S. K. Bhuyan, *Assam Buranji, S.M.*, p. 118.

ranta temple on the north bank. So a regular triangle can be constructed connecting Amrajuri-ghat and Itakhuli on the south bank and Aswakranta on the north. Ram Singha planned to enter Gauhati through the breach in the rampart at Andharubali with a detachment of his cavalry, by carrying his men and horses in boats across the river.

Chakradhawaj Singha, king of Assam, died in April 1670, and was succeeded by Udayaditya Singha. The leadership of the new monarch fell far short of the spirited exertions of his patriotic predecessor. The long continuance of hostilities without any decisive result produced some discontent in the Assamese camp. Ram Singha's demands for the restoration of the limits of 1639 received a more encouraging response from the Barphukan and his lieutenants; and the diplomatic negotiations became more cordial than before. But Atan Buragohain, the premier, did not support this change in the attitude of his colleagues. He pointed out that the resistance which they had offered to the enemy and which had caused such loss of men and provisions was absolutely meaningless if it was followed by their voluntary surrender of Gauhati. The premier characterised Raja Ram Singha's promises as 'a highway made of ashes' as they might not be accepted by the emperor of Delhi, or by the Raja's successor in the Assam command. The dislodgement of the Ahoms from Gauhati, said the Buragohain, might be followed by their expulsion from the capital Gargaon. King Udayaditya Singha confirmed the views of the Buragohain, and directed the commanders to bring the war to a victorious conclusion.[67]

Ram Singha's enthusiasm in the Assam campaign relaxed a great deal on receiving reports of his son's maltreatment at the hands of Emperor Aurangzeb. He also received a warning from his consort and his widowed mother to the effect that it would be impious to disturb the peace of Assam which resounded with holy recital and prayer, *Nama-kirtan*, and where lived cows, Brahmans and Vaisnavas in security and peace. "Remember also", concluded the royal ladies of

67. MS. Assam Buranji No. 14.

Amber, "that having invaded Assam Mir Jumla could not thrive long. So take heed, and do as you think proper". But as a Rajput of the famous Kuchchwa clan, Raja Ram Singha could not be untrue to the vow of loyalty and faithfulness taken by him before Emperor Aurangzeb; and he fought with great resolution to bring the Assam campaign to an end by forcing a decisive encounter.

He commanded a contingent of his cavalry to cross the Brahmaputra in boats and enter the plains of Gauhati by breaking through the opening at the Andharubali rampart. The breach was quickly repaired, and the Mogul boats steered back to the north bank. Lachit Barphukan was very ill at that time, and his soldiers missed the benefit of his personal command. They were doubtful of their success, and some boatmen loaded the boats of the Barphukan and the Buragohain with the object of sailing upstream abandoning the scene of contest. Lachit Barphukan sent messages from his sick-bed expressing his determination to die on the spot rather than desert his charge. He was removed on his bed to the gate-house from where he observed the fury of the attack made by the Moguls upon his boats and sailors on the waters of the Brahmaputra. On Churamani's declaration of the auspicious moment to initiate a counter-attack, Lachit Barphukan came down from the gate-house and boarded his boat accompanied by six other war-vessels.

The appearance of Lachit Barphukan on the Brahmaputra filled the hearts of his soldiers with animation and courage. He rushed towards the enemy with his seven boats and was soon joined by the Assamese fleet from both banks of the river. The Assamese war-ships entered into the thick of the Mogul fleet; and in the fight that ensued the Moguls could not stand the well-directed attack of the Assamese soldiers. The combat came to an end, and it was a decisive victory for the Assamese. This engagement is known in history as the battle of Saraighat. The Moguls were chased down to Pandu, and then beyond Assam's western frontier at Manaha; and the Ahoms retained their possession of Gauhati and Kamrup. Lachit Barphukan who was in high fever when he led the attack against the Moguls died soon after his memorable triumph at Saraighat.[68]

During the conflicts with Ram Singha, the premier Atan Buragohain proved his eminence as an intrepid soldier and a sage counsellor. He conducted the war operations on the north bank from his camp at Lathia Hill. As the Mogul forces had spread themselves in the villages and plains to the immediate west of his headquarter, the first brunt of the defence fell upon him. The failure of the Moguls to break through the Ahom fortifications on the north bank bears testimony to Atan Buragohain's gallantry and organisation. He infused fresh vigour into the wavering hearts of his colleagues; and checked their plans and measures whenever he found them to be ill-conceived, and hence detrimental to the best interest of his country. Atan Buragohain proved to be the brain of the organisation instituted by the Assamese for successfully resisting the imperialistic designs of the Moguls.

68. S. K. Bhuyan, *Assam Buranji, S.M.*, pp. 121-22; H. C. Goswami, *Purani Assam Buranji*, pp. 147-48.

CHAPTER VI

THE INFLUENCE OF PARAMANANDA SANNYASI

Raja Ram Singha being frustrated in his attempt to recover possession of Gauhati retired to the Mogul garrison at Rangamati, and waited there for an opportunity to reinvade Assam. In view of this eventuality the Ahom officers commanding the garrison at Gauhati and the posts lower down the Brahmaputra up to the Manaha river remained vigilant and watchful in their respective charges. At Gargaon, the capital, the king had to manage the affairs with the aid of inferior talents. The three ministers, the Buragohain, the Barpatra Gohain and the Bargohain, paid occasional visits to Gargaon, but their temporary intervention could not offer any effective check to the designs and machinations of ambitious and unscrupulous nobles. Rajmantri Atan Buragohain had thus a dual duty to perform, the supervision of the military affairs at Gauhati and also of the civil administration at Gargaon. He had to pay greater attention to Gauhati as Lachit Barphukan had died soon after the battle of Saraighat, and was succeeded in the Barphukanship by his elder brother Nimati, commonly known as Metakatalia Laluk Sola Barphukan.

The wisdom and foresight of Atan Buragohain came out in the advice he tendered to King Udayaditya Singha with regard to the proposed expedition against the Dafalas, a tribe living in the hills to the north of the present sub-division of North Lakhimpur. They used to come down to the plains on marauding excursions when they would capture Assamese subjects and properties. The Dafalas were however kept in check by the grant of blackmail from the Assam government, and by permission to use the services of the Dafala-Bahatias who were formed into a penal colony settled along the foot of the Dafala hills.

The Dafalas now complained that they were on the verge of starvation owing to the long delay in the delivery of the stipulated blackmail and the payment of the taxes due from the Bahatias; and under the leadership of Bar Gam, Radha Gam, Tami Gam and Bakara Gam, the Dafalas raided Gagaldubi village, killed three Ahom subjects, and carried off forty persons including women and children. Udayaditya Singha proposed to despatch a force against the Dafalas under Ao Gohain's son Ghorakowanr Barbarua, an officer of proved ability who had acted as an intermediary between the king and the Gauhati commanders during the conflicts with Ram Singha.

Atan Buragohain knew well that an expedition against the Dafalas was bound to end in a disastrous failure as they lived in inaccessible villages situated in the midst of dense forests and steep mountain defiles, and the hill-men could always evade the pursuers by flying from one shelter to another. It was besides difficult to maintain the line of supplies once an army entered into the interior of the hills. The Dafalas were experts in the device of rolling down boulders from hill-tops so as to fall on the opponents marching along the narrow jungle paths below. The Buragohain therefore dissuaded King Udayaditya Singha from despatching a force against the Dafalas, saying,—"There are instances in the past of the failure of our Dafala expeditions. The Dafala raiders can be captured only if an elephant can enter into a rat-hole. Their suppression can be effected only by tact and diplomacy".[69]

The monarch ignored the advice of the Buragohain, and despatched Ghorakowanr Barbarua against the Dafalas at the head of a considerable force. In May 1672, the Barbarua crossed the Subansiri river and halted at Rangamati from where he shifted his camp to Dulungmukh. Two Assamese commanders, Tua and Tita, were despatched to bring the Dafalas to submission. The agents of Bakara Gam met Tua and Tita and expressed regrets for having acted disloyally against the Ahom monarch. "We are mere monkeys", said

69. MS. Assam Buranji No. 5.

the Dafala agents, "and we have dared to rebel against the Maharaja! We are like domestic dogs biting our master's legs". Tua and Tita offered to secure pardon for the Dafalas, first from the Barbarua and then from the Swargadeo, and asked them to proceed to the presence of the Barbarua to pay their respects to him. The Dafalas however hesitated to appear before the Barbarua who, they thought, was swayed at that time by an ungovernable passion for vengeance.

Bakara Gam now appeared on the scene with fifty-two followers and continued the parleys with Tua and Tita. The Gam realised the insecurity of his position, and said,—"The Barbarua has come to kill us. How will it be possible on the part of elephants to proceed by paths meant for the passage of dogs and jackals?" Tua and Tita sent a secret message to the Barbarua asking him to fall upon the Dafalas during the continuance of the negotiations. The Barbarua sent a force who proceeded by boat, but the Dafalas had meanwhile left the venue of the talks on the pretext of coming back with the men and goods captured by them from the Assamese.

Tua and Tita were accused by the monarch for having put the Barbarua on a wrong track: they were chained with iron fetters and imprisoned. The rains then set in, and the Barbarua was compelled to suspend operations, which were made more difficult by the inaccessible character of the terrain. The hesitation of the Barbarua was construed by the Swargadeo as cowardice. The king sent a message threatening to kill the Barbarua if he returned to the capital without subduing the Dafalas. He asked the Barbarua to wear the skirt of a woman in the event of his further inaction.

Having heard this the Barbarua came from Dulungmukh to Barchetia, and then to Gangmukh, from where he sent a number of detachments under Khaga Hazarika, Kharagom, Chutia-kari Barua, and Chungi Barua who proceeded by different routes against the Dafalas. But the Ahom troops could not make any headway for difficulties of communications aggravated by the torrential showers of the monsoon season. After they had made some advance they were attacked by the Dafalas who had concealed themselves in the neighbouring jungles. The Ahom soldiers seized with panic dispersed down the slopes of the mountains. Large numbers were massacred by the Dafalas, some were carried off as slaves, and the rest were chased down to the plains. Khaga Hazarika and Kharagom were among the slain. The Barbarua then returned to his camp at Barchetia.

The king attributed this reverse to neglect and mismanagement on the part of Ghorakowanr Barbarua. Chaudang Barua Papang, under the orders of the monarch, brought Ghorakowanr back and kept him as a prisoner in the Hatisal along with the other surviving members of the expedition. The king accused the Barbarua of dereliction of duty which had resulted in the heavy loss of war-materials and men, and ordered him to be executed together with the other deliquents; but they got off through the intervention of the king's mother and wives. Ghorakowanr was however dismissed from office, and Charingia Pelan Phukan of Rangmahal fame was appointed Barbarua. After some time Ghorakowanr was readmitted into the good graces of His Majesty, and was made Bhitarual Phukan or the commander of the household troops. During the following dry season the Dafala leaders returned the goods and the men of their own accord.

But the most notable event of the period which had a far-reaching effect upon the subsequent history of Assam was the affair of a Sannyasi of Gakulpur who exercised great fascination on the mind of King Udayaditya Singha and was in consequence on the verge of superseding the authority of the original Vaisnava monks of the country. The Sannyasi who hailed from Gakulpur near Brindaban had first lived at Hajo with another hermit from Kalitakuchi in Kamrup. The Sannyasi from Gakulpur whose name was Paramananda then came to live at Kamakhya; but for some reason or other he soon changed his mind, and proposed to leave that place which was the stronghold of Saktaism in Assam. Paramananda saw a dream in which he was dissuaded by the goddess Kamakhya from leaving her sacred precincts, but he did not pay any heed to the dream-message. As he was coming down the main steps of the Kamakhya hill he was suddenly enveloped in darkness; and being unable to proceed any further he sat down on the spot. He soon discovered that he had at one stroke become completely blind. The inhabitants of Kamakhya erected a shed for the Sannyasi at the Hanumanta gate where he remained for some time offering prayers to his tutelary god. A large number of persons, both male and female, became disciples of the Sannyasi. He then set out on a pilgrimage to Bhramarakunda in Eastern Assam, and stayed for some time at Kalabari in the monastery of Banamali Gosain. Here also the Sannyasi charmed the people by demonstrations of his occult powers.

The fame of Paramananda Sannyasi had spread to the metropolis; and whether of his own accord, or on the invitation of the monarch he went to Gargaon, where he first lived under the protection of a Brahman official named Daha Barua who was greatly pleased with the manners of the Sannyasi, and with his learning and his devotions. The son of one Mora used to live in the house of Daha Barua. Having received proofs of the Sannyasi's great powers Mora's son reported the same to the king. The monarch also elicited, through Mora's son, additional proofs of the Sannyasi's powers. New buildings were constructed for the Sannyasi to which he shifted from the house of Daha Barua, and began to live under the care of Mora's son. The king brought the Sannyasi occasionally to the palace, and asked him questions on religious topics and other subjects which the Sannyasi answered to the satisfaction of the monarch. Udayaditya became greatly devoted to Paramananda, and constructed for him a large monastery near the entrance to the capital known as Chunpora-duar. His Majesty used frequently to visit in person the new residence of the Sannyasi.

The undue respect, amounting almost to subservience, shown by the king to a person whose antecedents, caste and family were completely unknown, was viewed with disfavour by the Assamese people who were accustomed for generations past to revere the old hierarchy of the indigenous religious preceptors,—Satradhikars, Gosains, Mahantas and Medhis. The people became further exasperated when the monarch forced his uninitiated subjects to become disciples of Paramananda Sannyasi. The three Dangarias, Atan Buragohain, Baghchowal Barpatra Gohain and Langichang Bargohain, and Laithepena Solal Gohain, and many Phukans, Rajkhowas and Baruas deserted the fold of their ancient preceptors and became disciples of Paramananda, obviously at the instance of the sovereign. The Sannyasi claimed to know, while sitting at his own Chunpora residence, everything that the king said or did in his palace. Claims of this nature enabled the Sannyasi to exercise great sway over the mind of the king and his court.

The ministers did not oppose the king's solicitude for the Sannyasi as they considered it to be a temporary phase of weakness in the monarchical mind which was bound to disappear in the light of reason. Besides, they were themselves overpowered by their conviction of the Sannyasi's great piety and erudition.

But things assumed a critical turn when King Udayaditya Singha in his eagerness to advance the prestige and influence of Paramananda summoned the twelve Vaisnava Mahantas of the Thakuria denomination and asked them to become disciples of the Gakulpuri Sannyasi in pursuance of his declared belief that none of the Mahantas was equal to the Sannyasi.[70] The Mahantas protested in a body; and their leaders, the Mahantas of Mayamara, Makajan, Silikhatal and Sesamukh were thrown into prison from where, the king said, they would be released only if they could satisfy him about their spiritual prowess by performing some miracle. The Mahantas replied in one voice,—"We are incapable of performing miracles. We pass our days in reciting and hear-

70. S. K. Bhuyan, *Assam Buranji, S.M.*, p. 126; MS. Assam Buranji No. 5.

ing the glory of the Great God, and in offering prayers for Your Majesty's welfare. Except this everything else is beyond our ken". The king reiterated his conviction of the omniscience of his Guru Paramananda, and the consequent propriety on the part of the Mahantas to become the Sannyasi's disciples.[71]

Now, the Thakuria Mahantas whose monasteries were originally founded by Bhavanipuria Gopal Deva were developed on somewhat separatist lines, and they had to function in the teeth of opposition from the orthodox church of Sankardeva and Madhabdeva. These tendencies fostered a spirit of militancy and protest in their articles of faith and their outward actions. The Thakuria Mahantas now stood as one man determined to oppose the king's design to convert them to the discipleship of Paramananda. In this they received the tacit support of the three Gohains who thought that the time for their intervention had arrived.

Lechai Debera now enters into the arena of Assam politics as the leader of the anti-Paramananda movement. He resolved to curb the influence of the Sannyasi and preserve the integrity and prestige of the Vaisnava monks of Assam. Being himself a disciple of the Makajan Mahanta of the Thakuria denomination, he knelt down before the Mahantas and solicited their blessings for the success of his enterprise, saying,—"Your Holinesses should only bestow upon me the dust of your feet, and I shall do whatever redress is necessary."[72] Debera was the son of Kharagom who had been killed in the Dafala campaign. He was a member of the Ahom Lukhurakhun clan, and he held the rank of a Hazarika. He hailed from Dakhinpat in Majuli.

The king got scent of the mischief that was brewing against him and his protegé; and, with the object of keeping Debera away from the capital for some time he ordered him to command an expedition against the Mishmi rebels living near Sadiya. The shrewd Debera gauged the real

71. MS. Assam Buranji No. 15.
72. MS. Assam Buranji No. 15.

intention of the monarch, and informed the Swargadeo that he would start on the expedition after three days as he was convalescent at that time having just recovered from polypus of the nose.

Debera was not the man to let the grass grow under his feet. On that very night he met the three Dangarias and persuaded them to support Sarugohain, brother of Udayaditya, in his attempt to seize the throne. Debera then broached the proposal to Sarugohain who readily accepted the offer. The prince gave vent to his resentment on the conduct of Udayaditya,—"The Bairagi has become to my brother, not a mere hermit, but an object of extreme veneration, the Saheb of his head. The Dangarias have also accepted initiation from the Bairagi, and the twelve Mahantas have been summoned. Justice cannot tolerate this impious situation."[73] With the help of Debera and his brother Mohan Deka, Ratanpuria Hazarika, Namgila Hazarika, and Tairai Dolakasharia Barua, the prince collected one thousand armed followers to assail and surround the royal residence at Haithaguri and seize the person of the reigning monarch.

Sarugohain armed with a gold-embroidered sword and shield, approached the palace at midnight. Charingia Pelan Barbarua and Papang Chaudang Barua who were on guard at the palace attempted to offer some resistance, but seeing Sarugohain properly armed they tried to leave the precincts of the palace. Sarugohain hurled his spear at the Barbarua and pierced him at his thigh. The prince then inflicted the finishing blows on the Barbarua and killed the Chaudang Barua as well.

After this, Sarugohain stationed himself at the king's audience-chamber, and despatched men to guard the several gates of the palace compound. Debera and Mohan Deka proceeded to remove the ladder leading to the royal apartments. The seven door-keepers who were guarding the entrances were killed by Debera and Mohan. Their chief, Pacha-simalu of the Dimaruguria unit, having offered resis-

73. S. K. Bhuyan, *Assam Buranji, S. M.*, p. 126.

tance was also killed, and the gates were broken open by Gajpuria Hatibarua and Parikshit Dhekeri by employing elephants. King Udayaditya, soundly asleep on his bed, heard faintly the uproar and commotion outside, but the body-guard on duty in the royal bed-chamber, who had already been tutored by Debera, informed the monarch that the disturbance was due to the elephants coming out of their stalls, and the attempt made by the Barbarua to bring them round. The king was satisfied with the answer, and refrained from making further enquiries. The details connected with this *coup d'etat* had been prearranged by Debera.

Those who opposed Debera and Sarugohain in the execution of their plan were instantly put to death by these two leaders or by their emissaries; and among the slain were Parvatia Chetia Tamuli, Daha Barua and his son, Simaluguria Phukan, Gomotha's brother, Dewai Goal Barua, and Chandal Barua and his two sons. The life of Maupia was spared in view of the sanctity attached to him for his being once a hostage living with the Moguls.

Having besieged King Udayaditya Singha in his bed-chamber and thus making it impossible for him to escape, Sarugohain, seated in the audience-hall, declared himself to be king. Ghorakowanr Bhitarual Phukan who had assisted the new monarch in his bid for the throne was immediately re-elevated to the office of Barbarua.

On the following day Udayaditya was placed on a sedan and led to Charaideo Hill. His mother beseached Sarugohain to spare the life of Udayaditya, or kill her along with the deposed monarch. Sarugohain consoled his mother saying that he and his brother would excercise joint domination, he from his headquarter at Gargaon, and Udayaditya from his capital at Charaideo. Udayaditya was put to death soon after his arrival at Charaideo. Before he breathed his last he had put a handful of rice in his mouth and said,—"An innocent is being killed! O, Great God, may retribution descend on him who is committing this crime!"

Sarugohain then killed Paramananda after having subjected him to insults and humiliations. The Sannyasi's corpse was placed on a barge which was made to float down the river as a warning to others who ever schemed to set up a new order.

The popularity of the Gakulpuri Sannyasi was certainly based on some inherent quality or accomplishment which he possessed, whether it be affability of manners or profound learning and erudition. The fact that he hailed from Gakulpur near Brindaban conferred additional charm and significance to his personality, as these two places, so intimately associated with the life of Sri-Krishna, were endowed with special sanctity in the imagination of the Assamese people as there is hardly a Vaisnava song, poem or drama in which they are not mentioned. Udayaditya's plan to bring the old Vaisnava monks of Assam under the influence of Paramananda was a political blunder of the highest magnitude as it tended to subvert the ancient regime. Udayaditya and Paramananda, the Sultan and the Darwesh, both perished in the whirlpool of retribution, though posterity will admit that the Sannyasi was a mere creature of circumstances over which he had no control.

The Assamese might not have tolerated the influence of Paramananda, but they were shrewd enough not to make use of his knowledge of Mogul India. Assamese Pundits wrote down what they heard from Gakulpuri, and incorporated his episodes in the *Padshah-Buranjis,* or chronicles devoted to the Delhi Badshahs, which were preserved in Assam in numerous versions.

In one such *Padshah-Buranji,* Gakulpuri is described as the narrator of an episode. The passage runs thus,—"The two monarchs Shah Jahan and Prithivi Shah met each other with their soldiers and retainers which were as large as the sea; and there did not occur any hitch or misunderstanding, for which the masters of the ceremonies belonging to the two monarchs were praised by all. Here is finished what was said by Gakulpuri". As there is no second Gakulpuri in Assam history, and the compiler was sure that the toponomous appellation would not mean any one else but the

Sannyasi of Udayaditya's reign, we can be almost positive that the narrator was Paramananda Sannyasi himself.[74]

The episode heard from the lips of the Sannyasi can be reproduced briefly as follows:—Shah Jahan desires to see a sovereign equal to his power and magnificence. Asaf Khan, his Wazir, consults the state papers, and reports the absence of two monarchs of equal strength during the period from the reign of Yudhisthira to that of Jahangir, but the Wazir informs the emperor that his peer is to be found in the person of Prithivi Shah, son of Chandra Raja, king of Kandor, which is contiguous to the empire of Delhi. Shah Jahan proposes to meet Prithivi Shah near the junction of the two states, and exchanges embassies for that purpose. The two monarchs, the Padshah and the Raja, meet at the appointed place to their mutual delight, and make presents of valuable articles and horses to each other. Two Rajput combatants fight a duel in the presence of the sovereigns and expire on the spot from the wounds mutually inflicted.

74. S. K. Bhuyan, *Annals of the Delhi Badshahate*, p. 191.

CHAPTER VII

THE ATROCITIES OF DEBERA BARBARUA

In November 1672, Sarugohain formally ascended the throne and assumed the Hindu name Ramadhwaj Singha. The new king tried to ease his conscience by instituting expiatory measures in atonement for the sin of fratricide. He appointed Brahmans to perform sacrificial rites at Galporaghat on which occasion he liberally distributed largesses to the priests and astrologers. He also assembled the Vaisnava devotees and arranged for religious music and recital which continued uninterrupted for seven days and nights.

As a disciple of the Narwa Thakur the king made every attempt to enhance his Guru's power and prestige, and became instrumental in obtaining more disciples for the Mahanta. A monastery was constructed for the Narwa Thakur at Gajpur under the orders of Ramadhwaj Singha.

As for Debera Dakhinpatia Hazarika,—he was seething with discontent for not having gained anything in the way of official preferment from out of Sarugohain's elevation to the throne. Debera had been responsible for the slaughter of a large number of officials and nobles; and the blood of the slain was crying for retribution. The power and resources of a Hazarika, a commander of one thousand, were inadequate to create round Debera a wall of protection against the vengeance of his enemies, and he did not count much on the support of Ramadhwaj Singha which was bound to fluctuate in tune with the counsels and warnings of the nobles, always anxious to bring home to the monarch the real state of affairs. The kingship of Ramadhwaj was in its turn like a castle built on sands as it was tainted by fratricide and massacre of innocents, and characterised by imbecility. Ghorakowanr, the holder of the office of Barbarua to which Debera aspired, was strongly intrenched in the favour of the monarch, and Debera realised his inability to oust Ghorakowanr from office in the normal way. By one stroke of villainy however, which combined the worst forms of perjury, Debera succeeded in getting himself appointed Barbarua, and in securing for his nephew Chengmung the position of Bargohain.

The most effective method of bringing about the downfall and ruin of an innocent rival was to prefer against him allegations of treason and disloyalty, and fabricate evidence in support of the allegations. As arranged by Debera, a number of influential nobles informed the monarch that Langichang Barukial Bargohain, in league with the disciples of the Mayamara Mahanta, was planning to kill Ramadhwaj Singh and place on the throne Moran Gohain Charing Raja, son of Udayaditya. Debera personally reported to the king about the existence of this conspiracy, and obtained His Majesty's orders to enquire into the truth of the allegations. During a visit to the Ahom shrine at Charaideo, the king was informed that the Charing Raja and the Bargohain had taken possession of the palace at Gargaon. The king despatched a messenger on horseback to ascertain the truth of the report; and himself hurried back and took shelter at Kathalbari fort. The messenger returned with the information that all was quiet at Gargaon. Debera explained away the discrepancy by saying that a horse had been sent by the Bargohain to the Charing Raja, but the prince did not come, for which reason the plan to storm the Gargaon palace had to be abandoned. Debera then produced witnesses to support the allegations of conspiracy which were now considered to be beyond doubt. The king had no other alternative but to despatch emissaries to the Bargohain's residence with orders to put him to death. The tragic fate of Langichang Bargohain was shared by Moran Gohain as well. No formal trial was held on either occasion.

Debera then accused Ghorakowanr Barbarua of being a party to the conspiracy and produced evidence in support, with the result that Ghorakowanr was removed from office and sent home, and Debera was appointed Barbarua instead. Debera's nephew Chengmung Gohain, who had married a princess of blood royal, and who was the son of Nakjoi Dulia

Barua, was appointed Bargohain. Some of the witnesses produced by Debera made depositions contrary to his tutoring, and they were all put to the sword. Ghorakowanr managed to obtain a Phukanship at Gauhati.

The death of Langichang Bargohain opened the eyes of Ramadhwaj Singha who had accorded the sanction for the execution virtually under compulsion. He realised the precarious situation of his kingship, and of his very life, both of which now lay at the mercy of the unscrupulous Debera Barbarua.

Debera had been at Gajpur supervising the arrangements for the consecration ceremony of the Narwa Thakur's monastery which the king had intended to attend. But the monarch fell ill being seized with an attack of dropsy. This compelled Debera to return to Gargaon before the completion of the arrangements. Debera informed the king that he had arranged for *Nama-kirtan,* or religious music and recital, at the Narwa Satra, and made rich presents to Brahmans for the Swargadeo's speedy recovery. Debera then employed expert physicians for the treatment of the king. It was at this time that Langichang Barukial Bargohain was executed for the alleged conspiracy to place Moran Gohain on the throne.

Ramadhwaj Singha's growing illness combined with the misgiving arising from the tragic end of the Barukial Bargohain prompted him to make timely arrangements for a peaceful succession in the event of his sudden demise. He summoned to his presence Debera Barbarua, Simaluguria Naobaicha Phukan, Dilihial Gohain-Phukan and the other leading nobles, before whom he suggested the names of Kalia Gohain, Narayan Gohain Tipam Raja, and Ban Gohain Namrupia Raja as his intended successors. Kalia Gohain was the son of Udayaditya Singha, and the other two were the brothers of Udayaditya and therefore of Ramadhwaj. The nobles who attended the deliberations in the royal bed-chamber, including Debera Barbarua, expressed their willingness to abide by the recommendations of Ramadhwaj Singha. But after coming out of the royal presence, Debera told his followers of his intention to oppose tooth and nail the elevation of either of the three princes as it would mean his own undoing. "In league with the reigning monarch Ramadhwaj Singha", said Debera, "we had deposed Kalia Gohain's father Udayaditya; now after ascending the throne will the son or brother of Udayaditya seek our well-being? We cannot therefore accept either of them as our sovereign." Debera tried thenceforward to enlist supporters to his cause.

On the other hand the following nobles expressed their determination to implement the king's proposal by placing on the throne his first nominee Kalia Gohain,—Tangachu Phukan and his two brothers, the Charingia Phukan and the Tipamia Phukan; Lai Sandikoi Phukan's son, Gargayan Sandikoi's son, Kandali Brahman Bezbarua, Bura Hazarika and his two sons, Luthuri's son Gandhia Barua, Dola Kowanr, Dulia Barua and his son, the two brothers of Ramdhan who was the chamberlain of the senior queen.

There were thus two factions in respect of the selection of a successor to Ramadhwaj Singh,—first, those who supported the nominations of the reigning monarch; and secondly, those who opposed them. The second faction was headed by Debera Barbarua.

Debera fully realised the consequence to himself if he allowed the opposite faction to grow in power and strength, and he therefore made up his mind to destroy his opponents at the very outset. He summoned to the king's bed-chamber all the Phukans and Hazarikas on the pretext of a serious turn to the monarch's illness, and he killed one by one, during the course of one single night, twenty-four Hazarikas and all the Phukans of the metropolitan establishment. The king came out of the bed, leaning on the person of his senior consort, and asked Debera about what was happening. The Barbarua justified the massacre of the Phukans and Hazarikas by pointing out that they were all enemies of His Majesty, and that he should not therefore feel aggrieved.

This was too much for the king to tolerate; and having decided to punish Debera with death he asked Tangachu Phukan to carry out the sentence in the name of the sovereign.

Debera had been living with great caution in a set of houses constructed by him in the immediate vicinity of the king's audience-hall, where he always remained properly armed, ready to encounter any attack upon his person. Tangachu Phukan was instructed by the king to come out of an audience with him, and then approach Debera on the pretext of delivering a royal message, after which the Phukan was to inflict the fatal blow.

But decisions affecting the vital interests of the state which are guarded so vigilantly from the knowledge of the public are staple topics of conversation amongst maids and lackeys who in their humble capacity attend the deliberations of sovereigns and potentates. Kingh Ramadhwaj Singha's direction to Tangachu Phukan to extirpate Debera Barbarua was overheard by a maid of the royal bed-chamber, with an unusual degree of interest and concern as the Barbarua had honoured her with his favours and attentions. She visited Debera's residence, and after having passed some time in dalliance with her paramour she said to him,—"This is the last occasion when I am seeing your face, for to-morrow you will be killed by Tangachu Phukan as he has been asked to do so by the Swargadeo." Debera received confirmation of the report from Saona Tamuli, grandson of Langichang, a member of the Lukhurakhun family to which the Barbarua himself belonged. Debera remained prepared for the event.

As previously arranged the two brothers of Tangachu Phukan, namely, the Charingia Phukan and the Tipamia Phukan, came out of the king's presence with swords concealed in rolls of mats, and asked Debera to listen to a message from His Majesty which they said they had been commissioned to deliver. As the two Phukans approached Debera he attacked them with his sword and killed them on the spot. Debera then asked his personal attendants, Namdangia, Chungi, Ramjoi and Tajubaju, to rid him of his enemies, and they killed whomever they could lay their hands upon among whom were included numerous Phukans, Rajkhowas and Hazarikas. The principal victims of this second orgy of massacre were,—Tangachu Phukan's two sons Chatai Kukura-chowa Phukan and

Chenkham Raidangia Phukan; Lai Sandikoi Phukan's son, Dolakasharia Barua and his two sons, Luthuri's son Gandhia Barua, Ramdhan Bhandari Barua's two sons, the three sons of Charal Hazarika, Lehu Gargayan Sandikoi, Dulia Barua and his son, Lai Deka, and Lecham Khanikar Barua. The following had their eyeballs extracted under orders of Debera,—Kandali Brahman Bezbarua, Gomotha Parvatia Bhandari Barua, and Bhelai's son who was a Brahman. The heart of another Brahman named Ranga Bez was ripped open, and the liver extracted and made over to Debera for his close inspection. The king came out of his room and obtained particulars of the massacre. He then returned to his bed with consternation and grief, aggravated by a consciousness of his inability to deal appropriately with the arch-fiend Debera.

Debera could visualise the consequences of the king's eventual recovery from his present physical prostration. Debera directed Saona Tamuli to ask Kharmaju Bez, a physician attending on the sick monarch, to mix poison with the medicine to be administered to the patient. Kharmaju had no other alternative before him but to obey the orders of Saona Tamuli which he knew had emanated from the Barbarua, and the next dose of medicine brought the mortal years of Ramadhwaj Singha to an end. The event took place in November 1674, three days after the second massacre of the Gargayan officials.

Ramadhwaj Singha's chief queen who was the daughter of Chaparakhowa Gohain was buried alive with her deceased consort, as well as Laiman Deka, grandson of Ao Gohain. Debera also buried in the vault a widowed queen of Swargadeo Jayadhwaj Singha for her refusal to share with him the comforts of his household.

Debera then placed on the throne a prince from Tungkhung, but he reigned only for twelve days. His name is omitted in most of the contemporary records as his elevation to the throne was the single-handed action of Debera Barbarua, and did not receive the concurrence of the nobles whose allegiance was necessary to vest a prince with the title of a sovereign. This Tungkhungia Raja was killed by Debera for some unknown reason. He now placed on the throne a prince of the Samaguria branch of the royal family. The new monarch was known as Suhung Raja, and was a descendant of Suhungmung Dihingia Raja during whose reign Assam was invaded by Turbak, a commander of the Gaur Padshah. Suhung was the nephew on his mother's side, of Kachalukhowa Solal Gohain and had lived at Khamjang for which he was also known as Khamjangia Raja.

The murder of Ramadhwaj Singha was a prelude to the brutalities of Debera which he now pursued with undiminished ferocity. The first victims were Ramadhwaj Singha's nominees to the throne. Narayan Gohain Tipam Raja having heard of his brothers' death had hurried from Tipam, and halted at Dalouguri on his way to Gargaon. As he was proceeding towards the capital with the hope of becoming king he was met on the road by Debera and his two lieutenants Ratanpuria and Dakhinpatia. The Tipam Raja was overpowered and he fell into the ditch. Debera assured the prince that he would be placed on the throne as Ramadhwaj Singha's rightful heir and successor; and having dressed the prince in the attire of a monarch Debera asked Ratanpuria and Dakhinpatia to promptly lead Narayan Gohain to Gargaon and install him as Raja. The two henchmen carried out Debera's hint and killed Narayan Gohain, and also Kachalukhowa Solal Gohain who had accompanied the prince. Ban Gohain Namrupia Raja was killed at Namrup by Chetia Patar, an emissary of Debera. The fourteen sons of Udayaditya Singha were put to death, and the whole family of Ramadhwaj Singha became extinct, except a daughter who lived till the reign of Rudra Singha.

A useful method of espionage is the employment of trusted women in the services of those about whose movements and intentions the employer wants to obtain prompt and accurate information. Several ladies were placed by Debera in the inner apartments of Suhung Samaguria Raja who served as secret agents and informants of the Barua. The Raja's senior consort was Pakhari Gabharu, daughter of

Momai-tamuli Barbarua and sister of Lachit Barphukan and Laluk Barphukan. She was first a junior consort of Jayadhwaj Singha, and became through that monarch the mother of Nangchen Ramani Gabharu who was presented to the Mogul harem by her father in fulfilment of the terms of the treaty with Nawab Mir Jumla. After the death of Jayadhwaj Singha, Pakhari Gabharu became the Barkuanri or chief consort of King Chakradhwaj Singha; but she was subsequently degraded from her Barkuanriship for having commented on the king's flirtations with a maid. Another wife of Samaguria Raja was Ahalya Gabharu, and the third was the daughter of Marangi Barua.

Pakhari Gabharu was specially instructed by Debera Barbarua to educate the king in the formalities and manners of his exalted office. Ahalya Gabharu used to tell Debera all that happened in the royal palace. Marangi Barua's daughter was asked to perform the same duties as were entrusted to Pakhari Gabharu; but she was advised not to admit her husband to the exercise of his connubial rights. The Barbarua had also in his employ several maids of the royal household.

Debera then began to kill the officers and nobles who were suspected of enmity towards him or who had means to effect his destruction. He planned to kill the Simaluguria Naobaicha Phukan, son of Chengdhara Barbarua of the Chiringdang family. The Phukan did not stir out of his house on the plea of illness. Debera engaged a woman of ill repute to visit the house of the Phukan on the pretext of rendering some domestic service. She came back and reported to Debera about the faked illness of the Phukan whereupon Debera sought opportunities to get the Phukan murdered. Gomotha Bhandari Barua was killed on this occasion.

The *modus operandi* adopted by Debera in his campaign of slaughter was as follows: when an official visited the court in connection with his duties, Debera would announce to him that the king was offended with him and had therefore asked him to renounce his office and retire to his house. The officer would then be deprived of his retainers and insignias of office. Ratanpuria and Dakhinpatia would then be instructed to escort the dismissed officer to his house. They would in their turn cut the officer into pieces on the way. In this way Debera caused the destruction of a large number of officials belonging to the establishment at Gargaon.

Debera's atrocities roused the attention of the Raja's chief queen Pakhari Gabharu. She pointed out to the monarch his reduction to a nonentity in view of the unbridled authority of Debera. Samaguria Raja having realised the significance of the Barkuanri's misgivings held secret consultations with her, and Simaluguria Naobaicha Phukan and Laitai Deodhai, and decided to kill Debera. The proceedings of this conclave were conducted in the Ahom language which was the original dialect of the Ahom rulers and which had now fallen into comparative obsoleteness owing to their adoption of Assamese as the language of the court. A maid in attendance at the meeting came to know about the plan, and she forthwith informed Debera of his impending destruction.

To avert his doom Debera contrived the death of Samaguria Raja by administering to him medicine mixed with poison. Debera said to the queen,—"You were formerly a Tamuli Kuanri or a junior consort of Jayadhwaj Singha, and I have elevated you to the rank of the Barkuanri of the Samaguria Raja. Now you have plotted with your husband to kill me! So please accompany your husband to enjoy eternal sovereignty with him!" Towards the end of April 1675 the queen was put to death, and the body was placed in the grave of her first husband Jayadhwaj Singha. The Simaluguria Phukan was also killed, but Laitai Deodhai's life was spared as he belonged to an Ahom priestly clan. Suhung Samaguria Raja ruled only for twenty days.

Debera then placed a Tungkhungia prince on the throne named Gobar Gohain, son of Saranga Gohain, and grandson of Suklenmung Gargayan Raja, king of Assam, 1539-1552 A.D.

By a series of cold-blooded murders Debera purged the capital of his opponents and rivals. But the real leaders of the country were stationed at Gauhati who would one day bring Debera to book for the slaughter of their colleagues and relatives, and for assuming dictatorial powers, and for appointing and dismissing officers at his own sweet will. Debera then turned his attention to the Gauhati nobles, and sent his agent Lao Deka, son of Momai-tamuli Barbarua, to Gauhati to bring to Gargaon, under the alleged orders of the king, a number of commanders including Ghorakowanr Phukan Ex-Barbarua, the brother of Tangachu Rajkhowa, Sologuria Rajkhowa and his son, Chanda Rajkhowa, Luthuri's son Opar-Dayangia Rajkhowa and his brother, and Medelial Rajkhowa of the Tamuli-Doloi family and his son. These officers were taken to Laotali where they were killed under instructions from Debera Barbarua, while a few others were released from captivity. Debera decided upon the destruction of Lao Deka as well, but his execution was postponed to an appropriate occasion in future.

The gravest fears of Debera sprang however from Laluk Sola Barphukan, the Ahom viceroy of Gauhati and brother of Pakhari Gabharu and Lao Deka, and from Atan Buragohain, the prime minister. The Barphukan and the Buragohain had continued to remain at Gauhati as the possibilities of fresh hostilities with the Moguls had not completely disappeared. The premier utilised the interval in repairing the old forts, and in constructing new ones in and round Gauhati. The fort of Shahburuz at Manikarneswar Hill in North Gauhati was constructed during this period.

Two agents of Debera, Kalanchu's son Betmela, and Lao Deka of Dihingia Khatowal Chetia family, were despatched to Gauhati to bring Laluk Barphukan to Gargaon. They were also accompanied by fictitious orders from the king. They were also instructed by Debera to take the Buragohain with them if possible. Betmela and this second Lao Deka reached Gauhati in time, and communicated the so-called royal orders to the Gauhati nobles at the Dopdar or the viceregal court. It was evening, and the officers retired to their respective camps having postponed their deliberations till the next day.

Khamtat Pachani, son of the Buragohain, arrived at Gauhati the next day, and he said to his father,—"I have also been deputed to take the Barphukan. If you seek your well-being I would ask you not to make over the Barphukan, nor should you go yourself. It is known how Lao Deka, son of Momai-tamuli, had taken Ghorakowanr and the Phukans and Hazarikas, and how they were killed. We three have been sent this time to take the Barphukan; it is also reported that you will also be captured and killed. I have nothing more to suggest. You should act as the situation demands." Khamtat gave a vivid picture of the atrocities committed by Debera Barbarua, and the Gauhati officers decided to take action.

The climax in the tempo of Debera's diabolical activities was reached in his despatch of emissaries to capture and kill Laluk Barphukan and Atan Buragohain, the two most powerful nobles of the realm. Debera had started as the champion of a popular cause, namely, the movement against Paramananda Sannyasi; and he would, have been honoured and respected as a patriotic leader if he had stopped there. But he committed one enormity after another, slaughtered princes, nobles and queens; and to protect himself from the vengeance of the survivors he instituted a ceaseless and unscrupulous campaign of massacre, till ultimately bloodshed and brutality became an easy affair with him; and chaos, anarchy, confusion and darkness became the only elements in which his depraved propensities found a congenial atmosphere. The restoration of order and justice meant his sure destruction, and Debera planned deliberately to subvert the constitution, as we know from a declaration he made to his lieutenant Jengani Bakal Namgila Hazarika,—"The Ahoms are enjoying their sovereignty through the blessings of their tutelary image of Chengdeo, they have enslaved all people by the black letters enscrolled on paper; and trained men are employed to seduce wild elephants from the jungles. Therefore, know thee, O, Namgila, I shall throw the Chengdeo image into water, release the elephants, and set fire to the state documents."[75]

The Chengdeo, the state elephants, and the official records constituted three principal accessories and symbols of

75. S. K. Bhuyan, *Assam Buranji, S.M.*, p. 131.

Ahom sovereignty. The image had remained in possession of the Ahom kings since the days of the first conqueror Sukapha, and an officer called Chengdhara Barua used to look after its preservation and worship. It was also called *Chomdeo* or *Chom-cheng.* Its blessings and influence are thus described by Atan Buragohain,—"Sovereignty does not desert the possessor of Chomdeo, as the image is the abode of the goddess of prosperity. It confers other blessings as well."[76] Elephants were necessary for the movement of the monarchs, and they formed an indispensable part of all ceremonial processions. The state documents constituted the record of precedents, and of the arrangements for the administration of the country. In declaring his intention to destroy these three accessories Debera simply gave vent to his plan to destroy monarchy and set up an authoritarian regime with himself as the dictator and the sole dispenser of affairs.

A similar revolutionary sentiment was subsequently expressed by a rebellious prince Bhudhar Singha Gohain, grandson of King Rajeswar Singha. It was directed, not towards the subversion of the constitution, but towards the destruction of the reigning monarch Lakshmi Singha, his mother, his junior consort, his heir-apparent, and his favourite officers,—"About the Swargadeo," the prince said, "I shall first put the Black Tiger [Lakshmi Singha] in a fish-trap, and kill him by keeping him immersed in water for a number of days. As to the queen-mother, I shall first slice off the nose and ears of that old hag, and then pluck out her eyes, and set her at large at Amguri forest. As to the Tamuli Kuanri, a mere paddy-husker, I shall cut off her nose and ears, and then make her over to a Naga or to a scavenger. As to the Gohaindeo, the heir-apparent, I shall mete out to him condign punishment, and relegate him to a nasty place where he will be supplied with only two-and-a-half seers of rice a month. As to Kalita Phukan, he will be impaled, and the spear will pierce through his body from head to foot with repetitions of this process. As to Kam, Lephera, Pijali and

76. S. K. Bhuyan, *Deodhai Asam Buranji*, p. 89.

Lakhar, these four will be killed by being hooked in water like fish."[77]

Now to turn to Debera.—The inaction of the Gauhati nobles in the matter of Debera's excesses can be easily explained. The affair at Gargaon in spite of its horror and its dislocation of the normal machinery of government was after all a domestic distemper which could be righted at any moment. Matters of graver consequences had kept the Saraighat veterans fully occupied during the period, and under no circumstances could they be persuaded to relax their efforts, the threat of a foreign invasion still looming large before them as Ram Singha had continued to remain at Rangamati with the hope of resuming hostilities with Assam. The veterans had to choose between two alternatives,—suppression of the disorders at Gargaon, and adherence to their military responsibilities at Gauhati; and naturally, as all patriotic leaders would do, they chose the second alternative. Moreover, with Ram Singha knocking at the door of Assam, they abhorred the idea of giving to him the solacing impression of their engrossment in internecine feuds which Ram Singha also desired, and which he would himself like to stimulate by all means in his power. The history of the subsequent years will prove the wisdom and foresight inherent in this attitude as lack of vigilance at Gauhati produced the most tragical results tending to overthrow the independence and integrity of the country.

Towards the beginning of 1675, Ram Singha became impatient of waiting for an opportunity to attack Assam, and he reported to Emperor Aurangzeb about the futility of his further halt at Rangamati. The breaking up of the preparations of Ram Singha, of which the Ahom commanders of Gauhati received timely information, encouraged them to relax their vigilance at Gauhati, and turn their thoughts to the happenings at Gargaon.

77. MS. Assam Buranji No. 23.

CHAPTER VIII

REHABILITATION UNDER ATAN BURAGOHAIN

The Ahoms were adepts in the art of rehabilitation. The measures they devised for this purpose mingled diplomacy with force as the exigency of the situation demanded. The Gauhati nobles whose patriotic instincts had enabled them to frustrate the designs of Emperor Aurangzeb could now easily combine to put an end to the autocratic regime of Debera Barbarua who, in the language of the Assamese, was a mere mosquito buzzing inside a bed-curtain. Being fully acquainted with the deterioration that had taken place in the affairs of Gargaon, and being partially relieved of their Mogul worries, they decided to proceed in person to the capital to bring the situation under control and put a stop to the diabolical activities of Debera.

The Phukans and Rajkhowas of Gauhati assembled at one place, and deliberated on the situation of Assam. They concluded that matters had developed beyond the limits of endurance, and that the continuance of the anarchy at the metropolis was fraught with the risk of total collapse of the administration which was bound to react on their efforts to keep the Moguls at a distance. Prompt and vigorous action, they decided, was therefore necessary for the security of the kingdom, as well as for their own personal safety.

Laluk Sola Barphukan, accompanied by the Phukans, Rajkhowas, Hazarikas and other commanders stationed at Gauhati and the neighbouring garrisons, went in a body to the camp of the prime minister Atan Buragohain, and pointed out to him the gravity of the situation at Gargaon, and asked him to take the lead in setting matters right. They placed themselves entirely at his disposal, and suggested the necessity to march to Gargaon with a view to capture Debera and mete out to him and his associates the punishment they deserved.

The appeal of the Gauhati commanders made to the premier ran as follows: "We are falling at your feet centering all our hopes on Your Excellency's intervention. We beseech you not to make over the Barphukan. Debera is indulging in the game of setting up a monarch at his own sweet will and in subsequently putting that monarch to death by his own hand! Now, Debera has sent orders to take the Barphukan in order to kill him! What authority has that slave of a Debera to do all this? Such acts can be done only under the authority of His Majesty. Should that villain Debera act in his way? At Gargaon he has exterminated practically the whole race of Phukans, Baras and Buruks, and others, high and low, nobles and commoners. He had besides managed to take from Gauhati Ghorakowanr Barua and a number of Phukans, Rajkhowas and Hazarikas, and he has contrived their death. He is now planning to capture and kill us as well. We therefore seek the protection of Your Excellency. Interregnums had existed in the past,—for seven years in the days of Tyao-Khamthi Raja, and for five years in the days of Sutupha Raja. During those periods the administration was conducted by the Bargohain and the Buragohain. We now implore Your Excellency to protect the people in the same way. In the event of Your Excellency's refusal the whole country is doomed to destruction. We propose that we should all go up to Gargaon under the leadership of Your Excellency and capture Debera. Your Excellency will then institute a regular trial of the offenders, and punish those who deserve punishment.[78]

Atan Buragohain who had been animated throughout his career by a high sense of patriotism was not willing, as the chief minister of the state, to sit complacently as the government was being gradually liquidated by the excesses of Debera Barbarua. The premier had, besides, at his disposal the resources mustered at Gauhati to combat the Moguls.

78. S. K. Dutta, *Assam Buranji*, p. 37; and S. K. Bhuyan, *Assam Buranji, S.M.*, p. 31.

He accepted the proposal of the Gauhati commanders and agreed to assume full responsibility for restoring the equilibrium of the government. But before taking any action in pursuance of the proposal he extracted a promise from the Gauhati commanders and soldiers that they would obey his instructions to a man and to the minutest detail. The Buragohain said,—"I shall protect you provided you do not deviate from my instructions. I shall institute necessary measures for the security of the kingdom to the best of my ability and intelligence. As the people have looked upon me as their protector and saviour at this critical juncture I shall never leave them in the lurch."

The Phukans, Rajkhowas and others of the Gauhati establishment entered into a solemn league and covenant to abide by the directions of the Buragohain, and adhere to each other of the confederacy in all circumstances and events. They placed before them articles sacred to the Vaisnavas,—the manuscripts of *Gita, Bhagavat* and *Ratnavali; Salagram,* copper, and the *tulasi* or basil plant; and in the presence of Brahmans they took the following oath,—"If we act contrary to the plans and orders of Your Excellency all the merits which we have earned hitherto will be nullified, our ancestors will be doomed to perdition, and we shall also go to hell. Besides, we promise not to desert one another."[79]

Arrangements were then made for the march of the Saraighat veterans to Gargaon. The affairs of Gauhati were placed in charge of Guimela Gohain-Phukan of the Bargohain family; Cheregual Gohain-Phukan of the Buragohain family; Kamalabaria Amuncheng Neog; Gajpuria Kalanchu Neog; Paniphukan, son of Phulbarua; and Kirkiria Phukan of the Duara family. The officers attached to the garrisons lower down the Brahmaputra continued in their respective charges, namely, Bar-Abhaypuria Rajkhowa Sen Gohain at Barepaita, Saru-Abhaypuria Chetia Rajkhowa at Bhogpur.

79. S. K. Bhuyan, *Assam Buranji, S.M.*, p. 131. *Ratnavali*, or *Bhakti-Ratnavali* of Vishnupuri Sannyasi in Sanskrit, translated into Assamese verse by the great Vaisnava reformer and poet Madhabdeva.

Orders were despatched to Chandranarayan Dharma-raja of the North Bank, Krishnanarayan Raja, Madurial Laithepena Solal Bargohain, and Kaliabaria Barchetia to get ready with their respective contingents to accompany the Buragohain to Upper Assam. The triple set of militia, *mul, dowal* and *tewal*, under the Kaliabar and Marangi commanders, were properly raised, and they remained prepared to accompany the force. The Buragohain's object was to raise the force necessary for his Gargaon expedition from among the waiting militia so that the old standing army employed in the Gauhati garrisons might not be the least disturbed, though a temporary withdrawal of some of the old Gauhati commanders was imperative to officer the new contingents.

The leading figures of the anti-Debera confederacy were: Laluk Sola Barphukan; the senior Duara Phukan; Pani-Abhaypuria Rajkhowa; Phulbarua's nephew; Pani-Dihingia Lehetia Phukan; Opar-Dayangia Datakaria Rajkhowa; Lari-gohain, brother of the Namdayangia Buragohain; Lalun, son of Pani-Dihingia Rajkhowa Lapeti Phukan; Mecha Rajkhowa of the Rangachila Duara family, and their subordinate Hazarikas and Saikias. It is said in one contemporary chronicle that the Phukans and officers of Gauhati did not remain satisfied by simply making Atan Buragohain their leader, and that they made him the Raja, and vested him with full sovereign power.

The expedition under Atan Buragohain left Gauhati early in April 1675, and proceeded by land as well as by water. Debera Barbarua made preparations to encounter the Saraighat force. He erected stockades on the south bank of the Dikhow river extending from the Kharikatia gate to the bank of the river; and on the north, from the Hahcharaghat to the proximity of the Darika river. He collected all available men, equipped them with arms and weapons, and posted them to guard the entrances and walls of the capital. He also assembled the Bangals or up-country men who had been residing at Takoubari, had them trained as sipahis with swords, shields and horses, and kept them by his own side. Debera himself took charge of the Mechaghar Duar; Chengmung Bargohain was in charge of the Barakhowa Duar; and Achuk Barpatra Gohain of the Bahgara Duar. Gobar Raja was made to stay at a camp near Chatai-ali. Arrangements were also made for guarding the several river-gates.

As an additional safeguard Debera retained in his custody the sons and nephews of the Gauhati Phukans and Rajkhowas, as well as the eldest son of Laithepena Solal Gohain, and declared his intention to decapitate them and throw the dismembered limbs to their parents and uncles if he had to face an eventual defeat at their hands.

Debera was living at that time with his wives and women near the temple of Chomdeo. Having heard of the approach of the Gauhati army he left his residence in battle-array solemnising the occasion by beheading Lao Deka, brother of Laluk Sola Barphukan, at the principal entrance of the capital city of Gargaon.

Debera realised the futility of resisting the army of the Gauhati veterans, and tried to prevent their progress by making diplomatic overtures. His henchman Dakhinpatia Tajubaju Neog was despatched with presents to meet the commanders at Kaliabar. The presents consisted of gold and silver articles,—dishes, jugs, bangles, earrings and necklaces, and garments, graded according to the position and status of the recipients, the best assortment being reserved for the Buragohain and the four principal Phukans. He also sent suitable presents for each Rajkhowa and Hazarika.

Debera, shrewd as he was, was not slow in discovering the weak point in the plan of the Buragohain and his adherents, namely, the relinquishment of their commands at Gauhati while the Moguls were still loitering at the frontier, and the risk taken by the Gauhati commanders only for curbing the activities of one single subject of the Swargadeo. Debera therefore asked the Gauhati nobles to return to their commands, and remain prepared as before for counteracting the Moguls. "The kingdom of the Ahoms," said Debera in the message accompanying the presents, "is a veritable casket of gold. Why should it be left to the mercy of the enemy for the sake of one single individual? They should remain where they were, and send only the Buragohain to conduct the affairs at the capital. I shall do whatever they ask me to do. Why should they undergo troubles on my account?"

The Gauhati commanders and their men were shrewd enough to see through the game Debera wanted to play. The soldiers sent this reply to Debera,—"Having had to serve at Saraighat we have not seen our sons and nephews for a long time; and we shall be happy to see their faces when we go up to Upper Assam." The four principal Phukans added,—"Having received such valuable presents it is not proper that we should not have a meeting with our generous friend." The reply of the Buragohain pointed out the inner reality of the situation,—"The enemy has entered into the very casket of gold! What is the harm if the outskirts of the kingdom are now exposed to hostile attacks?" The Gauhati force then resumed their march to Gargaon.[80]

Demoralisation began to set in the camp of Debera when it was learnt that the Gauhati commanders were within an easy reach of the capital. Debera's followers did not fail to foresee the inevitable termination of the reign of terror which their master had inaugurated taking advantage of the absence of the stalwarts from Gargaon. On their arrival at Jhanji, Chengmung Bargohain deserted his post at Barakhowa gate and went over to the camp of the Buragohain. The Baruas and Baras posted at Bahgara gate deserted their charge and took shelter within the walls of the palace compound.

Further defection took place on the arrival of the Gauhati force at Namdang. During the course of the very same night the remnants of Debera's partisans stationed at different places abandoned their respective posts and took to their heels. Debera himself fled to some unknown destination.

From Namdang the Gauhati commanders proceeded to Sakbari, on the bank of the Dikhow river, and they fixed their headquarters at the local Naosal or dockyard.

Emissaries were then despatched to different quarters to trace the whereabouts of Debera Barbarua. He was found

80. S. K. Bhuyan, *Assam Buranji, S.M.*, p. 132.

ultimately in his hiding at Thukubil near Dilih where he was captured. He was put in a pig-cage with his senior wife seated on the top of the cage, and he was brought in that array to the camp of the Gauhati commanders at Sakbari Naosal. He was then kept for a time on a raised bamboo platform erected at the Naosal. His junior wife who was a princess by birth was made to sit on his shoulders when he was brought to the presence of Laluk Barphukan to stand his trial. Debera had to remain in that posture during the entire course of the criminal proceedings.

During the trial which was presided over by Laluk Barphukan, Debera was asked to state the reasons which had led him to commit such barbarities. Debera's reply to the Barphukan was significant and prophetic,—"Have you not heard that we are composed of the same elements? I have composed some verses of the *Dasama*, and you in your turn will compose the rest."[81] The first half of the *Dasama*, or the tenth canto of the Bhagavat, was translated into Assamese by Mahapurush Sankardeva, who allowed the subsequent half to be translated by his disciple Ananta Kandali. The book deals with the life and teachings of Sri-Krishna, and was very helpful in propagating the Vaishnava faith, known also as *Bhagavati Dharma* in Assam. Sankardeva and Ananta Kandali were inspired by the same motive,—the glorification of Sri-Krishna, and Sankardeva's injunction to Ananta Kandali to complete the translation was to prove the identity of their souls though they were lodged in separate bodies. Debera could see that Laluk Barphukan, a Lukhurakhun like himself, had the making of a traitor and a villain as much as he himself had; and subsequent events will prove the significance of Debera's prophecy.

Laluk Barphukan then informed Debera of the impending sentence of death. This gave an opportunity to Debera to amplify his prophecy regarding the fate of the judge himself, and he said,—"I am going to be killed by you, a man; but you are destined to die at the hands of women belonging

81. S. K. Bhuyan, *Assam Buranji*, S.M., p. 133.

to your own household. No purpose is served by attributing blame to me. What is decreed by Fate is bound to take place." Laluk Barphukan passed against Debera the verdict of the extreme penalty of law to be accompanied by insults and tortures.[82]

It was proposed to press Debera to death between wooden cylinders. The culprit was abused and reviled all the way as he was led to Rajahat to undergo the sentence. Two men died in the meantime under the weight of the rollers as they were being carried to the place of execution. This mode of punishment was given up, and it was now decreed that Debera should be killed by being hoed from foot to head. As victims in Sakta worship are first anointed with holy water before they are tied to the sacrificial pillar, Debera's junior wife was made to relieve her kidneys upon her husband's person.[83] Debera's body was then cut, slice by slice, with a hoe, starting from the feet, and ending at the head. The gruesome task was performed by a Hari or a man of the scavenger caste.

Thus died Debera Barbarua who for the space of thirty months had proved himself a terror to kings and queens, princess and nobles, and masters and serfs. In the whole recorded history of Assam Debera occupies the topmost place among political intriguers and murderers. His championship of the cause of the Assamese Vaishnava monks, and his attempts to curb the influence of the thaumaturgic Sannyasi of Gakulpur constituted a highly patriotic move; but he exceeded the limits of necessity when he intrigued with Sarugohain in bringing about the deposal and murder of Udayaditya Singha. Having committed this first crime Debera proceeded to other misdeeds to protect himself from the consequences of his initial act of villainy. The subsequent murder of the princes and of Ramadhwaj Singha himself made Debera's position odious and intolerable. He realised that his life was safe only in a state of civil commotion, and that his opponents would

82. S. K. Bhuyan, *Assam Buranji, S.M.*, p. 133.

83. MS. Assam Buranji No. 14.

stay their hand of retribution only if he made himself an object of terror who would not allow anybody to thwart his will. Debera's case was not one of "motiveless malignity", as continued absorption in machinations and murders was necessary for his very preservation. He developed revolutionary propensities, and stopped the functioning of the normal government, the restoration of which would spell disaster to himself.

Debera's accomplices shared the fate of their master. The sentence of death was passed on Bacha Hazarika, Chungi Hazarika, Ramjoy, Namgila Hazarika, Dewai Bamun, Lai Bacha and Tetera Kari. The sentences were carried out at Rajahat. Tajubaju Neog who had been confined at Kaliabar was executed at that place. Another lieutenant of Debera, Nara by name, was tied with a rope round his neck, and made to wear cock-feathers on his head. He was then asked to account for his crimes. "Who am I to do anything?", said Nara, "There was Debera Barbarua, and I did as he asked me to do. It is wise for an individual to act as he is directed by a stronger man." Nara was released for the candid exposition of the situation. The closest male relatives of Debera were traced out, captured, and put to death in consonance with the legal maxim of the Assam government,—"The shoots as well as the roots of a bitter plant are equally bitter."[84] The remaining adherents of Debera were gradually captured and put to death.

Atan Buragohain then set upon himself the task of replacing some of the old officers by new ones which was necessary in order to cleanse the government of the sinister traditions of Debera's regime. The sons and nephews of the Phukans who had been killed by Debera were now admitted to the rank of Phukans and Baruas.

84. Bhandari Gohain made this observation when King Pratap Singha asked him as to how to deal with the daughter of Akhek Gohain who had been condemned to death for treason. She was accordingly executed. Bhandari Gohain had to share a similar fate for the capital offence and conviction of his sons.

The major appointments were as follows:—Ramcharan Cheng Gohain, son of Chapa Patra and son-in-law of Atan Buragohain, was appointed Barpatra Gohain in place of Achuk, deceased; Guimela Laluk Gohain-Phukan was appointed Bargohain in place of Chengmung, dismissed from office; Kirkiria Phukan, son of Rangachila Duara Phukan, was appointed Barbarua in place of Debera, executed; Tepartalia Gohain of the Buragohain family was appointed Deka-Phukan in place of Simaluguria Phukan. The following were appointed Phukans: Bhatdhara, brother of Laluk Sola Barphukan, in place of Tangachu Phukan; Mecha, the younger son of Rangachila Duara Phukan, in place of his brother Kirkiria, promoted to the office of Barbarua; and Lalukia Gohain of the Bargohain family. The following were appointed Rajkhowas: Kari Deka, brother of Laluk Sola Barphukan, was appointed Dikhowmukhia Rajkhowa, in place of Kalanchu; Kekora Sandikoi as Pani-Sologuria Rajkhowa in place of Tangachu; a brother of Kirkiria Barbarua as Tarua-Dihingia Rajkhowa. Lao Deka Harkina Barua of the Khatowal Chetia family was appointed Barchetia in place of Okanimaria Barchetia.

Debera's nominee on the throne, Gobar Raja, had meanwhile been deposed, and kept in confinement at Haithaguri. He was now put to death at Bhogbari along with his brother Nisaranga Gohain. This happened on Wednesday, the 23rd May 1675. Gobar had become Raja for about three weeks.

The throne now became vacant for want of a successor. The Phukans offered the kingship to Atan Buragohain; but he declined the offer in a summary manner, saying,—"I am a minister, and hence I cannot become the king. A reed-pole cannot stand the weight of a buffalo-thigh, and a Sudra cannot wear the sacred thread of a Brahman."[85]

Atan Buragohin, in the company of his four sons, searched for a suitable prince for the throne, and they found one at Dihing, who was a member of the Namrupia royal family.

85. MS. Assam Buranji No. 39; S. K. Bhuyan, *Kamrupar Buranji*, p. 89; H. C. Goswami, *Purani Assam Buranji*, p. 152.

The prince's name was Arjun, and he was the grandson of Swargadeo Pratap Singha, and son of Namrupia Gohain who had been a co-disciple of the premier.

The Buragohain then reminded his adherents of their old promise to support him, and communicated to them his intention to place on the throne Arjun Kowanr, the prince from Dihing. The nobles reiterated their promise to support the Buragohain in all circumstances, and said,—"Why should we not pay our homage to a prince who is found fit to receive Your Excellency's allegiance?" Arjun Kowanr, the Dihingia prince, was accordingly declared as king, and the nobles knelt down before him and took their oath of allegiance at Sakbari Naosal. The prince is known as Dihingia Raja, as his home was at Dihing.

The government of the country was thus restored to peace and order. A crude contemporary chronicle specifically mentions this fact in the following words,—"The people and the country became well settled, and the government functioned according to the usages of the past." Laluk Barphukan and the other Gauhati commanders returned to their respective posts leaving Atan Buragohain in charge of the affairs of the metropolis.

In November 1675, the coronation ceremony took place at Barnaosal at a newly constructed Singarighar, without which function no prince attained the status of a full-fledged sovereign. The Dihingia Raja, who was then forty years old, assumed the Ahom name Sujinpha. The Gohains, the Phukans, the Rajkhowas, the Baruas, and other officials, as well as the populace, were given appropriate presents, and the festivities continued for seven days.

Atan Buragohain's refusal to accept the exalted office of a monarch offered to him by the nobles in their free-will and volition, and his selection of the Dihingia prince for succession to the throne, were viewed with great satisfaction by that prince, and he expressed his gratefulness to the Buragohain by saying,—"The nobles and the populace recognised the Bahgaria Buragohain as their king, but he declined to accept the honour. On the other hand, in consultation with his colleagues he appointed me as king. In appreciation of this fact, and as a token of my esteem and regard for him I should give him some presents and confer upon him some distinctions." Arjun Raja then presented to the Buragohain a pair of long earrings, a pair of bangles, a *bata* or tray with a stand, a lime-pot and a mirror, each of these articles being made of gold; a headwear with gold embroidery, a necklace of pearls, a suit of garments, two elephants and two ponies. The Buragohain was also given a large plot of fertile land, and twenty *paiks* or retainers of the Kaivarta caste to attend on him when he would go out on his sedan. Sixty more *paiks* from Mulatali were also allotted to him. The *paik* allotments were in addition to those to which he was ordinarily entitled as Buragohain and Rajmantri.

Arjun Raja's mother was a daughter of the Khatowal Chetia family. The Raja had married the two daughters of Kekora Sandikoi; the elder was made Barkuanri, and the younger Parvatia Kuanri. The Barkuanri was the mother of four sons,—Kalia Gohain, Dighala Gohain, Dhala Gohain and Saru Gohain.

The king and the Buragohain lived and worked in harmony and friendship; and their relationship became specially intimate and cordial as they were both disciples of the Mahanta of Moramara Satra. They constructed a temple at that monastery, and the ceremony of its consecration was attended by the king and the prime minister.

The premier interviewed the monarch after every eight or ten days; and he used to be accompanied on those occasions by a body of armed men, consisting of archers, shieldsmen, musketeers, swordsmen, spearmen and clubmen, as was the custom of the nobles when they went out of their residences. The wisdom and influence of Atan Buragohain made the officers of all ranks and positions to look upon him as the corner-stone of the government, and they paid frequent visits to his residence for consultation and advice. It became a practice with the nobles and officers to first pay court to the Buragohain at his residence on their way to the secretariat and the tribunal of justice where they had to go in connection with their daily duties. The Vaisnava monks also considered the Buragohain as the receptacle of all temporal power, and hence their sole patron and protector.

Peace was thus restored to the land, and the king and his ministers applied themselves wholeheartedly to the institution of measures for the well-being of the people. Atan Buragohain was not a mechanical practitioner in the art of government; he was an idealist, and he held definite views regarding the achievement of human happiness and the ultimate end of sovereignty, as we know from the chronicle written by him. He speaks of the *Satya-yuga* or the Golden Age,—"Love was the order of the day: men used to take food from the same dish like sons of the same mother: nobody entertained any jealousy or hatred towards any other person." Speaking of the reign of Khunlung's son, an early Shan king who was an ancestor of the Ahom race of monarchs, the Buragohain says in his chronicle,—"During his rule the miseries of the people came to an end, and they became happy as before. The king governed his subjects as his own sons. There was no taxation in his time. He lived in the ways of righteousness, according due punishment to every guilt, and reward and honour to virtue and merit." These sentiments must have formed the Buragohain springs of action in his administrative measures.[86]

86. S. K. Bhuyan, *Deodhai Asam Buranji* p. 89

CHAPTER IX

DIHINGIA RAJA QUARRELS WITH THE PREMIER

The reign of Arjun Dihingia Raja supported by the wisdom and foresight of Atan Buragohain promised to be one of prosperity and peace. As the grandson of Swargadeo Pratap Singha, Dihingia Raja inherited the refinement, sobriety and patriotism of his illustrious sire. Arjun Raja was in his domestic relations a man of peace, and he dissociated himself from anything which bordered on arrogance and autocracy. Grateful in disposition he was unwilling to take harsh measures against his supporters and friends, even when such measures were urgently called for. At the same time he was by temperament incapable of opposing the intentions of his immediate associates though he realised that their projects had emanated from pride and selfishness. The Buragohain resembled the monarch in many respects; he was dominated by a high sense of patriotism, and he totally eliminated self in his private and political dealings. He could look squarely at facts, and get into the inner reality of things, and he never hesitated to state his convictions before his colleagues who entertained contrary views and opinions. In the light of developments it was generally found that the Buragohain was right and his opponents were wrong.

The Swargadeo and the Buragohain were determined from the very beginning to employ all their resources in the achievement of the good of the people, and for this purpose they resolved to live in amity and concord. But men were not wanting in the palace and in the court who disliked this combination, more specially they abhorred the growing power of the Buragohain. Most of the nobles had directly or indirectly participated in the machinations of Debera, and conspiracy and treachery had become the very soul of their being which they could not shake off in a moment. These nobles now realised that their secret ambitions and plans could be accomplished only when the king could act independently, unaided and unhampered by the counsels of the astute Buragohain. So, discord between the king and his premier became the principal objective of a section of the nobles, as that situation was favourable to the accomplishment of their selfish designs.

Dihingia Raja was a perfect gentleman, but his character suffered from lack of vigour and initiative. He dared not offend anybody, more specially if the parties were his intimates amongst whom he had to pass most of his time. He lent his ears to the whisperings of his womenfolk which proved more irresistible at times than the casual and formal counsels of the Buragohain.

Just as the officers of Gauhati were arranging to leave the metropolis on the termination of the Singarighar celebrations, Dihingia Raja, with a view to secure the throne for his own sons, put to death the princes descended from Suklenmung Gargayan Raja. The Buragohain and his colleagues submitted their protest to the monarch expressing their disapproval of this ruthless slaughter of princes.

The hero in the ensuing drama of estrangement between the king and the premier was Lao Deka, *alias* Harkina Barua, of the Dihingia Khatowal Chetia family, who had been sent by Debera to Gauhati to bring Laluk Barphukan to Gargaon, and who had been subsequently promoted to the office of Barchetia by Atan Buragohain. He had free access to the palace as a near relative of the king's mother. The Barchetia succeeded in rousing the maternal fears of the Barkuanri by warning her of the evil days that were in store for her four sons if the Buragohain was allowed to wield unbounded power as he was doing at present. The queen, in order to enlighten her husband on the dangers of the situation as pointed out to her by the Barchetia, said,—"The Buragohain and the Phukans have sworn steadfast adherence to one another, and they therefore oppose your intentions and actions. They do not entertain any good-will towards our four sons. Do you think the princes' lives will be secure when you will be no more? It would have been much better if we had continued to live in our own village by ploughing our fields than to lead this life of subordination to others." The four princes supported their mother, and gave vent to similar misgivings, adding,—"Our sovereignty is only in name as the Buragohain monopolises all power in himself." The king declined to interfere with the exercise of power by the Buragohain in view of their mutual professions of friendship and co-operation. The Barchetia was thus frustrated in his first attempt to antagonise the king against the premier.

Two sons of Arjuna Raja had once, in the excitement of a hunting excursion, obstructed the path of the Buragohain. The consequences of this discourtesy were exaggerated by Lao Barchetia, and stern measures against the princes were reported as being contemplated by the Buragohain. They now planned to kill the premier when he was asleep in a neighbouring camp. Lao Barchetia having apprised him of the plot the Buragohain made good his escape and went home. This is how the double-faced Barchetia deepened the estrangement between the royal family and the premier.[87]

Lao Barchetia now harnessed the services of a senior female attendant of the royal household. It was her duty to bring daily to the Buragohain twenty trays of presents from the king. One day she warned the premier of the preparations made by the king for his capture, and she asked the premier to remain similiarly prepared for an eventuality. The Buragohain dismissed the lady after asking her to tell him more about the plot and promised to advance her rank. She then went to Dihingia Raja and told him that the Buragohain was making elaborate preparations for attacking the monarch. The Raja believed the maid's story, and remained vigilant and prepared with his four sons. He posted additional men to guard the entrances of the palace, and appointed spies to keep watch over the movements of the Buragohain and his adherents.

The Phukans came to know of the preparations made by the king, and they went in a body to the Buragohain and

87. MS. Assam Buranji No. 39.

suggested to him the advisability of attacking the king before the latter completed the preparations. The Buragohain, as a constitutionalist, did not support the proposal made by the Phukans, and he said,—"What you have said is not dictated by canons of propriety. Your proposal, if carried out, will result in the total annihilation of our families. Rebellion is to be shunned as an impious move. We should, instead, enquire of the monarch as to the persons who have created this distrust and suspicion." The Buragohain and the Phukans proposed to go to the palace and meet the king for clarification of their doubts.[88]

Lao Barchetia in his turn gave a different colouring to the honest desire of the Buragohain and his friends for an audience with His Majesty for the purpose of reconciling their differences. The Barchetia was no doubt afraid that the proposed meeting of the king and the nobles would result in the discovery of the part he was playing in fomenting the estrangement. He therefore resolved to prevent the meeting, and thereby upset the Buragohain's apple-cart of reconciliation. The Barchetia persuaded the Barkuanri to warn the king of the dangers of an interview with the nobles, as it might give them an opportunity to accomplish some prearranged plan for the destruction of the monarch. The assumedly friendly advice of the Barchetia was duly communicated by the gullible queen to her husband and king. The Barchetia, however, continued to remain on friendly terms with the Buragohain, and even supported the latter's plans.

A few days later, the Buragohain accompanied by the Phukans proceeded to the Barchora or the council-chamber, wherefrom they deputed the Majumdar Barua, the king's private secretary, to convey the following message soliciting an interview with His Majesty,—"Well, Majumdar, please tell the Swargadeo as follows,—In the primordial days Mahadeva swallowed poison to save the gods and the demons from fear. We have come to meet the king in his palace just to enquire as to who amongst us have said anything untoward

88. S. K. Dutta, *Assam Buranji*, p. 40.

to the princes, and when and how we have disobeyed the orders of His Majesty. The person who has created this misunderstanding should be asked by the king to support his allegations by proper evidence. If His Majesty is convinced of our guilt we should be dismissed from office and expelled; and if the allegations are found to be baseless then the person who fabricated them should be removed from association with His Majesty. If this is done the king and ourselves will be rid of mutual fears and suspicions. We are prepared to take fresh oaths and repeat our homage to His Majesty in proof of our fidelity. The king should invite us to a friendly banquet and assure us that we have no reason to fear from his quarter."[89] The Majumdar Barua duly communicated to the king the message of the nobles, but Dihingia Raja who had implicit faith in the warnings of the Barchetia refused to come out. He said he was unwell, and asked the nobles to go home. From this incident the nobles realised the hostile attitude of Dihingia Raja. The virus of distrust of the Buragohain implanted in the king's heart by the intimate associates of the palace thus began to work its way.

Dihingia Raja then actively engaged himself in preparations to seize the persons of the Buragohain and his supporters. He equipped the attendants of the palace with *daos*, shields, bows and arrows, and mounted guns at the several entrances. The four princes took charge of the preparations. A spy was set against each partisan of the Buragohain to watch his movements and actions.

Tepartalia Ram Phukan, Dilihial Langi Phukan, Kalanchu Phukan Govinda and Bhitarual Phukan Betmela pressed the Buragohain for immediate action to counteract the king's designs which, they were informed, would be put into operation the next day. The Phukans asked the Buragohain to take the lead in their contemplated attack on the palace, saying,—"If you do not come out you shall earn eternal demerit as the slayer of our wives and children." The Buragohain was unwilling to adopt hostile measures against the sovereign

89. S. K. Dutta, *Assam Buranji*, p. 40.

which he described as "dire treason, an action destined to destroy the sustenance of the entire family, a step to be shunned at all costs."[90] That day was Saturday, eleventh Ashar, 1598 *Saka*, or June 25, 1676 A.D. or near about. As no momentous step should be taken on a Saturday, which is an inauspicious day, the Buragohain asked the Phukans to wait till the following night. The Phukans then fell prostrate at the premier's feet, and appealed to him in the name of his gods and ancestors, and entreated him to come out. They caught hold of the premier's hand, and put him in the sedan. The premier had thus no other alternative but to lead the party of the Phukans. He was accompanied by his attendants and followers all properly armed. The Buragohain asked his son-in-law Ramcharan Barpatra Gohain to join the party with his followers; but Ramcharan evaded immediate compliance, and promised to join up after having a bath. He however allowed half his men to accompany the Buragohain retaining the other half with himself. The premier and the Phukans with a force of armed men entered the palace enclosure shortly after midnight.

The Buragohain halted for some time at the principal gate of the palace; and then he proceeded on his sedan to the entrance of the Barchora where had assembled Laithepena Solal Gohain, Lao Barchetia, and the other leading officers and nobles. Bhatdhara Phukan entered the precincts of the palace by the gate leading to the queens' apartments, and removed the ladder to prevent any escape. Kirkiria Barbarua left the scene in the company of a few attendants, and proceeded to Kharikatia.

Having heard the commotion and uproar Dihingia Raja issued out of his room attended by the armed guards of the palace, and killed whomsoever he met on the way. A shieldsman of the Swargadeo named Chatai-kukura, brandished his sword as he walked by the side of the king, and managed to put twelve men to death. Betmela Phukan snatched away

90. S. K. Dutta, *Assam Buranji*, p. 40.

the king's waterpot, made of gold, from its bearer Chengpetu Jaradhara.

Having seen the king, blazing with fury and revenge, the Buragohain got down from his sedan, and stood at the open space near the Barchora. The Swargadeo approached the sedan in darkness and inflicted on it a few blows with his sword thinking that the premier was seated inside. The Buragohain then left the scene and fled down the river to Dilih in a dug-out taken from the boat-house at Lechang. Proceeding down the Dilih the Buragohain came to Salkowanr; there he collected his followers and came to Jakaichuk where he remained prepared. From Jakaichuk the Buragohain shifted his camp first to Govindapur and then to Lakhau and Dergaon. Ramcharan Barpatra Gohain who had followed the premier to the palace returned to his residence after the flight of his father-in-law.

In the meantime Guimela Laluk Bargohain, Lao Barchetia and Laithepena Solal Gohain rushed to the presence of the king. The monarch got frightened, and stepped forward sword-in-hand to meet the three nobles. The latter explained their action to be in pursuance of their loyal anxiety to come to the aid of the monarch in that emergency. Dihingia Raja got terribly nervous, and could not be easily pacified. The Solal Gohain reminded the king of the necessity to become steady by controlling himself, saying,—"If Your Majesty becomes upset at this trivial affray how could you expect your subjects to remain cool and steady under trials and ordeals?" The Solal Gohain then placed the Dihingia Raja on his lap and tried to soothe him. The king was very restless, and he gnashed his teeth in excitement and rage. He was then bathed when he became somewhat composed. The king was then taken to the Barchora and placed on a wooden seat covered with a carpet. Guards were posted at the gates, and the nobles passed the remaining portion of the night by the side of the sovereign.

On the following morning the king assembled the leading nobles, and expatiated before them on the attack made by the Buragohain which he characterised as unfriendly and unprovoked, as the premier himself had brought the prince from his ancestral home and seated him on the throne. "I could have killed the Buragohain," said Dihingia Raja, "but I refrained from taking his life as we are co-disciples and have thus jointly attained pious companionship under the spiritual teachings of the same Guru."

During the course of the deliberation on Sunday morning the king asked the officers and nobles to reaffirm their allegiance to him by taking the necessary oaths, according to both the Hindu and Ahom forms. The Hindu oaths were administered by Rama Misra and his son and other Brahmans in the presence of Lakshminarayan *Salagram, Gita, Bhagavat,* copper vessels and the basil plant. The Ahom oaths were taken in the presence of the Bardhak, or sacred drum, where pigs and fowls were sacrificed. The officers were given appropriate presents by the monarch after which they retired to their respective quarters. The king then arranged to go to Teliadonga in the company of the following officers,—Ramcharan Barpatra Gohain, Laluk Bargohain, Lalukia Gohain-Phukan, Lao Barchetia, Kirkiria Barbarua, and Laitao Bhitarual Phukan, brother of Baghchowal Barpatra Gohain. The Hazarikas and other officers were despatched in advance to wait for the Dangarias at Gajpur.

With the restoration of reason the king began to recollect the services rendered to him and his family by the Buragohain who had raised the prince from the position of a farmer to that of a full-fledged sovereign whose territories extended from Sadiya to the frontiers of Bengal. He realised the precarious nature of his own position as a monarch without the friendship and support of the Buragohain who was held in great respect by the nobiliary and the populace. Besides, the Buragohain at large was a positive danger to his own security.

Animated thus by sentiments of gratitude and motives of self-preservation, Dihingia Raja promised to forgive the Buragohain for all that he had done, both wilfully and under pressure, and asked the Bargohain, the Barpatra Gohain and the Barchetia to institute a search for the Buragohain and procure his return to Gargaon.

Soon after his flight from the capital, the Buragohain sent Dilihial Gohain-Phukan and Ram Tamuli to Gauhati with a request to the Phukans and Rajkhowas stationed there that they should march up to his aid in fulfilment of their old promise to stand by one another in emergencies. He added in his message,—"When Debera indulged in killing men ruthlessly, my colleagues at Gauhati entered into a solemn covenant not to desert one another. On this assurance I had Debera executed and the Dihingia prince placed on the throne, and thereby preserved the government. A year has not elapsed, and the king now wants to kill me! I have left everything at the capital and have now taken refuge at Salkowanr. I shall survive only if my compatriots now come to my rescue in remembrance of their respect for their manhood, the dictates of truth and their solemn promises."[91] The Phukans and the Rajkhowas decided to proceed to Salkowanr in remembrance of their oaths of fidelity to the Buragohain, and urged by the necessity to protect their own selves. They said in one voice,—"We had made the Buragohain our Raja, but he conferred the sovereign power on the Dihingia prince. The Buragohain has now been reduced to such a plight! Is it possible that the king will hesitate to contrive our destruction as well?" They then reiterated their oaths of adherence to the common cause in the presence of *Salagram*, copper vessels, the basil plant and Brahmans, and made arrangements for proceeding to the Buragohain's camp.

The following officers were left in charge of the affairs of Gauhati,—Landabi Phukan; Thanua Deka-Phukan; Cheregual Gohain-Phukan; Kamalabaria Amuncheng Neog; Pani-Sologuria Rajkhowa Kekora Sandikoi; Tar-Sologuria Rajkhowa Chakrapani; Gajpuria Rajkhowa Kalanchu, commander of the garrison at Bhogpur; and Saru Abhaypuria Rajkhowa Bandar of the Lanmakharu Chetia family, commander of the Barepaita garrison. The following officers of the Gauhati command were despatched in advance to meet the Bura-

91. S. K. Bhuyan, *Assam Buranji, S.M.*, p. 134.

gohain,—Tarua-Dihingia Rajkhowa Mecha, elder son of Rangachila Duara Phukan; Bar-Abhaypuria Rajkhowa Japang Sen Gohain; Pani-Dihingia Rajkhowa Alun, son of Lapeti Phukan; Pani-Abhaypuria Rajkhowa, nephew of Phulbarua; Opar-Dayangia Rajkhowa Datakaria; Nam-Dayangia Rajkhowa Bihparua of the Buragohain family; and Dikhowmukhia Rajkhowa Kari Deka.

After some time the main body of Gauhati officers and nobles marched up to the Buragohain's camp under the leadership of Laluk Barphukan. The party consisted of,—Panphukan, son of Phulbarua; Dihingia Sandikaoi Phukan; Chengkham, son of Laithepena Solal Gohain; Maupia Abhaypuria Rajkhowa, son of Rajasahur; Phaguna Majiu-Abhaypuria Rajkhowa; Harkina Dayangia Rajkhowa, a kinsman of Laluk Barphukan; Lechai-kalia Kajalimukhia Barua of the Mechagharia Bargohain family, and the Rajas of Darrang and Beltola.

Meanwhile, Dihingia Raja anxious to compose his differences with the Buragohain, had been sending emissaries to meet the latter at his camp. The king first deputed the son of the Sakta priest Katyayan Bhattacharyya to Jakaichuk with messages of friendship and good-will, and desire for reconciliation; but the Buragohain had already left Jakaichuk. The king then sent one Pathak Chandra Kataki, but on approaching the Buragohain's camp, the Kataki was forbidden to enter the gate. The Barpatra Gohain, the Bargohain, the Solal Gohain, Lao Barchetia, and the Mahanta of Moramara were then deputed by the monarch to the camp of the Buragohain with the object of bringing about a reconciliation; but they were not allowed to enter into the enclosures of the camp. The mission of Banamali Gosain of Dakhimpat, and of Ramakrishna Bapu of Bengena-ati Satra proved equally unsuccessful. The Swargadeo became greatly alarmed, and regarded the persistent refusal of the Buragohain to meet the deputies as a clear indication of the premier's unfriendly disposition. The Gohains together with the Barchetia were sent again to initiate negotiations with the Buragohain for his return to the capital.

The deputies were instructed to convey the following message of the king to the Buragohain,—"I solemnly promise that if I do any harm to the Buragohain, and touch even a cock-feather of his house, I shall be guilty of the sin of murdering my servants, wives and children." The four nobles were allowed to take only three boats each. The Gohains proceeded to Dergaon accordingly, and were received by the Buragohain at the Hatisal of the local temple. They communicated the royal message to the premier who asked them to wait for the next day when the discussions would be resumed. He observed that a wife, however pure she may be, is never trusted by her husband if once she becomes adulterous.[92] During the course of the very same night the Buragohain held a secret conference with his supporters, and it was decided that the king's summons should be ignored and rejected. The advance body of the Gauhati nobles had approached meanwhile the vicinity of the Buragohain's camp.

The Buragohain was a master-genius in penetrating into the depth of complex situations. The animation and vigour with which the Gohains pleaded the king's cause enabled the Buragohain to realise at once that his interests would be ill served by their continuance as the immediate advisers of the monarch, factious and intriguous as they were. He did not anticipate any trouble from the harmless and good-natured monarch. But Arjun Dihingia Raja was a weak-kneed gentleman who did not possess sufficient strength and stamina to resist the solicitudes and entreaties of his intimate associates and the members of his household, who might consider the restoration of the Buragohain to position and power as a menace to their own safety as they had demonstrated their lack of sympathy to his cause. Meanwhile, the Buragohain had received information of the approaching arrival of the principal Gauhati stalwarts. Atan Buragohain therefore considered the use of force as the only way to decide the issue between himself and the Swargadeo.

92. MS. Assam Buranji No. 39.

In the meeting of the Gohains next morning the premier assumed an attitude of humility, and expressed regrets for his long absence from the capital and his inability to pay his customary obeisance to the monarch. He however informed the Gohains that he was waiting for the subsidence of the first wave of the king's indignation, adding at the same time that it was also necessary for him to consult his remaining Gauhati colleagues who were expected to soon arrive at his camp.

The Buragohain then entered into an examination of the situation at Gauhati which was exposed to Mogul attack, its vulnerability having increased owing to the absence of the senior and more experienced commanders. Mecha Rajkhowa, as arranged in the secret meeting of the Buragohain's partisans held on the previous night, suggested that the Bargohain and the Solal Gohain should march posthaste to Samdhara and Kaliabar to command the local garrisons, and that the Barpatra Gohain and the Barchetia should remain with the Buragohain at Dergaon. The proposal received the approval of the premier. The Barpatra Gohain, who was the son-in-law of the Buragohain, admitted his common fate with the premier, and pointed out the analogy of a boat the sinking of whose stern is followed by that of the prow. "But", added Ramcharan Barpatra Gohain, "I have come here with the Bargohain and the Solal Gohain; and it will not be proper if I now desert them and remain with the premier." The Buragohain despatched the Barpatra Gohain to Samdhara, and detained Lao Barchetia in custody at Dergaon.

Having received intelligence of the developments at Dergaon, Dihingia Raja repaired the fort at Chinatali, and remained there with a considerable force. There was a royalist garrison also at Gajpur. In the meantime Laluk Barphukan and the leading Gauhati commanders arrived at the Buragohain's camp at Dergaon. The premier deliberated with his supporters, and decided to launch an attack upon the royalist forces at Gajpur and Chinatali.

On Wednesday, the twenty-ninth Ashar, 1598 *Saka,* the forces of the Buragohain boarded the boats at Dergaon and sailed up to Gajpur. The king's soldiers deserted the Gajpur garrison and retreated to Chinatali where they were attacked by the premier's forces. There ensued a severe contest at Chinatali both on land and on water, with heavy casualties on the king's side, at which the monarch expressed his regret that so many men had to perish only for the safety of his person, his sorrow being aggravated by the internecine character of the conflict as opposed to hostilities with foreigners. He then retreated to Singhaduar, the principal gate of the capital, and encountered the ministerialists in an engagement on the river.

The contest lasted till the evening when the royalist force was completely routed. The four sons of the monarch had participated in the fight, but they could not improve the situation. Kirkiria Barbarua and Kalia Gohain protected the gate till the last moment, but they were soon defeated. The princes deserted the battlefield and fled to unknown destinations. The gate or *duar* of the city being now open after the defeat of Kirkiria Barbarua of the *Duara* family the Buragohain said,—"We have got possession of the *duar* after *Duara* [literally, a door-keeper] had relinquished it."[93]

Dihingia Raja had meanwhile left the scene of contest in a boat by which he sailed down a short distance, and stopped near a camp. The king got down from the boat, and an ostler from Bangaon spread his cloth before the king to walk upon. The Swargadeo left his camp on horseback accompanied by a Tamuli, his personal attendant, whom he proposed to encourage by a reward in cash. The king alighted from the pony at the gate of the camp, and had a box of coins brought to him. He asked the Tamuli to make a receptacle with the ends of his cloth. Dihingia Raja then poured into the Tamuli's cloth four handfuls of silver rupees. The king then asked the Tamuli to leave his company and offered to him a cloth-piece worn by himself, saying—"Tamuli, you have some years more to live, and I give you this cloth from my own body as a token of my affection for you. The texture of your cloth on which I poured the rupees is as fine as gossamer, but still it did not give way under the weight of the

93. S. K. Bhuyan, *Assam Buranji, S.M.*, p. 136.

coins; it is not therefore proper that you should die with me." The Tamuli began to weep like a child, and then left the company of the king with a heavy heart; and Dihingia Raja rode companionless to his doom. He took shelter in his palace at Gargaon to pass a few hours that might still be spared in the company of his wives and children. The king was kept under watch and guard at his palace in charge of Bhatdhara Phukan.

The Phukans and nobles pressed the Buragohain to assume sovereign power, adducing the additional reason that his refusal to do so on the previous occasion, after the death of Gobar Raja, had involved his friends in such woeful predicaments. The Buragohain who was an upholder of the constitution refused the offer with the remark,—"I am not entitled to undertake sovereign responsibility. A scion of a king is alone entitled to kingship, and the offspring of a saint should alone become a saint. Others are not entitled to these offices."[94] He then instituted a vigorous search for a prince worthy of occupying the exalted office of a sovereign. For a period of three fortnights the Buragohain himself controlled and guided the affairs of the kingdom without the intervention of a monarch.

Atan Buragohain then found a prince living near Charaideo Hill, and proposed to place him on the throne. He was a descendant of Deka-Raja. The Buragohain in seeking the concurrence of the nobles reminded them of their promise to support him in all eventualities. They reiterated their consent to pay their homage to any prince whom the Buragohain considered fit for the throne. The prince selected by the Buragohain was now brought from his residence at Charaideo Hill and the nobles and other officers paid their homage to the new monarch. He was known as Parvatia Raja from the fact of his residence at Charaideo Parvat. He assumed the Ahom name Sudoipha.

Parvatia Raja and his ministers then discussed the method of disposing of the deposed sovereign Arjun Dihingia

94. MS. Assam Buranji No. 5.

Raja. His continuance as an able-bodied person would provide a handy material for insurrection and trouble, and so it was decided to disable him by extracting his eye-balls, as a mutilated limb was considered to be a disqualification for holding the office of a monarch. Bhatdhara Phukan and Betmela Phukan were entrusted with the execution of the decree. Arjun Dihingia Raja was waiting for the approach of the two Phukans with the manuscript of the sacred book *Ratnavali* tied to his breast, and his youngest son seated on his lap, hoping thereby that his person would be held sacrosanct and therefore unassailable, touched as it was by a sacred book and an innocent child. But the heat of political antagonism eliminates all considerations of humanity, compassion and chivalry. Bhatdhara removed the manuscript with his feet, threw off the child from his father's lap, and dragged the deposed Raja from his seat, after which he applied to the Raja's eyes the apparatus for extracting eye-balls. Having carried out his mission Bhatdhara battered the blinded prince, agonised with shock and pain, with the butt-end of a gun, and Arjun Raja died in consequence. Bhatdhara then entered the ladies' apartments, and ravished the queen just widowed.

The Buragohain disapproved of the excesses committed by Bhatdhara, and expelled him from the conference of the nobles held at the premier's residence next day. Bhatdhara was allotted a seat in the open space outside the conference-chamber. He was also refused admittance to the secret deliberations of the Phukans held later in the inner apartments of the Buragohain's house.[95]

According to another version, Arjun Raja suffering from excruciating pain as a result of the blinding operation put an end to his life by striking his head against a stone, uttering imprecations on his destroyers. His two sons Dhala Gohain and Saru Gohain shared the fate of their father; and the blinded princes Kalia Gohain and Dighala Gohain remained the only survivors.

95. MS. Assam Buranji No. 15.

Thus died Arjun Dihingia Raja after a reign of fourteen months. He was predominantly a man of peace; and he abhorred harshness and cruelty except when his impetuosity led him to actions which brought him to repentence with the revival of reason. He was grateful by disposition and upbringing, and he hesitated to disbelieve the counsels of his immediate associates lest he offended their sentiments by his distrust. But he lacked the qualities of quick decision and prompt action which are so indispensable to a man of affairs. Passing his days in Dihing in the leisurely comforts of a gentleman-farmer he was suddenly called at the age of forty to assume the onerous responsibilities of a sovereign for which he had practically no training except the normal experiences of a prince's surroundings. The problems of the state and the intrigues of the period proved too complicated for him, and he constantly referred to his palmy princely days passed in Dihing in contrast to his thorny life at Gargaon as the head of the state. The prince, this Ahom Cincinnatus, lost his throne and his life as a retribution for his imbecility as a sovereign, however unsurpassed he might have been in the sphere of refinement and good breeding.

CHAPTER X

MURDEROUS ASSAULT ON PARVATIA RAJA

As was the practice of the age, Sudoipha Parvatia Raja, soon after his elevation to the throne, married a number of wives from the families of his supporters in order to strengthen his political alliance with the bonds of family attachment. The Buragohain's daughter became the Barkuanri; and Laluk Barphukan's daughter the second consort or Parvatia Kuanri. The king also married the daughters of Mecha Barbarua and Bhatdhara Phukan, and the sister of Betmela Phukan.

The assumption of office by the new monarch was followed by a partial overhauling of the official personnel which was carried out on the advice of Atan Buragohain who naturally wanted to promote his adherents to power in place of those who had opposed his plans.

The major changes were as follows:—Kola Patar was appointed Barpatra Gohain in place of Ramcharan, dismissed from office; Japang Sen Gohain was appointed Bargohain in place of Laluk Guimela, dismissed; Mecha Rajkhowa, son of Rangachila Duara Phukan, was appointed Barbarua in place of his brother Kirkiria, transferred to Gauhati as Deka-Phukan; Mau Gohain was appointed Neog Phukan in place of Garudharia Neog; Atan Buragohain's elder brother was appointed Naobaicha Phukan in place of Mad-nokhowa; Dilihial Dighala Gohain was appointed Bhitarual Phukan; Tepartalia Ram was appointed Deka-Phukan of Gargaon, and Kirkiria Duara as Deka-Phukan of Gauhati. The following officers were appointed as Phukans: Betmela, son of Kalanchu; Phulbarua's son; Miri Sandikoi's son; and Bhatdhara at Gauhati.

Soon after the accession of Sudoipha Parvatia Raja the Gauhati commanders left the capital for resuming charge of their respective posts. They however placed 5,000 men at the disposal of the Buragohain to enable him to meet any eventual crisis. The detachment consisted of one thousand men from each of the following units,—Ghuria shieldsmen, Namanial Bacha, Medelial Kari, Rabhi and Kharangia.

The king had stayed for some time at Sakbari from where he shifted his camp to Bokanagar and then to Barkola. The Singarighar-utha ceremony was performed at Chunpora Nagar in the midst of the usual pomp and splendour. Appropriate presents were given by the monarch to his officers and nobles and others, and the festivities and rejoicings continued for seven days.

It was at this time that reports reached the new monarch about the harbouring of Dighala Gohain, a surviving son of Arjun Dihingia Raja, by Sundarishan Medhi of Sologuri Satra. Tepartalia Ram Phukan who was deputed for investigation arrested the prince; his eye-balls were extracted, and Dighala Gohain died in consequence. The three dry months of November, December and January were spent by the monarch in fishing and hunting excursions staying at his camp at Pabkata on the north bank of the Brahmaputra. At the end of his holiday the king returned to Gargaon.

Sudoipha Parvatia Raja, in the manner of his predecessor, expressed his gratefulness to the Buragohain for having secured the throne for him, though the premier himself could have taken possession of it if he had so desired. Parvatia Raja gave valuable presents to the Buragohain consisting of sedans, carpets, swords, golden trays and ornaments, elephants and horses, lands in Charaideo Hill, and an estate in Dulung with eighty servitors. The monarch issued an order to the effect that the estates settled on Atan Buragohain should be enjoyed in perpetuity by him and his descendants as long as members of Sudoipha Parvatia Raja's family remained in occupation of the Ahom throne. The wife of the Buragohain was honoured by the monarch with the gift of a Kekora-dola, a sedan which could be used only by the king and the Dangarias.

The relations between Parvatia Raja and Atan Buragohain proceeded on a cordial basis for some time. But feelings of estrangement and mutual distrust had been in evidence meanwhile, first, on account of the alleged deviation of the Buragohain from the time-honoured customs of the land; and secondly, for his dismissal of the Barbarua without obtaining the previous consent of the monarch.

According to the custom of the Ahoms it was necessary for the Buragohain, the Barpatra Gohain and the Bargohain to pay their homage to a new king and his chief consort by prostrations repeated seven times. King Sudoipha received the homage in due form; but when the Buragohain and his two colleagues approached the seat of the Barkuanri, who happened to be the Buragohain's daughter, she left her seat being unwilling to see her father kneeling down before her. The nobles then left the room there being no one in that place to receive their allegiance and homage.

The king took the Buragohain to task, saying,—"The Dangarias paid their homage to me in the usual form; but why did they retire to their residences without kneeling down before the Barkuanri ? They have thus violated a significant and time-honoured custom of the land. They have made me Raja because I am a descendant of the royal family. What am I here for if the Dangarias renounce the old customs of the country? Let them select any one as their overlord, and I shall retire to my village to live there as I did in the past." To this the Buragohain replied,—"We have made him the dispenser of our bodies and of our minds, and we have knelt down before him accordingly. We went to pay our homage to the queen as required by custom, but she left her seat on our approach. Whom are we to salute in an empty place? This has been our only transgression; otherwise we are not the men to relinquish the usages of the past. Let His Majesty appoint another day for the salutation ceremony, and we shall proceed accordingly to pay our homage."[96]

Parvatia Raja rebuked the Barkuanri as well for the unqueenly demeanour shown by her in her unwillingness to

96. MS. Assam Buranji Nos. 5 and 39.

receive the obeisance of her father; she was described by her royal consort as the daughter of "a king-making and king-unmaking rebel". The king also gave vent to his suspicions about a possible move on the part of her father and his two henchmen, Ram Phukan and Betmela Phukan, to set up a new monarch. The queen reported the whole matter to her father, the Buragohain, and he felt extremely mortified.

The Buragohain then invented a double-edged device to get over the delicate situation. The Barkuanri kept before her a raised tray on which was placed the sacred book *Ratnavali* and received her father's salutation in that position. The queen's filial conscience was eased by the thought that her father's obeisance had been paid to the sacred manuscript, and not to herself; while the exacting monarch construed the salutation as being meant for his consort which thus removed his grievance against the Buragohain.

The second trouble centred round Mecha Barbarua. He had a number of wives from the royal family, first, the widowed Parvatia Kuanri of King Ramadhwaj Singha who was the daughter of one Laho. Mecha had also married two other widowed queens. His own daughter who had been married to Parvatia Raja became a favourite of her husband in supersession of the other consorts. Proud of his royal connections Mecha began to show discourtesy to the Buragohain. He never visited the premier's residence and ridiculed the nobles who paid court to the Buragohain. Ram Phukan and Betmela Phukan complained to the Buragohain about the arrogance and hauteur of Mecha Barbarua with whom the premier had already been offended for having married ex-queens. "From which royal family has Mecha Barbarua sprung," enquired the Buragohain, "that he dares to make wives of widowed queens ?"

Mecha even refused to attend the official dinners at the residence of the prime minister where important matters of state were discussed over the meals. He further offended the Buragohain and some of the Phukans by making uncomplimentary references to their religious preceptors, the Mahantas of the Thakuria denomination.

Being convinced of the habitual arrogance of Mecha the premier held consultations with Ram Phukan and Dighala Phukan, and dismissed him forthwith from his office, and appointed Chakrapani Tar-Sologuria Rajkhowa as Barbarua. The matter was reported to Parvatia Raja for approval. The king observed that the reference should have been made before the dismissal of Mecha and the appointment of Chakrapani as his successor. The monarch however was not willing to interfere with the new appointment as it was an accomplished fact. The king said,—"Now that the Gohain does not like Mecha he may be sent away to his village where he can live by ploughing his fields". Mecha was then ordered to go to his village in Dihing.

According to another account, Mecha's affronts were brought to the notice of Parvatia Raja; and following a hint from the monarch the Phukans seized the person of Mecha and produced him before the Buragohain during the progress of a banquet. The premier did not approve of the summary manner in which the Phukans were handling the situation. The Phukans pointed out to the Buragohain the impropriety of allowing Mecha to continue as Barbarua. The premier accordingly reported the matter to the king, saying,—"Mecha Barbarua ridicules us as disciples of the Gosains of the Thakuria denomination. He is besides living as husband and wife with the widow of the younger Charingia Raja [Ramadhwaj Singha] and the daughter of a Deodhai priest. It is we who have made him Barbarua. His Majesty should now remove him from that office". Mecha was accordingly dismissed, and ordered to live at his home at Laphabari in Dihing.

The prostration episode had seemed to end peacefully, but it left a canker in the rose. Parvatia Raja's indictment of the Buragohain as "a king-making and king-unmaking rebel" meant an accusation of the premier's supporters as well. They interpreted it as the opinion entertained by the king about the Buragohain and his adherents, in spite of the monarch's expressions of gratitude and good-will. The king, they thought, could at any time come upon them and cause their destruction and ruin.

The two enterprising nobles Tepartalia Ram Phukan and Betmela Bhitarual Phukan took up the gauntlet. They blamed the Buragohain for nominating princes who always proved hostile in the long run, and they expressed their determination to accord one more illustration of the practice of king-making and king-unmaking of which they had been accused though the accuser owed his elevation to their support. Secret consultations were held between Ram Phukan and Betmela Phukan and the latter's son Chikan Tamuli. The Tamuli, who was a personal attendant of Parvatia Raja, undertook to see to the annihilation of his royal master. The support of Betmela's sister who was a junior consort of the monarch was enlisted for the execution of the plan. The chronicles are mute as to whether Atan Buragohain had been cognisant of or promoted this design.

As prearranged Chikan Tamuli entered the palace at night by crossing the earthen wall situated behind the rows of the rear apartments. He crawled into the king's bed-chamber, and put out the light. His aunt removed the cloth which covered the king's person and exposed it to the blows of the assassin. Chikan Tamuli then inflicted four blows on the body of the king with his axe-shaped *dao,* one on the head, another on the left arm, a third on the back, and a fourth on the palm of the right hand. The king had meanwhile woke up, and he raised his left hand to resist further blows, and lost the thumb in consequence. The inmates of the palace then got up from their sleep, and there ensued a great uproar and commotion. The assassin had meanwhile escaped leaving the *dao* in the king's bath-room.

Having heard of the attack the Buragohain and the Phukans tightened the watch in the palace, and engaged expert physicians to attend to the wounds which were rapidly healed, and Parvatia Raja soon returned to his normal health and disposition. Chikan Tamuli fled down to Gauhati during the course of the same night. Laluk Barphukan's brother Marangi Dola-kasharia Barua, and Ramdhan Tamuli Rajkhowa, who had been confined at the Hatisal under the king's orders before the incident of assault, proceeded on their release also to Gauhati.

The king and the nobles then assembled in a meeting to enquire into the matter. The ministers questioned the monarch about the features of the assassin so that he might be identified and traced. The king was not able to give precise and full details as the attack had been made after the light had been extinguished. From what little he could see he described the man as being pockmarked and dark-complexioned. The description fitted in with Jadu Tamuli, an attendant of Mecha Ex-Barbarua; and Betmela Phukan confirmed the suspicions by pointing out that on the day before the assault the Phukan had seen Jadu Tamuli on the road, but the Tamuli avoided the contact by darting off into an adjoining lane, and that the Tamuli was an intimate friend of the principal door-keeper of the palace who was found missing. The Buragohain and the nobles then concluded that the assault had been engineered by the dismissed Barbarua Mecha who had deputed emissaries from Dihing with instructions to carry out the attack. The king ordered detailed investigation into the matter.

Mecha's daughter who had been married to Parvatia Raja secretly communicated the developments at the capital to her father then living in exile at Dihing. Mecha was afraid of what would come upon him as a result of the suspicions of complicity in the assault, and he fled in a fishing boat to Gauhati, concealed in a pile of nets. He was accompanied by a handful of household retainers. At Gauhati, Mecha met his old friends Laluk Barphukan and the other officers to whom he dilated on the happenings at Gargaon. The Phukans in their turn guaranteed full protection to Mecha as he came within the orbit of the old promises of mutual help and collective security.

The emissaries despatched to Dihing to capture Mecha and his alleged accomplices came back with the report of the Ex-Barbarua's flight to Gauhati. It was represented by the nobles as a confirmation of Mecha's guilt; while the king held that the attack could not have been made by men from Dihing without the connivance and support of confederates living at the capital, as the entrances to the palace were vigilantly guarded at night. Jadu Tamuli was found at the house of the door-keeper, and both were arrested; they were then subjected to severe tortures with a view to extort their confessions, but no incriminatory information came out of their lips. Jadu Tamuli was beheaded with his brothers and relatives, as well as a number of alleged suspects captured at Dihing. The king had to give his consent to these proceedings against his will as he did not possess the stamina to oppose the wishes of his nobles.

Parvatia Raja then despatched Kalia Kataki to Gauhati to bring up Mecha, but the Phukans of that place refused to part with him. They informed the monarch that the culprit would be found somewhere at the capital if the Dangarias and officers instituted proper enquiries, and that they would take the Ex-Barbarua with them when they would themselves go to Gargaon. The Kataki then returned from Gauhati to Gargaon. Another messenger, one Bahbaria Ramkrishna Kataki, was next sent to Gauhati to bring Mecha, with threats of severe punishment if his mission failed. The nobles of Gauhati reaffirmed their determination not to make over Mecha, and detained Ramkrishna at Gauhati.

Matters developing at Gauhati and Gargaon indicated the formation of two political factions each running counter to the other. The Gargaon party represented the government of the day, as it consisted of the premier and his two colleagues, the Barpatra Gohain and the Bargohain, and the other principal heads of the administration. The decisions and actions of this party bore the stamp of authority and law, and they received the ready concurrence of the sovereign who was not strong enough to oppose the recommendations of his ministers, nor could he withdraw his confirmation of their accomplished decrees. At Gauhati, by virtue of its distance from the capital, the Phukans and Rajkhowas could easily evade compliance with the orders of the government if such compliance militated against their interests and their security.

Their strength lay in the armed forces which had been placed at their disposal to encounter the Moguls, and which could be diverted at any moment for the suppression of their opponents at the capital. The Gauhati party could, in any conflict, easily score over their rivals at Gargaon. Besides, in the eye of the people the Gauhati party received always special consideration and respect by virtue of their responsibilities connected with the maintenance of their country's independence, and the fact of their exile from their kith and kin in the interest of the state.

The refusal of the Gauhati nobles to part with Mecha Ex-Barbarua, in violation of the orders of the sovereign, offered a delicate problem to the government. Betmela Phukan and Kaupatia Bhandari Barua consulted Chakrapani Barbarua who asked them to seek the advice of the Buragohain to whom they explained the gravity of the situation, referring to the way in which the prime minister had protected Laluk Barphukan from the murderous intentions of Debera Barbarua. "Now, this very Laluk Barphukan", said Betmela and Kaupatia to the Buragohain, "is acting in contravention of His Majesty's orders and flouting the wishes of the Buragohain. Should the Barphukan act in this manner? We should now proceed to Gauhati in pursuit of the Barphukan and capture him. We are only waiting for Your Excellency's concurrence."

The prime minister was unwilling to sanction the application of force against Laluk Barphukan for one obvious reason.—The Moguls had not totally given up their intentions to recover Lower Assam even though Raja Ram Singha had left Rangamati. The enemy would readily take advantage of an internal dissension in Assam by pitting one party against the other. Besides, local feuds would prevent the Ahoms from offering a united front to the enemy. So it was necessary, thought the Buragohain, to settle the domestic differences of Assam in a peaceable manner, and not in a spectacular form by the despatch of an armed expedition against the viceroy of Gauhati. The prime minister wanted to convey to the Moguls an impression of internal solidarity in Assam so that the enemy might consider it difficult to break through the barrier of one common undivided purpose.

The thoughts of the Buragohain were based on fresh complications with the Moguls which had developed meanwhile and which foreshadowed the possibilities of renewed hostilities. About the beginning of 1678, Lanmakhru Bandar Chetia Saru-Abhaypuria Rajkhowa, the commander of the Ahom garrison at Barepaita, had permitted a number of Bengal traders living in Khuntaghat Pergana to buy rice from Assam. The merchants crossed the Manaha and committed excesses upon Assam subjects; they even transgressed the Assam outposts taking advantage of Bandar Rajkhowa's absence at Gauhati on account of illness. The Assamese living on the frontier villages retaliated by entering into Bengal where they captured a number of Mogul subjects. Minor skirmishes then ensued between the Assam and Mogul subjects living on the frontiers of the two territories. Laluk Barphukan reported the matter to Nawab Mansur Khan, Thanadar of Rangamati, who dismissed the affair as a normal border encounter which should not disturb the amicable relations between the Swargadeo and the Delhi emperor.

This explanation by Nawab Mansur Khan was considered by Parvatia Raja as reasonable and proper; and the Paniphukan who commanded the fleet on the Brahmaputra was directed to convey to the Nawab the Swargadeo's acceptance of the explanation. In communicating the royal message to Mansur Khan, the Paniphukan expressed his own conviction that the Nawab did not have any hand in the matter, and the clashes represented the private actions of a handful of mischievous Mogul subjects. The Paniphukan further expressed his hope that the Nawab should not be surprised if the Barphukan adopted measures to punish the Bengal miscreants wherever they could be found. A small Ahom party then attacked Jhaobarigaon in Khuntaghat. All the villagers deserted their homes leaving only one man behind. Nothing further happened at the moment, but the Buragohain knew very well that matters would not stop at that stage, and that the Rangamati Thanadar was sure to adopt measures of retaliation.

Atan Buragohain's apprehension of a possible attack by the Moguls was not due to his over-anxiety for the security of his country, nor was it invented to serve as a pretext to suspend vigorous measures against Laluk Barphukan. The new complications with Nawab Mansur Khan were interpreted in terms of a demand made by Sultan Azamtara about September 1677. The prince had halted at Rajmahal with 1,00,000 horses and 300 elephants on his way to Dacca to take charge of the musnad of Bengal. He ordered Abu Nasr Khan, son of Nawab Shaista Khan, to ask Laluk Barphukan to surrender Gauhati and Lower Assam to the Moguls in fulfilment of the terms of the treaty enacted between Allah Yar Khan and Momai-tamuli Barbarua, for which Raja Ram Singha had pressed so hard, though unsuccessfully. "The Ahoms will remain in their old limits, and we shall remain in ours", said Sultan Azamtara in his message to Laluk Barphukan, "and if this proposal is rejected the Barphukan alone will have to answer for whatever loss is caused to the cows and Brahmans. An early reply is solicited." Reference was made in the letter to the number of Azamtara's horses and elephants. This epistle, written in Persian, together with another written in Bengali by Nawab Shaista Khan, was sent to Laluk Barphukan in October 1677, by Abu Nasr Khan, Fauzadar of Rangamati. The letters were delivered by one Ghansam who was accompanied by a courier belonging to the establishment of Baduli. A *sirpao* was sent with the letters as a present to the Barphukan.

Laluk Barphukan had submitted a report to the Ahom king and the Buragohain through Kalia Kataki pointing out the hostile intentions of the Moguls. Atan Buragohain objected to the present of the *sirpao* which was a sewn piece, as it was not customary to send such an article to the officers of an independent state. The premier also took exception to the insertion of Shaista Khan's name over that of the Barphukan on the ground that they were viceroys of equal status. A reply was sent in the name of the Buragohain in which it was said,—"The territories referred to by the Sultan do not belong to the Moguls. They are enjoyed by those on whom God is pleased to bestow them for the time being. The prince's claim is therefore unjust and improper, and has obviously been made without much deliberation. He has also made mention of horses and elephants in order to give us an impression of his military strength, but these animals do not deserve any mention whatsoever, for the horses may be horses to him, but to us they are as useless as deer, for they cannot shoot arrows nor can they fire guns."[97] The presents and epistles sent by the Moguls were returned alongwith. Baduli's man died at Gauhati. This happened in November 1677.

To the proposal of Betmela Phukan and Kaupatia Bhandari Barua to attack Laluk Barphukan at Gauhati the premier Atan Buragohain therefore gave the following reply,—"The enemy is lurking in our immediate vicinity; and hence it will not be advisable to pursue the Barphukan and capture him, whatever may be the differences between ourselves. Such an action will give the enemy an additional encouragement. There is also the risk of an eventual reverse. We shall therefore deliberate with His Majesty and do what is expedient under the present circumstances."[98]

The premier's mind was filled with apprehension of a possible invasion by the Moguls before which the Barphukan's refractoriness faded into insignificance. The Buragohain realised the dangers of the defenceless condition of the territory round the capital. Between Samdhara and Gargaon there was no fortification of any strategic importance, and hence it had been possible for Nawab Mir Jumla to march straight to the capital practically unopposed. The premier therefore planned to construct a rampart facing the Brahmaputra river from where it would be possible to obstruct the progress of the enemy at a safe distance from

97. S. K. Bhuyan, *Kamrupar Buranji*, p. 90; and MS. Assam Buranji No. 6.

98. MS. Assam Buranji No. 5.

the capital. The proposed rampart was to touch Dighmuria village near the Brahmaputra at one extremity, and Murkata, Soraguri and Tulasijan near Gabharu Parvat on the other. The Buragohain first explained the details of the proposal to his colleagues and obtained their support. The king having approved of the same asked the Barbarua to make a preliminary survey of the alignment of the rampart by planting sign-posts at regular intervals. On receiving the report from the Barbarua the king ordered him and the Buragohain to raise levies of labourers for executing the work. The construction of the rampart proceeded in full swing during the early part of the year 1678. The king named the rampart Laimati-garh, but it became popularly known as Chintamani-garh.

CHAPTER XI

GAUHATI SURRENDERED TO THE MOGULS

Mecha Ex-Barbarua and Marangi Dolakasharia Barua, after their arrival at Gauhati, described to Laluk Barphukan the state of affairs at Gargaon which, they alleged, were going from bad to worse owing to the high-handed actions of Atan Buragohain and his adherents. The two fugitives pointed out the imminent danger to the safety of the Barphukan himself. Laluk Barphukan, as a result of the representations made by Mecha and Marangi, realised the necessity of making himself strong and powerful so that he might successfully oppose the reported designs of the Buragohain.

The Barphukan held secret consultations with his two brothers Bhatdhara Phukan and Marangi Barua about the means to avert their destruction which was inevitable if the Buragohain was allowed to continue in the unfettered exercise of his power. They decided to invite their uncle Baduli, then living at Dacca, to come to Gauhati with a powerful force with the help of which it would be possible to remove Atan Buragohain from his position and influence. They kept this decision as a close family secret, and the Phukans and Rajkhowas of Gauhati were simply given a general idea of the alleged mal-administration of the Buragohain.

The circumstance which gave an incentive to the plan of the three brothers was Sultan Azamtara's demand for the restoration of Gauhati. Raja Ram Singha had returned to Delhi in the middle of 1676 being unsuccessful in his attempt to reoccupy Gauhati. One of the tasks imposed by Emperor Aurangzeb on Sultan Azamtara, the new governor of Bengal, was the recovery of Gauhati which Ram Singha had failed to achieve. So, from his camp at Rajmahal, Azamtara sent a letter to Laluk Barphukan demanding the restoration of the limits fixed in 1639 by Momai-tamuli Barbarua and Allah Yar Khan. The prince in his letter had referred to Laluk as his Moma-sahur, or maternal uncle-in-law, hoping thereby that he would be able to induce the Barphukan to comply with the demand on account of the family ties subsisting between the two. The Barphukan reported the matter to the Swargadeo; and Atan Buragohain, as has been stated before, sent a sarcastic reply to Sultan Azamtara comparing his war horses and elephants to a herd of innocent deer useless for the purpose of fighting operations.

As a highly responsible officer of the Ahom government the Barphukan had no other alternative but to discountenance outwardly the proposal of Sultan Azamtara; he therefore sent the epistle promptly to the Swargadeo and also its reply to the Sultan. But, in their secret conference the three brothers Laluk, Bhatdhara and Marangi, decided to exploit this demand of Azamtara for their own advantage. They were prepared to make over Gauhati to the Moguls provided Azamtara promised to send an adequate force to Assam to crush the Buragohain and install Laluk on the throne of Assam. Their scheme, they hoped, would be promoted by the expected intercession of their niece Ramani Gabharu, consort of Azamtara. Besides, Baduli, their uncle at Dacca, would be able to throw in the weight of his personality to induce the prince to accede to the proposal of Laluk which was highly advantageous to the Moguls and to Azamtara himself as it would raise his prestige and importance before Emperor Aurangzeb.

In pursuance of the decision arrived at at the family conclave the Barphukan sent three messengers to Baduli,—Kedar Brahman of Hajo, Radha of Kowanrbhag, and Nazar of Samaria, with the message,—"We shall meet each other here, and he should come to this place". Of course, the messengers were instructed to elaborate the cryptic request embodied in the epistle. The despatch of an armed force from Bengal to Assam would necessitate the consent and permission of the governor of Bengal. Baduli was unwilling to take any action in the matter as he did not place any reliance on the three messengers who were natives of the frontier territory of Kamrup and who might act as agents of the

Moguls. Laluk Barphukan then sent to Baduli two new messengers, Kalia of Buruk and Chengaya Bangal, with the same message, and sent alongwith a lime-pot and a ring both made of gold and inlaid with gems, and a fan made of peacock-feathers with a golden handle, as presents in order to impart the stamp of genuineness to the deputation.

Laluk Barphukan's anxiety to secure the intervention of his uncle Baduli deserves more than a passing reference, for there is a great deal of similarity in the careers and ambitions of the uncle and his nephew. During 1658-60, Baduli had fought gallantly in expelling the Koches and the Moguls from Kamrup, and in carrying the banner of victory to the neighbourhood of Dacca. During Nawab Mir Jumla's invasion, Baduli had opposed the imperialists at different places, and he continued his resistance after the Moguls had occupied Gargaon. But, having seen Mir Jumla firmly intrenched in Assam, Baduli became friendly with the general with a view to strengthen his own position with the help of the Moguls. He offered to make over the Swargadeo and the principal nobles, and to procure the submission of the people, provided Mir Jumla promised to make him Raja of Assam. He posed as the supreme commander of the Assamese forces, and assured the Nawab that after his submission opposition to the Moguls would completely disappear. Mir Jumla conferred upon Baduli the Subedarship of the country between Gargaon and Namrup with the title of Deka-Raja. He was allowed to use some of the insignias of the Ahom sovereigns and to live in the royal palace. Some junior commanders and officers no doubt followed the example of Baduli, but the Assamese as a whole did not relinquish an iota of their ground. They continued their hostilities with undiminished vigour acting under the directions of their patriotic leaders as well as of the king issued from his retreat in Namrup. Mir Jumla and his lieutenant Diler Khan soon realised the baseless character of Baduli's vauntings. On the conclusion of the treaty the Ahom king insisted on Baduli's continuance in Assam, but Mir Jumla took him to Bengal with his relatives and dependants hoping that his presence at Dacca as a Mogul protegé would be of use in future dealings with Assam. He settled at Dacca where he was allotted an estate with a comfortable income. Baduli was therefore not unused to the dream of converting the Lukhurakhun clan into a dynasty of sovereigns; and as such he was expected to promote his nephew's designs to become the Raja of Assam.

The Paniphukan and the Miri Sandikoi Phukan came to know about the despatch of Laluk Barphukan's emissaries to Baduli, and they reported the matter to Atan Buragohain. The premier realised the seriousness of the situation, but he did not want to create an alarm by permitting the report to be accepted as a fact, whatever might be his inner conviction. He dismissed the report by saying,—"The Barphukan is a sensible man, and why should he be engaged in such a disloyal move? The informants must have communicated a false report". The Buragohain then turned his attention to the completion of the Chintamani rampart.[99]

The construction of Chintamani-garh which passed through well-settled villages was explained by the Phukans of Gauhati as a preparation to prevent their entrance into the metropolitan area. "What is the necessity of erecting this rampart in the heart of the country", said the Phukans, "unless it is meant as a base for attacking and capturing us? If ramparts are to be erected to oppose the march of the Moguls they should be constructed at Gauhati and Samdhara. There is an army to fight within the fortifications of Gauhati. We would therefore proceed to the new fortifications at Chintamani-garh and remain there in readiness to fight". This hostile attitude of the Gauhati commanders was favourable to the promotion of the Barphukan's designs as he could now make a common cause with them against the prime minister.

About this time Laluk Barphukan despatched two messengers Likchow Garia Bakas, and Betphalia, Ahina Mudoi's son, to Nawab Mansur Khan, Fauzadar of Rangmati; the presents for the Nawab consisted of elephants' tusks, agar wood, silk cloths and gold. The messengers deputed to Rangamati

99. S. K. Bhuyan, *Assam Buranji, S.M.*, p. 138.

were sent up to Dacca with Mansur Khan's recommendations for the acceptance of the Barphukan's proposal.

The terms of the offer made by Laluk Barphukan in the appeal sent to Dacca were as follows: some two hundred Mogul horsemen and a flotilla consisting of about twenty boats should make their appearance in front of Saraighat on the western outskirts of Gauhati; the Barphukan would make a show of resistance to the Mogul invaders by firing a few shots, after which he would evacuate Gauhati and proceed upwards to Kaliabar; the Moguls should then occupy the deserted garrison of Gauhati where they would not meet with any opposition; in return for this bloodless surrender of Gauhati the Barphukan is to be made Raja of Assam; he would hand over to the Moguls the Ahom nobles who are his avowed enemies and those who are expected to oppose his plans.

The proposal when carried out would place the Moguls in possession of Gauhati and Lower Assam which would be a virtual reversion to the *status quo ante* of 1639, and for which Ram Singha had fought so hard. The Assamese under Lachit Barphukan had fought valiantly to prevent Gauhati from falling into the hands of the Moguls; and his elder brother Laluk Barphukan now proposed to deliver Gauhati at his own sweet will, just for a mess of pottage!

Laluk Barphukan had to indulge in many face-saving devices in his attempt to conceal his real intentions from the knowledge of his Gauhati colleagues, and they were known only to his two brothers Bhatdhara and Marangi. The Barphukan impressed his friends of the urgent necessity to curtail the growing power of the Buragohain, and the question of obtaining military aid from the Moguls was carefully concealed from the Gauhati commanders. The embassies sent to Rangamati and Dacca were described by the Barphukan as originating from the necessity to settle inter-territorial problems and commercial disputes; but the envoys were entrusted by him to further his proposal to surrender Gauhati for the stipulated promise of Mogul aid to make him Raja of Assam. The envoys were also instructed to verbally communicate the personal message of the Barphukan and bring replies thereto.

In addition to the deputations sent to Baduli and Mansur Khan, Laluk Barphukan despatched two trusted envoys directly to Sultan Azamtara,—Madhabcharan of Kaupati, son of Sola Kataki, and Jadunandan of Gajpur, son of Sanatan Kataki. The mission was a secret one, and the papers connected therewith were kept in the personal custody of Laluk himself, and they were found in his house when it was searched, after his death, under the orders of King Gadadhar Singha.

As the success of Laluk Barphukan's plan to become the Raja of Assam depended upon the result of his direct deputation to Sultan Azamtara, he despatched with Madhabcharan and Jadunandan valuable presents to the governor and to his Assamese consort Rahmat Banu, and to the senior Begum. The presents to the two consorts included four elephants beautifully caparisoned and decorated. Madhabcharan Kataki was plied with heavy presents, as his visit to Dacca was expected to be as fruitful in result as that of the Barphukan himself.

Laluk Barphukan's messengers to Baduli, Mansur Khan and Azamtara were sent in quick succession after the despatch in November 1677 of the Assam government's reply to the Padshahzada's demand made from his camp at Rajmahal three months before. From Rajmahal, Sultan Azamtara proceeded to Dacca, and lived for some months in his camp at Khizirpur, at a distance of nine miles to the east of Dacca, as the viceregal palace in that city was still occupied by the interim governor Fidei Khan Koka who was then seriously ill. It was after the death of Fidei Khan, towards the end of May 1678, that Azamtara occupied the Subedar's quarters at Dacca. Madhabcharan and Jadunandan encamped therefore at Khizirpur to meet there the Subedar of Bengal

The visit of the two Assamese messengers was not in conformity with the usages of the Dacca court, as they had gone directly from the Barphukan without any forwarding epistle from the Rangamati Fauzadar. Besides, the taunting reply of Atan Buragohain to Azamtara's demand for the restoration of Gauhati, communicated through Laluk Barphukan, had made the prince suspicious of the real motive of any overture from Assam. Madhabcharan and Jadunandan presented themselves before Mulukchand Dewan, minister of the Dacca Subedar wielding the departments of revenue and finance. The Dewan told Sultan Azamtara about the envoys' request for an interview. Azamtara was not satisfied with the credentials of the two messengers, and ordered the Dewan to confine them.

King Jayadhwaj Singha had presented to his daughter a faithful servant named Moina at the time of delivering her to Nawab Mir Jumla in 1663. This Moina had accompanied Rahmat Banu in her wanderings from one Mogul capital to another, and had now come with her to Dacca to stay in the viceregal palace of the city. Moina saw with his own eyes the plight of his two countrymen who were led to the prison under the orders of Azamtara. He ran to Rahmat Banu in her inner apartments and told her all that he had seen. She in her turn immediately met her husband and interceded on behalf of Madhabcharan and Jadunandan. The two envoys were released forthwith, and arrangements were made for their accommodation and food. They were given audience with the Sultan seven days later. The envoys were attired on this occasion in the dress usually worn by Mogul officers of the corresponding rank. The prince was satisfied with the pleadings of the two envoys, and after considering the entire situation he said,—"I solemnly promise to elevate my uncle to the throne of Assam". Azamtara also promised to give the Barphukan a sum of rupees four lakhs as a reward for the evacuation of Gauhati.

However enthusiastic the governor of Bengal might have been in accepting the offer of Laluk Barphukan he was not authorised as a rule to launch an expedition against an independent neighbouring country or enter into important negotiations with foreign states without the concurrence of the Mogul emperor; because such actions might bring in complications which could be met only with the help of the central authority of the Moguls. Sultan Azamtara submitted his proposal to Emperor Aurangzeb, and the latter gave his approval of the project.

Preparations were then set on foot at Dacca and the neighbouring naval headquarter at Khizirpur for the expedition to Assam, and they were completed towards the end of 1678. Sultan Azamtara invited the agents of the English and Dutch factories at Dacca to help him with some European artillery-men to accompany the Mogul force to be despatched to Assam. The factors pleaded their inability, and Azamtara did not press for the fulfilment of the demand. He however accepted a sum of rupees 21,000 from the English as consideration for the grant of the Nishan or order for a free trade without the payment of duties,—"the customs of all goods, exported and imported, bought or sold, belonging to the English company to be released".[100]

Sultan Azamtara then issued orders to Nawab Mansur Khan to proceed to Gauhati and take delivery of the town from Laluk Barphukan. Mansur Khan was selected to lead the expedition for his intimate knowledge of Assam affairs first acquired as a commander under Mir Jumla, and subsequently, as Fauzadar of the Mogul outpost of Rangamati, wherefrom he had to conduct the Mogul relations with Assam.

The prince also wrote a letter to Laluk Barphukan conferring upon him the kingship of Assam. The letter was written in Persian in golden ink, and illuminated borders, and bore Sultan Azamtara's *hasta-panja* or impression of his palm. It ran as follows: "To Raja Barphukan, who deserves our favour and condescension, and who is a leader amongst the heroes, with greetings. You should know it for certain that I hereby confer upon you the kingdom and the kingship of Assam. You should now be steadfast in your resolution, and take as many soldiers as you want from Imin Husain Khan who will accompany you in the expedition. You should act in a way which will enable you to expel the Buragohain and the Bargohain, and to establish and consolidate your sovereign authority". This letter is dated Ashar, 1600 *Saka*, or June-July 1678.[101]

100. Charles Stewart, *History of Bengal*, 1910, pp. 333-34.

101. S. K. Bhuyan, *Kamrupar Buranji*, p. 93: MS. Assam Buranji No. 6.

It is interesting to study the reaction produced in the mind of the Assamese princess Rahmat Banu by the machinations of her uncle Laluk Barphukan. He had also written a letter to her couched in very affectionate language wishing thereby that she should intercede on his behalf before her husband Sultan Azamtara. In her reply Rahmat Banu referred to the rich presents brought by Madhabcharan and Jadunandan for her and her sister-begum as having enhanced her prestige at the viceregal harem and court. She had left Assam in 1663, and she had no opportunity till now to communicate with her kith and kin in Assam, or to hold personal contacts with the inhabitants of her land of birth; nor had any of her relatives made enquiries about her health and welfare though she was separated from her parents when she was a child of only six. The opportunity to meet her two countrymen — Madhabcharan and Jadunandan — after fourteen years of absence from home made her recollect the vicissitudes through which she had passed in the company of strangers and people of 'other minds and other eyes'. She had plenty of things to tell her people; some she revealed to Madhabcharan; and she asked her uncle to take Moina to Assam as he would tell all about her and her surroundings. Rahmat Banu's letter was dated Bhati, or Khizirpur, 1599 *Saka,* and was probably written in March 1678.[102]

The secret overtures of Laluk Barphukan could not obviously remain concealed from the knowledge of Rahmat Banu. She must have known all about them from her intimate talks with the two Assamese envoys, and from the reports of the parleys at her husband's court. She was the consort of Padshahzada Sultan Azamtara, governor of Bengal, and the daughter-in-law of Emperor Aurangzeb; and as an important member of the Mogul imperial family she was bound to support the plans of the emperor and the Bengal Subedar. At the same time, she was the daughter of the

102. MS. Assam Buranji No. 6. For the full text of the letter, see Appendix E of this book; and also, S. K. Bhuyan's *Ramani Gabharu,* pp. 38-40 and 72-76.

Assamese monarch Swargadeo Jayadhwaj Singha, grand-daughter of the illustrious statesman Momai-tamuli Barbarua, and niece of the great hero Lachit Barphukan; and she therefore thought it to be her duty to avert, if possible, the impending catastrophe of her country involved in the loss of Gauhati and Kamrup in a bloodless and disgraceful manner, as was contemplated by her ambitious uncle Laluk Barphukan. An open request to him to abandon his nefarious project would however amount to interference in the plans of the Mogul government.

She however managed to throw a hint in her reply to her uncle's letter by saying that his proposed desertion of Gauhati would be unbecoming and abominable, and he should therefore wait till he meets Moina who would be posted with full information from which he would be able to judge the propriety of his plan to evacuate Gauhati. The sentence in the Persian letter of the Begum ran as follows: "Take Muina nazde suma narasad yi na-shayesta hargiz nakhahad kard", which can be translated as,—till Moina reaches your place you should never do this unbecoming and abominable act. But Laluk Barphukan who had staked everything upon the execution of his plan was not the man to be cajoled into inaction by the laconic injunction of his amiable niece.

The two Assamese envoys returned from Dacca in the company of Azamtara's messenger Govindaram, and duly handed over the letters from the Padshahzada and his consort. The Barphukan then deputed some men to Nawab Mansur Khan to lead him safely to Gauhati. The Nawab, accompanied by Baduli, Ali Akbar and Satmal Dewan, crossed the frontier of Assam and entered into Kamrup. His march was deliberately slow as he apprehended the possibility of some dirty trick being played upon him by the wily Assamese.

Laluk Barphukan, as if innocent of the whole matter, deputed Dikhowmukhia Kataki to Gargaon to report on the entrance of the Moguls, asking the king to send reinforcements of men and provisions for expelling the invaders. The Barphukan also appealed to the Buragohain as the only person who could save the situation. The Buragohain replied,—"We have received the untoward news. If it be true I shall myself proceed to Gauhati accompanied by the other nobles. May he be the Padshah's son or the Padshah himself, why should we leave him alone?" [103] The Swargadeo's proposal to send provisions to Gauhati was opposed by the Buragohain who said that the materials could not do the fighting, and that if the Moguls had actually entered into Assam he and his colleagues would in person take the field.

The Buragohain then instituted measures to ascertain whether the Moguls had actually entered into Assamese territories. The launching of an expedition was expensive and hazardous, and it could not therefore be undertaken on mere reports; besides, instances were not wanting in the past of similar reports proving ultimately unfounded and baseless. The despatch of a force against the recalcitrant viceroy would only precipitate matters, and the Chintamani rampart upon which the Buragohain had counted so much was not yet completed. The absence of the able ministers from the capital was fraught with the possibility of a recurrence of misrule and anarchy. So the Buragohain hesitated and paused in spite of the persistent demands made by the Gauhati commanders to despatch fresh reinforcements and supplies.

Khanikar Dolakasharia Barua was sent down to Gauhati to enquire into the truth of the report. The Phukans of Gauhati took the Barua to the vicinity of the Mogul camp and pointed out to him the Mogul soldiers halting in their camp in Kamrup. The Barua returned to Gargaon and reported on what he had seen with his own eyes.

Kalia Kataki was then deputed to Gauhati to ascertain whether the Moguls had come to Assam of their own accord or whether they had come at the invitation of the Gauhati nobles. Kalia Kataki was similarly shown the camps of the Moguls, but he could not be sure of the reasons which had induced the Moguls to come to Assam. Kalia Kataki duly returned to Gargaon and reported his findings to the Swargadeo and the Buragohain.

103. S. K. Bhuyan, *Assam Buranji, S.M.*, p. 139.

The Buragohain, the Barpatra-Gohain and the Bargohain then tried to find out the real motives of the Mogul force. "If the Moguls had come of their own accord", the Dangarias pointed out to the Swargadeo, "they would have marched straight to attack Gauhati; but from their protracted halt in Kamrup it can be surmised that they have come to Assam on an express invitation from some one".

Gajpuria Hati-Barua was then sent to Gauhati to make enquiries on the above lines. The Hati-Barua came back after some time and reported to the king,—"I had a glimpse of the Moguls, but I could not be sure whether they have come as friends or as enemies. I have not seen any preparations on our side in respect of boats and provisions. The boats of the Gauhati Phukans are fully loaded with their personal goods, and their prows are facing upstream with a view to sail up from Gauhati at any moment". The report of the Hati-Barua convinced the monarch of the gravity of the situation, and he asked the Buragohain to suspend work on the Chintamani rampart, and to march to Gauhati instead at the head of an adequate force. The Buragohain was to be accompanied by the Barpatra Gohain, the Bargohain, Dihingia Phukan, Ram Phukan, Betmela Phukan, and the Naobaicha Phukan who was an elder brother of the premier.

Laluk Sola Barphukan had succeeded in keeping his designs concealed from his colleagues, the Phukans and Rajkhowas of Gauhati. They were therefore dismayed when they heard of Mogul forces appearing at Agiathuri near Gauhati. They enquired as to why the officers of the frontier outposts had failed to send prompt information of the advent of the Moguls. The Barphukan explained that the Moguls were following close on the heels of the frontier guardsmen who could not therefore give information in advance. The Phukans and Rajkhowas were not satisfied with this explanation; and they appealed to the Barphukan, as their chief, to do all that was needful, and promised to act as directed by him. Laluk Barphukan then dilated on the advantages of leaving Gauhati for the present as the fortifications of that place had not been repaired. The Barphukan added,—"We should therefore sail up to Kaliabar and launch our offensive operations from that place". The Paniphukan and the Miri Sandikoi Phukan then sent a message to the Buragohain through the Khanikar Barua, and it ran as follows,—"We have reported times without number about the advent of the Moguls, but no body has attached any credence to our reports. Now, Baduli has actually come; let the Buragohain now do what he can".

Mansur Khan had been staying with his force for some time at Agiathuri outside the western approaches of the Gauhati fortifications. He hesitated to enter into the fortified zone of Gauhati fearing some trap might be laid by the Ahoms for his destruction. Marangi Barua, dressed in a black attire, then proceeded in a boat to Mansur Khan's camp and told him of the arrangements made for his safe entrance into Gauhati. Marangi went so far as to cudgel a few Mogul soldiers to force them to cross through the line of Gauhati fortifications. Kalia of Buruk who was a trusted agent of the Barphukan also persuaded the Moguls to enter into Gauhati without hesitation. Mansur Khan then sailed up to Gauhati, and took possession of the town and its fort already vacated by Laluk Barphukan. It was Wednesday, the fourteenth day of Phalgun, 1600 *Saka*, or the 26th February, 1679.

The Barphukan had left Gauhati in a boat three days earlier in the company of the Phukans and Rajkhowas. At the time of sailing from Gauhati the Barphukan had cited a Sanskrit *sloka* which can be translated as follows: "I know Sita, the offspring of Janaka, and I know Rama, the slayer of the demon Madhu". In the language of the feelings uppermost in the mind of Laluk Barphukan at that dramatic moment, the *sloka* can possibly be rendered as follows: "I have put my whole faith in my niece Rahmat Banu Begum, the daughter of Jayadhwaj Singha, and in her husband Sultan Azamtara who alone is capable of destroying my arch-enemy Atan Buragohain".

Laluk Barphukan had proceeded in the rear of the Phukans and Rajkhowas. He had left instructions for Baduli to march at the head of a small force to seize the person of Atan Buragohain. Mansur Khan in the meantime established himself securely at Gauhati, and his task was made easy as he was assisted by several Mogul officers who had participated before in the administration of Lower Assam and were thus fully acquainted with the customs and manners of the people and the general situation of the place.

The occupation of Gauhati by Nawab Mansur Khan acting under the instructions of Sultan Azamtara, was considered in Delhi to be a great victory; and the prince was rewarded by his father Emperor Aurangzeb with costly presents. This is how the *Maasir-i-Alamgiri* records the event,—"On the 29th Muharram, 1090, Shahrukh, a servant of Prince Muhammad A'zam, brought a report to court which contained the account of the conquest of Gawahatti by His Majesty's troops. The messenger received a reward of Rs. 1,000; and a necklace of 91 pearls, valued at 25,000 rupees, was sent to the Prince as present".[104]

Baduli Phukan who had come to Gauhati with Nawab Mansur Khan soon realised the atrocious character of the treachery committed by Laluk Barphukan. Sixteen years of exile in Bengal had opened the eyes of Baduli to the realities of the situation in Assam. The impregnable fortifications of Gauhati had offered protection to Assam from the attacks of the enemy; and Mansur Khan now walked through them without meeting the slightest opposition! A big slice of Assam was now cut off and the enemy intrenched himself in full military strength in the heart of the kingdom! From Gauhati the Moguls could at any time march up to Gargaon as did Nawab Mir Jumla! Neither had Laluk Barphukan achieved for the present any personal advantage from his treachery. He did not press Mansur Khan for the promised reward of four lacs of rupees. In the meeting which took place at Laotali, Baduli gave vent to his feelings by saying to Laluk Barphukan,—"What have you done? The fortifications of

104. H. Blochmann, *Kuch Behar and Assam*, J.A.S.B., 1872, p. 99, reference to *Maasir-i-Alamgiri*, p. 105.

Saraighat cannot be penetrated into even by the immortals. What are the reasons which impelled you to desert them? Though you are the son of Momai-tamuli Barbarua, you have renounced your honour and your prestige of your own sweet accord! You have not even taken from the Moguls the four lacs of rupees promised to you! No good has come out of this affair! Besides, I used to take pride in telling the Padshah that my nephew is a great warrior—a true Kshattriya, and the days of my prestige acquired by praising your valour are also over!"[105] Baduli passed the night with Laluk Barphukan, and he left his nephew's company the next day by sailing down the Brahmaputra with the object of returning to Dacca. Baduli's reprimands, patriotic though belated, failed to produce any change in the ambitious bosom of Laluk Barphukan who had been dreaming dreams of installing himself as the crowned head of the kingdom.

105. S. K. Dutta, *Assam Buranji*, p. 48; MS. Assam Buranji Nos. 15 and 39.

CHAPTER XII

A BOY-KING PLACED ON THE THRONE

After having evacuated Gauhati, Laluk Barphukan sailed up towards Kaliabar. He then sent a report to the Ahom monarch about the entrance of the Moguls into Gauhati and its environs, obviously concealing the part he had played in the game.

The Ahom government had now to face a complex two-fold situation. It was necessary to curb the treacherous activities of Laluk Barphukan; it was still more imperative to oust the Moguls from Gauhati. Parvatia Raja despatched a considerable force under Betmela Bhitarual Phukan, Kalanchu Phukan Govinda, Tepartalia Ram Phukan, Mau Gohain-Phukan, Japang Gohain, Laithepena Solal Gohain and Kola Patar Barpatra Gohain, with Atan Buragohain at the head. The contingent sailed down the river, and halted at Biswanath for some time in order to form an accurate estimate of the situation.

Laluk Barphukan then sent a message to the Buragohain advising him to stay at Biswanath and send up the Phukans to Kaliabar to join his forces in an attack upon the Moguls. The expulsion of the Moguls being the primary objective of the expedition of the Buragohain, he readily complied with the Barphukan's requisition, and despatched to his camp Govinda Phukan, Betmela Phukan, and Ram Phukan together with their soldiers and provisions. The Buragohain failed to detect the real motive of the wily Barphukan; he had firm faith in the sincerity of the Barphukan; and he considered it to be his solemn duty to stand by him in pursuance of the oaths mutually taken during the disturbances in the reigns of Gobar Raja and Arjun Dihingia Raja. In old contemporary records, the despatch of the Phukans has been attributed to the Buragohain's adherence to his promises of old; and in the same vein, Laluk Barphukan has been described to be a man of falsehood and a violator of his vows.

When the three commanders arrived at the Barphukan's camp at Kaliabar, he took them inside on the pretext of having a conference, and divested them of the soldiers under their commands. Govinda Phukan thereupon bit the flesh of his arm, and exclaimed,—"Just see, we are perishing like women having listened to the advice of the Buragohain. It is my life's regret that I have not been able to drop the head of Sola [Laluk Sola Barphukan] on the ground". The three Phukans, Betmela, Ram and Govinda, were then imprisoned at Duimunisila under the vigilance of Kirkiria Duara Phukan.

Having heard of these developments at Kaliabar, the Buragohain ordered his forces to sail down the river towards Kaliabar. The Barphukan had similarly sailed up to encounter the royalist party. They arrived at Duimunisila on the very same day. A hot contest ensued between the two forces in which the soldiers of the Buragohain were defeated and routed, and the principal leaders captured.

Laluk Barphukan then fixed his headquarter at Kaliabar where he began to act in an independent manner totally ignoring the authority of Sudoipha Parvatia Raja seated on the throne of Assam.

Tepartalia Ram Phukan, Govinda Phukan and Betmela Phukan who had been kept in the custody of the Duara Phukan at Duimunisila were taken to Kaliabar and confined. Betmela who had acted as the principal adherent of Atan Buragohain was lodged in a pig-cage. In May 1679, he was tried by the Barphukan at the Dopdar at Kaliabar. An attendent of Mecha Ex-Barbarua arraigned and vilified the Phukan, and spat on his head mouthfuls of chewed betel-nut, leaf and lime. Ram Phukan and Govinda Phukan were also subjected to vile abuses on this occasion. The three Phukans were then beheaded in a village in Samdhara near Kaliabar.[106]

106. The commanders Tepartalia Ram Phukan, Govinda Kalanchu Phukan, and Betmela Kalanchu Bhitarual Phukan, were three distinct and separate individuals. In some chronicles, only two names are men-

In fulfilment of the terms requiring Laluk Barphukan to make over his principal opponents to the Moguls, the following Ahom nobles were sent down as captives to Nawab Mansur Khan at Gauhati: from Latasil camp, Champa Paniphukan, son of Phulbarua; Dihingia Miri Sandikoi Kari-Deka; Bamuni-putek Dikhowmukhia Rajkhowa of Kalanchu family; Lechai-kalia Kajalimukhia Barua of the Mechagharia Bargohain family; from Kaliabar headquarter, Mau Gohain-Phukan of the Kuoigayan family; and Tepartalia Sonarimua Gohain Rajkhowa. Mansur Khan however sent back the captives to Kaliabar a few weeks later. The Barphukan kept with him Mau Gohain, Sonarimua Gohain and Bamuni-putek, and set the remaining prisoners at liberty with permission to return to their respective homes.

Laluk Barphukan then promoted his adherents and supporters to high offices. His brother Marangi was appointed as Barbarua; his son Jagara Kari-Deka as Paniphukan; Alun, son of Dihingia Lapeti Phukan as Khangia Phukan; Maupia and Bandar Lanmakhru Chetia as Phukans; Dulia Barua as Neog Phukan. He nominated Dighala Gohain-Phukan to the office of Buragohain.

The defeat of the Gargayan force at Duimunisila and the subsequent fate of his principal compatriots had placed Atan Buragohain in a tragical predicament. There were heavy casualties amongst his followers, most of them had been killed in the engagement or imprisoned by the Barphukan. The suppression of a civil war presents enormous difficulties as soldiers engaged in the task prove lukewarm in their duties on account of the presence of their friends and relatives in the camp of the insurgents. The Buragohain could not march against the Barphukan with the inadequate remnant of his army, nor could he return to the capital without being able to quell the Barphukan's uprising with which mission also he had been entrusted by the king. His further stay at

tioned,—Ram Phukan and Betmela Phukan. Govinda and Betmela were two brothers, and they belonged to the well-known Kalanchu Sandikoi family.

Biswanath was unsafe as the emissaries of the Barphukan had been scouring the villages to capture the enemies of their master. A considerable force had actually been despatched by the Barphukan to Biswanath to fall upon the Buragohain and his party.

Atan Buragohain therefore decided to leave Biswanath and proceed to the Naga Hills for temporary refuge from where he would come out when opportunities permitted. From Biswanath the Buragohain went to Gabharu Luit, and then to Jakaichuk in Darrang, but finding it unsafe he halted for some time at Kaupati near Mangaldoi. He then crossed the Brahmaputra near Biswanath with the intention of proceeding to the Naga Hills by the Satsaya route, and stayed for some days at Lejubaj in Kutikuchi in the house of Ramrai Rajkhowa. In March 1679, the Buragohain was captured in the house of the Rajkhowa and taken to Kaliabar along with his elder brother, the Naobaicha Phukan, who had been seized on the way. The two brothers were confined at Duimunisila and guards were posted to keep watch over them.

Japang Bargohain left Biswanath with his personal detachments and proceeded to the Barphukan's camp at Kaliabar, and so did Laithepena Solal Gohain. Kola Patar Barpatra Gohain having left Biswanath went to his home at Kenduguri. The Barphukan sent one Kera, a Bhakat or devotee of Sutarpara, to bring the Barpatra Gohain with his men to Kaliabar. On his arrival at Kaliabar the Barpatra Gohain was deputed by the Barphukan to repair the fort at Diju in the Kaliabar area, and the Bargohain was appointed to supervise the repairs of the other forts on the south bank of the Brahmaputra. About the middle of April 1679, the Barphukan brought the two Gohains back to Kaliabar being afraid that they might concert hostile measures against him, and kept them under surveillance. The Barpatra Gohain was

107. In one chronicle, Atan Buragohain is described as having concealed himself in a granary belonging to a Brahman Saikia of Gozlong who was a retainer of the Dangaria.

deprived of his personal contingent of Dikhowmukhia retainers.

According to the Ahom system of government the Buragohain, the Barpatra Gohain, the Bargohain, the Barbarua and the Barphukan constituted the *Patra-mantri*, or the pillars of the state. Within the space of two months Laluk Barphukan managed to bring the whole administration under his direct control by confining the three Gohains, and appointing Marangi, his brother and his creature, as Barbarua. The Swargadeo, the head of the state, was the only person now left for being dealt with. The Barphukan therefore turned his attention to the task of coming to an understanding with the monarch, and in reducing him to the position of a mere figurehead, as under the shelter of the king's authority the Barphukan could further his designs without obstruction till the time became ripe for him to throw off the monarch's overlordship and become Raja himself. Besides, the Swargadeo could at any time sentence the Barphukan to death, and hence a lip-deep allegiance and accommodation with the monarch was necessary for Laluk for maturing his own designs.

Arrangements were then made for visiting Gargaon. The Barphukan first wanted to feel the situation at the capital and to create an atmosphere favourable to his reception. Marangi Barbarua, Alun Phukan and Maupia Phukan were sent in advance to Gargaon. Parvatia Raja had heard of the developments at Gauhati and Kaliabar; he now found himself divested of the counsel and support of the three Gohains as they had been imprisoned at Kaliabar. He was therefore scared at the approach of Marangi Barbarua and the two Phukans, and he retreated to a shelter in the hills, from where he sent a message to the Gauhati representatives recalling the ease and comfort of his life as a farmer passed in the pastoral surroundings of his village in the days of his princehood, and disowning all connection with the regrettable occurrences at the capital during the brief period of his kingship. "I had been living as a ploughman," ran the message, "and I have been brought here and made a Raja, and I do not know anything. If they have any designs against me let them come and execute them here; they alone will share the blame or merit of their action."

Having received this message from the Dulia Barua at Chinatali the Gauhati nobles sent a reassuring reply to the monarch denying sinister intentions against him. They said,—"The Swargadeo is not justified in speaking to us in this way. The people have been subjected to unnecessary harassment by the construction of the rampart in the heart of the kingdom. We have captured the Buragohain and have come up in quest of those who have revolted against His Majesty. It is significant that we have left Gauhati which resembles a casket of gold. What is the good of fighting with our external enemies if enemies inside the country are allowed to act as they choose? If we cannot settle up these matters, what is the good of our remaining at Gauhati, separated from our women and wives, and eating coarse rice in our meals? We have come to mete out proper punishment to the rebels, and to pay our respects to His Majesty."[108] This reassuring message from the Barbarua and the two Phukans induced Parvatia Raja to return to Gargaon.

Laluk Barphukan then proceeded to the capital leaving Bhatdhara Phukan and Kirkiria Phukan in charge of the affairs at Kaliabar. In his first interview with the Swargadeo the Barphukan expatiated upon the reasons which had led him to leave Gauhati and come up to the capital. The Barphukan started by saying that he and his friends entertained no grievance against His Majesty, and that they had come to find out the culprits who had instigated men to commit the murderous attempt on the king's person, and those who had made false allegations against Mecha and procured his dismissal from the Barbaruaship. The construction of the Chintamani rampart, observed the Barphukan, had caused endless hardship to the people, and those responsible for it had neglected their state duties, and misrepresented the situation to the monarch for their own personal advantage.

108. S. K. Bhuyan, *Assam Buranji*, *S.M.*, p. 140.

The Swargadeo pointed to Atan Buragohain as the originator of the misdeeds, and instantly sentenced him to death. The execution of the order was however suspended owing to the intercession of the chief nobles. The king affirmed his suspicion of Chikan Tamuli as being the villain of the assault though he was not sure as the attack had been made in the darkness of the night. The Barphukan held that the attack could not be made except by an inmate of the palace: and hence it was probable that Chikan Tamuli who had been a palace-attendant had committed the crime. Chikan was arrested and then executed at Rajahat in Railung after his hands and legs had been cut off. His aunt the queen who had uncovered the king's person exposing it to the blows of her nephew was also put to death.

Having been admitted to the good graces of the sovereign Laluk Barphukan succeeded in persuading him to sanction and confirm the appointment of Marangi Dola-Kasharia Barua as Barbarua in place of Chakrapani; Dilihial Dighala Gohain-Phukan as Buragohain; Mecha as Bhitarual Phukan; Metekatalia Ramdhan Tamuli as Naobaicha Phukan in place of Atan Buragohain's elder brother; Laluk Barphukan's son Tholoka as Deka-Phukan; Bezdoloi Rangacharan as Bhandari Barua in place of Kaupati who had his ears and nose clipped.

The Barphukan suggested the advisability of sending an embassy to Dacca offering the Swargadeo's felicitations to Sultan Azamtara who was in a sense the son-in-law of the Assam king as he had married King Jayadhwaj Singha's daughter. The envoys, accompanied by epistles and presents left Gargaon on 19th Jaistha 1601 *Saka,* or 5th June 1679 or near about. Laluk Barphukan sent with the official envoys secret messages of his own reviving his claim for the Rajaship of Assam.

In appreciation of the promises of loyalty and support made by Laluk Barphukan and his colleagues, Swargadeo Parvatia Raja gave them rich presents, consisting of ornaments and cloths, whereupon they returned to Kaliabar to resume charge of their respective commands.

About this time Laluk Barphukan wrote to Baduli the following letter: "I write this letter to you with affection mixed with necessity. You have reminded me of Sultan Azamtara's demand for the release and expatriation of Sayid Sala, son of Sayid Piroz Khan, and other prisoners, and of the relevant letter of the Padshahzada bearing his hand-impression and accompanied by a *sirpao.* I had intended to release them long before the receipt of the above letter. If we could meet for a short while we could talk about the means of preserving the cows and Brahmans of both the territories, and the maintenance of cordial relations with the officers and men of the Mogul emperor. It would also give me an opportunity to hear from you about your sorrows and sufferings. Now that the emperor's son has sent to me an epistle with presents, I should ask you to send a trusted man of yours with our two envoys Madhabcharan and Jadunandan; I shall tell him all that I have to communicate to you. The persons who planned hostilities against us have been killed and eliminated, and your relatives as well as mine have become secure in consequence. With regard to your desire to return to Assam, I should point out that we have been saved during several upheavals and disorders only because you are in Bengal. Do you think we shall be let off if we three, uncle and nephews, meet and live together in one place? Be assured of our prayers for your long life; and we shall be in enjoyment of peace and happiness through your blessings. Act in a manner which will perpetuate the good name of our ancestors, and secure the preservation of the cows and Brahmans."[109]

The reconciliation between Parvatia Raja and Laluk Barphukan transpired to be momentary and superficial as far as the monarch was concerned. The king was weak, no doubt, but he had sense enough to realise the seriousness of the situation brought about by the Barphukan's high-handedness and autocracy. The king had allowed the Barphukan to leave Gargaon with professions of friendship and good-will,

109. MS. Assam Buranji No. 6.

but after his departure to Kaliabar the king instituted measures for the capture of that ambitions noble, and for the rehabilitation of the government. Mecha Bhitarual Phukan who had outwardly supported Laluk Barphukan under sufferance and compulsion now became the confidant of the monarch. "Who is this man," exclaimed the monarch, "that he surrenders Gauhati to the Moguls, imprisons my Buragohain and my Phukans, and dismisses and appoints my officers?" It was proposed to engage Kirkiria Phukan, brother of Mecha, to arrest the Barphukan.

One Parvatia Kukurachowa Bara was deputed to Kaliabar with presents from the king for Kirkiria Phukan, with an order that the Phukan should seize the person of Laluk Barphukan, and that Kirkiria's services in this connection would be rewarded by promoting him to the office of Barphukan. The king planned to arrest Marangi Barbarua and Ramdhan Naobaicha Phukan at Gargaon. Kirkiria Phukan was engaged at the moment in supervising the repairs of forts in the north bank. He expressed his inability to capture the Barphukan who, he said, was always guarded by an armed retinue. Kirkiria Phukan suggested at the same time that an important officer should be despatched to him from Gargaon to act in conjunction to carry out the king's orders.

Parvatia Raja then deputed Gargayan Sandikoi's son with presents to Kirkiria, on the plea of enquiring into the progress of the repairs, for submitting a report to the monarch. The Sandikoi was appointed Neog, and the king promised to make him Naobaicha Phukan if he succeeded in his mission. The Neog first went to Kaliabar to meet Laluk Barphukan, from where he proceeded to the camp of Kirkiria Phukan. The Phukan asked the Neog to keep the presents with himself, saying,—"It will behove me to accept the presents after I succeed in carrying out the orders of His Majesty. Let them remain with you for the present." When pressed for definite action, Kirkiria Phukan told the Neog that he and the Barphukan had taken solemn oaths together in the waters of the Brahmaputra, and that he could not, at least for the present, act contrary to the interest of the Barphukan. "If the Barphukan brings the Moguls to Kaliabar," added Kirkiria. "I shall take proper steps as directed by His Majesty." The Neog reported the matter to Laluk Barphukan.

The king had in the meantime arrested Marangi Barbarua and Ramdhan Naobaicha Phukan. They were accused by the monarch as follows,—"The beautiful land of Kamrup is my dominion, and it has been acquired by us with great difficulty and suffering. Under whose orders did you relinquish such a territory in favour of the Moguls? Besides, who appointed you to these high offices? It appears that the slaves of Lukhurakhuns have become all-in-all, and I am nobody!"[110] Marangi and Ramdhan were necked out of the court, and then chained with iron fetters and imprisoned in the Hatisal.

The king also proposed to arrest Dihingia Alun Khangia Phukan, but having come to know about it the Phukan crossed the city walls one night and fled in a boat to Kaliabar where he apprised the Barphukan of the happenings at Gargaon. The Phukan would have followed a different course had he not left behind an indelible proof of his sinister motive in the shape of his red *muga-dhuti* getting stuck in the pointed bamboos of the wall as he was crossing the same. Marangi and Ramdhan were released after ten days. Marangi fled to Kaliabar and reported to his brother on the developments at Gargaon. One Ram Saraswati Kataki also sent a secret message to the Barphukan warning him of the king's hostile attitude. Bhatdhara instructed Ram Saraswati to inform the king that he would undertake to capture his brother Laluk Barphukan provided he would be appointed to the consequent vacancy in the office of Barphukan. The king failed to see through the hoax, designed to extract definite information about the royal intentions; and he made the promise on the lines of Bhatdhara's proposal. Bhatdhara communicated the whole matter to his brother at Kaliabar who now became confirmed in his belief that the king was determined to effect his destruction.

110. MS. Assam Buranji No. 5.

The Barphukan decided to leave for Gargaon to frustrate the execution of the plan against himself and his adherents. The affairs of Kaliabar were left in charge of his brother Bhatdhara who was promoted to the office of Barphukan. Kirkiria was brought back from the north bank and directed to assist Bhatdhara in the administration at Kaliabar. Kirkiria had now become a suspect of Laluk as he had kept silent about the visits of the king's emissaries Parvatia Kukurachowa and Sandikoi Neog. Laluk Barphukan took away from Kirkiria the latter's personal contingent of Dihingia *karis*, and replaced them by men from the Barphukan's own contingent, who were secretly instructed to capture Kirkiria and despatch him to Gargaon on the receipt of advice to that effect. The Barpatra Gohain and the Bargohain were left behind at Kaliabar. The prisoners including Chengkham Gohain Hati-Barua, and Khamti Dayangia Rajkhowa, nephew and son respectively of Atan Buragohain, were left under the special custody of Bhatdhara who imprisoned them in a net used for entrapping deer.

Laluk Barphukan accompanied by Laithepena Solal Gohain, and several Phukans and Rajkhowas, proceeded towards Gargaon. The Barphukan fixed his headquarter at Sakbari dockyard. Kirkiria had in the meantime been brought to Sakbari as a prisoner. Sudoipha Parvatia Raja opposed the insurgents in an armed conflict, but his men were quickly dispersed with heavy casualties. The monarch then took shelter in the palace.

After this, a number of unusual occurrences took place in the vicinity of the palace portending the ill fate of the sovereign. A deer had inserted its head inside an improviso rice basket made by wrapping round a betelnut sheath, and it could not extricate its head from the basket. It ran about in that state round the city, and there was universal anxiety and uproar at this uncommon sight. A party of armed men was also seen at midnight as proceeding from the palace to the Ahom necropolis at Charaideo Hill in the pomp and array of a royal procession. The palace guards thought the king was in the procession, and they beat the royal drums accordingly. This procession must have been staged by the Sakbari commanders to give an indication of the approaching funeral procession of the monarch.[111]

The Gauhati Phukans and Rajkhowas, stationed at Sakbari, decided meanwhile to depose Sudoipha Parvatia Raja, and Laluk's brother Marangi was sent with a party of men to execute the decree. Marangi saluted the king with a golden tray in his hand, and said,—"O, Swargadeo, please leave the throne". The king in his fury kicked the tray, and began to curse the Lukhurakhuns, describing them as a cabal engaged in the game of making and unmaking kings. The king also hinted at the treacherous move of the Lukhurakhuns to seize the Rajaship of Assam, and he predicted their destruction as a punishment for their treachery. The Gauhati Phukans being masters of the situation, Sudoipha Parvatia Raja had no other alternative but to bow to their intentions. He was then formally divested of his kingly authority, and was in consequence deprived simultaneously of his personal guards and retainers and his usual supply of food articles. He then became a house-prisoner at the palace. The two brothers Mecha and Kirkiria were then blinded, and banished to a place called Nikari.

In October 1679, a prince of the Samaguria branch of the royal family, aged only fourteen years, was placed on the throne at Sakbari Naosal. A few days later, the deposed monarch Sudoipha Parvatia Raja was taken to Charaideo Hill for execution. On the eve of his approaching end, the unfortunate monarch thrust into his mouth a morsel of rice and quickly spat it back, saying, "Let there be a famine in the land as a punishment for this injustice and cruelty". He was then put to death by being made to drink poison. His two sons were also executed under the orders of the new king which were obviously inspired by Laluk Barphukan. The daughters of Mecha and Halwa who were the consorts of Parvatia Raja were also put to death.[112]

111. MS. Assam Buranji No. 5.
112. MS. Assam Buranji No. 5.

The new monarch first lived at the Hatisal attached to the quarters opposite the royal camp at Chunpora. The camp was protected by earthen walls on all sides which the astrologers, both Hindu and Ahom, had declared to be inauspicious, and advised the monarch to remove his camp to a place called Bahgara which was surrounded by bamboo walls. The king lived for some time at Lechang and then at Meteka near Alikekuri.

Laluk Barphukan then became Rajmantri Phukan, or His Majesty's Minister, vested with executive power over the whole administration. This office was created in emergencies to provide for the association of a man of exceptional ability with the government of the kingdom.[113] Laluk then appointed his supporters to positions of responsibility. Sandikoi Neog was appointed as Dakhinkulia Phukan, Bandar Chetia Phukan as Deka-Phukan; Bihparua as Neog Phukan; Jatakari Hazarika as Bhitarual Phukan. Dihingia Kari-Deka and Anka, both related to Laluk, were sent down to Kaliabar with the rank of Phukans. Laluk dismissed many old officers and appointed new ones in their place.

The new monarch assumed the Ahom name Sulikpha and the Hindu name Ratnadhwaj Singha. But he is commonly known as Lora Raja, or the boy-king, on account of his tender years.[114] On the appointment of Bhatdhara as Barphukan, followed by the elevation of his brother Laluk to the office of Rajmantri Phukan the latter ceased to be called Barphukan. As he was sufficiently advanced in years he was thenceforward known as Bura-phukan, or the aged Phukan. In the Mogul epistles of the period Laluk Phukan is referred to as Rajmantri Phukan.

To cement the friendship of the royal house of Samaguri to which Lora Raja belonged, and the Lukhurakhun clan of which Laluk Buraphukan was a member, the latter's daughter

113. Badanchandra Barphukan was similarly appointed Rajmantri Phukan after the first Burmese invasion in 1817. The office of Rajmantri was usually held by one of the three Gohains.

114. Lora Raja was also known as Samaguria Raja and Kathalguria Raja.

who was bald-headed was given in marriage to Lora Raja as well as Bhatdhara's daughter. Laluk's daughter was aged only five years, and Bhatdhara's daughter, described as being on the verge of youth, was twelve years. These matches between minors were intended to increase the Buraphukan's hold on the monarch, and also to serve as a medium through which the Buraphukan would receive prompt intimation of what was going on at the palace.

During the king's residence at Meteka the Buraphukan fixed his abode in its immediate vicinity. He mounted guns on the walls of his compound, and lived with great vigilance and caution. The Phukans and the other officers had to attend the court of the Swargadeo and the Rajmantri Phukan, and pay their obeisance to both. They had thus to serve two masters. The king could be ignored as they would receive protection for their anti-royal disposition and actions from the Buraphukan; but the displeasure of the Buraphukan was fatal to the interests of the nobles as the king was impotent to protect them from the consequences.

CHAPTER XIII

LALUK BURAPHUKAN DONS THE REGALIA

After having consolidated his position at the capital Laluk Buraphukan took active measures to fulfil his old dream of becoming the Raja of Assam.

The atrocities of the Buraphukan were not committed for the mere pleasure of suppressing his rivals and annihilating his foes. They were deliberate and planned, aimed at accomplishing one single purpose and design. After setting up the puppet Lora Raja on the throne, Laluk Buraphukan became the virtual head of the administration, and this was signalised by his assumption of the title of Rajmantri Phukan. But he had been cherishing the hope of becoming the actual ruler of Assam. This ambition was assiduously concealed from his supporters and friends, as he knew very well that no one in Assam would countenance this preposterous proposal.

Since the conquest of Assam by the Ahoms under Sukapha in the early part of the thirteenth century no person of non-royal origin had ever been admitted to the office of the Swargadeo. Ministers had no doubt run the administration during the interval between the death of one monarch and the accession of another, though the interval at one time had extended up to seven years, but these were stop-gap arrangements and of the nature of caretaker governments, and the throne remained vacant on all such occasions for being occupied by a suitable prince when he could be found. Atan Buragohain had refused to wear the crown voluntarily offered to him by the ministers and nobles, with the remark,—"I am a minister, and I cannot become a king. The crown should be placed on the head of a prince of royal blood." About a hundred years later, when a Moran leader Ramakanta sat on the throne by expelling the Ahom monarch Lakshmi Singha, the Dangarias remarked,—"We see that a

Moran has assumed sovereign power. The Heavenly King has also been removed from the throne; the Mahantas also have been made to pay money under compulsion; the Dangarias, the Baruas and the Phukans have been murdered, dismissed or expelled. The Morans have set up an independent sway. Since the advent of King Sukapha till now only the members of the royal family have become kings, and not others of inferior blood."[115] These remarks of high-ranking Ahoms, as quoted above, represent the constitutional usage sanctified by uninterrupted practice which debarred a commoner and a non-royal patrician from succeeding to the position of a sovereign.

But Laluk Buraphukan, like his predecessor Debera Barbarua, had come to break the law and not to respect it. Laluk was possessed with an obsession for power which obliterated before his mind's eye his limitations arising from his origin and descent, and the combined opposition of precedent and custom. The picture of himself seated on the throne, attired in the purple robe of the Swargadeo, with the crown on his head, and the glittering image of Chengdeo hanging down from his neck, with the nobles prostrating seven times before him, constantly haunted Laluk's distorted imagination; and the dream in process of sublimation and concentration lost the shock and horror which the novelty and imposture inherent in the very idea would have produced in the mind of a balanced and rational individual.

A man of Laluk Barphukan's temperament is not slow in inventing arguments to justify his intentions and actions, and the thoughts which must have surged in his mind at that moment can be thus represented in an imaginary soliloquy:—

"I must become the Raja of Assam, and convert the sweltering summer of my obscurity into a golden autumn of my sovereignty. The present circumstances are most favourable to my enterprise. There will be opposition no

115. S. K. Bhuyan, *Tungkhungia Buranji*, O.U.P., p. 72.

doubt, but I have resources enough to suppress it with vigour and speed.

"But why should there be opposition at all? It is true I am not of royal blood, but have not non-princes ever adorned the throne? Look at Sher Shah, he became the emperor of Delhi. In our own days, has not Shivaji, the son of a Jagirdar, and the grandson of a tiller of the soil, become an anointed sovereign—a Chhatrapati ?

"Now, examine my claims. My father Momai-tamuli Barbarua was first a humble farm-labourer, but he became ultimately a Barbarua and a general; and my brother Lachit was a Barphukan. By being a Barphukan myself I have simply repeated the honour once attained by the Lukhurakhun family. Now, the crown of my family has been reached in me, and I must climb a step higher to maintain the prestige of our line in an ascending scale.

"It was my father who fixed the Barnadi and the Asurar Ali as the western limits of the Ahom kingdom, transferring Lower Assam to the Moguls. The Ahom kings had no doubt recovered possession of Lower Assam, but it was the feat of my younger brother Lachit. Gauhati and Kamrup therefore constitute our family demesne. By surrendering the Gauhati fort to the Moguls thereby permitting them to reoccupy Lower Assam, I have honoured the sacred stipulations of my illustrious sire. Gauhati had been acquired by Lachit; and I as his elder brother can restore it to the Moguls to whom it had been originally allotted by my father.

"Besides, Kamrup which is contiguous to the Mogul boundary is no bed of roses; claims and counter-claims, and aggressions and reprisals, give no peace to the Ahom rulers. So it is better that their kingdom should be contracted that they may govern their truncated dominions in continued peace and security.

"My nephew Sultan Azamtara is near at hand, and he has promised to see me through the initial difficulties; and if he hesitates to implement his promises I have my uncle Baduli to urge the prince to support me, as my elevation is to his advantage. Aurangzeb Padshah is infirm and old, and my nephew Azamtara is sure to succeed to the throne of Delhi, resourceful and valiant as he is: and then the mighty support of the Mogul emperor will be harnessed for the security of our family.

"The Barpatra Gohain and the Bargohain are prisoners at Kaliabar, and Atan Ex-Buragohain, the greatest thorn in my way, is awaiting his doom at the very same place. The Barbarua is my own brother Marangi, and I am the Rajmantri Phukan, the undisputed head of the government. As for Lora Raja, — let my plans be fully matured under the shadow of his sovereignty, and when the moment comes he will be cast away without any ceremony and compunction. The princes who are impediments in the path of my ambition are in the process of being liquidated one by one, thanks to the energy and vigilance of my emissaries.

"So this is my time, the meridian of my fortune, my zenith and my heyday, and hence I must rise to the clarion call of my opportunity, or languish in the limbo of oblivion and obscurity. So, hail Laluk, hail to thee, the founder of the Lukhurakhun dynasty of Ahom Swargadeos, hail!"

These thoughts which took a final shape in the reign of Lora Raja must have dawned on Laluk's mind sometime in 1677. Azamtara had demanded the restoration of Gauhati; and he had gone so far as to say that he would be satisfied if Gauhati was placed in his possession only for a few seasons. The Padshahzada's sole aim was to gain prestige and importance in the eye of his exacting father Emperor Aurangzeb, and to strengthen thereby his claim to succession to the throne of Delhi. There was nothing which Azamtara would not be prepared to do to achieve his object; and a promise to confer on Laluk Barphukan the Rajaship of Assam was too small a price in view of the momentous character of the achievement if the Padshahzada could obtain from that Barphukan the evacuation of Gauhati. As a shrewd politician and schemer Laluk Barphukan did not fail to study this attitude of Sultan Azamtara, and exploit it to his full advantage.

The offer to surrender Gauhati had originated from Laluk himself, and on the completion of the necessary arrangements he evacuated that town making it easy for the Moguls to occupy it unopposed. He then installed himself as virtual dictator of affairs at the capital, and reduced the monarch Parvatia Raja to a mere nonentity. It was now Laluk's time to work for the culmination of his dream with determination and vigour.

During his first visit to Gargaon, Laluk Barphukan, as we have seen, had persuaded Parvatia Raja to establish friendly relations with Sultan Azamtara and send an embassy to him with rich presents. The Barphukan said,—"We hear that Your Majesty's son-in-law Azamtara has come to Dacca with our princess. It is difficult to fathom the real drift of *Moguli-fandi,* or the tactics of the Moguls. It is therefore desirable that Your Majesty should send some ambassadors to the Padshahzada conveying your affection and friendship in order to ascertain his real intentions". Parvatia Raja asked the Barphukan to nominate the envoys. This was the opportunity sought for by the Barphukan, as his object was to utilise the official embassy for the purpose of communicating his own secret message to Azamtara.

The Barphukan had peacefully surrendered Gauhati to the Moguls, and had thus acted up to the promise made by him. But the Padshahzada had not done anything to implement the promise on his side to make Laluk the real Raja of Assam except conferring the title and the kingdom in a mere epistolary scroll. It was for this reason that the Barphukan now inspired Parvatia Raja to send an embassy to Dacca composed of his own nominees and confidants. These trusted emissaries were Madhabcharan and Jadunandan whose fathers Sola and Sanatan had also been employed in diplomatic missions to the Mogul court. A knowledge of the manners and usages of the Mogul court was therefore a tradition in the families of the two ambassadors, and it was handed down from father to son. The Barphukan said to the king,—"Sola and Sanatan had served as envoys in our missions to the Moguls. Their two sons are Madhabcharan and Jadunandan who should therefore be sent now as envoys to Dacca". The king accordingly made over the epistles and presents to the two envoys for being delivered to Sultan Azamtara.

There were presents also for Rahmat Banu, and for Shuja's daughter; and for the second Assamese consort, the daughter of the Tipam Raja. Presents were also sent to the nobles of the Dacca court, including Sayed Ali, Manowar Khan, and the Barphukan's uncle Baduli. Separate presents were sent to Mansur Khan at Gauhati through Kanthabhushan Kakati. The articles sent to Dacca represented the best that nature and art produced in Assam; and they consisted of agar wood, elephants' tusks, musks, cowtails; rings, earrings, bangles, waist-bands, and necklaces, and made of gold; and embroidered cloths, including *mekhelas* or skirts, and *rihas*, or pieces to cover the upper part of the body, which are the special wear of Assamese ladies.[116] A secret letter was also sent to Sultan Azamtara reminding him of his old promise to make Laluk the Raja of Assam. "I have surrendered Gauhati", wrote the Barphukan, "and you should in your turn fulfil your old promise". The Barphukan asked the Padshahzada to address him as Raja of Assam. This embassy left the Ahom capital on the 19th Jaistha, 1601 *Saka*, or June 2, 1679 A.D.

In the meantime Sultan Azamtara had received orders from Emperor Aurangzeb to proceed to Rajputana where fresh disturbances had raised their head. The prince proceeded to Jodhpur by the route through Banaras, Agra and Ajmer, and met the emperor at Mewar on December 16, 1679.

On August 14, 1679, the very day of the arrival of the Assamese envoys at Dacca, Sultan Azamtara had left that place on his way to Rajputana making over the governorship of Bengal to Nawab Shaista Khan.[117] The Katakis submitted the letters and presents to the new Subedar. Owing to

116. S. K. Bhuyan, *Ramani Gabharu*, pp. 52-54, for a complete list of the presents.

117. Stanley Lane-Poole, *Medieval India*, Vol. II, p. 261, published by Susil Gupta, 1951.

troubles brewing meanwhile in Rajputana and the Deccan, Shaista Khan was unwilling to get himself entangled in fresh embroils by sending an expedition to Assam to install Laluk on the throne. He therefore sent a mere letter to the Barphukan running as follows,—"We write to Raja Barphukan. In fulfilment of our promise we confer on you the Rajaship of Assam. You are to continue as Raja by exterminating your foes or sending them to our place. We have not as yet received your enemies, nor the son of Sayed Piroz. They should be sent to us in pursuance of the old stipulations. The emperor will be pleased when this is done".[118] The letter was sent to Assam with the Subedar's envoy Govindaram who accompanied Madhabcharan and Jadunandan on their return journey; the envoys were also instructed to verbally elaborate the written message.

The embassy arrived at the Ahom capital within a few months of the commencement of the reign of Sulikpha Lora Raja when the Barphukan had got himself appointed as Rajmantri Phukan. The Barphukan, now called Buraphukan, obtained full particulars from the three envoys, and ascertained from them that the letter brought by them had been addressed to him and not to the monarch.

This was a great occasion for Laluk Rajmantri Phukan. There was an embassy for him from Nawab Shaista Khan, Subedar of Bengal, brother of Shah Jahan's immortal consort Mamtaz Mahal, and uncle of Emperor Aurangzeb, and its object was to confer upon Laluk the Rajaship of Assam. He therefore made elaborate arrangements to accord a fitting reception to Shaista Khan's envoy Govindaram. A large area was cleared up near the boat-house at Sakbari. A pavilion was constructed where the Buraphukan would sit with the

118. In some chronicles, the reply from Dacca is attributed to Sultan Azamtara, and is of the same tenor as his first letter conferring the Rajaship on Laluk. The date of Azamtara's departure from Dacca is given by Charles Stewart as August 14, 1679, and in another account as October 12, 1679. See Stewart's *History of Bengal*, p. 335, and Jadunath Sarkar's *History of Bengal*, Vol. II, pp. 230, 382.

pomp and splendour of a sovereign. The seven canopies which were hung one above the other at the king's reception of foreign envoys were now brought from the royal store, and hung over the dais. Tassels and lamps were suspended from the borders of the canopies. The whole place assumed a spectacular appearance, and was thronged with elephants, horses and men.

Laluk Rajmantri Phukan dressed himself in the robes and ornaments worn by Ahom monarchs. He had managed to bring the crown formerly used by Parvatia Raja, and wore it on his head. The Rajmantri Phukan, endowed with the title of Raja of Assam conferred upon him by the Moguls, behaved on this occasion as a virtual sovereign. Govindaram was formally ushered into the presence of the "Raja"; the envoy delivered the presents and epistles, and gave replies to the questions put to him in the diplomatic style of the Ahom court. At the end of the formalities, Govindaram was allowed leave to retire to his camp after being informed that the result of his visit would be communicated to him later. After a few days Laluk made over presents and epistles to his envoy Bhushan Kandali Kataki for being delivered to Nawab Shaista Khan. The Assamese envoy then left for Dacca in the company of Govindaram.

Laluk thus became the Raja of Assam through the instrumentality of the Mogul Subedar of Dacca. As Lower Assam was in possession of the Moguls the title was obviously used in reference to Upper Assam which was still independent. The Moguls had no title over Upper Assam, and could not therefore pass it on to another party. The Moguls were not prepared to back up the distinction by sending an armed force to the help of Laluk with which he could occupy the throne or get himself acknowledged as Raja. His Rajaship was at best a titular distinction, a token of the good-will of the Moguls shown towards an Ahom quisling who had made them masters of Gauhati treacherously and bloodlessly.

The Buraphukan could not make much fuss about his Rajaship for the Ahoms would not tolerate any one on the throne who was not a direct descendant of Sukapha on the male line. To Laluk the title proved to be a matter of secret satisfaction which, when published, would mean his sure and immediate destruction, for he would have the whole country arrayed against him. "The Lukhurakhun dynasty of Ahom Swargadeos" figured only in the perverted imagination of Laluk Sola Rajmantri Phukan; and his foreign allies lived too far from him and were too much engrossed in vital matters of their own to come to his rescue in the event of an emergency.

CHAPTER XIV

MURDER OF ATAN BURAGOHAIN AND JAIMATI

The crown-wearing of Laluk Buraphukan at Sakbari Naosal was at best a serio-comic performance designed to gratify his vanity and to give an impression of his importance to the envoy of the Bengal Subedar. There was the lawful sovereign Lora Raja on the throne, and two kings cannot rule in one kingdom at the same time.

But Laluk Baruphukan thought it otherwise. He considered his Sakbari 'crowning' to be a preliminary to his formal and lawful coronation, when the Dangarias, the Phukans and the Rajkhows, and the other officers and potentates would prostrate themselves seven times before him offering their homage and allegiance, amidst the multitudinous shouts of the populace, the yellings of the elephants and the beatings of trumpets and cymbals; when his new name and title would be written by the court Pundits in letters of gold with golden pens, and newly minted coins bearing his superscription would be distributed for the first time amongst the assembled gentry and the masses. The Sakbari affair, designed obviously as a shock-absorber, accustomed the people to see the Buraphukan in royal pomp and attire, and as such it was calculated to rob the subsequent formal ceremony of much of its odium and novelty. Lora Raja was a mere puppet, and when the preparations would be completed Laluk Buraphukan could smother the embers of the boy-king's life in the twinkling of an eye.

The Buraphukan knew well that his dream could not see its final consummation as long as Atan Buragohain was alive. The Buragohain was well-known throughout the land for his sober statesmanship and disinterested patriotism, and he therefore commanded the confidence and respect of the nobiliary and the populace. The Buragohain would by no means tolerate the elevation of a commoner to the exalted rank of a sovereign, and his views on this subject were definite and pronounced, as he had given vent to them when the nobles, including Laluk, had pressed him to wear the kingly crown. The Buragohain was now a captive at Duimunisila, but popular as he was, he could, if he intended seriously, escape from his incarceration at any moment when opportunities were favourable.

Laluk Buraphukan, after the Sakbari ceremony, turned his attention to Atan Buragohain who had been languishing as a prisoner along with his elder brother. During his first visit to the capital after the surrender of Gauhati, Laluk Barphukan had manipulated to obtain Parvatia Raja's approval for the execution of the Buragohain; but the nobles interceded, and the king finally withdrew his orders. Besides, at that time Laluk had not fully consolidated his power, and the execution of a popular and respected leader like Atan Buragohain would place the Buraphukan in bad odour with the nobles and the masses; and like Herod the tetrarch, Laluk Buraphukan spared the Buragohain's life, not for love, but for fear of the multitude.

But when Lora Raja became king, the Buraphukan's position was very much strengthened, and he considered himself capable of crushing any popular disturbance that might follow the execution of the Buragohain. The craze for wearing a crown, not stolen from the royal store, but offered to him solemnly by the willing consent of the nobles, made Laluk blind of the consequences of his actions. He now renewed his plan for the destruction of the Buragohain. "A number of men, including the Buragohain, are confined at Kaliabar", said Laluk, "what is Your Majesty's intention with regard to these prisoners?" The boy-king who understood the drift of Laluk's question had no other alternative but to order their execution. The nobles did not perhaps know anything of the royal orders; and even if they knew their impotent subservience to the Buraphukan would not permit them to utter a word of protest.

Two emissaries, Metekatalia Khona Chaudang Barua of the Bargohain family, and Rangason Chaorak Saikia of the

Banchengia Barpatra Gohain family, were despatched to Kaliabar to carry out the orders of execution. The Chaudang Barua was the officer in charge of the Chaudangs, a community of sturdy and able-bodied men specially employed by the Ahom government in duties connected with the apprehension and punishment of offenders. The toponomous appellation 'Meteka-talia' applied both to the Buraphukan and the Chaudang Barua shows that they both lived at Meteka and were thus neighbours.

On the arrival of the Chaudang Barua and the Chaorak Saikia, the two prisoners Atan Buragohain and his elder brother were brought from their place of confinement at Duimunisila and taken to the garden of the Solal Gohain at Kaliabar. Atan Buragohain was strangled to death with the help of a *tangali*, or waist-scarf. His brother was also put to death in that garden by the Chaudang Barua and the Chaorak Saikia. It was the second day of the bright fortnight of Agrahayan, 1601 *Saka*, sometime in November-December 1679 A.D. Langkham Deka, son of the Buragohain, was taken as prisoner to his family residence at Bahgara near Gargaon where he was subsequently put to death under the orders of the king.

History is mute about Atan Buragohain's life of captivity at Duimunisila, and the last scene at the Solal Gohain's garden. One can imagine the thoughts which must have passed through the mind of that patriot — his unending efforts to restore his motherland to tranquillity and peace, though frustrated by the renewed machinations of unscrupulous nobles. But these musings we leave to the creative imagination of our future poets and dramatists.

Atan Buragohain perished by the orders of Lora Raja Ratnadhwaj Singha, but everybody knew that it was Laluk Buraphukan who had put the sword in the hangman's hand,— the hand was the hand of Esau, but the voice was the voice of Jacob. Even the crude chronicler of the age records the tragic circumstances with an evident touch of regret,—"The Buragohain who had been confined at Kaliabar was killed under royal orders with his whole family by Khona Gohain of the Bargohain family who had been despatched thereto for this purpose. All did whatever the Buraphukan made them to do."[119]

The other obstacles in the path of Laluk's ambition were the princes of royal blood, all descended from King Sukapha, the first Ahom conqueror of Assam. They were scattered in the districts adjoining the capital. Suhungmung Dihingia Raja, 1497-1539 A.D., placed the estates of the princes on a regular footing by establishing his four sons at Charing, Dihing, Tipam and Tungkhung. There were also establishments of princes at Samaguri and Namrup. The head of each of these six royal families was given an estate or *mel* together with a contingent of retainers for the maintenance of himself and his dependants; and these heads were known by the title of Raja or Gohain, and they were distinguished from each other by the addition of the names of their respective estates, *e.g.*, Charing Raja, Tungkhungia Gohain, Samaguria Gohain, and Namrupia Raja. There were many princes who went without any estate and distinction, and who had therefore to depend for their bread on the heads of their respective families. In course of time the appellations Charingia Raja, Tipam Raja and the Namrupia Raja became titular distinctions conferred on the nearest male relatives of the reigning sovereign, the distinction Charing Raja being ordinarily reserved for the heir-apparent.

Every one of the princes could trace his descent from some one in the past who had actually sat on the Ahom throne. The nearer the descent the stronger would be his claim to the throne; thus the son of a king would be preferred to a grandson, and a grandson to a great-grandson. But this priority was of no avail if a prince failed to back up his claim by the support of some one in power; and a prince who belonged to the seventh degree of descent from a previous king could compete for the throne if his cause was taken up by an influential potentate. Thus every prince, whatever might be his position or status, could look forward to kingship provided he was

119. S. K. Bhuyan, *Assam Buranji, S.M.*, pp. 142-43.

perfect in all his limbs, and provided he could enlist the active support of a noble. The potentates, and even the heads of monasteries, harboured princes with a view to raise them to the throne when opportunities permitted themselves; and if the supporters succeeded in their attempt they would acquire great influence and power through their nominees on the throne.

Owing to the presence of this numerous body of princes, each of whom was a positive material for insurrection, and a rallying point of miscreants and rebels, no Ahom king could sit on the throne safely and complacently. It was for this reason that Debera Barbarua, to secure the position of his royal protegés, and vicariously of himself, pursued the ruthless plan of massacring all able-bodied princes. It was more necessary in the case of Laluk Buraphukan, not for the safety of Lora Raja, but for his own security when he would become king as that glorious event was, according to his calculation, bound to take place sooner or later.

Laluk Buraphukan accordingly instituted a vigorous search for the princes; and he despatched emissaries to different quarters to scour the villages and the princely establishments. Those whom the Buraphukan's agents could lay their hands on were captured and killed, or let off after mutilation thereby disqualifying them for succession. This is how this fact is recorded in a contemporary chronicle,—"At that time the Barphukan [Laluk Buraphukan] after having informed the monarch, caused the death of Bahgaria Gohain and his brother at Kaliabar. After this he searched for princes and killed all those he could get." In order to escape from the hands of the Buraphukan's agents, most of the princes left their homes, lived disguised in the houses of their relatives and friends, wandered incognito in remote districts, or even crossed the borders of Assam.

The principal target of Laluk Buraphukan's campaign of massacring princes was Gadapani of the Tungkhungia royal family, *first,* because he was the son of Gobar Raja who had sat on the Ahom throne thereby making his son Gadapani's claim just and unassailable; *secondly,* because Prince Gadapani was reputed for his personal vigour and energy thereby rendering his candidature readily acceptable to the nobles and officials.

Being fully aware of Laluk's designs against him, Prince Gadapani left his ancestral home at Tungkhung, and roamed from place to place as a fugitive, assuming disguise when necessary. "At the time when Samaguria Lora Raja, Momaitamuli Barbarua's sons Laluki Barphukan and Marangi Barbarua were residing at Meteka," says an old chronicle, "a search was made in the families of kings; being afraid of this he [Gadapani] left his home and orchard, and wandered about in the north and south banks, in hills and forests, and in numerous villages, both in Assam and outside."[120] His two sons Lai and Lechai, aged about fourteen and twelve, were kept by him in a retreat in the Naga Hills out of fear for Laluk Buraphukan who would not spare even the lives of minor princes.

The agents of Laluk Buraphukan reported to their master their inability to trace Gadapani or obtain any information about his whereabouts. Laluk could not feel secure till he knew precisely about the movements and intentions of Gadapani. The emissaries led by one Gidagathi Hazarika of Dakhinpat instituted a more vigorous search for Gadapani and came upon his wife Jaimati who, they thought, must be aware of her husband's refuge. This lady is believed to be the daughter of Laithepena Bargohain, though this fact has not been fully corroborated till now.

It was perhaps not possible for Jaimati to know about Gadapani's precise whereabouts as he had left home a long time ago; and therefore, when questioned about Gadapani she pleaded her ignorance of his movements. Gidagathi Hazarika was not satisfied with the answer, and he inflicted tortures on Jaimati to elicit from her information about her husband. The princess stuck to her old plea of ignorance, and she replied to the increasing tortures by silence and

120. MS. Assam Buranji No. 16.

patient forbearance. She was *enceinte* at that time, and the chastisements gradually became unbearable to her, and she breathed her last in the midst of her tortures.

Jaimati resembles Shakespeare in one respect: the incontrovertible facts about their life can be represented in a few sentences, in spite of the gradually expanding volume of apocrypha in either case. The facts about Jaimati as given above are all that can be learnt or reasonably deduced from contemporary chronicles where we come across only two statements about her. The first chronicle says,—"Previously to this, out of fear for the Buraphukan he [Gadapani] had kept his two sons in a Naga village. His wife died in a state of pregnancy in the midst of punishments and tortures." In the second chronicle we read,—"At that time [after the departure of the Bengal envoy Govindaram] the Barphukan, after having informed the monarch, caused the death of Bahgaria Gohain and his brother at Kaliabar. After this he searched for princes and killed all those he could get. Having failed in his search for the Burha-Raja [Gadapani, afterwards king Gadadhar Singha, commonly known as Burha-Raja], and having got his wife, Dakhinpatia Hazarika Gidagathi killed her by punishments and tortures."[121] The contemporary chronicles hitherto discovered do not say anything further about the circumstances connected with the death of Gadapani's wife, and her name is not even mentioned in the chronicles we have come across.

But the dry bones of Princess Jaimati's death as found in contemporary records have been replenished by traditions circulated amongst the Assamese people. She is adored as an ideal wife who sacrificed her life for ensuring safety to her husband by wilfully withdrawing information regarding his whereabouts and movements. She was subjected to all forms of torture, but she stuck heroically to her determination not to give any clue which might lead to the capture of her husband. Gadapani who survived Jaimati only through her self-sacrifice ultimately sat on the throne, and restored peace,

121. S. K. Bhuyan, *Assam Buranji*, S.M., p. 145; MS. A.B. No. 5.

and tranquillity in the country. He became the founder of a long line of kings whose reigns terminated only with the advent of the Burmese, followed by that of the British. Jaimati's son King Rudra Singha was an ambitious and powerful sovereign, who patronised learned and religious persons, subdued the neighbouring chieftains of Cachar and Jayantia, established friendly relations with the Rajas of Hindusthan, and launched elaborate preparations to unfurl the flag of victory in Bengal, and to continue his victorious progress as far as Delhi. He constructed the Jaisagar temple and the Jaisagar tank which can still be seen at Rangpur, the capital founded by that monarch. It is believed that the temple and the tank were constructed by King Rudra Singha to perpetuate the memory of his mother Jaimati and the site where they stand indicates the venue of her torture and death. These circumstances have created a halo round the memory of Jaimati, and poems and dramas have been written bringing out the central theme of her immolation for her husband's safety, with varying details about the attendant circumstances. The first cinematographic venture of the Assamese centred round the story of Jaimati. Celebrations are held every year on the death anniversary of Jaimati in the vicinity of Jaisagar tank, and throughout the Assam Valley, and other places where there are organised Assamese societies.

The details of Jaimati's torture and death were recorded by Mr. J. M. Foster of Nazira in his article on the temple of Jaisagar published in 1874 in the Journal of the Asiatic Society of Bengal, where he refers to old Assamese chronicles describing the sacrifice of Jaimati, though there is some room for confusion in respect of the causes of her husband's flight and some sources of his information; *secondly*, by Dutiram Hazarika in his metrical chronicle of the Tungkhungia rulers, known as *Kalibharat Buranji*, the materials for which were obtained by the author from Raja Purandar Singha; *thirdly*, by Harakanta Barua Sadar-Amin in his revised and enlarged version of the Assam Buranji by Radhanath Barbarua and

Kasinath Tamuli Phukan;[122] *fourthly*, by Ratneswar Mahanta who had heard the story from Indibar Barua Shirastadar of Sibsagar;[123] and *fifthly*, by the present writer from information obtained from Srijut Umanath Gohain who in his turn had got it from Srijut Kripanath Phukan of Sologuri. Mr. Phukan's source of information is reported to be an old Shan chronicle, named *Lailek Buranji*, which he had read during a visit to the Northern Shan States of Burma.[124]

In Mr. Foster's version of the story, King Gadadhar Singha, after sustaining a defeat at the hands of the Moamarias, escapes to the jungles. The Moamarias then set up Lora Raja as king. Gadadhar's wife Jaimati Kuanri was captured by Lora Raja to give information about her husband's refuge. "In the centre of the Jaysagar Tank, a post now stands", says Mr. Foster, "and it was at this spot she is said to have been daily flogged, but without its producing the desired effect. On being questioned as to his whereabouts, and a promise being made that she should be liberated if she would give the necessary information, she replied that she had not seen him for a long time. Gadhadhar Singha hearing of this presented himself one day in disguise before her, and asked her why she did not point him out to his enemies. She at once recognised him, but refused to betray him. Addressing him as a friend of her brother, she told him to leave her to her fate, as his submission to the Lora Raja could be of no advantage to either. Three times this scene was repeated, and finally Jaymati Koorie told him she would insult him if he troubled her any more. He at length left for the jungle, and she, faithful to the last, died

122. S. K. Bhuyan, *Asamar Padya-Buranji*, wherein is incorporated Dutiram Hazarika's *Kalibharat Buranji;* and Harakanta Barua's enlarged version of the Assam Buranji by Radhanath Barbarua and Kasinath Tamuli Phukan.

123. Ratneswar Mahanta, *Jaimati Kuanri and Langi Gadapani* in *Jonaki, Calcutta*, Vol. III, p. 321-26.

124. S. K. Bhuyan, *Asam Jiyari*, Part II, for a thorough examination of the sources of information about Princess Jaimati; and also, Batori. Jorhat, issue of April 4, 1931.

under her tormentor's hands. Now Gadhadhar Singh's sister was married to the Bor Phukan, who lived at Gauhati and was an ally of the Lora Raja; Gadhadhar Singh took refuge in his house, and was so well disguised, that he remained there in safety, being known to his sister only, for two years or more. Ultimately, a misunderstanding between the Bor Phukan and the Lora Raja occurred. The wife then revealed all to her husband; he and Gadhadhar Singh raised strong forces, marched to Ghargaon, captured it; killed the Lora Raja, and reinstated Gadhadhar Singh on the throne of his ancestors. With true oriental gratitude, he was no sooner firmly seated than he put to death his brother-in-law, the Bor Phukan, and two others of the highest officers of State who had also assisted him, alleging as his reason that as they were powerful enough to depose and kill the Lora Raja, they might possibly serve him in a similar manner, should any quarrels arise between them. He did not live long after his restoration and was chiefly occupied in restoring order throughout the country; and he strictly enjoined his son Rudra Singh to build a temple on the spot where his mother was put to death, and to call it after her name. This was done, and Jaysagar Dhol is doubtless the finest specimen of stone architecture in Upper Assam."

Mr. Foster is evidently mistaken when he attributes Gadadhar's flight to his defeat by the Moamarias.[125] The first insurrection of the Moamarias took place in 1769 during the reign of King Lakshmi Singha as a result of which the insurgents assumed the reins of government imprisoning Lakshmi Singha in the Jaisagar temple. As is well known, it was as a prince that Gadapani had fled from his home, out of fear for Laluk Buraphukan who had instituted a campaign

125. Ratneswar Mahanta had committed a similar mistake when he first described the circumstances of Princess Jaimati's torture and death as having occurred after the alleged flight of King Lakshmi Singha in consequence of his defeat by the Moamarias. A corrected version was subsequently compiled by Mahanta with the help of materials furnished by Indibar Barua Shirastadar of Sibsagar. See *Jonaki*, Calcutta, Vol. III, pp. 200-205 and 321-26.

of mutilating and killing all possible claimants to the Ahom throne. The name Gadadhar Singha was assumed by Gadapani on his accession in 1681.

Mr. Foster refers to the reign of King Rudra Singha, son and successor of Gadadhar Singha, as mentioned by William Robinson on page 168 of his *Descriptive Account of Assam,* 1841. After quoting the relevant passage, Mr. Foster writes within inverted commas: "In an old Assamse Bulanji [Buranji] it is said that Jaymati Koorie was taken into custody by the Lora Raja, carried to the place where Jaysagar now is, and was caned and whipped to death under a large pipal tree, which was in the same place where the pillar in the centre of the tank now stands". Curiously enough, the above passage is not to be found in Robinson's book.

Mr. Foster then reproduces the following passage alleged to be on page 34 of the *Assam Buranji* by Radhanath Barbarua and Kasinath Tamuli Phukan: "On the 14th Phalgun, 1617 (A.D. February 24th, 1695) Raja Rudra Singha went to the Singree Ghur at Ghargaon, and there assumed the name of Sooklungphaw [Sukhrungpha] and, according to his father's command, memorialized the death of his mother Jaymati Koorie by digging the large tank called Jaysagar, and erecting three temples in and about the place where she was murdered". This passage is also not to be found in the aforesaid chronicle by Radhanath Barbarua and Kasinath Tamuli Phukan in the edition published by the American Baptist Mission in 1844, or in the edition published by authority in 1906. As Mr. Foster was obviously dependent on his Assamese helpers for the references to Assamese chronicles, he was probably misled by them as to the original provenance of the passages quoted by him.

It must however be admitted that in spite of the mistakes committed by Mr. Foster in citing and locating his sources of information, the fact is undeniable that he had access to old Assamese Buranjis which contained accounts of Jaimati's death in the midst of tortures inflicted upon her for refusing to give any clue to her husband's whereabouts, the punishment having taken place in the centre of the Jaisagar tank which was constructed by her son Rudra Singha in commemoration of his mother's name. We are confident that Assamese Buranjis, as were consulted by Mr. Foster, will be recovered sooner or later, as owners do not generally allow Buranjis to be lost though they are somewhat unwilling to show or part with their treasures to casual acquaintances.

According to Dutiram Hazarika's version, Jaimati was taken to the royal court with her young daughter, and was there questioned about the whereabouts of Gadapani. Though subjected to inhuman tortures, the mother and the child refused to give any clue whatsoever. The prince moved from place to place under the alleged name of Gothor. He had taken shelter in the house of a female hawker named Ramani Pohari, and thus evaded discovery for some time. Having heard of the death of his daughter and the precarious condition of her mother he visited in disguise the place of punishment and indirectly asked his wife to save herself by giving the clue asked for. Jaimati hinted back that he should seek his safety by leaving the place. The princess breathed her last soon after her husband's departure. The responsibility for the chastisement and death of Jaimati is laid at the door of Lora Raja alone.

In Harakanta Barua's version, which was compiled with the help of old chronicles and the oral reports of reliable Ahom nobles, the basic fact of Jaimati's death in the midst of tortures inflicted on her for refusing to mention the whereabouts of her husband remains the same, though the attendant circumstances are different from the other versions. Lora Raja killed or mutilated all the rival princes. Gadapani, out of fear, fled from his residence with his wife and took shelter in the forest where they built a hut with leaves and twigs. Once at midnight the princess heard the voice of a group of persons whom she suspected to be the emissaries of Lora Raja. She persuaded her husband to leave the hut in disguise, and she waited alone to face the royal agents. When questioned about Gadapani she pretended complete ignorance. She was then subjected to various tortures. Gadapani visited the place of torture, and for this dare-devil act he was indirectly and politely reprimanded by his dying wife. After Jaimati's death Gadapani resumed his wandering life. This version gives an impression that the punishment of Jaimati was the action of the emissaries, and that the king or any noble had neither ordered, nor authorised the brutalities.

Ratneswar Mahanta's version agrees substantially with that of Dutiram Hazarika, though Mahanta does not make any mention of the daughter. Jaimati was taken to the presence of Lora Raja, and on her refusal to say anything about her husband she was made over to the Chaudangs with orders to extract the required information from her, and punish her if she proved incorrigible. The princess remained adamantine, and she bore with fortitude the tortures inflicted upon her in consequence. Gadapani had heard of his wife's plight during his wanderings in the Naga Hills, and he visited the place of torture disguised as a Naga tribesman. His indirect hint to Jaimati to speak out met with a polite rebuff from her, accompanied by a request that he should immediately leave the spot infested as it was with his cruel and unrelenting foes. Jaimati died in the midst of tortures which had continued for fifteen or sixteen days. The *Nag* or wooden pillar in the centre of the Jaisagar tank marks the place where Jaimati breathed her last. The tank and the temple were constructed by Rudra Singha to perpetuate the memory of his mother. The boy-king Lora Raja alone is held responsible for Jaimati's summons to court, her punishment and her death. Mahanta also uses the name Jaimati, and it has now been accepted universally. There is a great deal of similarity between the versions of Mahanta and Foster.

Mention may be made of the version of Srijut Kripanath Phukan for whatever worth it may have, as we had not the opportunity to personally interrogate him, nor have we been able to examine the *Lailek* chronicle on which his account is reported to have been based. According to Mr. Phukan, Jaimati's father was Laithepena Bargohain who had thirteen daughters and twenty-four sons, of course through his twelve separate wives. Jaimati's mother was Chandradaru, daughter of Lecham Buragohain of the Kuoingayan family; while Gadapani's mother Siddheswari was a daughter of the Lahan family. Jaimati's lamentations before her death have been put by Mr. Phukan in a number of homely couplets.—She regrets for not seeing her mother and her mother-in-law once before her death. She hands over her two sons Lai and Lechai to Siddheswari, and predicts the elevation of her husband Gadapani to the Ahom throne. She desires that Gadapani should marry her younger sister Jayeswari with whom he would pass many long years in enjoyment of his sovereign power.

In none of the above four versions any mention is made of Laluk Buraphukan. The search for princes is said to have been made by Lora Raja for his own safety who also ordered the punishment of Jaimati. This is quite in conformity with historical truths as they were known to the masses at the time. The necessary orders for the arrest of princes were issued in the name of Lora Raja, and as their prime mover Laluk remained concealed behind the scene, the average contemporary had no opportunity to know that he was the inspirer in all these matters. Traditions have grown round the current reports which pinned the whole blame on Lora Raja even though he was a stripling of only fourteen years. But the critical compilers of the chronicles and others who lived in intimate touch with the court knew that Lora Raja was a mere instrument in the hands of the ambitious and wily Laluk.

In our opinion which is based on the testimony of contemporary records and the incontrovertible logic of events, it was Laluk Buraphukan who initiated the search for and the massacre of princes, the most powerful of whom was Gadapani, son of Gobar Raja. To punish a lady for her refusal to communicate useful information was a very unusual and serious step according to the Ahom code of chivalry; and it must have been undertaken by Gidagathi Hazarika at the instance of Laluk Buraphukan on their own initiative, and not under the formal orders of the government. Jaimati's death in the midst of tortures consequent upon her refusal to supply any clue which might lead to her husband's capture is unchallengeable in view of the evidence of contemporary documents and the unanimous verdict of age-long traditions. The Assamese people are perfectly justified in holding up Jaimati before the world as an example of wifely devotion and unshaken determination, who like the extremely limited few of her sisterhood, thought "What death can be sweeter than the death for one's beloved ?"

CHAPTER XV

THE NEMESIS OF LALUK BURAPHUKAN

As Laluk Buraphukan was indulging in the commission of the most heinous crimes of murder, usurpation, treachery and imposture, the inevitable hand of retribution was working invisibly to bring about his destruction and doom. The splendour of the Sakbari ceremony satisfied the vanity of the imitation Swargadeo, but it helped to open the eyes of the Assamese people to the realities of the situation. "A commoner has now become the virtual dictator of Assam, and his unbounded powers are being used not for the good of the people but for his self-aggrandisement, thus bringing the country to anarchy and confusion. He has bartered away Gauhati to the Moguls not for any advantage to his country but for furthering his own self-interest". This was exactly what the Assamese felt about Laluk Buraphukan; and when he killed Atan Buragohain, their most respected leader, and princess Jaimati, an *enceinte* lady of high rank and status, most unceremoniously and cold-bloodedly, they thought the time had come to put a stop to the Buraphukan's career of crime and treachery.

It was not easy to commit any personal violence upon the Buraphukan for he remained vigilant being always attended by armed men. No outsider could therefore approach him, and any plan of assault could be effected only with the co-operation and support of his body-guards and personal attendants, and the inmates of his house. An opportunity offered itself when the Buraphukan dismissed some of his household retainers possibly for some sympathetic response on their part to an outside attempt to tamper with their loyalty. This disgruntled body of cashiered retainers could now be incited to commit a murderous attempt on their whilom master in secret league with their old friends who were still in service in the Buraphukan's establishment.

A fresh circumstance now developed in the metropolis when a stalwart and enterprising retainer of the Buraphukan was led to a situation in which he had to choose between two tragic alternatives—his own death or the death of his master, and the instinct of self-preservation which dominates all human enterprises actuated him to decide in favour of the second alternative—the death of Laluk Buraphukan.

The government was now on the verge of collapse, life and property were insecure, and the Moguls were masters of Gauhati and Kamrup. The people in general realised the necessity to restore the country to peace and order. This responsibility was shared by all, but as nobody was prepared to take the lead it was shelved in cold storage: the discontent however wide-spread it might be was ineffective as long as a leader did not come out to harness that discontent to positive remedial measures. The Deodhais or the orthodox Ahom priests who considered themselves to be the guardians of the throne, and of the peace and prosperity of the kingdom, now took action in their time-honoured theocratic manner. The gods, they thought, were indignant with Assam because they had not been duly propitiated for a long time. The Deodhais therefore advised Lora Raja to offer human sacrifices to the Kechaikhati temple at Sadiya as the goddess worshipped there had not tasted the blood of victims with full satisfaction. "The miseries of the people", said the Deodhais, "do not seem to come to an end. The time has now come to offer human sacrifices." The king asked Laluk Buraphukan to search for suitable men for being offered as sacrifices at the Sadiya copper-temple.

Now it so happened that a fortnight before the king issued the order to Laluk Buraphukan, a wild bear had entered into the latter's compound and killed two of his men. Many people contrived to kill the animal, but they all failed in their attempt.

In the establishment of the Buraphukan there was a man of remarkable courage and dash, named Bhotai Deka Saikia, a Kalita by caste. He was a member of the Kharangi Khel of Nowgong, and had attained considerable notoriety because of the help he had rendered to Nawab Mir Jumla to penetrate into the Kaliabar district, which he did at the instance of Rajasahur Barphukan. He, like Meleager of the Argonautic expedition, now took upon himself the task of slaying the bear, and asked the Buraphukan as to what reward would be given to him in the event of his success. The Buraphukan promised Bhotai to present to him gold earrings and other articles and also to elevate his rank. Bhotai then tightened his cloth round his body, and armed himself with a shield and a sword. He chased the bear in the Buraphukan's garden, came upon it ultimately, and killed the animal by thrusting the sword into its mouth. The Buraphukan praised the bear-slayer for his intrepidity, and gave him the promised reward of gold earrings, and presented to him a wife in addition, perhaps to act as an agent to secretly report on Bhotai's movements and designs.[126]

But an ambitious man of Laluk Buraphukan's stamp who had risen to power and influence by unworthy means is always suspicious of gallantry and merit. By giving a practical demonstration of his boldness Bhotai Deka proved the possibility of his being an instrument of the Buraphukan's destruction. Outwardly, Bhotai's action was praised by the Buraphukan; and inwardly, he was devising means to kill the heroic bear-slayer. The Buraphukan therefore selected Bhotai as a victim to be sacrificed at the Sadiya temple. "In view of the extraordinary boldness of this fellow," said the Buraphukan, "he will be a fit person to be sacrificed at the Sadiya temple. His heart is suited for being offered to the gods. Who will fathom the designs he will hatch and execute if he is allowed to live? He dares to fight with a wild bear!"

Having received intelligence of the Buraphukan's intentions, Bhotai Deka enlisted the support of his two colleagues Madha Tamuli and Aghona Kachari, and devised with them the means to frustrate the designs of the Buraphukan which if carried out would result in the extermination of all able-bodied persons amongst the Hindus. "A large number of

126. S. K. Bhuyan, *Nagayan Saikia Bhotai Deka,* inserted in *Buranjir Vani,* 2nd edition, pp. 116-125.

stalwarts", said the trio, "were offered last year as sacrifices to the gods. He proposes to sacrifice a fresh lot this year as well! It is not known who will be selected for this purpose. If strong and robust men are offered as sacrifices every year how would it be possible for good Hindus to survive? All right, with God's blessings we shall see what we can do."

The three leaders took into their confidence several women serving in the Buraphukan's household. With their assistance they entered the sleeping apartment of the Buraphukan in the stillness of the night, and pierced him to death when he was fast asleep. The ladies of the house started a hue and cry, but they were silenced by the threat of immediate decapitation. Angara, Tholoka and Jagara, the three sons of the Buraphukan, were summoned to come to their father's residence, together with the Jatakaria Phukan, on the pretext of a faked invitation; and they were killed by Bhotai and his adherents. They also put to death Chungi Hazarika. The Buraphukan's brother Marangi Barbarua was hotly pursued, but he escaped by taking shelter in the palace enclosure. He was afterwards captured and imprisoned in his brother's Hatisal. These events took place on Tuesday, the tenth Agrahayan, 1602 *Saka,* or November 24, 1680 A.D.[127]

Thus perished Laluk Buraphukan, and with his death the dream of setting up the Lukhurakhun dynasty of Ahom Swargadeos vanished for ever. The prediction made by Debera Barbarua that Laluk would attain the same notoriety as himself and meet with an ignoble end through the instrumentality of his own women was fulfilled to the letter. There was one difference, however: Debera never dreamt of becoming a crowned monarch, whereas the assumption of sovereign power, both *de facto* and *de jure,* constituted the principal motive of Laluk's atrocities and crimes. The fact that there were men in Assam who would not permit Laluk to culminate his inconceivably preposterous claim to sovereignty, and

127. S. K. Bhuyan, *Assam Buranji, S.M.,* for the events prior to and after the murder of Laluk Buraphukan.

to continue uninterruptedly his regime of terror, reflects credit on their patriotism and their profound solicitude for their national integrity.

Bhotai Deka and Madha Tamuli received universal applause for putting to death Laluk Buraphukan and thereby ridding the country of a common foe and a very sinister influence. They were hailed as patriots and saviours. Encouraged by their success the two leaders began to dictate the affairs of the capital, and no one dared to oppose their plans and actions. They brought the personal contingent of the deceased Buraphukan, and fixed their headquarters in his residence which had all the equipments of a fortified garrison. The immediate supporters of the monarch could not view with complacency the growing influence of Bhotai and Madha; and the royalists threw up their camp inside the palace-enclosures ready to encounter the forces of Bhotai and Madha when the occasion arose.

The two leaders then began to appoint officers of their own accord. Gidagathi Hazarika was appointed as Barphukan; and Hulou, grandson of Pikchai Chetia, as Gargayan Deka-Phukan. These high-handed actions on the part of Bhotai and Madha militated against the authority of the Swargadeo, but no harsh measures could be adopted as the two leaders were at that time the idols of the people. Lora Raja's advisers therefore proposed to deal with Bhotai and Madha with consideration and tact.

The Phukans attending on the monarch sent two envoys Madhabcharan Kataki and Ananta Kataki, in the company of four Hazarikas, to ask Bhotai and Madha to come to the palace and offer their submission to His Majesty. The accompanying message ran as follows: "Bhotai and his friends have rendered a signal service to their country by killing Laluk Buraphukan who was an enemy of the whole world. Owing to the excesses which they have committed without the concurrence of the Swargadeo they should now come to the palace-enclosures and kneel down before His Majesty. We shall intercede on their behalf, and beg the Swargadeo to grant them pardon; and we shall abide by what they propose."

Bhotai Deka interpreted this invitation as a contrivance for the destruction of himself and his adherents. They lived thenceforward with greater vigilance and caution. Bhotai remained armed with his sword all the twenty-four hours. The Kharangi unit of Nowgong to which Bhotai belonged were asked by the Swargadeo to capture the leader in default of which they were threatened with wholesale slaughter.

Bhotai had a woman in his house with whom he lived as husband and wife even though they had not entered into formal wedlock. She was approached by the Kharangis who begged her to persuade Bhotai to offer his voluntary submission to the Swargadeo. They said, "O mother, you should bestow on us our lives. The king will not do any harm to your husband, for by killing the Buraphukan your husband has ensured the well-being of us all. He should throw off his sword and his shield, and proceed to the palace to kneel down before His Majesty." The lady broached the subject to her husband after having offered him a dose of betel-nut and betel-leaf seasoned with tobacco; she then pressed him to surrender to the monarch. Bhotai, whose recent actions were directed to the good of the people, resolved to go to the palace, as he thought that by doing so he would save the lives of his comrades of the Kharangi Khel.

Before taking the final step Bhotai held consultations with Madha Tamuli and other leaders, and drew up the following conditions of surrender: *first*, the appointments made by Bhotai and Madha should be confirmed by the Swargadeo; *secondly*, Marangi Barbarua who had been imprisoned by Bhotai's party should be released; and *thirdly*, a Phukan should come to take Bhotai and his compatriots to the presence of the king giving them assurances of pardon by His Majesty.

The king accordingly sent Gargayan Sandikoi Phukan to escort Bhotai Deka and his adherents to the palace. The insurgents first released Marangi Barbarua and then proceeded to the palace. They were however arrested on approaching His Majesty. They were allowed to kneel down before the Swargadeo and solemnly affirm their allegiance, whereupon they were set at liberty. Bhotai Deka Saikia and Madha Tamuli were however dismissed from their respective offices and sent home without further punishment. Marangi Barbarua fell prostrate at the feet of the Phukans and begged for mercy: he was let off after having his ears clipped. The following appointments made by Bhotai and Madha were left undisturbed for the time being; Bandar Lanmakharu Chetia Phukan as Rajmantri Phukan; Dihingia Alun Phukan as Barbarua; Maupia as Naobaicha Phukan; Khona Chaudang Barua as Dihingia Phukan; Gidagathi Hazarika as Barphukan at Kaliabar in place of Bhatdhara; Hulou Hazarika, grandson of Pikchai Chetia, as Deka-Phukan.

In obedience to the orders of the king Bhotai Deka left the Ahom capital and proceeded to his home in Nowgong. As he was sailing down to Kaliabar his boat was sighted by Hulou Deka-Phukan who signalled to the oarsmen to steer Bhotai's boat towards his own barge. The Phukan transferred Bhotai to his boat, and sent a report to the king on the inadvisability of allowing Bhotai to be at liberty in full bodily fitness and vigour. The Phukan said,—"The liberation of Bhotai Deka by the Swargadeo is equivalent to permitting a tiger to roam at large after having sliced off its tail." Hulou Phukan, with the permission of the monarch received meanwhile, cut off the ears and nose of Bhotai, and plucked one of his eyes. Though the chronicles are mute about the fate of Madha Tamuli, he was in all probability subjected to the same punishment as his comrade Bhotai. Nothing more is heard about Bhotai after the mutilation of his limbs by Hulou Deka-Phukan; he became obviously too disabled to play any active and prominent part in the affairs of the time worthy of being recorded in contemporary chronicles. The village Bhotai-gaon, situated at a distance of three miles to the east of the present town of Nowgong, is believed to be named after the gallant hero who had put to death the treacherous betrayer of Gauhati and the murderer of Atan Buragohain and Princess Jaimati.

The death of Laluk Buraphukan and the submission of Bhotai Deka and his associates restored the capital to tranquillity and order; and the nobles now turned their attention to Laluk's brother Bhatdhara who, they feared, might now proceed to Bengal to bring a Mogul force to invade Eastern Assam. The appointment of Gidagathi Hazarika as Barphukan of Kaliabar was short-lived as he was soon replaced by Bandar Lanmakharu Chetia. Dighala Buragohain, Alun Barbarua, Bandar Barphukan and the Dihingia Phukan sailed down to Kaliabar to take charge of the affairs of that place, with special instructions to capture Bhatdhara, and to repair the fortifications at Samdhara on both banks of the river.

The officers deputed to Kaliabar met on their way the envoy Bahbaria Kataki from whom they learnt that Bhatdhara had already left Kaliabar in the company of his son Madha and a considerable body of men. The Kataki who had been sent by Laithepena Solal Gohain to communicate to the Swargadeo the information about Bhatdhara's flight then continued his journey to the capital. The king heard the whole story from Bahbaria Kataki, and sent presents to Bandar Barphukan and his colleagues who had by this time reached Kaliabar. Sen Bargohain was asked to return to Kaliabar from the passes leading to the Dafala Hills where he had been putting the outposts in order. The officers of Kaliabar who in fact constituted the stronger elements in the administration relieved Bandar Barphukan of his additional responsibility of the office of Rajmantri Phukan; appointed Khamchang, son of Phulbarua, as Paniphukan in place of Chakrapani; and Kari-Deka of the Miri Sandikoi family as Kaliabaria Deka-Phukan. The remaining Phukans and Baruas continued in the offices to which they had been appointed by Bhotai and Madha. In distributing the royal presents, sent through Bahbaria Kataki, the new Barphukan, Bandar Chetia, made no discrimination between the Gohains and the Phukans. Sen Bargohain was seriously offended and he left the Dopdar or viceregal council in protest.

Meteka where the royal residence was situated at that time was considered to be a tainted place as it had been the venue of Laluk Buraphukan's crimes. The officers of Kaliabar advised Lora Raja to shift the capital to Gargaon. The continuance of the daughters of Laluk and Bhatdhara as royal consorts was likely to perpetuate the traditions of their parents, and it was possible that the two ladies would give timely warnings to Bhatdhara and his followers of measures contemplated against them. The Kaliabar officers therefore recommended their replacement by the daughters of Laithepena Solal Gohain and Alun Barbarua who would rank as Barkuanri and Parvatia Kuanri respectively. It was arranged that the Barbarua should return to the capital to deliver to Lora Raja the message of the Kaliabar Phukans, and remain by the side of the monarch for consultation and advice.

Sen Bargohain who was a spirited noble, had been partially tainted by the machinations of the previous years. He refused to return to Kaliabar despite the repeated invitations of Bandar Barphukan and his colleagues. The Barphukan then deputed the Dihingia Phukan to fetch the Bargohain who had meanwhile initiated plans to capture Bandar to avenge the insult meted to him at the Kaliabar Dopdar by offering him presents inferior to what his rank deserved. The Bargohain slapped the Dihingia Phukan on his face and on his head, and turned him out of his presence. The Bargohain then went to the house of Miri Sandikoi Phukan for assistance to carry out his designs against Bandar Barphukan. "I belong to your house," said Miri Sandikoi Phukan, "and I shall do as you ask me to do. You should bring over the Paniphukan to your side." Sen Bargohain then proceeded to the Paniphukan's camp. As it was late in the evening the Paniphukan asked the Bargohain to pass the night at his house so that they might resume the talks next morning, to which the Bargohain agreed. The Paniphukan then sent a secret message to the Barphukan informing him of the detention of the Bargohain. The Gohain was accordingly arrested by the Barphukan, divested of the insignias of his office, and sent up to Gargaon to stand his trial for the triple offence of conspiracy to seize the Barphukan; physical assault on the Dihingia Phukan; and his visits to the houses of subordinate officers, namely, the Miri Sandikoi Phukan and Paniphukan, with a view to promote his criminal designs.

The Barphukan in consultation with his colleagues proposed to appoint Laithepena Solal Gohain as successor to Sen Bargohain. Laithepena refused to accept the offer as it was made by the Phukans who had no authority to do so, and as his acceptance would mean contravention of the prerogative of the monarch who alone could sanction such superior appointments. Laithepena however expressed his willingness to accept the office of Bargohain if the offer came from His Majesty, and provided his eldest son was made Solal Gohain. The Barphukan accordingly sent up the proposals to Gargaon. Sen Bargohain's dismissal was confirmed by Lora Raja; and Laithepena was appointed Bargohain, and his son as Solal Gohain.

Bhatdhara had in the meantime arrived at Gauhati where he met the Mogul Fauzadar Nawab Mansur Khan and narrated before him the happenings in Assam. "The enemies", said Bhatdhara, "have killed my brothers and friends and all the members of my family. You should now give protection to me as I have come to you for shelter and help. I have no men or soldiers at my disposal. If you give me an armed force I can undertake to attack and subjugate the Ahoms." The governor of Gauhati could not obviously concede to the petition of Bhatdhara, as such compliance would lead to serious complications with the independent kingdom of Assam however curtailed might be its dimensions at that time. Mansur Khan therefore asked Bhatdhara to proceed to Dacca, and submit his appeal personally to the Bengal Subedar. Bhatdhara went to Dacca accordingly, and with a cloth tied round his neck he entreated the Nawab to give him military aid to attack the Ahoms. The Subedar of Bengal asked Bhatdhara to wait at Dacca for sometime for knowing the result of his petition. Having failed to receive any favourable reply though he remained at Dacca for several months, Bhatdhara returnd to Assam with his son Madha by the route through Jayantia. On his arrival at Kaliabar in June 1681, he was captured by the Phukans stationed there and sent up to Gargaon.

CHAPTER XVI

GADAPANI DECLARED KING AT KALIABAR

What was the condition of Assam about the year 1680? Atan Buragohain was killed in December 1679, Laluk Buraphukan in November 1680, and the death of Princess Jaimati took place sometime between these two dates. Lora Raja still occupied the Ahom throne. On account of his immaturity the monarch was incapable of exercising any check upon the machinations of his nobles, and he could hardly be expected to co-ordinate the activities of the different departments of the government. He acted on the advice of his ministers, but his judgment was too undeveloped to enable him to find out whether the advice was tendered for the good of the people or for the self-interest of the adviser and his friends. Besides, a powerful minister could always coerce his colleagues to give him support even though such acquiescence militated against their conscience and their own conviction. In that case the advice had the appearance of a united counsel, and it therefore became irrebuttable by the monarch.[128]

Bhotai Deka and Madha Tamuli did no doubt rid the country of the common enemy Laluk, and in their enterprise they received the tacit concurrence of the superior officials. But the subsequent actions of these two leaders constituted a direct challenge to the lawful authority of the sovereign. The fact that a pack of desperadoes could dictate affairs at the capital and thus paralyse the government gave a clear indication of something being rotten in the state of Gargaon.

Under these circumstances, the people had to pass their days in a condition of insecurity and fear. They could not rigidly define their personal attachments and political leanings, for their adherence to a particular noble would jeopardise

128. J. P. Wade, *Account of Assam*, p. xiv,—"The opinion of an eloquent man frequently influences the decrees of the Gohains".

their position when his rival would come into power. Unworthy persons, vested with "brief authority" through the support of their friends and allies, were tempted to utilise their opportunities for their own self-aggrandisement, totally ignoring the interests of the people and the canons of propriety and justice. For temporary advantages, if not for permanent security, the common people were compelled to attach themselves to one noble or the other, and to promote his selfish designs; as on their refusal to do so they would be subjected to pin-pricks, harassments and oppressions, deprivation of property, mutilation of limbs, and other forms of punishment and degradation. The sufferings of the people became so acute that the priests were compelled to suggest to the monarch the necessity to assuage the wrath of the gods by offering to them sacrifices of mortals.

The Moguls under Nawab Mansur Khan had intrenched themselves at Gauhati with their domination spread over to the Manaha river; and they could at any time march up and bring the rest of Assam under their subjection. Complications arose owing to the undefined character of the Mogul limits, for their present occupation was the result of their collusive arrangement with a private citizen, and not in pursuance of any treaty stipulations in which case the mutual boundaries would have been demarcated and fixed. Encroachments on the part of the Moguls became the order of the day; and they could be prevented only by armed resistance, which neither the Ahoms nor their vassal chieftains were capable of offering at that time owing to the prevalence of internal disorders and strifes.

Reports were received about the excesses committed by Mansur Khan's officers, specially in connection with the Kheda or elephant-catching operations in Darrang in the areas round Singari, Balipara and Bargaon; and rumours were afloat that Mogul forces had invaded the territories of the Darrang Raja.

The encroachments were the result of a claim deliberately set up by the Moguls that their present occupation of Assam was in consonance with the terms of the treaty of 1639 enacted between Allah Yar Khan and Momai-tamuli Barbarua, and the subsequent one of 1663 between Nawab Mir Jumla and Swargadeo Jayadhwaj Singha, and that it was in consequence a reversion to the *status quo ante* of 1639 and 1663.

The Ahoms repudiated this claim by pointing out that the repeated demand of the Moguls for the restoration of the limits fixed in 1639 and 1663 had been successfully opposed by the Swargadeo. In 1669, Raja Ram Singha, equipped with a large force, had pressed for the fulfilment of the demand; "but he could not", said the Ahoms, "even approach the fortifications of Gauhati though he tried hard for one full year."[129] In 1677, the demand was reiterated by Sultan Azamtara, but the Ahoms dismissed it with taunts and rebuffs. The Padshahzada having thus failed in his diplomatic efforts entered into a secret conspiracy with Laluk Barphukan, and obtained possession of Gauhati on promise of making the Barphukan Raja of Assam. The Barphukan was not vested with any authority or title to transfer the domination of Lower Assam to the Moguls as he was a mere servant of the Swargadeo. The occupation of Gauhati by the Moguls, held the Ahoms, therefore constituted an act of aggression, and it had no semblance of legality about it. The Mogul claims and the replies of the Ahoms are embodied in the diplomatic correspondence of the period.

However sound the arguments of the Ahoms might be it is clear that they would not have been able, in 1680, to oppose the Moguls if the latter had decided to press their claims by launching hostilities. But one thing must be said to the credit of the Ahoms: there was always a body of sane and patriotic men amongst them who could read the signs of the times, and measure the true extent of the consequences if the weakness of the government was permitted to continue for long. Once they gauged the situation correctly they never failed to adopt prompt and vigorous measures to restore the equilibrium of the government. We have seen how the

129. Letter from the Assam Barphukan to Nawab Mansur Khan, *saka* 1603, MS. Assam Buranji No. 6.

Gauhati nobles succeeded in rehabilitating the administration when the enormities of Debera Barbarua had brought it to the brink of catastrophe and collapse. Disorders followed by rehabilitation constituted the principal redeeming feature of the Ahoms throughout their long sway in Assam; and their total collapse came only when men of sufficient stamina and foresight were wanting to marshall the resources of the country for recouping the effects of past disasters, as in the period of the Burmese invasions in the second and third decades of the nineteenth century. In the common parlance of the Ahoms the kingdom of Assam, their demesne and their stronghold, was compared to a casket of gold which they wanted to preserve at all cost; and the entrance of an outside element into that casket was an abomination and a humiliation of the most intolerable character. Urged by instincts of self-preservation the Ahoms sank their differences, and put their united might on the task on undoing the effects of their past indifference and callousness.

The ravages of the years from 1672 to 1680 roused the attention of the patriotic section of the Ahom nobles to the imperative necessity of restoring peace and order in the kingdom; this they considered to be an essential prerequisite to the successful prosecution of measures for the expulsion of the Moguls from Gauhati and Kamrup. Gargaon the capital was not convenient as a venue of their deliberations in which they would have to discuss the effects of the imbecility of the reigning sovereign Lora Raja and the treacherous propensities of many persons who still wielded influence at the metropolis. Besides, according to the custom of the Ahom government the Dangarias could not meet one another, nor could the Phukans visit the residences of the Dangarias, except under the orders of the monarch. Under these circumstances the patriots decided to hold their deliberations at Kaliabar, the headquarter of the Barphukan since the occupation of Gauhati by the Moguls.

After the flight of Bhatdhara the affairs of Kaliabar, as we have seen, were administered by Bandar Barphukan, He was assisted by two very influential and spirited nobles,—

Chenkak Gargayan Sandikoi Neog Phukan and Khamrak Charingia Phukan. The Phukans held preliminary discussions amongst themselves in which they decided to launch hostilities against the Moguls at Gauhati; and to replace the boy-king by a monarch of maturity, vigour and enterprise. They said,—"The country is now restored to peace, and we have an abundance of resources to fight the Moguls who are intrenched in our immediate vicinity. Our only need is a powerful leader; how can an imbecile monarch and a weakling protect the kingdom?"[130] Animated by these patriotic sentiments the Kaliabar Phukans invited the principal nobles and officers of Gargaon to come to Kaliabar where the plans would be further discussed and steps taken to implement the decisions. The deposal of a monarch and the appointment of a successor required the consent of the Gohains, and the Phukans of Kaliabar considered themselves unauthorised to take final action in the matter.

The following nobles and officials of Gargaon accordingly left for Kaliabar,—Dighala Buragohain; Laithepena Bargohain; Champa Paniphukan, son of Phulbarua; Chenglai Phukan of the Dilihial Buragohain family; and Namdangia Phukan, son of Keo Sandikoi. They declared their object to be the expulsion of the Moguls from Gauhati, and they thereby obtained from the monarch all materials that were necessary for the success of their expedition. Their primary object of appointing a strong man to replace the boy-king was assiduously concealed from Sulikpha Lora Raja. The nobles were accompanied by a large number of subordinate officials, Rajkhowas, Baruas and Hazarikas. The Barpatra Gohain and Maupia Phukan alone remained with the king at Gargaon. Dihingia Alun Barbarua was also taken down to Kaliabar.

Chenkak Gargayan Sandikoi Phukan and Khamrak Charingia Phukan had decided to press the claims of Prince Gadapani for appointment as king in the place of Lora Raja.

130. S. K. Bhuyan, *Kamrupar Buranji*, p. 93; MS. Assam Buranji No. 14.

This selection was not dictated by any consideration of past friendship or any hope of future benefits. By his lineage, character, experience and personal valour Gadapani was the most capable, among the surviving princes, to wield the authority of a sovereign, and pilot the government through hazardous adventures. He was the son of a reigning monarch, Gobar Raja. The latter was the grandson of Swargadeo Suklenmung Gargayan Raja, who in his turn was the son of Suhungmung Dihingia Raja. By his royal and dignified presence Gadapani commanded the respect of all who came near him. He was reputed for his giant stature, physical vigour, intelligence and valour. Stories are still current about the enormous size of his rings, the unusual richness of his diet, and his voracious and carnivorous appetite. He is said to have strangled a wild buffalo into inaction by merely twisting its horns as it rushed to attack him.

Gadapani, after his flight from Tungkhung, wandered from place to place, disguised as a Naga, a petty trader, and sometimes as an ordinary cultivator. Many places in Assam, including the Naga Hills, claim to have been visited by the fugitive prince, and stories of his escapades from the enemies, and of his wanderings, thrilling and colourful, like those of Odysseus, form part of the legendary lore of the Assamese people. While in the Naga Hills he is said to have saved himself by hiding behind a huge boulder. A Naga lady is said to have protected him once by concealing him inside her skirt. During his stay in the house of Aghoni Bai at Sologuri, the emissaries of Laluk Buraphukan approached the house in a most unexpected manner. Aghoni Bai made Gadapani lie flat on the ground like a dead man, and then covered him with a shroud.[131] She invited two ladies from her immediate neighbourhood, Rahdoi of Raha, and Bhadoi of Tipam, and the three started a wail and cry by catching one

131. This incident has led to an oft-cited Assamese doggerel to illustrate the lack of relationship amongst persons who pretend to have common interests, and the names of Rahdoi, Bhadoi and Aghoni Bai are woven into the verses.

another's neck as if they were mourning for the death of a common and near relative. The emissaries left the "dead man" alone. Amours with women at different places form part of the Gadapani legends and traditions. Gadapani met one Arjun, a Daivajna astrologer, who predicted his kingship. He lived for some time at the house of another Daivajna named Mayur who gave him shelter at imminent risk to himself. He also lived for some time as a trader in betel-leaves in the house of the Chandkuchia Barua in Kamrup; and in the monastery of the Jakhalabandha Gosain in Kaliabar.

It was perhaps during his wanderings in Kamrup, Darrang or Nowgong, that Gargayan Sandikoi Phukan and Charingia Phukan established contact with Gadapani. They advised him to proceed to Dakhinpat Satra and seek the assistance of the Satradhikar to further his plans to occupy the throne. Prince Gadapani accordingly proceeded to Dakhinpat Satra in the company of Tekela Bara Niran of Silpani and Ramdhan of the guild of bow-makers, and stayed there for some time. Bandar Barphukan and Lora Raja were both disciples of the Dakhinpat Gosain. The Gosain was requested to ask Bandar Barphukan to cast the weight of his influence and office in favour of the fugitive prince. The Gosain refused to promote the plans of Gadapani as they aimed at the undoing of his own disciple Lora Raja. The Gosain apprised the Barphukan of his ideas on the subject, and asked the latter not to act in opposition to the interests of his royal co-disciple.

Gargayan Sandikoi Phukan and Khamrak Charingia Phukan then sent messengers to bring Gadapani to Kaliabar where he was first lodged in a boat, and then transferred to the house of Burha Duara Phukan. The two Phukans, Chenkak and Khamrak, now openly declared their intention to place Gadapani on the throne; and their colleagues both of Kaliabar and Gargaon, expressed a desire to have a look at the prince. Gadapani was brought to the Dopdar where he was made to give proofs of his skill in archery. The officers were satisfied with Gadapani's performance with the bow, and they declared forthwith,—"This strong and robust man will be able to give us protection."[132] The prince was then kept in the house of Dayangia Rajkhowa, brother of Bandar Barphukan. The Kaliabar officers however hesitated to confer the kingship upon the prince straight away, as this step would be exposed to the offence of high treason against the reigning monarch Lora Raja. They therefore proposed to make him Charing Raja, or a principal duke, but Gadapani declined to accept this title saying that he had been brought from his exile to be made a king, and not a duke; and he asked leave to return to his old life of a wanderer and a fugitive. His two best friends Gargayan Sandikoi Phukan and Khamrak Charingia Phukan succeeded however in making him accept the office of Tipamia Raja as an interim dignity.

In the meantime Dighala Buragohain and Laithepena Bargohain had arrived at Kaliabar. The nobles were divided into two sections with regard to the replacement of Lora Raja by Gadapani. The first section, led by Gargayan Sandikoi Phukan and Khamrak Charingia Phukan, supported the candidature of Gadapani; and the second, led by Bandar Barphukan who acted on the advice of the Dakhinpat Gosain, opposed the elevation of Gadapani to the throne. The strength of the first group lay in the popularity of Gadapani and the urgent necessity to have a change in the monarch; and the second group gained their strength from the eminent position and influence of Bandar Barphukan who was the head of the Kaliabar establishment.

Bandar Barphukan then sent presents to all the Kaliabar nobles with a request to desist from any plan to depose Lora Raja and place Gadapani on the throne. The presents were accepted by all the nobles except Gargayan Sandikoi Phukan and Khamrak Charingia Phukan. These two Phukans now expressed their determination to carry through their project at all cost. Bandar Barphukan got frightened, and remained

132. The late Srijut Hiteswar Barbarua was of opinion that Gadapani was Charing Raja before he became a fugitive, and hence his wife Jaimati was called a Kuanri. See *Avahan*, Calcutta, Vol. III, No. 7.

in his residence fully guarded and prepared to encounter any display of force on the part of the two staunch supporters of Gadapani. The Barphukan however soon realised the unanimous disposition of his colleagues in favour of Gadapani, and he gave way in consequence a few days later.

The nobles now assembled in one place at Kaliabar and had Prince Gadapani brought to their presence. He was first relieved of his dukedom as Tipam Raja, and was then declared as king. Bandar Barphukan, as the highest official of the Kaliabar establishment and as an example to his whilom anti-Gadapani partisans, was the first to kneel down before the new monarch and pay his homage. The other nobles then followed suit. This event took place on Thursday, the 20th of Sravan, 1603 *Saka,* or 5th August 1681 A.D.[133]

The nobles of Kaliabar then sailed up the Brahmaputra in swift boats taking with them the newly appointed sovereign Gadapani, and reached Gargaon on Thursday, the 27th Sravan. On that very day they deposed Lora Raja, and re-affirmed their allegiance to Gadapani who now assumed the name Gadadhar Singha. Lora Raja was taken to Namrup on the pretext of being made Namrupia Raja; but he was put to death shortly afterwards.

The refusal of Chota Banamali Bapu, the Satradhikar Gosain of Dakhinpat Satra, to support the claims of Gadapani needs more than a passing reference, as it influenced that prince's subsequent attitude towards the whole body of Vaisnava monks. Banamali Gosain was reputed for his extraordinary piety and devotion. He had first lived in Cooch Behar which had provided an asylum to Sankardeva and his immediate apostles. Banamali Gosain came to Assam on the express invitation of Swargadeo Jayadhwaj Singha, who in 1658 A.D., established a monastery for him at Rangalibahar, which was subsequently known as Dakhinpat Satra. Banamali Gosain ministered to the spiritual needs of three successive Ahom sovereigns, Jayadhwaj Singha, Chakra-

133. S. K. Bhuyan, *Assam Buranji, S.M.*, p. 145; MS. Assam Buranji Nos. 14 and 15.

dhwaj Singha and Udayaditya Singha. He attended the death-bed of the first two sovereigns and made them utter the final *mantras* to secure the peace of their souls in heaven. Udayaditya continued to be an ardent devotee of Banamali Gosain till he came under the influence of Paramananda Sannyasi. At the instance of the nobles Sulikpha Lora Raja had also become the disciple of Banamali Gosain. The Gosain was asked on several occasions to remain at the capital to assist his royal disciples in the administration of the country by his advice and guidance; but the Gosain resolutely and systematically declined the offer on the ground that spiritual leaders should remain aloof from meddling in temporal matters which are highly complicated and distracting. He, like the other Gosains, looked upon himself as the well-wisher of his disciples; and as such he felt bound to prevent the deposal of Lora Raja, and to counteract the move in favour of Lora Raja's rival Gadapani.[134]

During the prince's stay at the Kalabari Satra in Darrang he was shown scant courtesy by the Gosain. Gadapani was not allowed to reside with the Bhakats, or the permanent body of disciples who live inside the Satra premises and participate in the daily round of recitals and devotions. He was allotted a place outside the barracks occupied by the first rank of Bhakats. The articles of food supplied to him were also of an inferior order, and not appropriate to the dignity of a prince. He had once an altercation with Ramdeva Deka Gosain or the deputy Satradhikar, during which he was subjected to severe abuses. The Deka Gosain had once spat the excretions of chewn betel-nut which accidentally fell on a cloth worn by Gadapani leaving red marks on it. It was a great insult, and the prince preserved the cloth to remind him of the need of vengeance in future.[135] In showing cold shoulders to Gadapani the Deka Gosain acted in consonance with the pro-Sulikpha attitude of his chief Banamali Gosain,

134. S. C. Goswami, editor, *Vanamalidevar Charit,* by **Ramakanta** Dwija, Asam Sahitya Sabha, Jorhat.

135. S. K. Bhuyan, *Assam Buranji, S.M.*, p. 145.

though in his extreme zeal for discouraging Gadapani, he violated the rules of hospitality and the principles of tolerance and equanimity which every Gosain must necessarily uphold and honour. At the same time, the Deka Gosain's refusal to harbour a rival claimant to the throne was in accord with the laws of Assam, because such harbouring, if detected, would bring the offender to very severe punishment.

Having heard of the march of Gadapani and the Kaliabar nobles towards Gargaon the Deka Gosain came down the river from Kalabari to persuade the Phukans to abandon their project. Gadapani was then encamping at Biswanath, from where he saw the boat of the Deka Gosain. He despatched a man to bring the Gosain to Biswanath for giving blessings to him for the success of his mission. But the Deka Gosain refused to leave his boat, and he continued his journey. On the arrival of the Kaliabar fleet at Dakhinpat, Banamali Gosain met Bandar Barphukan and asked him again to give up the idea of conferring the kingship on Prince Gadapani pointing out that the Barphukan and Lora Raja were fellow disciples of the Dakhinpat Satra, and that one should protect the interest of the other. The Barphukan pleaded his inability to accede to the request on the ground that the deposal of Lora Raja and the enthronement of Gadapani had been agreed upon by the whole body of nobles, and that he as an individual could not deviate from the unanimous decision of his colleagues. The Barphukan's refusal is said to have resulted in the severance of his friendly relations with the Dakhinpat Gosain. The meeting ended in the utterance of mutual imprecations in which one wished the extinction of the power and influence of the other.

While living at Dakhinpat Satra, Gadapani had witnessed the wealth and grandeur of the Gosain. He was specially struck by a golden image which had been made by Banamali Gosain. The Gosain had a graded hierarchy of officials and servitors, and all other paraphernalia of a regular sovereign. He also saw similar magnificence at Auniati and other Satras. He began to ponder whether religious leaders should be permitted to acquire such wealth and influence, and whether they did not thereby divert the allegiance and devotion of the subjects which should be paid to the monarch alone. These notions shaped his policy towards the Vaisnava monks of Assam, and he gave a practical shape to that policy after he consolidated his position on the throne.

Banamali Gosain died in 1683 at the age of 107 years. He had founded a number of Satras which are flourishing till this day, *viz.*, Jakhalabandha Satra in Kaliabar, Jatakara Satra in Ahatguri Mauza in Majuli; Dakhinpat or Baikunthapur Satra in Majuli to the south of the Ahom royal camp Rangali-bahar; and Achyutpur Satra at Kalabari in Tezpur Sub-division. After the demise of Banamali Gosain in 1683 his nephew Ramdeva Goswami was appointed the Adhikar of Dakhinpat Satra.

Now to return to the new monarch Gadadhar Singha.—Having seen for himself the plight to which the country was reduced through the imbecility of the preceding sovereigns, King Gadadhar Singha began to rule with an iron hand, meeting out justice with sternness and impartiality. His wanderings throughout the kingdom as a fugitive prince were a blessing in disguise, as he acquired by that process an intimate first-hand knowledge of the conditions of the people in various places, in various grades of society and in various walks of life. The credit for the selection of Gadapani, for the manipulation of the support of the nobles, and for the subsequent measures to get him properly installed on the throne, was due to Chenkak Gargayan Sandikoi Phukan and Khamrak Charingia Phukan. A contemporary chronicle records this fact in no unmistakable language,—"In the matter of Gadapani's elevation to the throne, the two Phukans [Chenkak and Khamrak] were the prime movers: the rest were mere twigs and leaves [accessories and helpers.]"

Soon after ascending the throne Gadadhar Singha sent officers to search the residence of Laluk Barphukan at Kaliabar, where they came upon several secret letters exchanged between the Barphukan and Sultan Azamtara, including the Padshahzada's letter appointing Laluk as Raja of Assam, and Rahmat Banu Begum's letter to her uncle

Laluk, and also the inventory of articles presented by Laluk to the Nawabs and Begums of Dacca. The papers were sent by Bandar Barphukan to Gargaon through one Ramkrishnai Kataki. Sometime afterwards, when the king wanted to inspect the letters they could not be traced and found. The Swargadeo asked his secretary Mayur Majumdar to enquire of Madhabcharan Kataki, but the latter affirmed that the papers were somewhere with the monarch himself. Gadadhar Singha asked Madhabcharan to come near the throne, and made him swear by kneeling down, touching the sacred thread with one hand and the king's knee with the other. "The papers are near about the Swargadeo somewhere", repeated Madhabcharan, "and if I be found to conceal the truth, will there be any paucity of punishment for me?" The king then had the articles and goods found in Laluk's residence brought before him from the royal store, and had them thoroughly examined. Mayur Majumdar who conducted the examination came upon a bundle of papers wrapped up in a piece of cloth, and the lost documents were among these papers. The king praised Madhabcharan for his truthfulness, gave him a sacred thread of gold, and married him to the daughter of Kalia Kataki.[136]

The first act of the reign of Gadadhar Singha was the stamping out of the possibilities of disloyal manouvres on the part of the nobles. This he did by inflicting exemplary punishments on those who had participated in the machinations of the previous regime, or had exhibited symptoms of rebellious and traitorous disposition. Bhatdhara Ex-Barphukan who had helped his brother Laluk in the surrender of Gauhati and who had subsequently approached the Subedar of Bengal for an armed force to attack the Ahoms had been in confinement with his son Madha. They were now taken out; slices from their bodies were now cut off and made into curries like other edible meat. The father was made to eat the flesh of his son, and *vice versa*. The heart of the son was then ripped open with an axe, and the liver extracted

136. S. K. Bhuyan, *Ramani Gabharu*, pp. 77-78.

and given to the father to eat. Bhatdhara was then beheaded. The capital punishment was also inflicted on his brother Marangi Ex-Barbarua. The other relatives and kinsmen of Laluk Barphukan, including Aka Phukan, were traced out, captured and killed; and some were allotted to the contingent of the Barpatra Gohain, Similar punishments were also accorded to the relatives of Debera Barbarua, and some of them were settled at Cheunibacha. The king also traced out all persons of rebellious propensities, including a number of princes, and had them all captured and executed. Japang Bargohain and Ahina Mudoi's son were victims of this purge. Those who had helped the king in his wandering life as a fugitive prince were amply rewarded. Arjun Daivajna was presented a golden sacred thread, and appointed astrologer to His Majesty. Mayur was appointed Majumdar Barua whose duties combined the functions of the king's Private Secretary and Lord Chamberlain.

In March 1682, Gadadhar Singha was formally crowned. The Majumdar Barua wrote his name with a golden pen and announced it to the public. The king married the daughters of the leading nobles, and thereby established friendly alliances with them. Laithepena Bargohain's daughter became the Barkuanri; Miri Sandikoi's daughter became the Parvatia Kuanri; another daughter of Miri Sandikoi became Barmahi Kuanri. Gadadhar Singha also married the daughter of Rup Sandikoi, Dhuliabata Barchetia and Bhakati Paniphukan.

CHAPTER XVII

FINAL RECOVERY OF GAUHATI

King Gadadhar Singha soon established his reputation as a stern and unrelenting disciplinarian who would not permit any delinquent to go with impunity, or tolerate any move likely to disturb the smooth sailing of the ship of state: his words were to be regarded as laws, and violation thereof would be promptly and rigorously suppressed. This impression had a salutary effect upon the intriguous nobles, and it ensured the purity of the administration, the peace and prosperity of the people, and the success of his arms in any eventual conflict with an enemy.

Having thus prepared the background, Gadadhar Singha turned his attention to the task of expelling the Moguls from Gauhati. A conference of the nobles was held in March 1682 to discuss the ways and means. The king opened the deliberations by saying,—"What have you got to say regarding the proposal to expel Mansur Khan from Gauhati. It is the duty of a king and a country to fight; and it is not proper that we should continue in a state of subordination to the enemy." The ministers exclaimed in one voice,—"We have no other opinion but what has been expressed by His Majesty. We shall carry out the Swargadeo's command and fight till the last breath of our life, and thereby repay the debt we owe to His Majesty for the salt and rice." The astrologers predicted the month of Bhadra to be an auspicious season for the campaign. "The Swargadeo is destined to achieve victory over the Moguls and enjoy the sovereignty of Kamrup," said the astrologers, "it was at this stellar conjunction that Ramchandra crossed the sea to Lanka and discomfited Ravana."[137]

On the completion of the preparations the Ahom army set out for Gauhati in three divisions; Bandar Barphukan and Champa Paniphukan proceeded by water on the Brahmaputra; Gargayan Sandikoi Neog Phukan and Khamrak

137. S. K. Bhuyan, *Assam Buranji, S.M.*, p. 146.

Charingia Phukan by the Kalang river on the south bank; and Hulou Deka-Phukan and the Namdangia Phukan by the north bank of the Brahmaputra. On the approach of the Ahom forces the Moguls evacuted their advance garrisons at Kajali, Panikhaiti and Kurua for fear of being outnumbered, and they concentrated at their stronghold at Itakhuli or Gauhati.

All was not well in the camp of Mansur Khan, the Mogul Fauzadar of Gauhati. The Nawab was lying prostrate with illness, and the imperial troops, impatient at the delay in getting their pay, had gone to Dacca to seek redress of their grievances, but they were disappointed. On their return to Gauhati they planned to set fire to the imperial stores where the provisions and weapons had been deposited, and they had to be pacified with great difficulty. The soldiers even proposed to capture Mansur Khan, and he out of fear ceased to stir out of his residence.[138]

The Nawab however managed to get together a force to resist the Ahoms. Fighting took place at Bahbari, Sonapur, Sarania, Jaiduar and Shahburuz. The Moguls mounted their guns at Umananda, an island in the Brahmaputra river opposite Gauhati. Their principal garrison of Itakhuli or Sukreswar Hill at Gauhati was attacked by the land and river forces of the Ahoms. One Jayanta Singha, a Mogul commander, displayed unusual bravery. Mansur Khan had already deserted Itakhuli and pitched his camp further to the west of Gauhati. Ali Akbar, the commander of Itakhuli, being unable to withstand the onslaught of the Ahoms fled in a boat to Mansur Khan's camp. The Fauzadar left his camp and retreated to Rangamati. The Ahoms chased him as far as the Manaha river which from that time became the westernmost limit of Assam, and remained as such till the occupation of the kingdom by the British. The battle of Itakhuli took place in September 1682. The Moguls were

138. Speaking of the Deccan wars of Aurangzeb, Stanley Lane-Poole says,—"The Mughal army was enfeebled and demoralised; 'those infernal foot-soldiers' were croaking like rooks in an invaded rookery, clamouring for their arrears of pay".—*Medieval India,* II, p. 275.

thus expelled from Gauhati after they had been in its occupation for three years and a half.

The Ahoms took possession of the large quantities of provisions and war materials left behind by the Moguls in their hurried flight from Gauhati: they consisted of horses, buffaloes, bullocks, guns, swords, daggers, boats, and gold and silver. It is believed that the materials obtained by the Ahoms on this occasion far exceeded in quantity and value all the spoils obtained by them in previous victories. Each of the captured guns was re-inscribed to contain this superscription,—"This war-weapon was obtained by King Gadadhar Singha after having vanquished the Yavanas in the year 1604 *Saka.*" Guns with this superscription have been found in several parts of Assam and they are being discovered even now. The battle of Itakhuli represents the last contest between the Ahoms and the Moguls.

From the report of an interview held at Dacca on October 29, 1682, between Nawab Shaista Khan and William Hedges, Governor of the English Factories in the Bay of Bengal, it appears that the Nawab was very busy at that time "in despatching and vesting divers principal officers sent with all possible diligence with recruits for their army lately overthrown in Asham and Silhet, two large plentiful countries, eight days journey from this city." The idea of a fresh war with Assam was perhaps abandoned ultimately by Shaista Khan in view of the strengthened position of the Ahoms in Lower Assam, and Mogul preoccupation in other parts of India, specially in the Deccan.[139]

Being free from foreign worries the Ahom nobles became again busy in their old game of political intrigues. Bandar Barphukan and Champa Paniphukan had not from the beginning viewed the elevation of Gadadhar Singha with favour, and they had supported it only because they found themselves in a hopeless minority. After the victory at Itakhuli they engaged themselves in covert acts to overthrow the monarch.

139. *Diary of Sir William Hedges in Bengal*, 1681-88, edited by Col. H. Yule, Hakluyt Society's publication, 1877-79, Vol. I, p. 43.

The two Phukans were promptly arrested, whereupon they confessed their guilt. The king proposed to inflict upon them the severest punishment, but the three Gohains and the other nobles interceded on their behalf, and the Swargadeo, in remembrance of their past services, let them off by merely dismissing them from their offices. Chenkak Gargayan Sandikoi Phukan was appointed Barphukan, and Bhakati of the Dihingia Phukan's family, brother of Alun Barbarua, was appointed Paniphukan.

A similar conspiracy led by the Phukans of Gauhati were promptly detected and suppressed. The principal culprits were Khamrak Charingia Phukan, Bhakati Paniphukan, Chengrai Phukan, and Khamchin Phukan. They harboured a prince with a view to place him on the throne. The king himself proceeded against the Phukans, and encamped at Kaliabar. The Phukans were brought by a stratagem to Kaliabar where they were accused of their guilt. They were first dismissed from office, and also Dighala Buragohain who had helped the conspirators. Khamrak Phukan and Khamchin Phukan were then executed. Bhakati Paniphukan was spared his life through the intercession of his brother Alun Barbarua. Another culprit, Namdangiya Phukan, was subsequently arrested and executed. The Barbarua was dismissed from office for his inability to exercise proper control over his brother Bhakati Ex-Paniphukan. Bhakati was subsequently executed. By prompt and vigorous measures the king thus suppressed the two conspiracies, and thereby eliminated all possibilities of their recurrence in future. King Gadadhar Singha gave the name Manpur to the royal camp at Kaliabar.

The Vaisnava monasteries or Satras next engaged the attention of King Gadadhar Singha. These institutions were the offshoots of the Vaisnava upheaval which swept over Assam in the latter part of the sixteenth century under the teachings of Sankardeva, Madhabdeva, Damodardeva, Gopaldeva and other reformers. By virtue of its simple faith, uncomplicated by rituals and ceremonies, and supported by a humanistic literature, music, recital, and drama, and emulated by the examples of devout saints and preachers, Vaisnavism came to be deeply rooted in the soil. The masses looked upon their Gurus with great reverence; and in some cases the allegiance due to a monarch was considered to be of lesser importance than the respect to which a spiritual head was entitled. Some of the monasteries were established under the patronage of kings and nobles, who were the disciples of one Gosain or the other. The Gosains grew in wealth and power through the tithes of their disciples, and presents, endowments and grants made by kings and potentates. Their food and garments and their ways of living were of a very simple character befitting holy men and saints, but the articles they used in their audience chambers and their prayer halls, the magnificence of their processions when they went out, and the receptions held in their honour, and the numerical strength of their devotees and attendants bespoke their kingly pomp and array. To an astute politician, the existence of so many centres on which popular respect was concentrated and focussed was bound to assume the shape of a prominent danger spot which at any time might disturb the solidarity and integrity of the governing power. Gadapani was greatly concerned over the influence and wealth of the Satras, and his attitude was coloured by his own experiences at Dakhinpat, Auniati and other Satras during his wanderings as a fugitive.[140]

It is believed that the mildness of the Vaisnava cult and the simple dietetics which its sponsors practised and advocated did not appeal to the vigorous habits of Gadadhar Singha. The spread of Vaisnavism among the members of the ruling race of the Ahoms was considered by Gadadhar Singha as a menace to the continuance of their domination in Assam for Vaisnavism, he thought, encouraged the growth of a spirit of submissiveness which ran counter to bodily vigour and martial ardour so much needed by rulers. Gadadhar Singha therefore exhibited pronounced Sakta proclivities, and entertained a stepmotherly if not a positively hostile attitude towards Vaisnavism.

140. S. K. Bhuyan, *Assam Buranji, S.M.*, p. 145.

Gadadhar Singha's anti-Vaisnava tendencies were fanned by one Rangacharan Bhandari Barua of the Bezdoloi family, son of Manthir Bharali Barua who had figured in the invasion of Mir Jumla. Rangacharan pointed out to the monarch the redundant character of the wealth possessed by the Gosains. "Why should there be wealth and grandeur in the establishment of a religious devotee?", said Rangacharan, "A few grains of rice constitute his only article of necessity, and that even is given to him by his devotees and disciples. If His Majesty desires I can obtain this wealth for the royal coffers." The king approved of Rangacharan's proposal, and despatched him in the company of two lieutenants, Kana Chekerai and Achubulia, to seize the persons of the Gosains and confiscate their property. The golden image of Dakhinpat was removed and melted, and made into a pitcher for being placed on the turret of the temple at Charaideo. Ramdeva Gosain of Dakhinpat had his eyeballs extracted. Keshabdeva Gosain of Auniati had his property confiscated and himself banished to Sadiya. A number of Thakuria Mahantas were executed at Namrup. The other Gosains and Mahantas were removed from their localities and settled at Namrup, Tokolai and Cheuni, after having their property seized and confiscated. The stories of oppressions and extortions committed upon the Gosains by Rangacharan, Kana Chekerai and Achubulia figure in the records and chronicles of the leading monasteries of Assam.[141]

As we have said, Gadadhar Singha regarded military efficiency to be the first and foremost requisite of a powerful state; he therefore disfavoured the non-aggressiveness and passivity of the Vaisnava faith, though in fact the exterior mildness and humility of a Vaisnava devotee was a cloak to conceal his inner vigour and energy which he had conserved by self-discipline and restraint. Gadadhar Singha patronised the performance of Sakta rites, and his Sakta advisers, if not preceptors, were Katyayan Bhattacharyya and Mukalimuria Gosain. Records do not show that he received initiation from any particular Sakta preceptor.

141. MS. Assam Buranji No. 15.

There is a section of people who think in the same way as Gadadhar Singha; there are others who go a step further and believe that non-flesh-eating people are hardly competent to govern. But about Assamese Vaisnavism two things come out prominently,—*first,* during the glorious period of the rule of the Ahoms when they successfully resisted the imperialistic menace of the Moguls the kings were disciples of Vaisnava Satradhikars, and Vaisnavism was predominant in the land; and, *secondly,* Assam attained a widespread reputation in India for the religious-mindedness of the people as evinced in the universal practice of musical recital of the name of Hari which was the direct result of Vaisnava preachings. The widowed consort of Mirza Raja Jai Singha of Amber and the wife of the Mirza Raja's son Ram Singha wrote to the latter then engaged in a deadly conflict for the subjugation of Assam,—"We have learnt that there is universal *nama-kirtana* and *nama-dharma* in that country, and that cows, Brahmans and Vaisnavas are living there in peace and comfort; by invading it, Oh, how long did Mir Jumla thrive? Consider these facts and act as you think proper."[142]

The sternness of Gadadhar Singha's rule improved the tone of the administration. Punishments were inflicted on offenders irrespective of their rank and position; the voice of rupture was promptly suppressed; officials were prevented from oppressing the subjects; corruption and slackness were eliminated; and in consequence the people lived in peace and security.

Chenkak Gargayan Sandikoi Barphukan, the Ahom viceroy of Gauhati from 1681 to 1695, proved to be a worthy pro-consul of a worthy sovereign. He administered the affairs of Lower Assam with vigour and tact. He did not permit any insubordination or disobedience on the part of his junior officials and commanders; and he succeeded in avoiding friction with the Mogul neighbours. The Siva temple at Umananda was constructed by Sandikoi Barphukan.

142. S. K. Bhuyan, *Lachit Barphukan and His Times*, pp. 78, 116-17, 140-41; *Kamrupar Buranji*, p. 87; *Assam Buranji, S.M.*, p. 121; H. C. Goswami, *Purani Assam Buranji*, p. 147; MS, Assam Buranji No. 7.

A Mogul of Secunderabad, named Muhammad Ali, who had belonged to the staff of Nawab Mansur Khan, continued to live at Gauhati even after the expulsion of his patron in 1682, enjoying that respect and esteem to which learned men are entitled all over the world. He had been entrusted with the education of Mansur Khan's sons for which he received an honorarium of one hundred rupees per month. He was greatly versed in Persian and Arabic. Gargayan Sandikoi Barphukan appointed Assamese scholars to take down from the lips of Muhammad Ali facts and information about Mogul India. Only one episode heard from Muhammad Ali has been preserved in an old Assamese chronicle dealing with the Sultanate of Delhi.[143] The story relates to the conquest of Secunderabad by Siliman Padshah, and its substance is reproduced below:

Sekendar Shah, Padshah of Iran, who accumulated 40,50,000 rupees per year, founded Secunderabad. After some time Sekendar Padshah returned to his native country, which was at a distance of three months' journey from Delhi, leaving Ghalib Khan Nawab, a commander of 9,000, as ruler of Secunderabad, which measured 220 *kros* in length and 103 *kros* in breadth. Pearls and gems were sold in the city; sea-horses basked on the shores, and men domesticated and sold them at prices varying from 1,000 to 1,500 rupees. Siliman Padshah lived at the port of Farang. Taking advantage of the absence of Sekendar Padshah, Siliman proposed to invade Secunderabad, but he doubted his success in view of the impregnable fortifications. Siliman was advised to take recourse to strategy on the following lines,—500 soldiers of Siliman should become employed as servants at Secunderabad, secretly to reconnoitre its military position, while others should proceed there as merchants with ships and boats; and a damsel, represented as the grand-daughter of Siliman Padshah, should be presented to Ghalib Khan with instruction to poison that ruler.

143. S. K. Bhuyan, *Annals of the Delhi Badshahate,* Chapter VI,

Accordingly Siliman despatched a letter to Ghalib Khan seeking the latter's friendship and alliance, on the ground that both of them were exposed to invasion by the Pathans. Ghalib Khan, delighted to receive the message, offers his daughter Gulmakhmal to Siliman Padshah's son. In return, Siliman sends to Ghalib Khan his niece, who was a learned and cunning lady; Ghalib Khan marries her. Siliman sends 500 soldiers to live at Secunderabad as spies; they offered their services to Ghalib Khan who enlisted them in his army as they looked handsome and energetic. Farangi merchants traded at Secunderabad; their leader had offered valuable presents to the viceroy Ghalib Khan who had permitted them to trade in his territory. The merchants possessed five ships loaded with attractive commodities. Their boats were covered with bags stuffed with fish-scales, and arrangements were made to carry elephants and horses on boats. The girl-scholar sent by Siliman, who had now become the Begum of Ghalib Khan, laid a poisonous cloth on the body of the Nawab when he was asleep, and he died in consequence. The Nawab's general fought with the soldiers of Siliman who had now gone to Secunderabad personally, but the contest remained undecided. Siliman issued secret instructions to his merchants to act within the city, and they set fire to the bazar, and riding on horse-back they began to kill men. Secunderabad was then occupied by Siliman Padshah.

At the end of the narrative it is recorded,—"From the territory of Siliman Padshah, Delhi is situated at a distance of three months' journey. Muhammad Ali is a Mogul of that place. He is a very great scholar, and knows all the *loghats* or languages, Arabic and Persian. He taught the sons of Mansur Khan, and for this he received an honorarium of full one hundred rupees per month. The above incidents have been heard from his mouth."

Muhammad Ali also furnished to Gargayan Sandikoi Phukan a list of the kings of Delhi from Yudhisthira down to Aurangzeb. The mention of twenty-six years as the then reigning period of Aurangzeb indicates that Muhammad Ali brought the list up to the year 1684 when possibly he made it over to Sandikoi Barphukan's scribes.[144] Whatever may be the historical value of the list, it at least furnished the Assamese a working knowledge of the chronology of Delhi sovereigns as an aid to the acquisition of further knowledge. We also believe that Muhammad Ali supplied numerous other facts to the inquisitive Assamese including the relative distances of the important towns and cities of India.[145] A full knowledge of Mogul India was necessary to the Assamese not only for widening their mental horizon, but also to serve as an effective aid to the counteraction of imperialist designs.

The necessity to make the best use of Muhammad Ali's stay at Gauhati by collecting information from him about Mogul India was imperative at that time in view of the possibility of a renewal of hostilities. The independence of Assam was a canker in the rose of Mogul supremacy in India, and the Moguls could not remain at ease till they could settle their differences with Assam. The Ahoms had worsted the Moguls on numerous occasions; and they could at ease sail down from their garrisons situated on the upper rapids of the Brahmaputra. This was a positive menace to the security of the Moguls in Bengal.

After their defeat at Itakhuli in September 1682, the Moguls were engaged in exploring the possibilities of attacking Assam. Their plan this time was to bring Mahindra Narayan, Raja of Cooch Behar, to complete submission, and persuade him to invade Assam on behalf of the Moguls. The son of the Subedar of Bengal himself visited Cooch Behar with an armed force, and a number of influential nobles of Cooch Behar who cherished hostile intentions against the Raja joined the Moguls at Bagduar. The Raja became a virtual prisoner of the Moguls. He was asked to invade Assam, and to pay a tribute of rupees ten lakhs. The Raja did not agree to either of these proposals.

144. May 23, 1658 was the official beginning of the first year of Aurangzeb's reign. See Professor Jadunath Sarkar's *Short History of Aurangzeb*, 1954, pp. 95, 464.

145. In an old Assamese chronicle there is "a statement of the distances from Delhi to other places having thanas", see S. K. Bhuyan's *Annals of the Delhi Badshahate*, pp. 173-75.

The Raja, in his desperation, wrote a letter to Gargayan Sandikoi Phukan suggesting the need of combining the resources of Cooch Behar and Assam in a joint expedition against the Moguls "who are the common enemies of both of us." The Raja even suggested the plan of operation. "You should", wrote Mahindra Narayan to Gargayan Sandikoi Barphukan in June 1684, "despatch a large force to attack the Rangamati garrison; and after having captured it, your soldiers should proceed by boat to attack Dacca. In our turn, we shall proceed by the route through Ghoraghat, and attack Dacca after having defeated Kumar Bhavani. Our two forces will then meet at a junction, and hurl a joint attack on Nawab Shaista Khan at Dacca. You should act in a manner which will lead to the destruction of your enemy as well as of mine."

In March 1685, Mahindra Narayan, Raja of Cooch Behar, wrote to Sandikoi Barphukan, informing him of the reported intention of the Moguls to invade Assam, after having first brought Cooch Behar under their domination. The Raja reiterated his plan of a joint and simultaneous attack on Mogul territories. "You should march to Rangamati," wrote Mahindra Narayan, "and then we can easily expel the Mogul force from Bagduar." The Moguls had forcibly occupied Bahirbund extending from Bagduar, and Mahindra Narayan considered himself incapable of single-handed action to dislodge the aggressors.

About his determination not to yield to the Moguls, the Raja declared,—"Bahir-vilat extending from Bagduar is in the hands of the Moguls. I spoke to the Moguls in words of friendship, but they expressed their unwillingness to part with the territories occupied by them. On the other hand, they have asked me to proceed to Dacca and offer my submission to the Subedar there. Now, I have made up my mind not to submit to the Moguls again even though I have to lose my kingdom. May the Padshah do whatever he likes."[146]

146. MS. Assam Buranji Nos. 3 and 8.

The attitude of the Ahoms towards the proposals of the Cooch Behar Raja can be easily imagined. They had just emerged from the successful termination of their long-drawn hostilities with the Moguls, and were therefore unwilling to try the force of their arms in foreign soil by launching offensive operations at the request of a neighbouring Raja whose representations might be exaggerated, and whose requests might be dictated by his own necessity. It was obvious that the request of the Moguls that Cooch Behar should take up arms against Assam was designed to create discord between the two Hindu states in order to prevent their alliance for any anti-imperialistic purpose. The alleged Mogul plans of invasion of Assam might be exaggerated, if not fabricated, by the Koch Raja himself to induce the Ahoms to attack the Moguls. The Ahoms had a systematic and efficient machinery for collecting information about Mogul manoeuvres, and they were not going to act on the mere statement of the Cooch Behar Raja. An expedition against the Moguls was at best a hazardous enterprise, and it was not known how far the promised co-operation of the Raja would be effective in view of his limited resources owing to the recent curtailment of his territorial limits. There were instances in the past of Cooch Behar's non-compliance with similar requests made by the Ahoms in crises of their own; and the Ahoms were under no diplomatic obligation to help Cooch Behar in its difficult hour. Besides, the relations between the Barphukan and the Mogul officers of the Bengal frontier were of a friendly nature at that time as we know from the frequent exchange of embassies.

The Ahom attitude therefore was one of present inaction as far as offensive operations were concerned, accompanied by watchful vigilance. Gargayan Sandikoi Phukan in his reply sent in October 1685 thanked Mahindra Narayan for his refusal of the demands made by the Moguls. About Mogul plans to invade Assam the Barphukan observed,—"All of you are aware of the repeated reverses suffered by the imperial forces at our hands. In recollection of our age-long friendship we desire your continued independence undisturbed by your enemy. You have desired that no quarters should be given by us to the Moguls. Sympathy towards them is a very remote contingency; on the other hand, you will be apprised of our prowess and might through our actions and proceedings. In respect of your solicitude for unity between our two territories,—the continuance of our mutual friendship will be tantamount to this unity." The Koch-Ahom relations became comparatively dormant during the remaining years of Gadadhar Singha's reign, owing to the difficulties of communication as were alleged by the Koch Raja. They were revived by Rudra Singha twenty-eight years later when he sought the alliance and support of the Cooch Behar Raja Rup Narayan to prosecute his plan to invade Bengal.[147]

Gadadhar Singha died in 1696 and was succeeded by his elder son Lai Gohain, who assumed the Hindu name Rudra Singha. The new king inherited from his father an orderly government and a peaceful kingdom; and he had therefore the opportunity to formulate new plans to elevate his kingdom to the rank of a first-rate power in India.

As we have said elsewhere, "Rudra Singha began by reforming the internal administration of the land with a view to secure the highest degree of efficiency. With the resources of a fully developed state at his command he proposed to unfurl the flag of victory in the neighbouring Mogul territories, and if possible to seize the throne of Delhi. He restored the Vaisnava monks to their original Satras, encouraged art, literature and music. The neighbouring territories of Cachar and Jayantia were subdued, and their chiefs made promises to help the Ahom monarch with men and provisions when such aid would be solicited. The vassal chieftains on the Assam frontier, the Sat-rajias and Panch-rajias, were bound by treaty terms to render timely assistance to their liegelord.

147. MS. Assam Buranji Nos. 3 and 8. Letter from Raja Mahindra Narayan to Gargayan Sandikoi Barphukan, Jeth 16, 1606 *saka*, and *Chaitra* 1, 1606 *saka;* from the Barphukan to Raja Mahindra Narayan, Aswin 1607; and from Raja Rup Narayan of Cooch Behar to King Rudra Singha of Assam, Jeth, 1635, received at the Ahom court on Ashar 29, 1636 *saka*.

Rudra Singha deputed agents in the garb of itinerant hermits to different places in India to study the customs of those places and collect information regarding their resources and strength.

"He despatched trusted envoys to the Rajas of different parts of India asking them not to offer him any resistance in his expedition against the Moguls. The messengers came back with a reply from the Rajas that they would render all possible co-operation to the powerful Swarga-Maharaja of Assam if he attempted to occupy the throne of Delhi as the indignities hurled at them by the Mogul Badshahs were becoming more and more intolerable. When the preparations were completed the king left the capital Rangpur and marched to Gauhati where his army was joined by those of his allies and the frontier chieftains. Rudra Singha mobilised at Gauhati an army of 4,00,000, and he planned to march into Mogul territories in the harvest season in November 1714. An advanced force already proceeded to the Manaha river where they waited for the signal to enter into Bengal. When the preparations were on foot for the march of the expedition Rudra Singha died suddenly at Gauhati in September 1714.

"If the greatness of a man is to be judged by the greatness of his designs, and his conscious and rigorous efforts to uplift his country apart from any success which finally meets his endeavours, Rudra Singha can be called Rudra Singha the Great. It will be easy to imagine the impression that would have been made by the dash and gallantry of the tribesmen and mountaineers who constituted the backbone of Rudra Singha's army upon the ease-loving and discontented hosts of the Timurid generals. Emperor Aurangzeb had died seven years before; and Delhi, now reduced to a theatre of contest between rival powers, ultimately excited the cupidity of transborder invaders."[148]

148. S. K. Bhuyan, *Tungkhungia Buranji*, O.U.P., Introduction, pp. xx-xxi; and also, *Studies in the Literature of Assam*, for the analysis of *Tripura Buranji*.

CHAPTER XVIII

ATAN BURAGOHAIN AS A HISTORIAN

Atan Buragohain, the statesman and warrior, was also a historian. The chronicle compiled by him was entitled "Sri-Sri-Swarga-Maharajar-vamsa-nirnaya", or an account of the Ahom kings of Assam, the word *vamsa,* originally meaning a family, being applied also to a history or a narrative of a ruling dynasty, or of a celebrated organisation or institution.

It was the practice of the Ahom court to record the events of a monarch's reign, and historiographers were appointed for this purpose, and were given access to the papers deposited at the state archives and other necessary sources of information. The leading nobles and officers were also engaged in compiling chronicles when they found that by doing so they would be able to rescue neglected facts from oblivion, or interpret the details from a new angle of vision. The existence of a vast number of chronicles mostly contemporaneous have given to the Assamese people and their literature a unique distinction and prestige.

It is believed that copies of Shan chronicles were brought into Assam by Sukapha; and so late as the reign of Swargadeo Gaurinath Singha, 1780-95, "a commission of Nara astronomers and other learned persons was deputed to Mogaung to examine the histories of their race in possession of the Shan Buddhist priests of that place, and to verify the books (or traditions) brought into that country by Chau-ka-pha [Sukapha]. The examination completed, the commission rewrote the Ahom history in Assamese, and extended it backwards from Sam-lung-pha's conquest of Assam to the founding of the first Ahom capital on the Shweli river."[149]

149. Ney Elias, *Introductory Sketch of the History of the Shans,* quoted in J. G. Scott's Gazetteer of Upper Burma and the Shan States, Vol. I, Part I, pp. 214-15. My attention was drawn to this passage by Srijut Padmeswar Gogoi, M.A.

Atan Buragohain's chronicle begins by stating that it was dictated and expounded by His Majesty's prime minister Bahgaria Buragohain, who was no other than Atan Buragohain himself, as the toponomous epithet "Bahgaria Buragohain" is applied to Atan Buragohain alone, no other member of the Bahgaria branch of the family having ever been appointed to the office of Buragohain.

Atan Buragohain gives in his chronicle an outline of the history of the Ahom sovereigns of Assam from the first conqueror Sukapha, 1228-1268 A.D., up to the reign of Swargadeo Pratap Singha, 1603-41. He avoids the details which are to be found in the ordinary chronicles, justifying the omission by the remark that those details are to be found in other chronicles. He concentrates on the significant events bringing out mainly the contacts and intercourse of the Ahoms with other races and tribes, and laying special emphasis on the occasions leading to the adoption of new measures and innovations. The statesman-historian attempts also to indicate *en passant* the features of good government. The chronicle is therefore idealistic in tone, and not a mere dry-as-dust narrative of wars and embassies, and punishments and rewards. It embodies the modicum of the knowledge of precedents which, according to the standard of those days, every member of the ruling class in Assam was expected to possess for the efficient handling of political affairs.

An abstract of the chronicle can be presented as follows: This chronicle is to be preserved in a secret manner. It should be shown only to a friend who is not hostile in disposition. Before the great deluge, Brahma made three unsuccessful attempts to create man. He then planted a sapling of a gourd, and from its fruit issued out men who were ignorant and beastlike. Indra then sent down a priest who gave proper instructions to men, and from that time they became conversant and aware. The *Satya-yuga,* or the Golden Age, was passed in amity and love. Men used to take food in the same dish like sons of the same mother; and nobody entertained any jealousy or hatred towards any other person. Disputes and strifes became rampant with the advent of the *Treta-yuga*: and the strong wanted to oppress the weak. Men offered their prayers to Indra, and the god sent down his two grandsons Khunlung and Khunlai to rule over this earth. A quarrel ensued between the two brothers in consequence of which Khunlung returned to heaven.

Khunlai and his descendants ruled over this earth for eleven generations after which they were expelled by a Naga subject of theirs named Mene. During Mene's rule the people became very miserable suffering constantly from epidemics and misfortunes. A descendant of Khunlung was then searched out and placed on the throne. During his rule the sufferings of the people came to an end, and they became happy as before. He governed his subjects as his own sons. There was neither extortion nor any taxation in his time. He lived in the ways of righteousness according due punishment to every guilt, and reward and honour to virtue and merit.

Then it came to pass that the two sisters of the king of Nara, or Mogaung in Upper Burma, became *enceinte* through divine intervention. Sukranpha was born of the first sister and Sukapha of the second. Sukranpha became king of Nara, and Sukapha proposed to try his fortune elsewhere. Sukranpha agreed to this proposal, and extracted from the younger prince a promise to pay a yearly tribute. The latter was furnished with the usual paraphernalia of a sovereign,—soldiers, nobles, scriptures, Pundits, ornaments, bows and arrows, and elephants and horses. Sukapha was also given a replica of the tutelary stone image of *Chomdeo*, which was believed to confer uninterrupted sovereignty and unbounded prosperity upon the possessor. But Sukapha managed to bring with him the original image. On the discovery of this fact Sukranpha despatched his emissaries in the pursuit of Sukapha, but the latter had crossed the Sri-Lauhitya, or Chindwin river, and his pursuers retraced their steps to Nara.

Sukapha then wandered from place to place in a career of conquest. He first subjugated a large number of Naga villages. Those who were met on the way were admitted to his company. Many Chutias, Morans, Kacharis and Barahis joined his ranks. It was about this time that Sukapha ordered his Pundits "to write down all particulars, whenever an incident takes place and when a person dies, and when we acquire new followers".

The victor then travelled through Tipam and Namrup, and the country on both the north bank and the south bank, and gave new names to the places he visited, and to the articles presented to him by the vanquished. He sometimes permitted the retention of the older nomenclature. This led to the duplication or triplication of names. He also conferred honours and distinctions upon his supporters and gave them titles according to the character and quality of the services they rendered. The Chutias, Barahis and Morans became more endeared to Sukapha than his original adherents and followers. Since that time there was an admixture of blood, and children were of mixed origin as the first Ahoms had not brought their wives when they came from Nara, and they accepted wives only when they came here.

Sukapha then sailed up the Dikhow and Dilih rivers, and found villages inhabited by Kacharis, Barahis and Morans; and the prince proposed to deal with them one after the other as he feared that a possible combination on their part might render his conquest a difficult task.

He sent an appeal to the Barahis and Morans and asked them to come to him for the pleasure of a meeting. "We have come from the east," said he, "and you are the *sthana-giris*, or indigenous lords. We are guests, and you should show us the villages and lands and tell us all about them." One Thamithuma, the *Adhikar* or chief of the Barahis and Morans, offered him co-operation and help. Sukapha was informed of the circumstances leading to the expulsion of the Kacharis from Mahang by the Nagas, and of their new settlement on the other side of the Dikhow river. Thamithuma suggested that the site of their tribal shrine, sacred to Khai-Nakuri, would be appropriate for the capital of the new conquerors. Sukapha was pleased with Thamithuma and asked him to repeat his visit. The Barahis and Morans undertook to supply vegetables and fuel to Sukapha's household. They accepted the domination of the conquerors and expressed their belief as follows:—"These are not men of ordinary lineage. These are the Ahoms famed as *Deo-manuh* or god-men. Others are not *sama* or equal to them."

King Sukapha then took four wives from the Barahi and Moran tribes. A Barahi queen having given evidence of her superior culinary skill, the king appointed her brothers and nephews as cooks. He also reformed the dress of the Barahis. The Morans however proved less amenable to changes.

Sukapha's successor Suteupha subdued the Kacharis by a stratagem. The next king Subinpha asked the Bargohain and the Buragohain to feed the royal household by rotation. On being reprimanded by the king for shortage of supplies, the Buragohain, named Thao-ruru, left the capital, and his whereabouts could not be traced. Some years later, a sword belonging to the fugitive Buragohain was found in possession of a young man born of a Moran woman through that noble. The Moran youth was appointed Buragohain. After an interregnum of eight years, an Ahom prince who had been brought up in a family of Brahmans was placed on the throne; and his old-time associates, the seven sons of his Brahman fosterfather, were provided with elephants and horses and given the honorific title of *Kowanrs* or princes. The Ahoms gradually succeeded in establishing their domination over the Kacharis, the Barahis, the Morans and the Nagas; and the king of Kamata presented princesses to the Ahom monarch.

During the reign of Dihingia Raja, his generals carried their victorious arms as far as the Karatoya river. A temple was erected on the bank of that river and some quantity of earth from the Gaur kingdom was brought to Assam. Biswa Singha, the new king of the Koches, offered his submission to the generals of Dihingia Raja, and entered into an agreement to pay a yearly tribute. The Ahom forces returned to Assam in the year 1427 *Saka*. Gargayan Raja sat on the throne after having killed his father Dihingia Raja. Here says the chronicler,—"The remaining events are to be found in other chronicles. Having killed the king, his son the Gargayan Raja ascended the throne, and his history is narrated in other writings."

Gargayan Raja was succeeded by his son Khora Raja. His reign of fifty-one years is dismissed with a mere reference to the wars with Cooch Behar. The Ahoms were discomfited, and the king fled to the hills. The withdrawal of the victorious Koch army was obtained by an offer of tributes and hostages. Here also the chronicler says,—"These facts are narrated in other writings, and I have therefore made a brief mention of the events."

Pratap Singha succeeded Khora Raja. His reign of thirty-eight years is full of significant events, and numerous innovations and reforms, which established the solidarity of Ahom rule in Assam. But our chronicler leaves out the other details of the reign, desiring to concentrate on the wars with the *Bangals* or Moguls. He says,—"His [Khora Raja's] son Burha Raja Pratap Singha became king. I shall omit the other details of his reign. I shall speak of his conflicts with the Bangals."

The river Bharari formed the boundary between the Ahom and the Koch kingdoms. After the death of the great Koch king Naranarayan, and of his brother Sukladhwaj or Chilarai, and of Chilarai's son Raghudeb, there was a serious dispute between Naranarayan's son Lakshminarayan, and Raghudeb's son Parikshit. Lakshminarayan appealed for mediation to Emperor Jahangir. The emperor deputed Mukarram Khan to seize Parikshit and send him to Delhi.

Swargadeo Pratap Singha asked Parikshit to meet him when they would jointly deliberate on the plan to fight the Moguls. He also made arrangements to help Parikshit with money, and it was raised by levying taxes on fisheries, markets and ferries. Payment of taxes in money was introduced only from this time. But Parikshit declined to go to the Ahom court as he thought that his presence at Delhi was imperative. Mukarram Khan occupied Parikshit's territories which extended up to the Bharari river on the north bank and Khagarijan or Nowgong on the south. His brother Balinarayan sought the protection of the Ahoms, and King Pratap Singha gave him articles and provisions worthy of a prince. Syed Abu Bakar was then the Mogul Fauzadar stationed at Hajo.

The outbreak of hostilities between the Ahoms and the Moguls took place about that time. The Ahoms obstructed the trading activities of the Moguls though conducted in their own limits. A vassal Raja of the Moguls named Satrajit plundered the Ahom royal stores at Sola, and captured two dancing girls belonging to the temple at Biswanath. The king himself conducted the operations from his camp in Darrang. During the first stage of the conflicts the Ahoms could not achieve much success.

Akhek Gohain, an Ahom noble who had lived as a fugitive in the Mogul camp, informed the Ahoms that the Moguls were in the habit of keeping awake during the first part of the night, and that the proper time for attacking them was the late hours of the night. The Ahom forces led by their ablest commanders and 120 war-elephants made a surprise attack upon the Moguls both by land and water in the early hours at dawn. The Moguls unprepared for the eventuality were routed, and Satrajit fled from the scene of contest. Syed Abu Bakar, the Mogul commander, was slain; and several Rajas and Nawabs were killed or captured. The princes belonging to the family of Parikshit paid their homage to King Pratap Sing; and so did Mangal Raja of Dimarua, and other chiefs of the southern passes.

The office of Barphukan was created about this time, with Langi as the first incumbent. In the subsequent wars with the Moguls, Mirza Nathula, said to be the brother of the Mogul emperor, was defeated by the Ahoms. Several Assamese merchants were executed at that time for carrying on unauthorised negotiations with the Nawab of Dacca. The narrative continues to the battles which took place near Agiathuri, a few miles to the west of Gauhati on the north bank. One Madharaja was the Barphukan of Gauhati at that time. The wars came to an end when a treaty was enacted between Momai-tamuli Barbarua and Nawab Allah Yar Khan fixing the boundaries of Assam and Mogul India.

A postscript appended to the chronicle deals with the creation of the office of Barpatra Gohain during the reign of Dihingia Raja, the first Barpatra Gohain being Kancheng, son of the Ahom monarch.

The last event of note described in the chronicle is the subjugation of the Chutias who lived in the territory round Sadiya. The narrative ends with the remarks,—"Our king, Dihingia Raja, went round the Chutia Raja's capital where he obtained a large quantity of goods and articles. They were loaded in boats and sent down to Dihing. Phachengmung Bargohain also came back with the Swargadeo. I have written here a brief description of the events of the war. I have not described them in detail as they are already recorded in the war-papers or military despatches." A list is given of the spoils obtained in the Chutia campaign. The Ahom king also brought from Sadiya a large number of Brahmans, Kayasthas, Kalitas, Daivajnas, bell-metal workers, goldsmiths and men of other professions. A brief mention is then made of the introduction of houses with two gable-ends; known in Assamese as *dutupia-ghars*, from the model furnished by a bird-cage presented to the king by the Barahis. Such houses, it was however decreed, could be constructed for the use of monarchs alone. The chronicle ends with a reference to the flight of the rebellions Aitania Naras from Sadiya on the approach of the Swargadeo's forces.

The original Assamese text of the chronicle of Atan Buragohain has been incorporated in *Deodhai Asam Buranji*. Small though in bulk it helps the reader to understand the trend of Ahom history from the conquest of Sukapha to the reign of King Pratap Singha. The author has deliberately eleminated many events, or has made only a passing reference to them as they are to be found in other chronicles. The eclecticism displayed by him in the selection of events for treatment is based on a well-planned desire to communicate the essential landmarks connected with the gradual expansion and consolidation of Ahom power in Assam. These essentials were calculated to furnish the rudiments of historical knowledge embodied in the Buranjis which were voluminous and numerous. He emphasises on those events which depict the manner in which the early Ahom conquerors subjugated the original inhabitants of Assam, and made their rule acceptable to the latter. He also brings out the origin of certain customs and practices. History-writing began from Sukapha's injunction to his Pundits to note down the names of his followers and record all important happenings. The Ahoms gave new names to the places and articles they first came across here in Assam. They did not bring with them their womenfolk when they first came from Nara; they married wives only when they settled in Assam. The Barahis were employed as cooks on account of their knowledge of the art of cooking. Payment of taxes in money was introduced in the time of Parikshit. The offices of Barpatra Gohain and Barphukan were created in the reign of Dihingia Raja and Pratap Singha respectively. The conflicts between the Ahoms and the Moguls have been dealt with in greater detail as their knowledge would furnish the background of the Assam-Mogul relations of the period of Atan Buragohain's premiership. A knowledge of the war-methods of the Moguls was helpful in counteracting the imperialistic menace in thwarting which the Buragohain himself played a conspicuous part.

The personal connection of the author has been maintained throughout the entire chronicle. He controls the length of each narrative; and abridgements or mere references are justified on the ground that fuller descriptions are to be found elsewhere, meaning thereby that the reader should refer to the other chronicles if he seeks further enlightenment. The historian thus keeps himself within the rigid bounds of his self-imposed limitations. He has thus given us sentences which can be expanded into paragraphs, paragraphs into chapters, and chapters into books.

The details of the Mogul wars of Assam in the reign of Pratap Singha are to be found in other chronicles. But the text of the condensed version of the Buragohain taken as a whole is nowhere to be found, though it is reminiscent of other texts.

The language of the book is realistic and racy. In the earlier portion of the narrative we come across some old-fashioned words and expressions. It is known from the introductory lines that the book was compiled by Atan during his Buragohainship which extended from 1662 to 1679; and as such the chronicle constitutes a literary specimen showing the condition of the Assamese language as it was spoken and written in that period by the dignitaries of the state.

The chronicle is a very significant example of the historical literature of the Assamese people; and its value is enhanced by the fact that the author was a master of precedents, and an illustrious statesman and patriot who wielded the affairs of his country in the most critical period of its history.[149a]

149a. In a second manuscript of the Buragohain's chronicle, the narrative continues up to the reign of Arjun Dihingia Raja, 1675-77. There are also ampler details of the reigns of King Pratap Singha's predecessors,—Dihingia Raja I, Gargayan Raja and Khora Raja, 1497-1603. The manuscript has recently been unearthed by Shri Lila Gogoi of Cherekapar, and a transcript prepared by him from the original which is in possession of Shri Jaichandra Bargohain of Chunpora in Sibsagar District.

CHAPTER XIX

REFLECTIONS OF ATAN BURAGOHAIN

The reflections and observations of Atan Buragohain Rajmantri Dangaria are scattered in contemporary chronicles where they appear in apposite contexts in the narratives concerned. They are brought together in this chapter to enable the reader to study them in a chronological form with a view to obtain an accurate glimpse of the Buragohain's personality and character.

The dominant feature of Atan Buragohain's utterances was his courage of conviction. His arguments were irresistible, and they were generally accepted by his colleagues; and in the event of rejection, the consequences usually proved disastrous in the end. He stated his views boldly, whether the parties addressed were his royal masters, or his colleagues in the cabinet. Coming from the prime minister, the highest functionary in a monarchical regime, the Buragohain's views shaped the policy of the government both in domestic concerns and in foreign relations.

It must be remembered that Assam's affairs during the eventful period of the Buragohain's premiership were no bed of roses. The Assamese prime minister, like Winston Churchill in 1940, "had nothing to offer but blood, tears, toil and sweat." A mistaken word and an ill-timed measure would place the country in jeopardy and disgrace. The equilibrium of the government and the contentment of the people were the special responsibility of the Buragohain, and his utterances smelt at every step of his deep anxiety for his country's welfare, prestige and prosperity.

Pericles, the great Athenian statesman, said of his fellow citizens that they were noted for being most adventurous in action and most reflective beforehand, as acts are doomed to failure when undertaken undiscussed. But there are situations when the pace of reflection and discussion must be accelerated, and inhibitions and scruples must be brushed aside; and a line of action, as determined by the exigency of the situation, must be adopted without vacillation, and executed with expedition and enterprise. Hamlet, the prince of Denmark, failed to realise the supreme necessity of prompt decision and action, and he had to pay the inevitable penalty; and so did Atan Buragohain; and character is destiny.

Reflection emanates from the passion to do the right thing; but what is the right thing? Different answers will be advanced from different quarters. Expediency will lay down one set of solutions, while absolute justice will dictate another set. The hero, the protagonist will be torn between the horns of a dilemma; and minor and unimportant issues, to the utter oblivion of the imperative ones, will appear before him in full blaze to be vital and incontrovertible. Thus it happened with Atan Buragohain. He had entered into a covenant with Laluk Barphukan and the Gauhati veterans to stand by each other in all emergencies, and how could the Buragohain now send a force to Gauhati against Laluk whom he had once solemnly promised to support? The prime minister stuck fast to his vows, while Laluk acted in a contrary manner. Even the chronicler in those uncritical days had to characterise Atan Buragohain as "an observor of vows," and Laluk Barphukan as "a man of falsehood." The fetish of consistency in political conduct has been regarded as a mark of supineness and imbecility, however high its position may be among the cardinal virtues. The result was Atan Buragohain's imprisonment and execution, and Laluk Barphukan's short-lived aggrandisement though followed by quick retribution.

By upbringing and temperament Atan was a deep-rooted constitutionalist. He would not wear the crown as he was a mere noble without any strain of royal blood in his veins; he refused to encourage the malcontents in their treasonable move to attack the monarch; and he was mortified when the king accused him of violating the ancient usages for his inability to salute the chief queen owing to a peculiar and delicate circumstance.

Atan Buragohain's reflections and observations illustrate his probity and foresight, his love of precedents and his adherence to consistency and truth. These qualities are essential in normal times, but their full-fledged utility in a crisis has not remained unquestioned.

Atan Buragohain's utterances can be divided into three parts: *first,* utterances made on crucial occasions in the way of counsel to the monarchs, or advice and instruction to his colleagues and subordinates; *secondly,* observations recorded in the chronicle written by him where his emphases and comments give us positive clues to his predilections and outlooks; and *thirdly,* his representations in his epistles to foreign courts, where the position taken up by him is the view-point of the government in the formulation of which Atan Buragohain, as prime minister, naturally contributed a major share.

The utterances which take us through the entire gamut of the great prime minister's views on the political issues of the day are here collected for the first time. The utterances of the first category are reproduced below; while the second and the third series are inserted in two Appendices. The background of each utterance of the first category is also briefly indicated so that its real drift may be readily appreciated.

UTTERANCES ON CRUCIAL OCCASIONS

DURING THE REIGN OF KING JAYADHWAJ SINGHA

1. *Atan Khanikar Barua appointed Buragohain:* The appointment of Bahgaria Atan Gohain Khanikar Barua as Buragohain or prime minister of Assam is thus recorded in old Assamese Buranjis or chronicles:

"Having heard of the approach of Nawab Mir Jumla, King Jayadhwaj Singha appointed Manthir Bharali Barua of the Bejdoloi family, as commander-in-chief of the Ahom forces, and despatched him against the Moguls. The Barphukan of Gauhati became unmindful and indifferent to his responsibilities being chagrined at the appointment of Manthir, [who has meanwhile been raised to the rank of Parvatia Phukan]. Similarly, the three Ahom commanders, Baduli

Phukan, Phulbarua Phukan and Lapeti Phukan, stationed at Pancharatna, Baritola and Hatichola, abandoned their respective garrisons, and withdrew themselves to Manaha, saying, "We are not going to fight: let the Hindu Parvatia Phukan do the fighting". The king was duly informed of the three Phukans' withdrawal to Manaha, and he deputed messengers to accuse the Phukans of delinquency and desertion. He then gave to the three Dangarias a banquet at the palace, and despatched Lecham Buragohain of the Kuoingayan family to the front. As the Buragohain was coming down the steps of the king's residence he slipped his foot on the ladder and fell. He however sailed down and halted at Sonai Noi where he died after a short illness. The king then appointed Bahgaria Atan Gohain Khanikar Barua as Buragohain, and despatched him as commander of the army on the north bank: Ao Gohain was also sent to Samdhara on the very same day. The forces of the Ahoms and the Moguls fought at Samdhara both on water and land. The Moguls were about to be routed, when a man belonging to the contingent of Bhotai Deka of Nowgong showed the way to the Moguls by the route through the Diju river."[150]

2. *A contemporary resumé of Mir Jumla's invasion*: An abstract of the details of Mir Jumla's invasion is thus given in an old chronicle: "Having been victorious at Gauhati and Samdhara, Mazum Khan Nawab [Mir Jumla] marched from Sola, and occupied Gargaon. The king [Swargadeo Jayadhwaj Singha] retreated to Namrup, and Mazům Khan Nawab pursued the monarch as far as Bakobari and Tipam. There was also a severe contest at Murkata. The Ahom commanders, including the Buragohain, were routed to the four quarters. The Ahoms used to come out of the woods to attack and kill the enemy. The Maharaja in consultation with the counsellors and ministers, offered his own daughter, and the sons of the three Gohains, and also Maupia Deka, son of the Rajmantri, who in turn was the son of Neog, as hostages to the Moguls,

150. S. K. Bhuyan, *Assam Buranji, S.M.*, p. 94; and MS. Assam Buranji Nos. 5, 8, 10 and 15.

and thereby procured the retirement of Mazum Khan Nawab to Gauhati. The king then came back to Bakata where he gave vent to his anger towards the Baras and Buruks [for their recent delinquency and slackness]. The king also expressed his anger towards Barukial Bargohain, and imprisoned him at his own residence. Then King Jayadhwaj came from Bakata to see the capital, and after his return to Bakata he died at that place in Kati 1585 *Saka*."[151]

3. *Atan Buragohain's optimism*: On Mir Jumla's approach to the capital Gargaon, King Jayadhwaj Singha left the city and fled to the wilds of Namrup. During the flight, many of his camp-followers, including Baduli Phukan, deserted him. The Buragohain despatched messengers to different quarters and brought back the deserters and sent them to the royal camp. The king spoke sorrowfully of his plight. The Buragohain comforted him, saying,—"His Majesty should not be aggrieved over his present condition. Victory and defeat are both to be encountered. When God becomes well disposed, we shall be able to vanquish the Moguls under the inspiration of His Majesty's prowess." The king said in reply,—"O Gohain, your words have brought solace to me."[152]

4. *Treachery of Baduli and Manthir*: During the stay of the Mogul forces at the Ahom capital Gargaon and its vicinity, Baduli Phukan, a leading Ahom noble and commander, went over to the side of the enemy and made friends with the Moguls. Following the example of Baduli, Manthir Bharali Barua started friendly negotiations with the enemy. The Buragohain observed,—"See how the slave of a Hindu is courting his destruction like a Muga silk-worm shrouding itself in the threads emitted from its own mouth." Manthir was executed for his treason.[153]

5. *Open warfare not possible with the Moguls*: The Moguls, during their stay in Assam, were subjected to endless

151. S. K. Bhuyan, *Kachari Buranji*, 1951, p. 50.
152. MS. Assam Buranji No. 15.
153. MS. Assam Buranji, No. 8.

suffering and harassment, but still they remained in occupation of a vast area of the country. Atan Buragohain expressed his regret and said,—"We cannot vanquish the Moguls in open warfare."[154]

6. *A country's preservation is the first necessity*: The Moguls proposed that the Ahoms should deliver three lacs of rupees and ninety elephants and that they should also send as hostages the sons of the Buragohain, the Bargohain, the Barpatra Gohain, and the Rajmantri Phukan, who would be repatriated only after the complete delivery of the above indemnity. The Buragohain said in reply,—"Their proposal is accepted in view of the necessity to protect our country. They in their turn should return to us Baduli and other deserters, as well as the territories upto the western boundaries of Barnadi and Asurar Ali."[155]

7. *Full indemnity to be paid later*: The Moguls, as has been said before, pressed for an indemnity of three lacs of rupees and ninety elephants. To this Atan Buragohain replied,—"Out of fear for the enemy, our subjects have taken shelter in the hills and forests. The Moguls have also taken possession of the treasures deposited in the royal stores. They should first retire from the land, and we shall deliver the indemnity in full after making a proper search for the money and the elephants."[156]

8. *Udaygiri and Astagiri*: The Ahoms agreed to the indemnity of ninety elephants and three lacs of rupees. Mir Jumla asked the Assam king to present a daughter of his to the imperial harem. King Jayadhwaj Singha was severely mortified at having to part with his daughter even after agreeing to pay so much money and deliver so many elephants. Atan Buragohain said to the monarch,—"His Majesty should not be sorry over this arrangement. Our first object is the protection and preservation of the people of the land,

154. MS. Assam Buranji No. 8.
155. MS. Assam Buranji No. 8.
156. MS. Assam Buranji No. 15.

and of its cows, Brahmans and saints. We should promptly deliver the stipulated indemnity, and thereby secure the withdrawal of the enemy from our country. After having established friendly relations with the Mogul emperor we shall ask for the restoration of our old boundaries. For the elephants and money which will remain undelivered at the moment, we shall send the sons and nephew of the Dangarias to remain as hostages with the Moguls. His Majesty the Swarga-Maharaja of Assam is endowed with divine attributes being a lord over men. He is the Padshah of Udaygiri, the mountain of sun-rise; and the Delhi emperor is the Padshah of Astagiri, the mountain of sun-set. The Swargadeo's daughter will adorn the palace of the Padshah of Delhi, and our people will be preserved. This news will gladden the hearts of men in countries far and near, and the Padshah of Delhi will also be happy. It is however left to His Majesty to determine the line of action."[157]

9. *Jayadhwaj Singha's longing to see Gargaon*: After the departure of Nawab Mir Jumla, King Jayadhwaj Singha left his retreat in Namrup, and lived for sometime at Bakata at some distance from the capital Gargaon. The capital had been in occupation of the Muslim invaders for about ten months, and it was a tabu to enter an abandoned city without the sanction of the customary priestly advisers. Atan Buragohain therefore said,—"All right. Let me ask the Deodhais, Bailungs and Daivajnas to find out whether the moment is auspicious for the king's visit to Gargaon."[158]

10. *Death of Jayadhwaj Singha*: The astrologers examined their treatises and gave their verdict in the negative mainly because Gargaon was an abandoned city still unsanctified. The king disregarded the prohibition of his ministers and astrologers, and proceeded from his sick-bed at Bakata towards Gargaon. On arrival at the principal gate

157. S. K. Bhuyan, *Assam Buranji*, S.M., pp. 98-99; MS. Assam Buranji, No. 5.

158. MS. Assam Buranji No. 8.

of the capital, Atan Buragohain and Chengdhara Barbarua said to the monarch,—"It is not proper that His Majesty should enter the capital. His visit has been interdicted by the priests." Being frustrated in his desire to see Gargaon where he had lived in pomp and power for fifteen years, he cast a longing lingering look at the city through the entrance-door, and then began to shed bitter tears, after which he fainted. His malady became aggravated at the shock, and he died at his Bakata camp nine days later.[159]

DURING THE REIGN OF CHAKRADHWAJ SINGHA

11. *Minor faults are to be ignored*: It was the practice of the Raja of Jayantia to send five letters at a time to the Ahom court, the first addressed to the Swargadeo, the second to the Buragohain, the third to the Bargohain, the fourth to the Barpatra Gohain, and the fifth to the Barphukan. The Assam king and his ministers sent five letters in reply all addressed to the Jayantia Raja. Towards the end of King Jayadhwaj Singha's reign and after the departure of Nawab Mir Jumla from Assam, Jasamatta Rai, Raja of Jayantia, suggested that henceforward he should receive the letter from the Assam king, and that the letters of the Assam ministers should be addressed to the corresponding dignitaries of the Jayantia court. This suggestion was broached verbally by the Jayantia envoy Ramai, though it was not embodied in the Raja's epistle the tenor of which was very friendly and sympathetic, inasmuch as regrets were expressed on Assam's discomfiture at the hands of the Moguls, and an offer of substantial military aid was made in the event of renewed hostilities. The suggestion regarding the letters however offended the Assam nobles as it implied a deviation from time-honoured practices; and the Jayantia envoy Ramai was necked out of the reception chamber. King Jayadhwaj Singha died soon after, and was succeeded by Chakradhwaj Singha. The Jayantia envoy was received by the new monarch, and

159. MS. Assam Buranji No. 8.

Atan Buragohain palliated Ramai's offence by saying,—"The letter of the Jayantia Raja is absolutely faultless. A minor blemish should not be taken seriously in the midst of a multitude of redeeming circumstances. The envoy's suggestion may be his own brain-wave. We should give him leave to depart by sending with him our messengers and epistles." At the instance of Atan Buragohain our two envoys Komora and Narayan were sent with Ramai with appropriate epistles and presents.[160]

12. *Imperial envoys Dor Beg and Rustom Beg*: Emperor Aurangzeb sent two *ahadis* to Assam, Dor Beg and Rustom Beg, with the present of a sirpao for the monarch Jayadhwaj Singha. The king was then lying on his sick-bed at Bakata, and as he died soon after the two imperial envoys returned to Gauhati from their camp at Dergaon. They came again with the present and offered it to the new king Chakradhwaj Singha, and insisted on his advancing from the throne a few steps in order to receive the sirpao, and donning it in their presence. Atan Buragohain gave vent to his disapproval of this humiliating proposal, and said,—"Should the slave of a Mogul speak in this fashion? Through our ill-luck, the Moguls have become victorious this once only, and should we, on this account, renounce the time-honoured custom of our land and receive the sirpao of the Mogul Emperor in violation of our age-old practices? Please make over the sirpao to our men, and our Maharaja will wear it afterwards in due manner." The articles were then sent for being deposited in the royal stores.[161]

13. *Emergency knows no law*: King Chakradhwaj Singha held a conference of his ministers to discuss the situation arising from the sirpao, and he said,—"My ancestors on this throne have never been subordinate to others, and I cannot wear this sirpao sent by the Moguls. The envoys should be made to return forthwith from their camp at

160. S. K. Bhuyan, *Jayantia Buranji*, 1937, p. 26.
161. MS. Assam Buranji No. 15.

Dergaon." Atan Buragohain realised that an attitude of hostility at this juncture would prove fatal to the interest of the country, and he said,—"If His Majesty proposes to act in this manner then our devastated country will become still more devastated, and that beyond reparation. During an emergency we must behave in a way as may be dictated by the demands of the situation even though such behaviour may not be sanctioned by customary practices, so that the integrity of our land can be protected and preserved. And hence, the two envoys should be received properly and given handsome presents, and the sirpao should be kept in a suitable place. The envoys should be sent back after we have satisfied them fully."[162]

14. *Atan Buragohain's speech on war provisions*: King Chakradhwaj Singha held repeated meetings of his ministers and nobles to devise ways and means for the speedy recuperation of the country which had now been reduced to virtual vassalage under the Moguls. On one occasion in 1664, he spoke out his feelings as follows,—"My ancestors had never been subordinate to others, and I cannot tolerate this subordination any longer, as death is preferable to a life of subordination to foreigners. I enjoin upon you to give me back my citadel of Gauhati after expelling the Bangals from that place." The Gohains, the Barbarua and the Phukans jointly deliberated on the situation, and declared,—"The ancestors of His Majesty had never been subordinate to foreigners, and our present plight has occurred just for our ill-luck. If the king desires we shall proceed to fall upon Gauhati."

But Atan Buragohain knew full well that immediate resumption of hostilities at that juncture would not be a politic step because the preparations were still negligible and inadequate, and he elaborated his views as follows,—"It is the legitimate duty of a sovereign to restore the old limits of his dominions by defeating and destroying his enemies. His success in war can alone enhance his glory and renown. So,

162. MS. Assam Buranji No. 15.

His Majesty's proposal is just and proper. We have been enjoying absolute and uninterrupted sovereignty from time immemorial, and the high-handed imperiousness of the Moguls has transcended the limits of our forbearance. His Majesty has only voiced the sentiments of his ministers when he declares that we should fall upon the Moguls this very moment if possible. But we must provide the army with sufficient quantity of food provisions and war materials, and must hold in stock sufficient reserve to enable us to replenish the stores of the expeditionary army as soon as they become empty. This task of supplying reinforcements will become a matter of frequent occurrence.

"The country has become depopulated owing to the flight of the villagers from their homes during the last war with Mir Jumla. His Majesty has recently procured their return to their country and settled them in different places. We shall have to enquire whether these people have been able to obtain their rice and food. Rice is the most indispensable of all the necessaries of life; and if it fails nothing will succeed. The officers who have to supply the allotted quota of boats, sailors and provisions, will now assert, on enquiry being made by Your Majesty, that they have got all the equipments ready, and that they will be able to deliver them whenever they will be required to do so. But it may be, they will fail just at the time when we shall badly need them; and nothing will come out even if we kill or chastise the officers in default. We shall have to face dire disaster in the eventual failure of boats and provisions. Unless we have sufficient surplus in the store at present how shall we meet the situation if war has to be prolonged for two or three years? We must take the necessary steps now and arrange for all future contingencies. In the event of failure of supplies even torture or death will not help us in overcoming an emergency.

"A *kari paik,* or a humble subject of Your Majesty, buys an earthen pot to boil his coarse rice for the trifling sum of two *cowries.* Lest the rice and the pot, the total value of which will not, in any case, exceed twenty *cowries* or one pice, be spoiled, he tests the soundness of the vessel by striking it with the fingers at the bottom and the sides two or three times before making the purchase.

"A bird erects a nest on high where she hatches to life her young ones. She takes them round from one bough to another after they have grown up a bit. They are brought down to the ground when they can fly. If they are let loose before they become full-fledged they are eaten up by dogs and jackals. The mother-bird leaves them only after they can pick up and eat their food themselves.

"Similarly, when the three batches of rowers, posted at the middle and the two extremities of Your Majesty's barge, strike their oars simultaneously, the sight becomes beautiful to look at, the oarsmen feel inspirited, the boat moves swiftly, and the helmsman wields the steering with ease and comfort. But, if on the other hand, there is no harmony and synchronism in the strokes of the three batches of rowers, the helmsman is inconvenienced in steering his shaft, the boat does not make any headway, and the spectators are far from being delighted.

"If the king directs his measures on the lines indicated above then only he will be able to vanquish his enemies and extend his territories to the old limits."[163]

15. *Moguls expelled from Gauhati*: During the course of the preparations King Chakradhwaj Singha came out of the palace daily, and supervised the training of the army. To satisfy himself about their efficiency, he made the archers to shoot their arrows, and the musketeers to fire their guns. He also paid frequent visits to the dockyards and arsenals, and saw to the proper storing of the provisions of war. When the preparations were completed, he announced to the ministers and nobles,—"It is my intention now to attack the Bangals. What do you say?" "Yes", concurred Atan Buragohain, "it is now time to attack the enemy, but before doing so we should hold a final manoeuvre of the army, and

163. MS. Assam Buranji Nos. 7 and 15.

it must be done without the knowledge of the enemy." "How do you propose to do it?", asked the monarch. To this the Buragohain replied,—"We should get a road constructed between Teliadonga Pukhuri and Jhanji with the help of our soldiers, and we shall by that means obtain an evidence of their mettle." Being satisfied with the vigour and agility of the soldiers, King Chakradhwaj Singha despatched an army against the Moguls. They sailed down to Gauhati, and during the course of a night they succeeded in dislodging the Moguls from the garrisons at Itakhuli, Pandu and Sarai. The enemy were then pursued up to beyond the river Manaha. Having received the news of victory, King Chakradhwaj Singha shouted out in exultation,—"It is now that I can eat my morsel of food with ease and pleasure."[164]

16. *Reward for loyal services*: The recovery of Gauhati and Western Assam was followed by strenuous preparations to resist the Moguls as renewed hostilities were considered to be inevitable. Atan Buragohain was engaged in the work of bringing the fortifications round Gauhati to a state of perfection. During the construction of a rampart from Asurar Ali to Romoiroka, the Raja of the principality of Rani prayed to Atan Buragohain and Baghchowal Barpatra Gohain for allotting him a plot of land inside the military enclosures where he could keep his family and children in safety and peace, as he would be absent most of the time in the emergency service of the Swargadeo. The Buragohain and the Barpatra Gohain encouraged the Raja by saying,—"If the Raja of Rani can give us satisfaction by the efficient discharge of his duties we shall intercede on his behalf at the feet of His Majesty. Land is after all a very trifling thing: he can expect to be rewarded with more valuable gifts." In the conflict that followed the Rani Raja proved to be a trustworthy and valorous fighter.[165]

17. *Ram Singha demoralised at Assam's fortification*: Emperor Aurangzeb despatched Raja Ram Singha of Amber

164. MS. Assam Buranji No. 15.
165. S. K. Bhuyan, *Assam Buranji, S.M.*, p. 111.

to recover Gauhati from the Ahoms. The Raja expressed his admiration and wonder at the sight of the impregnable wall of defence round Gauhati. It led Atan Buragohain to promulgate this message to the army,—"You are to note carefully that at the sight of our fortifications demoralisation has already crept into the enemy's camp. His enthusiasm is already on the wane." The officers and men gave a valiant response to the message by saying,—"The Barphukan should only remain inviolate in his command, and we shall fight to the last drop of our blood."[166]

18. *Ultimate victory is to be our goal:* Ten thousand Assamese soldiers lay lifeless in the battlefield when they confronted the Rajput cavalry of Raja Ram Singha in the plain of Alaboi near Hajo. The Ahom general Lachit Barphukan sat depressed in his camp at the loss of so many men during the course of a single day. Atan Buragohain raised the drooping spirit of the general by saying, "Well, general, such a reverse should never shake your confidence in our ultimate victory. Eventualities of this nature are normal in a protracted warfare. When you agitate the waters of a pond for catching large fishes, the fish-catchers will be pricked by the thorny scales of the smaller fries. You should judge your success by the number of large catches." The Alaboi disaster, however disheartening it might be, failed to dislodge the Assamese from their determined resistance to the Mogul invaders.[167]

DURING THE REIGN OF UDAYADITYA SINGHA

19. *Gauhati cannot be abandoned:* Raja Ram Singha attempted to obtain the restoration of Gauhati by armed conflicts and diplomatic negotiations. Having failed in the first line of action, he resumed his efforts in the second direction and pressed his demand with redoubled vigour and tact. Some Assamese commanders including Lachit Barphu-

166. S. K. Bhuyan, *Assam Buranji, S.M.*, p. 115
167. MS. Assam Buranji No. 5.

kan appear to have countenanced the Raja's views though the exact reason for the change of attitude is not known. Atan Buragohain dissented from the proposal for the peaceful evacuation of Gauhati, and he expressed his opinion as follows,—"What you have said can be considered in this way also. If you want to abandon Gauhati at this stage, then, what was the good of fighting so long causing such loss to our men and provisions? Ram Singha has pressed his demand for the restoration of the old limits with oaths and promises. Even if we agree, it is not known whether the Mogul emperor will ratify Ram Singha's proposal which is like a highway made of ashes. There is also no guarantee whether Ram Singha's successor in the Assam command will respect the stipulations of his predecessor. What shall we do then? Besides, where shall we go if we abandon Gauhati? We shall have to abandon Gargaon as well, and take shelter in Namrup. We cannot therefore part with Gauhati." The Buragohain's views were approved by the king, and the Ahom commanders of Gauhati remained ready for action.[168]

20. *Ram Singha's admiration of Atan Buragohain*: Raja Ram Singha was full of admiration for the intrepidity and tactfulness of the Assamese commanders, and he asked his envoy Punditrai, who had frequently visited the Ahom camps, to give him an idea of their character and antecedents. To this Punditrai replied,—"The Barpatra Gohain, the Bargohain and the Barphukan have all impressed me as wonderfully capable commanders presenting a rare combination of handsomeness, accomplishment, valour and wisdom. As to the Buragohain, he is young in years, fair and attractive in features, sober and deep in intelligence, dexterous in all matters, and he rivals all others in the soundness of his counsel". Ram Singha commented,—"It is really wonderful that a man can be so intelligent when he is so young". Punditrai added,—"The Buragohain is also an arch-diplomat". Ram Singha concluded,—"Who will be able to cope with such a minister when he comes

168. S. K. Bhuyan, *Assam Buranji, S.M.*, p. 120; MS. Assam Buranji No. 15.

to years? Pride should be the heritage of the land where such a counsellor has taken his birth".[169]

21. *Assam's victory at Saraighat*: In a desperate and final attempt to occupy Gauhati, Raja Ram Singha plied his boats and cavalry across the Brahmaputra. The Assamese watched the progress of the enemy inactively as they were waiting for specific orders to hurl their missiles. The Moguls came very near the sandbanks of Gauhati, but the Buragohain thought it was not yet opportune to launch an attack. He issued this peremptory order,—"Let the Moguls approach Gauhati. No one should now shoot an arrow or fire a musket." Soon afterwards the Buragohain came out fully prepared for action. He issued the signal for attack, and the Assamese boats spread themselves on both sides of the river. In the contest that followed dead bodies floated on the stream like drift-wood in a spate. It was a decisive victory for the Assamese, and the engagement is known as the battle of Saraighat.[170]

22. *Buragohain's attendants punished*: The delay in launching an attack on the invading Mogul forces was construed as an act of hesitancy, and Atan Buragohain's boats were loaded, and they turned their prows eastward so that they might immediately sail up the river when necessary. This was done at the instance of one Hati-Barua Deka. On the successful termination of the contest, the Buragohain accused the Hati-Barua Deka, the water-carriers and cooks by saying,—"How dare you bring such disgrace upon my head? People will think that you loaded my boats having received specific orders?" They were punished accordingly.[171]

23. *An elephant in a rat-hole*: The difficulty of conducting military operations against the interior tribes of Assam was realised by Atan Buragohain. The difficulty was aggra-

169. MS. Assam Buranji No. 15.
170. MS. Assam Buranji No. 15.
171. S. K. Bhuyan, *Assam Buranji*, *S.M.*, p. 122.

vated by the inaccessible character of their habitats and the guerrilla methods of their warfare. In the year 1671 A.D., the Dafalas had raided an Assamese village in the Sabansiri area, and had taken forty persons as captives including a number of women and children. King Udayaditya Singha proposed to send a detachment against the Dafalas under Ghorakowanr Barbarua. But Atan Buragohain opposed the proposal by saying,—"There are instances in the past of the failure of our Dafala expeditions. The Dafala raiders can be captured only if an elephant can enter into a rat-hole. Their suppression can be effected only by tact and diplomacy." In disregard of the Buragohain's advice, a force was despatched against the Dafalas. The results proved unsatisfactory, and Ghorakowanr was dismissed from his office of Barbarua.[172]

DURING THE REIGNS OF RAMADHWAJ SINGHA TO GOBAR RAJA

24. *Machinations and intrigues, 1671-1680*: The decade following the battle of Saraighat, 1671-1680, was a period of internecine strifes and conflicts, brought to being by the imbecility of the monarchs and the ambitions and rivalries of the unscrupulous nobles and ministers. The ablest leaders of Assam were stationed at Gauhati in preparedness for eventual hostilities with the Moguls, and Gargaon became a theatre of contest for power and intrigue. Debera Barbarua was the first to rise to unbridled authority which he exercised in the furtherance of his own nefarious designs. The Gauhati veterans, generally known as Saraighatias, were themselves placed in jeopardy as Debera issued orders, in the name of the king, for their undoing. They in one voice implored Atan Buragohain to take the lead and give them protection from the machinations of Debera. "I shall see to your protection and to the protection of the country," said the Buragohain, "only on the condition that you will implicitly carry out my injunctions, and I in my turn will do all that I can according to my capacity and intelligence." The Saraighatias then took

172. MS. Assam Buranji No. 5.

a solemn vow to support the Buragohain and abide by his decisions in all circumstances.[173]

25. *Bangals inside and outside*: The Saraighatias then sailed up the river towards the capital, under the leadership of the Buragohain, with the avowed object of putting an end to the atrocities of Debera Barbarua and restoring the country to peace and order. Debera collected a small force of Bangals, or up-country soldiers, to resist the Saraighatias. As the party was advancing towards the capital, Debera sent presents to the leaders with a request for returning to their charges as Gauhati lay open to Mogul attacks during their absence. All non-Assamese, specially those cherishing hostile intentions against Assam, were called Bangals, and this term was applied analogically even to those Assamese who had treacherous and disloyal dispositions. The Gauhati leaders rejected forthwith the overtures of Debera, and their feelings found an echo in Atan Buragohain's reply,—"The kingdom of Assam is a veritable casket of gold. The Bangals have entered into this very casket. What is the harm if the outskirts of the dominion come to the possession of the Bangals?" The Buragohain implied that the components of Debera's forces and their master all belonged to the category of Assam's enemy.[174]

26. *Atan Buragohain declines the proffered crown*: Debera was hotly pursued after his defeat at the hands of the Saraighatias. He was subsequently captured, tried and executed, and his nominee on the throne, Gobar Raja, was removed from office and killed. The throne having now fallen vacant, the nobles, including the Phukans of the Gauhati establishment, offered the crown to Atan Buragohain, but he refused the offer in words which will be ever-memorable in the annals of Assam: "The proposal is grossly improper. We are ministers and counsellors from ages past, and we are not entitled to the exalted office of a sovereign. Only

173. MS. Assam Buranji No. 5.
174. S. K. Bhuyan, *Assam Buranji, S.M.*, p. 132.

a scion of the royal family should become a king. A shoulder-pole of reed cannot bear the weight of the thigh of a buffalo, and how can a Sudra wear the sacred thread of a Brahman? There is the prince Arjun Gohain, son of the Namrupia Gohain who is a co-disciple of mine; you should kneel down before him and pay him homage as your sovereign."[175]

DURING THE REIGN OF ARJUN DIHINGIA RAJA.

27. *Rebellion is an impious move, says Atan Buragohain*: In compliance with the wishes of the nobles, Arjun Gohain assumed the reins of government towards the end of June 1676. He showed his gratefulness to Atan Buragohain for his refusal to accept the kingly crown, and for elevating an obscure prince like himself to the office of a monarch. The growing popularity of the Buragohain was however viewed with misgivings by the wives and sons of Arjun Raja as their ears were poisoned by the whisperings of their relative Lao Barchetia. The estrangement between the king and his premier deepened gradually, and Arjun Raja fortified the palace and posted armed guards at the several entrances. The supporters of the Buragohain proposed to attack the king before he completed the preparations for defence. But the premier rejected the proposal, saying,—"What you have said is not dictated by canons of propriety. Your proposal, if carried out, will result in the total annihilation of our families. Rebellion is to be shunned as an impious move. We should, instead, enquire of the monarch as to the person who has sown the seed of this distrust and suspicion."[176]

28. *Atan Buragohain desires peace with the monarch:* In pursuance of his desire to clarify the situation, the Buragohain, accompanied by his colleagues, proceeded to the palace for an interview with the Raja. Atan Buragohain asked the

175. H. C. Goswami, *Purani Assam Buranji*, p. 152; S. K.Bhuyan, *Kamrupar Buranji*, p. 89; MS. Assam Buranji No. 39.

176. S. K. Dutta, *Assam Buranji*, p. 40.

king's private secretary, the Majumdar Barua, to inform the Swargadeo accordingly, saying,—"Well, Majumdar, please tell the Swargadeo as follows: In the primordial days Mahadeva swallowed poison to save the gods and the demons from fear. We have come to meet the king in his palace just to enquire as to who amongst us has said anything untoward to the princes, and when and how we have disobeyed the orders of His Majesty. The person, an enemy of mankind, who has created this misunderstanding should be asked by the monarch to support his allegations by proper evidence. If His Majesty becomes convinced of our guilt we should be dismissed from office and expelled; and if the allegations are found to be baseless then the person who has fabricated them should be removed from his association with His Majesty. If this is done, the king and ourselves will be rid of mutual fears and suspicions. We are prepared to take fresh oaths and repeat our homage to His Majesty in proof of our fidelity. The king should invite us to a friendly banquet, and assure us that we have no reason to fear from his quarter."[177]

29. *Treason is suicidal, says Atan Buragohain*: The petition for an interview was represented by Lao Barchetia as a device for launching a surprise attack upon the monarch, and Arjun Raja refused to give audience to the august deputation. On the other hand, he intensified his preparations for defence, and placed them under the management of his four sons. The prospect of reconciliation having thus failed the Phukans decided to attack the king's palace, and they pressed the Buragohain to accompany them. But he refused to accede to the request, saying,—"It is dire treason, an action destined to destroy the sustenance of our entire families, a step to be shunned at all cost. More specially, to-day is Saturday. So, please retire to your respective quarters for the night, and remain there ready for any eventuality."[178]

30. *Will a husband trust his faithless wife?*—Further entreaties having been of no avail, the Phukans caught hold

177. S. K. Dutta, *Assam Buranji*, p. 40.
178. S. K. Dutta, *Assam Buranji*, p. 40.

of the Buragohain's hand and forced him to the sedan waiting outside. During the melee that followed the king came out of his room, sword in hand, and killed whomever he met. The Buragohain got down from his sedan and loitered in the adjoining open space. Arjun Raja, in the darkness of the night, inflicted a few blows on the sedan thinking that the Buragohain was seated inside. The Buragohain then left the precincts of the palace, and proceeded in a boat to an interior village with a number of his supporters and retainers. The king did not fail to realise that a powerful and popular malcontent like Atan Buragohain at large was a positive menace to his security. Arjun Raja then sent batches of emissaries to the Buragohain's camp assuring him of pardon, with a promise that 'not even a cock-feather of the Buragohain's house will be disturbed.' Atan Buragohain was unwilling to place himself at the mercy of the credulous monarch, and he said to his confidants,—"Do you think that a husband will ever trust his wife, however virtuous she may have been, if she once deviates from the path of conjugal fidelity? I resign myself entirely to the will of God."[179]

31. *The Buragohain's reluctance to return to the capital*: Atan Buragohain assumed outwardly an attitude of humility and repentance, and said to the Gohains who had been sent by Arjun Raja to request him to return to the capital,—"I am interested that the Maharaja has asked me to return, and the Gohains have also spoken in the same vein. But I have gravely offended the monarch, and how can he be expected to forgive me? I would request my colleagues to take rest in their camp to-day, and we shall resume our talks tomorrow."[180]

32. *The Saraighatias resent the king's conduct*: Meanwhile, Atan Buragohain had deputed agents to Gauhati to inform the Saraighatias about the happenings at the capital, and to come to his aid in remembrance of their vows of mutual

179. MS. Assam Buranji No. 39.
180. MS. Assam Buranji No. 15.

support. The message of the Buragohain ran as follows: "When Debera indulged in killing men ruthlessly, my colleagues at Gauhati entered into a solemn covenant not to desert each other. On this assurance I had Debera executed, and the Dihingia prince placed on the throne, and thereby preserved the government. A year has not elapsed, and the king now wants to kill me! I have left everything at the capital, and have now taken refuge at Salkowanr. I shall survive only if my compatriots now come to my rescue in remembrance of the respect for their manhood, the dictates of truth and their solemn promises". The Saraighatias easily anticipated that the plight to which the Buragohain had been reduced would befall them as well. They repeated their oaths, and under the leadership of Laluk Barphukan, brother of Lachit Barphukan, they proceeded to the camp of the Buragohain.[181]

33. *The Buragohain awaits the arrival of the Saraighatias*: The prime minister had received intelligence of the approach of the Gauhati commanders; and emboldened by this prospect, he dismissed the king's delegates with this reply,— "I am living here in retirement out of fear for His Majesty. How long can I thus remain without saluting him? I am waiting for the subsidence of the king's anger. I have received reports of the approaching arrival of the Gauhati nobles; let me have an opportunity of hearing their views."[182]

34. *Atan Buragohain enters the capital victorious*: The Gauhati nobles, accompanied by a considerable force, arrived soon after at the Buragohain's camp. They deliberated on the situation and decided upon attacking the royalist forces posted at different garrisons in the areas round the capital. In the contest that followed the royalists were defeated, and Arjun Raja took shelter in his palace. The door of the capital was in charge of Kirkiria Barbarua, a member of the well-known Ahom Rangachila Duara family. He put up a brief

181. S. K. Bhuyan, *Assam Buranji, S.M.*, p. 134.
182. MS. Assam Buranji No. 5.

resistance, but he had to give way, and the door was flung open for the entrance of the victorious nobles led by Atan Buragohain. The Buragohain then exclaimed,—"We have got possession of the *duar*, after Duara [literally, a door-keeper, here meaning Kirkiria Duara] has opened it." It was decided to depose Arjun Raja, and mutilate him to render him unfit for the throne.[183]

35. *Atan Buragohain declines the crown a second time*: Atan Buragohain then discussed with the nobles about the selection of a new king. His supporters pressed him to wear the kingly crown pointing out the consequences of his refusal to do so on the previous occasion. They said,—"We had previously offered the sovereignship to Your Excellency. But, as you refused to accept it we were plunged into a disastrous calamity. We now accept you as our monarch." To this Atan Buragohain replied,—"You had previously promised, after taking due oaths, to act according to my injunctions, and now I want you to act as I ask you to do. About your intention to make me king,—I would say that the offer is a preposterous one. I am not entitled to hold this exalted office. A scion of the royal family can alone become a monarch, and similarly, the descendant of a saint can alone become a saint. Others are not entitled to these positions. There is a descendant of Deka Raja; I wish to make him king. I solicit your views on the subject." The nobles having agreed to the proposal of the Buragohain, the prince concerned was brought from his home at Charaideo Parvat and placed on the throne. The new king was known as Parvatia Raja.[184]

36. *Bhatdhara punished for his brutalities*: Two Phukans, named Bhatdhara and Betmela, were asked to carry out the mutilation of Arjun Raja. Bhatdhara, in an excess of frenzy, battered the deposed monarch to death after having subjected him to brutal tortures. Bhatdhara capped his inhumanity by outraging the queen just widowed. The

183. S. K. Bhuyan, *Assam Buranji, S.M.*, p. 136.
184. MS. Assam Buranji No. 5.

Phukans then assembled at the council chamber of the Buragohain. Having heard of the excesses committed by Bhatdhara, Atan Buragohain ordered,—"It is my express command that Bhatdhara should get out of this chamber, and sit in the space outside."[185]

DURING THE REIGN OF PARVATIA RAJA.

37. *A father's prostration before his daughter*: The new monarch, generally known as Parvatia Raja, bestowed honours and presents on Atan Buragohain for elevating him to the throne, after having sacrificed it for himself. Parvatia Raja married the daughter of the Buragohain and made her his Barkuanri or chief consort. According to the practice of the Ahom court, the three cabinet ministers, the Buragohain, Bargohain and Barpatra Gohain, had to pay their homage to the Barkuanri by kneeling down before her. As a loving and dutiful daughter, the Barkuanri was reluctant to see her father prostrating before her, and she therefore left her seat when the Buragohain entered the room to perform the obeisance. Having heard this the king accused the Buragohain of infringement of a time-honoured practice, specially as the prime minister was the custodian of the precedents and usages of the land. The king moreover referred in this connection to the Buragohain's recent participation in the monarchical changes. The Buragohain replied to the charges as follows: "We have made him the dispenser of our bodies and our minds, and we have knelt down before him accordingly. We went to pay our homage to the queen as required by custom, but she left her seat on our approach. Whom are we to salute in an empty place? This has been our only transgression; otherwise we are not the men to relinquish the usages of the past. Let His Majesty appoint another day for the salutation ceremony, and we shall proceed accordingly to pay our homage." The delicacy of the Barkuanri in receiving her father's prostration was obviated by the placing of the sacred book *Ratnavali* on the tray before her. The queen's filial

185. MS. Assam Buranji No. 15.

conscience was eased by the thought that her father's salutation was aimed at the scripture, and Parvatia Raja was satisfied that the queen was the recipient of the homage.[186]

38. *Mecha Barbarua dismissed and expelled*: Another consort of Parvatia Raja was the daughter of Mecha Barbarua, a member of the Ahom Rangachila Duara family. She was a favourite of the monarch, and encouraged by this circumstance, Mecha slighted the Buragohain and his colleagues, and cast aspersions upon their spiritual leaders. He also carried on liaison with ex-queens and daughters of priests. He even ceased to attend the official dinners at the residence of the prime minister. The Phukans complained to the monarch of Mecha's arrogance, and following a secret hint from the king they caught hold of Mecha, and produced him before the Buragohain during the progress of a banquet. Atan Buragohain shouted out,—"What is this change you are up to?" The Phukans gave vent to their reluctance to allow Mecha to continue as Barbarua. "If you do not like Mecha, I shall inform His Majesty accordingly", the Buragohain observed. He then reported to the king: "Mecha Barbarua ridicules us as disciples of the Gosains of the Thakuria denomination. He is besides living as husband and wife with the widow of the younger Charingia Raja and the daughter of a Deodhai. It is we who have made him Barbarua. His Majesty should now remove him from that office." Mecha was accordingly dismissed, and ordered to live at his home at Laphabari in Dihing.[187]

39. *Internal solidarity must be maintained*: The dismissal and expulsion of Mecha produced a new situation in the political affairs of Assam. The ex-Barbarua could neither forgive the monarch, nor the prime minister. A murderous attack was made on Parvatia Raja one night, and Mecha was suspected as having engineered it. The suspicions were confirmed by Mecha's flight to Gauhati, where he circulated

186. MS. Assam Buranji Nos. 5 and 39.
187. MS. Assam Buranji No. 15.

exaggerated reports of the happenings at the capital. The king's order to send back Mecha was ignored by Laluk Barphukan. The defiant and disloyal attitude of the Barphukan gradually became apparent, and the nobles at the capital requested the Buragohain to despatch a force for the capture of the Barphukan. The suggestion was not favoured by the Buragohain who said,—"Whatever differences there might exist amongst us, it is improper to send a force to Gauhati to capture the Barphukan, as our enemies the Moguls are loitering at the frontier with hostile intentions. Such a step will give a fillip to the designs of the enemy. There is also the possibility of a reverse in the event of our bad luck. We shall do whatever is necessary under the circumstance in consultation with the king. We shall meet him together."[188]

40. *Assam's taunting reply to Azamtara's demand*: Atan Buragohain's mind was then filled with apprehension of the possibility of renewed hostilities with the Moguls. About the year 1677, Sultan Azamtara, the third son of Emperor Aurangzeb, encamped for some time at Rajmahal on his way to Dacca to join his new appointment as governor of Bengal. From that place he instructed Nawab Shaista Khan to write to Laluk Barphukan for the restoration of Gauhati to the Moguls. A letter to that effect was accordingly written by Abu Nasr Khan, son of Shaista Khan, on the authority of his father. It was accompanied by a sirpao, and the name of Shaista Khan was inscribed in that letter above that of Laluk Barphukan. The letter was forwarded by the Barphukan to Atan Buragohain, who advised the former to send a reply to the following purport: "Sewn garments were never before sent to us. Why are they sent now in violation of the age-old practices? Shaista Khan's letter to the Barphukan should have been written in recognition of their equal status. Why should be Barphukan's name be written below that of Shaista Khan? The territories referred to by the Sultan do not belong to the Moguls. They are enjoyed by those on whom God is pleased to bestow them for the time being. The

188. MS. Assam Buranji No. 5.

prince's claim is therefore unjust and improper, and has obviously been made without due deliberation. He has also made mention of horses and elephants in order to give us an impression of his military strength; but these animals do not deserve any mention at all, for the horses may be horses to him, but to us they are as useless as deer, for they cannot shoot arrows, nor can they fire guns."[189]

41. *Laluk is a knowing man, says Atan Buragohain*: Laluk Barphukan had been planning meanwhile to check the growing power of the Buragohain, and he received an encouragement in the demand of Sultan Azamtara for the restoration of Gauhati. He then made overtures to Dacca offering the surrender of Gauhati on condition that he would be made Raja of Assam, and presented with a cash reward of rupees four lacs. His main supporter was his uncle Baduli who had been living at Dacca as a protegé of the Bengal Subedar. Atan Buragohain had received reports of these secret negotiations between Laluk Barphukan and Sultan Azamtara, but he did not consider the despatch of a force against Laluk to be desirable at the moment; and he therefore suppressed his reaction to the Phukans' proposal so that no one could get an inkling of the disruptive developments at Gauhati. To the Phukans who had communicated to him the treacherous move of Laluk, the Buragohain simply replied,—"The Barphukan is a knowing man, why should he act in this manner? The Phukans have perhaps been misinformed by their reporters."[190]

42. *Vulnerable defences in the environs of Gargaon*: Atan Buragohain's mind was working at that time in a different direction. He had realised the imperative necessity of instituting defensive measures for opposing the enemy in the districts round the capital. The defences of Assam ended practically at Samdhara, near Tezpur, and it was for this

189. S. K. Bhuyan, *Kamrupar Buranji*, p. 90; MS. Assam Buranji No. 6.

190. S. K. Bhuyan, *Assam Buranji, S.M.*, p. 138.

reason, thought the Buragohain, that the Moguls under Mir Jumla could advance easily towards the capital after the fall of Gauhati, Samdhara and Simaluguri forts. He therefore said to the Phukans who had pressed for the despatch of a force against Laluk,—"Let us first erect a rampart extending up to the Dihing river, and consolidate our position in that fortification. Having done this we shall be invulnerable to an eventual attack from the Gauhati side."[191]

43. *Construction of Chintamani rampart*: Atan Buragohain then submitted his scheme to Parvatia Raja, saying,—"Being afraid of punishment for committing the murderous assault upon the king, the elder Duara [Mecha Ex-Barbarua] has fled to Gauhati. We have also heard of untoward developments at that place. We do not see any place for defending our country if we once slip our hands and feet at Gauhati and Samdhara. During the last invasion of the Moguls we had no position of defence after the fall of Samdhara. I propose to construct a rampart linking Tulasijan and the Dihing in order to defend the country in the event of an attack. I am waiting for His Majesty's approval." The monarch having sanctioned the construction, the Buragohain employed men to do the work as quickly as possible. The rampart was called Laimatigarh, but it was known more popularly as Chintamanigarh.[192]

44. *Atan Buragohain's vacillation in attacking the Moguls*: Laluk Barphukan's treacherous negotiations for the surrender of Gauhati having matured meanwhile, Sultan Azamtara deputed Nawab Mansur Khan to receive Gauhati from the hands of its Ahom viceroy. It was duly reported to Atan Buragohain who said,—"Thanks for the information. After we receive corroboration of the report we shall ourselves proceed to Gauhati, and others will also go. Let the son of the Padshah or the Padshah himself come, why should we allow him to advance?"[193]

191. MS. Assam Buranji No. 15.
192. S. K. Bhuyan, *Assam Buranji, S.M.*, p. 138.
193. S. K. Bhuyan, *Assam Buranji, S.M.*, p. 139.

45. *The Moguls' entry must first be ascertained:* Reports were then received at the capital about the entrance of the Moguls into Kamrup. The king asked the Buragohain to despatch immediately men and provisions to Gauhati. As unfounded reports of this nature were received in the past, the Buragohain wanted positive confirmation of the same. He therefore said to the king,—"If the advance of the Moguls be a fact, the provisions alone will not be able to do the fighting. Should we not also go to the place? We should first ascertain whether the Moguls have really come or not."[194]

46. *The Moguls came on express invitation:* The agents of the Buragohain who had been deputed to Gauhati for this purpose returned with the information that the Mogul forces under Nawab Mansur Khan had advanced into the interior of Kamrup. "If the Moguls had come of their own accord," observed Atan Buragohain and the other Gohains, "they would have rushed to occupy Gauhati. What are they doing by lingering in the heart of the country? From this it appears they have come on express invitation." This is the last utterance of Atan Buragohain as recorded in contemporary Assamese chronicles.[195]

47. *The end of Atan Buragohain:* As prearranged, Laluk Barphukan surrendered Gauhati to Azamtara's deputy Nawab Mansur Khan. He then sailed up to Kaliabar where he began to act in a most autocratic manner. The king's forces under Atan Buragohain, having advanced to Duimunisila, near Kaliabar, encountered a detachment of the Barphukan at that place. The royalists were defeated, and the Buragohain sought refuge from place to place. He was finally captured and imprisoned at Kaliabar along with his brother the Naobaicha Phukan.

Laluk Barphukan then went to the capital, and explained to Parvatia Raja the real motive of his actions. After Laluk's return to Gauhati, the king realised the gravity of the situation

194. MS. Assam Buranji, No. 5.
195. MS. Assam Buranji No. 5.

brought about by the machinations of Laluk Barphukan, and he planned to mete out condign punishment to the traitor, saying,—"Who is this man that he surrenders Gauhati to the Moguls, imprisons my Buragohain and the Phukans, and dismisses and appoints my officers in league with Mecha Phukan?" In accusing Marangi Barbarua and Ramdhan Phukan, two staunch supporters of Laluk, the king said,—"The beautiful land of Kamrup is my dominion, and it has been acquired with great difficulty and suffering. Under whose orders did you relinquish such a territory in favour of the Moguls? Besides, who appointed you to these high offices? It appears that the slaves of Lukhurakhuns have become all-in-all, and I am nobody."[196]

Laluk sailed up again to the capital where he began to play the role of a virtual dictator. Parvatia Raja was deposed and killed, and a stripling of fourteen was placed on the throne. The new monarch was generally known as Lora Raja, or the boy king, on account of his tender years.

As for Atan Buragohain, we had better tell the story in the words of the contemporary chroniclers.—

In *one* chronicle we read: "Parvatia Raja then despatched a force against Laluk under Betmela Phukan, Tepartalia Phukan, and Mau Gohain Phukan, with Bahgaria Buragohain at the head. The contingent sailed down the river and halted at Sola [Biswanath]. The Barphukan then sent a message to the Buragohain asking him to stay at Sola, and send up the Phukans with their men and provisions to join the forces of the Barphukan. Buragohain Dangaria, in pursuance of the promises of old, sent [Govinda] Kalanchu Phukan, Tepartalia Phukan, and Betmela Phukan to the company of Sola [Laluk Barphukan]. On their arrival at Sola's camp at Kaliabar, he took the three Phukans inside on the pretext of having a conference, and imprisoned them, and took away by force the soldiers under their command. Kalanchu Phukan bit the flesh of his arm, and exclaimed,—"Just see, we are perishing

196. S. K. Bhuyan, *Assam Buranji, S.M.*, p. 142.

like women having listened to the advice of the Buragohain. It is my life's regret that I have not been able to drop on the ground the head of Sola." Having received this news, the Buragohain Dangaria left his camp and concealed himself in the granary belonging to the house of a Brahman Saikia of Gozlong who was his retainer. Sola Barphukan then instituted a search for the Dangaria, and succeeded in capturing the Buragohain and his son, Tepartalia Phukan and his son, Betmela Phukan and his son, the Naobaicha Phukan who was the elder brother of the Buragohain and his son, and got them all killed."[197]

In *another* chronicle we read: "At that time, Metekial Sola Barphukan [Laluk Barphukan], having entered into a conspiracy with the Moguls, surrendered the fort of Saraighat [Gauhati] without any war. At the same time he sent an information to the king about the arrival of the Moguls. Bahgaria Buragohain then sent a force under the command of Betmela Phukan, Tepartalia Phukan, and Mau Gohain Phukan, with Phukan-Gohain as their chief. They sailed down and halted at the place called Sola. Sola Barphukan then left Saraighat, and sailed up the river Brahmaputra. The Buragohain, in observance of his vows, refrained from entering into a quarrel with the Barphukan, who was a man of falsehood. Sola captured them all by a strategem. The Moguls came, and made nice utterances. The Barphukan then killed [a mistake, not as yet] the Buragohain and his son, Tepartalia Phukan and his son, Betmela Phukan and his son, the Buragohain's elder brother the Naobaicha Phukan and his son. The Barphukan then elevated the young Samaguria prince to the throne."[198]

In a *third* chronicle we read: "Laluk Barphukan then brought one Samaguria prince and placed him on the throne on Thursday, the fifth Aghon, 1601 *saka*. A few days later, Parvatia Raja was killed under the orders of the new monarch. He had reigned for three years, three months and five days.

197. MS. Assam Buranji No. 39.
198. MS. Assam Buranji No. 11.

The first residence of the Samaguria Raja [Lora Raja Sulikpha Ratnadhwaj Singha] was at Lechang. After this, Sola Phukan obtained the orders of the king for the despatch of two emissaries to Kaliabar, namely, Metekatalia Khona Gohain Chaudang Barua of the Bargohain family, and Khamchang Gohain Chaurukar Saikia of the Barpatra Gohain's family. By despatching these two officers, the Barphukan effected the execution of the Buragohain and his elder brother the Naobaicha Phukan and his nephew. The Buragohain's son Langkham Deka was brought up and killed at his residence at Bahgara. Langi Gohain of the Dilihial family was now made Buragohain. A camp was then erected for the monarch at Alikekuri of Meteka, and Sola Phukan continued to live in his residence as before."[199]

In a *fourth* chronicle we read: "The Samaguria prince was placed on the *henglang* [throne] at Barnaosal, and the nobles paid their homage by kneeling down before him seven times. The new king resided at the newly constructed camp at Lechang. After this, Sola Barphukan said to the monarch,—"The Bahgaria Buragohain and a large number of persons have been imprisoned at Kaliabar. What is His Majesty's intention concerning these prisoners?" The king ordered that they should be executed. The Buragohain was accordingly killed at the Solal Gohain's compound at Kaliabar by being throttled with a *tangali* [scarf hanging from the waist]. The Naobaicha Phukan, the elder brother of the Buragohain, and his brother and son were similarly killed. The orders for execution were carried out by two officers despatched from the capital, namely, the Chaudang Barua who was a member of the Metekial Bargohain family, and Rangason Gohain Chaurukar Saikia who was a member of the Banchengia Barpatra Gohain family. Langkham, the eldest son of the Buragohain, was taken up and killed at his residence at Bahgara. Langi Dighala Gohain of the Dilihial family was made Buragohain. In Baisakh 1602 *Saka,* the king was brought to the new camp at Meteka. Laluk Phukan,

199. MS. Assam Buranji No. 15.

now appointed Rajmantri Naobaicha Phukan, continued to live at his new residence at Meteka. After this, Kamal Kataki of Abhaypur was deputed to Kaliabar to bring the two Dangarias to the capital. In the same month of Baisakh, the bald-headed daughter of Sola Phukan, aged seven years, was made the Barkuanri. The daughter of Bhatdhara was then in her pre-puberty [guri-juvat] stage; she was now made Parvatia Kuanri. Chakrapani Barbarua was released from prison and made to reside in his own residence. Kaupatia Bhandari Barua was expelled after having his nose and ears sliced off; a member of the Bejdoloi family [Rangacharan] was appointed Bhandari Barua in his place."[200]

The account in a *fifth* chronicle is coloured by a tinge of regret: "Lora Raja then erected a residence at Lechang. His Barkuanri was a daughter of the Barphukan [Laluk], aged five years; and the Parvatia Kuanri, a daughter of Bhatdhara, aged twelve. On Friday, in Aghon 1601 *Saka*, the king came to Meteka. The Buraphukan erected an earthen wall round his compound, mounted guns, and lived cautiously. The Phukans and the Baruas used to serve in the residence of the monarch and also of Laluk. The Buragohain who had been confined at Kaliabar was killed under royal orders with his whole family by Khona Gohain of the Bargohain *phoid* who had been deputed to that place for this specific purpose. All did as the Buraphukan made them to do."[201]

200. MS. Assam Buranji No. 8.
201. S. K. Bhuyan, *Assam Buranji, S.M.*, pp. 142-43.

CHAPTER XX

CONCLUSION

The age of Atan Buragohain Rajmantri Dangaria is crowded with events of momentous significance to the destiny of the Assamese people. They emanated from a clash between the grim determination of the Assamese to maintain the integrity and independence of their country, and an equally insistent ambition of the Moguls to unfurl the Timurid banner over the fair and prosperous valley of the Brahmaputra. The study of these events gives us a glimpse into the redeeming traits of the Assamese people as well as of the weak points in their political behaviour. Such a study will lead to the strengthening of the strong points, and elimination of the dark ones, so that we may repeat the triumphs we had achieved, and avoid the blunders we had committed during our struggle with the Moguls.

Heroic exploits in the sphere of diplomacy, organisation and leadership figured side by side with mean intrigues and conspiracies. The spirit of Satan hovered over the land till the hand of justice brought the wicked to inevitable retribution, and man's noble soul returned once more to dominate the political scene. The events of the period present before us a panorama of the interaction of human passions,—wounded pride and suppressed jealousy, enkindled wrath and determined vengeance, and a ruthless search for opportunities of aggrandisement and seizure of power. We also witness the final entry of the tottering nation into the paradise of national consciousness.

Throughout the vicissitudes of the period, the Assamese were governed by their fundamental conception that reverses are bound to occur in the long history of a nation, and that we should take our inspiration from the great deeds which the nation has accomplished. As in the case of an individual, a nation in its collective capacity should not be down-and-out at the touch of a misfortune however grave and overwhelming it may be; on the other hand, it should adopt vigilant measures to rehabilitate itself so that it may regain its lost prestige and power. These sentiments constituted in brief Assam's policy towards the Moguls, and the success of this policy earned for them the observation of an English writer recorded about a hundred years ago,—"The Assamese were to the Moslems what the Numidians and Mauritanians were to the old Romans—*genus insuperbile bello*".[202]

The principle of recuperation comes out prominently in the letters exchanged between the rulers of Assam and Cooch Behar after the departure of Nawab Mir Jumla from Assam. "You should not feel distressed at having temporarily lost your dominion", wrote Raja Prananarayan of Cooch Behar to Swargadeo Jayadhwaj Singha of Assam, "since Ramchandra, Suratha and Yudhisthira could not escape such calamities. But their prestige has not been affected as they regained their kingdoms by dint of their exertions". To this King Jayadhwaj Singha replied,—"A king, when confronted by a powerful enemy, has no other alternative but to gain time by entering into a treaty. Appropriate measures can be adopted in due course only if there subsist the monarch and his country". Jayadhwaj Singha wrote again a few months later,—"Even when the sun is once eclipsed does it not make its appearance again?". The same determination was voiced by Jayadhwaj Singha's successor Chakradhwaj Singha when he wrote to Raja Prananarayan,—"You know for yourself all about the manner in which we have repeatedly dealt heavy blows upon the Moguls. If God has inflicted on us a reverse on this single occasion, does it mean that we shall be subjected to discomfiture again?". More than a hundred years afterwards a leading Ahom official, Kirti Chandra Barbarua, thus expounded Assam's policy of recuperation,—"When a king becomes subjected to the monarch of another country, diplomatic measures should be adopted so that the

202. *Calcutta Review*, 1867, Vol. XLVI, p. 78, article entitled *The Religious History of Assam.* The writer's name is not known.

conqueror may return to his own kingdom. On his retirement, the subdued prince should remain in preparedness with his army; and when opportunities present themselves he should act promptly and reinstate himself in his lost suzerain power".[203]

This policy of recuperation was carried into effect in a number of occasions during the period under review. The river Karatoya was the western boundary of Kamarupa in ancient Assam, and during the reign of Dihingia Raja, A.D. 1497-1539, the Ahoms conquered the territories up to that river; but having found it inconvenient they retracted further east, and fixed the Manaha river as the western boundary of their kingdom. During the reign of King Pratap Singha, 1603-41, after a protracted war with the Moguls, the boundaries between Assam and Mogul India were pushed further to the east, and they rested at Asurar Ali on the south bank and the river Barnadi on the north. Swargadeo Jayadhwaj Singha took advantage of the virtual evacuation of the Mogul garrisons as Sultan Shuja, governor of Bengal, had taken most of the soldiers and the *nawarra* with him for confronting his rival brothers in a bid for the throne of Delhi. "The whole territory up to the Karatoya river", said the king, "was conquered by our Gargayan Deka Raja [son of Dihingia Raja] who erected a temple and a tank there as a mark of victory. It subsequently fell into the hands of the Badshah. We should seize this opportunity and take it." The intrepid generals of King Jayadhwaj Singha then recovered the territory up to the Manaha river, and carried the banner of victory up to the neighbourhood of Dacca. Cooch Behar had similarly thrown off the Mogul yoke and assumed complete independence.

These affronts induced Emperor Aurangzeb to depute Nawab Mir Jumla to re-establish Mogul prestige in Eastern India. The Moguls occupied Cooch Behar, and then marched into Assam. Mir Jumla had comparatively a smooth sailing

203. MS. Assam Buranji No. 23.

up to the capital Gargaon. The eyes of the Assamese were now opened to the humiliation and disaster that confronted them. They organised a guerrilla warfare, consisting of ambushes and sudden attacks, thereby putting the invaders to unending sufferings. Mir Jumla however succeeded, by virtue of his unrivalled diplomacy, more than by his military strength, in compelling the Assam Raja to pay a heavy indemnity and tribute, and cede the territories up to the river Manaha. The Ahoms were thus reduced to a state of subordination to the Moguls.

King Jayadhwaj Singha, after having returned to his camp in the neighbourhood of Gargaon instituted measures of rehabilitation, but he died a few months later, his death-bed request to his ministers being,—"You should exert yourselves to extract the spear of humiliation thrust by the Moguls upon the bosom of our country." His successor King Chakradhwaj Singha shouted out from the throne,—"Death is preferable to a life of subordination to foreigners." Preparations were then made on an elaborate scale to expel the Moguls from Gauhati and Kamrup; and four years after Mir Jumla's departure from Assam, the Ahoms succeeded in recovering their lost dominions.

Emperor Aurangzeb then despatched a powerful army under the leadership of the far-famed general Raja Ram Singha, son of Mirza Raja Jai Singha of Amber, to invade Assam and reoccupy Gauhati. But the Mogul forces were completely crushed at the battle of Saraighat fought on the waters of the Brahmaputra at Gauhati. The Rajput chief halted for five years at the frontier Mogul outpost at Rangamati for an opportunity to re-attack Assam. But the Assamese were united to a man, and Ram Singha had to return to Delhi crestfallen and depressed. The Ahoms continued in possession of Gauhati till the year 1679.

The best leaders of Assam were concentrated at Gauhati in order to thwart an eventual Mogul attack. Their absence gave an opportunity to self-seeking nobles at the capital Gargaon to indulge in machinations and intrigues reducing the monarchs to mere puppets and the officers to a set of time-serving sycophants. The arch-villain was one Debera who had raised himself to the office of Barbarua. The Gauhati nobles, under the leadership of the prime minister Atan Buragohain, then marched up to the capital, brought the miscreants to book, and restored the country to peace and orderly government. They then returned to their respective military charges in Western Assam. The most notable event of the period was the offer of the crown to Atan Buragohain, and his refusal to wear it on the plea that he was not of royal descent.

Atan Buragohain administered the affairs of the capital with justice and moderation, gaining the appreciation of the king and the nobles, and the love and affection of the people. But the atmosphere was surcharged with the effluvia of conspiracy; and the nobles had discovered in factions an opportunity for quick rise to fortune and to power; and a strong and efficient prime minister was regarded as an insurmountable obstacle for the ascendency of underserved merit. Atan Buragohain's motives were misrepresented to the Gauhati nobles who, despite their lack of conviction, were persuaded to support their leader Laluk Barphukan in opposing the growing power of the prime minister. The Buragohain had the good-will of the king and the nobles behind him, but the Gauhati nobles were in command of the army; still, then the Buragohain could have crushed the conspiracy of Laluk Barphukan, but, he feared that any discord in the Assamese camp might give an encouragement to the Moguls who were still lurking in the frontier. Besides, the monarch being a weakling, the Buragohain would not get from him that amount of support which was necessary for the successful solution of the tangle.

Laluk Barphukan then turned to the Mogul Subedar of Bengal, Sultan Azamtara, for military aid to crush his opponents including the Buragohain. He played upon the Subedar's ambition to occupy Gauhati, a task which could not be accomplished by Raja Ram Singha. Besides, Sultan Azamtara had married the Barphukan's niece Ramani Gabharu, and he was naturally anxious to see his uncle-in-law placed in a high position. It was secretly arranged that the Barphukan would receive four lakhs of rupees as consideration for the surrender of Gauhati, and that he would be made Raja of Eastern Assam in recognition of his services to the Moguls. Things happened according to plan. Gauhati passed into the hands of the Moguls, and the Barphukan became all-in-all at the capital. The lives of princes and nobles were insecure, and the people groaned under the burden of oppression and tyranny. The Buragohain had already been liquidated, and similarly the rival princes who were likely to oppose the Barphukan's exercise of his unbridled power. He used to live and go about armed all the time, but Nemesis was working invisibly for the undoing of Laluk Barphukan. A couple of desperadoes entered into his bed-chamber one night, and killed him while asleep.

The plight of the country roused the patriotic instincts of the nobles. Gauhati and Western Assam were under the Moguls, and the government was completely shattered. If this sorry state of affairs was allowed to continue, the country would be plunged into irreparable ruin and destruction. Having foreseen the consequences, the nobles conferred secretly, and marched with the army to Kaliabar on the pretext of attacking the Moguls who were intrenched at Gauhati.

Swargadeo Chakradhwaj Singha's successors were all imbeciles hardly capable of exercising their sovereign power with any degree of authority, and the consequence was its usurpation by ministers and nobles. The king set up on the throne by Laluk Barphukan was a stripling of fourteen, and was generally known as Lora Raja, or the boy-king, on account of his tender years. He was the husband of two girls, one aged five, and the other aged twelve. The first was the daughter of Laluk Barphukan, and the second the daughter of his brother Bhatdhara. As the authority of the monarch was necessary for sanctioning executions, the Barphukan easily procured royal consent for his persecutions and tortures. The continuance of such a monarch was therefore regarded by the patriotic nobles as a principal impediment to the launching of measures for the country's rehabilitation.

Remote from the capital, and at a distance from the sight of the monarch and the associates of Laluk Barphukan, the nobles gathered at Kaliabar, and deliberated coolly and dispassionately upon the affairs of the kingdom. "How can an imbecile monarch protect his country"?—formed the main subject of their discussion. They therefore brought before them Prince Gadapani, who had been wandering as a fugitive to escape from slaughter at the hands of Laluk, and declared him to be the king of Assam. The prince had already acquired a reputation for physical vigour, and firmness and strength of character. They took Gadapani with them to Gargaon and installed him on the throne after having deposed Lora Raja.

Gadapani, now known as Gadadhar Singha, fulfilled the expectations of the nobles. The ravages of the preceding nine years had perverted the character and temper of the people. But once peace and tranquillity were restored, and recalcitrant tendencies suppressed with a strong hand, their sanity and foresight were restored alongwith. Nature in her turn did not cease to bestow her bounties upon Assam. The fertility of its soil, its copious rainfall, its numerous streams and rivers, its green forests, its sandbanks sparkling with gold-dusts, and its abundance of crops combined with an efficient administrative machinery, made recuperation an easy matter. After a year of his accession, King Gadadhar Singha, succeeded in expelling the Moguls from Gauhati, and the river Manaha remained the western boundary of Assam till the advent of the British. The stability introduced by King Gadadhar Singha in the affairs of Assam enabled his son and successor to dream of conquering Mogul India.

Now, let us turn to the unpalatable chapter of delinquency and treachery. It begins with the wilful desertion of the charges entrusted to the Ahom viceroy of Lower Assam, Rajasahur Chengmun Barphukan and his subordinate commanders, simply because a non-Ahom, Manthir Bharali Barua, was appointed general of the army over their head. Such an appointment, made at a critical juncture like Mir Jumla's invasion, was no doubt a serious blunder: the king ought to have anticipated the resentment of the Ahom commanders who were highly sensitive to their rights and privileges. Besides, these very Ahom commanders had just triumphed over the Moguls by recovering Kamrup and overrunning the territories up to the neighbourhood of Dacca. They were not expected to take their orders ungrudgingly from a new-fangled non-Ahom commander who had previously been a mere store-keeper. Though military discipline required them to do so, yet, in matters like this the influence of sentiments cannot be totally ignored. But, it was a mistake on the part of the Ahom viceroy and his lieutenants to allow their personal discontent to override the requirements of a grave national emergency. They might have afterwards demanded of the king to account for his indiscretion; but for the present their sole duty was to concentrate all their energy and resources in resisting the advance of Mir Jumla's army. Manthir himself proved later to be a traitor, and he was executed together with his brothers; and Chengmun Barphukan committed suicide to escape from punishment for his defection.

The next scene takes us to the camp of Baduli Phukan. As a brother of the great statesman Momai-tamuli Barbarua, and being himself a valorous commander, Baduli enjoyed the esteem and confidence of the king and the people; but thinking that the support of the Moguls would be at his life-long disposal, he made overtures to Mir Jumla promising to desert his command in the Ahom army, go over to the Moguls, and seize the persons of the king and his ministers, provided he was made Raja of Assam. Mir Jumla received Baduli with open arms, and promised to fulfil his wishes. The climax of treachery was reached when Baduli, at the head of a numerous Mogul contingent, fought with his Assamese countrymen in several pitched engagements, in which the Moguls were defeated. Baduli's example was followed by a large number of Assamese, and Mir Jumla received them all giving them hopes of preferment under the Moguls. Baduli with his family, and also the other betrayers were taken by Mir Jumla to Bengal.

The subsequent war in connection with the recovery and retention of Gauhati was a clean chapter, because the great general Lachit Barphukan nipped treachery in the bud by interdicting fraternisation with the enemy even on the slightest pretext. Immediate decapitation was his remedy for delinquency, faintheartedness and treachery. All devices at corruption, stored in the armoury of the Rajput Raja Ram Singha, failed to create an impression upon the resolute mind of the Assamese general and his colleagues. The result was the victory of the Assamese in the ever-memorable battle of Saraighat which witnessed the Assamese in the highest pitch of their abilities for organisation and discipline. But Lachit Barphukan died soon after this triumph, and was succeeded in the Barphukanship by his brother Laluk. A new chapter of sordid brutality and selfishness now begins in the history of Assam.

Chakradhwaj Singha's successor Udayaditya Singha developed an infatuation for a Sannyasi of Gakulpur in Brindaban. He declared that the Vaisnava Mahantas of Assam were not equal to the Sannyasi in spiritual eminence. He planned to get them initiated by the Sannyasi. One Debera Hazarika of the Lakhurakhun clan stood as a champion of the Assamese Mahantas, deposed Udayaditya Singha, and placed Ramadhwaj Singha on the throne. Aided by this initial popularity, Debera himself began a career of autocracy, and his enormities became gradually intolerable. Ramadhwaj Singha was killed, and also a number of innocent princes and nobles. The Gauhati commanders, under the leadership of the prime minister Atan Buragohain, then moved up to the capital Gargaon, captured Debera and executed him along with his accomplices. A new prince, Arjun Dihingia Raja, was now placed on the throne, and peace and order prevailed once more in the affairs of Assam. The commanders returned to Gauhati, leaving Atan Buragohain in charge of the affairs at the capital. The Buragohain steered the government with his customary probity and good sense.

But a fresh villain now appeared on the scene in the person of Lao Barchetia. He poisoned the ears of the king against the premier, and the estrangement that followed resulted in a battle between the royalists and the adherents of the Buragohain. The brutal manner in which Arjun Raja was blinded and murdered by Bhatdhara Phukan, brother of Laluk, will never fail to excite sentiments of sorrow and compassion. It was followed by a murderous attempt on the person of the new king Sudoipha Parvatia Raja, but the guilt could not be pinned on any one with dead certainty, though suspicions hovered round several persons.

Exaggerated reports of the happenings at the capital reached the ears of Laluk Barphukan at Gauhati. He attributed them to the alleged autocracy and high-handedness of Atan Buragohain. Determined to crush the power of the Buragohain and wield it by himself, Laluk sent proposals to Sultan Azamtara, the governor of Bengal, expressing his willingness to surrender Gauhati, provided he was made Raja of Eastern Assam. After a series of secret negotiations, the Moguls occupied Gauhati: Laluk's Rajaship became a mere titular distinction conferred on him by the Moguls, though he became all-powerful in the state. His reign of terror was however cut short by his death at the hands of a few gallants whom he had proposed to offer as sacrifices to the Kechaikhati Gosani at Sadiya.

The history of the age of Atan Buragohain is a drama of paradise lost and paradise regained. Delinquency and treachery became prominent at times; but patriotism and disinterestedness reigned supreme in the residual mind of the nobles and the people. A powerful and unselfish leader could alone bring about the awakening of the nobler traits, and his absence witnessed invariably a catastrophic relapse into personal vendetta and barbarism. If Assam had suffered, it was not due to any lack of resources, but to the lack of efficient leaders who could marshall the resources to the full advantage.

Mingimaha Bandula, the Burmese general, having witnessed the valour of individual Assamese fighters during his operations in Assam, expressed his opinion that Assamese reverses were due to the absence of able leaders. The indispensableness of able leaders had similarly been emphasised upon by the Buragohain of King Rudra Singha—"In the reign of Jayadhwaj Singha there was an abundance of provisions and men, and still he acquired the title of 'Bhaganiya Raja', or the 'Deserting king'; arms and ammunitions, materials and supplies are torpid and impotent: the followers and subordinates of the monarch are symbols of life and animation; they alone can infuse into the immobile war-provisions a dynamic force".

It is rightly said that history is the biography of great men. During this momentous period of Assam's history, 1662 to 1682, four persons come out prominently as their country's men of destiny—King Chakradhwaj Singha, Senapati Lachit Barphukan, Atan Buragohain and King Gadadhar Singha, as, without their patriotic inspiration and guidance, the affairs in Assam would have assumed a different shape altogether.

A king was regarded by the Assamese as the fountain of all energy and prowess; and slackness on his part always led to lukewarmness in high enterprises, to rapid growth of mutual jealousies and strifes, and to the formation of cabals and juntos. King Chakradhwaj Singha was a spirited monarch, and the obligation to pay the heavy tribute to the Moguls as imposed by Nawab Mir Jumla was too much for him to bear. When pressed by the Moguls to pay the balance of the stipulated tribute, King Chakradhwaj Singha cried out, —"Death is preferable to a life of subordination to foreigners". He personally supervised the preparations for attacking the Moguls at Gauhati, and warned the commanders that should they fail in their allotted duties he would find men enough to replace them. Victory was easily achieved and the Ahoms got back Gauhati after its occupation by the Moguls for a little more than four years. The king then exclaimed in self-satisfaction,—"It is now that I can eat my morsel of food with peace and happiness". The momentum of efficiency and discipline which Chakradhwaj Singha had initiated continued to work even after his death, and the Ahoms were able to thwart the Moguls in their formidable attempt to reoccupy Gauhati.

King Chakradhwaj Singha who had a keen eye for merit had selected Lachit Barphukan as the leader of the Gauhati expedition. Lachit proved to be a commander of rare courage and capacity for organisation. He discarded formalities which are handicaps in quick action which is vital for success in arms. He knew well that patriotism being more or less a moral quality its permeation cannot be guaranteed on easy terms, and it may at times fail to inspire implicit obedience to superior commands. But fear of physical injury or decapitation is an unfailing antidote, and he applied these draconic methods unhesitatingly in view of the emergency in which he was placed, and which he was asked to resolve. He also knew that temptation however trivial it may be, once admitted, leads to increasing vulnerability; and the Moguls and the Rajputs, who were past masters in the art, were always on the look-out for opportunities for corrupting the Assamese. Lachit Barphukan would not even allow his messengers to accept a pair of wooden sparrows from the Amber Raja. Patriotism was a religion with Lachit Barphukan, and fearless of consequences, he rushed to the thick of the enemy's boats with his brow sweating with the drops of high fever. Lachit Barphukan attained the crown of his glory in the victory of Saraighat, and his death a few days later arrested any eventual change which Fate and Time would have produced.

The soldier-statesman Atan Buragohain Dangaria appears on the scene when Mir Jumla's army was advancing towards Samdhara after having crossed the environs of Gauhati without any resistance whatsoever. His opposition was of no avail as he had to share the consequences of the commanders' defection of the preceding weeks. Mir Jumla occupied the capital Gargaon, but his stay of ten months was full of suffering and misery. The Buragohain was chiefly responsible for organising the campaign of harassments which compelled the enemy to accept the peace terms and retire from Assam. The quick rehabilitation of the country was mainly the achievement of Atan Buragohain who moved from one outlying village to another encouraging the fugitives to return to their empty homesteads. Besides, it was Atan Buragohain who erected the extensive fortifications at Gauhati on both banks of the Brahmaputra. Gauhati was soon recovered, and his sober counsel and direction enabled the Ahoms to retain its possession against the enormous pressure of the Moguls under such a reputed general as Raja Ram Singha. His wise leadership restored the equilibrium of the state when it was threatened by the atrocities of Debera Barbarua. His rejection of the kingly crown manifested his love of the constitution and his unparalleled self-restraint and spirit of sacrifice.

But the events which followed this evidence of the Buragohain's magnanimous character put his leadership to the severest trial. Laluk Barphukan had been carrying on secret negotiations with the Moguls for the surrender of Gauhati, in return for his recognition by them as the Raja of Assam. The Moguls when intrenched in their stronghold at Gauhati would surely march into Eastern Assam when it was necessary to give military aid to their protegé Laluk. The developments at Gauhati were duly reported to the Buragohain at the capital, and his colleagues proposed to attack the Barphukan. But the premier did not countenance their proposal on the plea that the Moguls who were lurking in the frontier would be encouaged by a rupture in the Assam camp. He however acted with foresight when he planned to construct a line of fortifications to defend the metropolitan zone. Outwardly, he expressed his disbelief in the treacherous move of the Barphukan who, in his estimation, was 'a knowing man'. The patriotic section of the nobles at both Gauhati and Gargaon were disappointed at the vacillation of their prime minister in baffling the manoeuvres of the Barphukan. To Atan Buragohain, the appearance of internal solidarity and the need for defensive fortifications near the capital were of greater moment than the adoption of appropriate measures for the immediate crushing of the traitor Laluk. He thus emphasised on a remote issue regardless of the emergency directly confronting him.

The Buragohain also delayed in despatching an army even when he was informed of Mansur Khan's entrance into Kamrup with a powerful force under the guidance of Baduli. The intentions of the Moguls were now apparent beyond any shadow of doubt; but the Buragohain deputed emissaries after emissaries to ascertain the facts. His supporters at Gauhati now exclaimed in one voice,—"We have been apprising the Buragohain of the situation here times without number, but nobody listens to us! Now, Baduli has come, what are we to do?" An intrepid Phukan even said,—"Having cast our lot with the Buragohain we are going to perish like so many women! I shall have to die with the regret that I have not been able to take off the head of Laluk and drop it on the ground."

The Buragohain was primarily a man of deliberation. His vacillation is the characteristic of most men of idealistic and reflective temperament who are incapable of detecting the real substance in the shadowy haze of contending issues. Something was rotten in the state of Assam; and even though the times were out of joint, Atan Buragohain could have cured the malady if he had acted with determination and firmness, shunning his delicate scruples and the fear of comparatively remote contingencies. Atan Buragohain, the premier of Assam, and Hamlet, the Prince of Denmark, both hesitated to strike at the proper hour, and Nemesis exacted from them the irresistible penalty. In both cases, to quote Goethe, 'a lovely, pure, noble and most moral nature without the strength of nerve which forms a hero, sinks beneath a burden which it cannot bear and must not cast away.'[204]

The height of Laluk Barphukan's despotism was reached in the murder of Atan Buragohain, and in a way it hastened his own destruction. The eyes of the patriotic nobles were now opened to the grave situation of their country, and they began to look for a prince, who, with a strong hand and master-

204. Goethe, *Wilhelm Meister*, reproduced in F. S. Boas's *Shakespeare and His Predecessors*, p. 387. Compare the famous soliloquay in *Hamlet*, Act III, Scene 1,—

" Thus conscience makes cowards of us all,
And thus the native hue of resolution
Is sicklied o'er with the pale cast of thought,
And enterprises of great pitch and moment
With this regard their current turn awry
And lose the name of action. "

ly organisation, would be able to restore equilibrium to the collapsing government.

Prince Gadapani was just the person capable of suppressing the intriguous propensities of the period. He had gathered wide experience having seen the different parts of the country as a fugitive. Gadapani was besides a man of extraordinary physical vigour. The nobles deliberating at Kaliabar selected Gadapani to be their sovereign in place of the boy-king who had been set up on the throne by Laluk.

Gadapani, now known as Gadadhar Singha, fulfilled the expectations of his supporters. The Moguls were expelled from Gauhati within a year of his accession. Rebellious tendencies were suppressed at the very outset; and he did not hesitate to deal sternly even with those who had elevated him to the throne. Owing to his strong and judicious administration Assam reached the acme of prosperity and peace, with the help of which his son and successor King Rudra Singha could expand his sphere of influence in neighbouring lands, and launch a scheme to oust the Moguls from authority and power.

A word must be said about the much abused monarch Jayadhwaj Singha. He was ridiculed by female hawkers during his flight from the capital Gargaon on the approach of Nawab Mir Jumla; he was dubbed 'Bhaganiya Raja', or the deserting king, and this appellation was reiterated in the war-council of King Rudra Singha fifty years later. It must however be admitted that his career before the invasion of Mir Jumla was one of unusual bravery and determination, and worthy of the heroic traditions of his race. He had put down a number of insurrections of princes and nobles, and had laid the foundation of royal patronage to Vaisnavism. He was quick in seizing the opportunity to re-annex Kamrup to his dominions, and his generals swept the territories up to the neighbourhood of Dacca 'with the broom of plunder.' Mir Jumla's initial success in Assam was the consequence of the defection of the Ahom commanders over which the monarch, situated at a distance, could not exercise any control. But Jayadhwaj Singha inspired vigorous resistance to the Moguls during their stay in Assam, and the discomfiture to which they were subjected compelled them to retire hastily from Assam. The king exerted every nerve to rehabilitate his country and prepare for redeeming his honour and prestige. His passionate love for his motherland comes out in bold relief when, lying on his sick-bed in his Bakata camp, near Gargaon, he expressed a deep longing to see Gargaon, where he had reigned in pomp and power. The ministers and the priests did not give their consent to the king's visit to an abandoned city; but Jayadhwaj Singha was firm and resolute. He proceeded to the gate of the city in a prostrate condition, and asked the warden to open the gate so that he could obtain a glimpse only without entering it. He peeped through the gate, and his old days in the city floated before his minds' eye. This recollection, and the sentiments it evoked, aggravated the king's malady, and he returned to his camp to die there a few days later. This incident reveals Jayadhwaj Singha's intense love for his motherland of which the capital was a fitting symbol.

This survey of the leading personalities of the age will not be complete if we omit to mention the names of two notables—Khamun Rajmantri Phukan and Chengmun Barphukan, both of whom were known as 'Raja-sahur', or the king's father-in-law. Khamun rose to be Naobaicha Phukan, or head of the navy, with the additional distinction of Rajmantri. Chengmun became Barphukan, or viceroy of Lower Assam. As Khamun lived mostly at Gargaon, he came to be known as Gargayan Rajasahur, while his brother was called Namaniyal Rajasahur. Khamun's two daughters were the consorts of King Jayadhwaj Singha, and the two Rajasahurs enjoyed great credit and influence at court. Chengmun Barphukan's defection owing to his supersession by Manthir Bharali Barua was responsible for Mir Jumla's easy passage through Gauhati. During the stay of the Moguls in Assam, Chengmun was allowed to participate in the defensive measures; but after the conclusion of the treaty with Mir Jumla, the king proposed to mete out proper punishment to his delinquent father-in-law. The verdict could be well anticipated, and Chengmun avoided his disgrace by self-immolation. Khamun Rajmantri Phukan was the medium of communications between the Ahoms and the Moguls during the negotiations for peace, and he was a signatory to the treaty enacted at Ghilajharighat. Khamun was later suspected of having organised a plot to obtain the succession for himself, or his grandson and nephews, during the interregnum that followed the death of King Jayadhwaj Singha. He was sentenced to death with his kith and kin, the prosecution being led by Laluk Dola-kasharia Barua. His two daughters, the widows of Jayadhwaj Singha, also perished with their father. Laluk was appointed Naobaicha Phukan, while the office of Rajmantri was conferred upon Atan Buragohain.

Besides the multiplicity of man-leaders and man-actors in the events of the period, three ladies come out prominently in all the noble susceptibilities of which they are capable. The first is the princess Ramani Gabharu, daughter of King Jayadhwaj Singha, and consort of Sultan Azamtara, third son of Emperor Aurangzeb. She was only six years old when her father parted with her in fulfilment of the terms of the treaty with Mir Jumla. Her passionate longing for her motherland comes out in that remarkable letter she wrote to her uncle Laluk; and in the unusual boldness shown by her when, living in the harem of the Subedar of Bengal, she warned her uncle against the consequences of his infamous proposal to surrender Gauhati.

The next lady was the daughter of Atan Buragohain who had become the chief consort of the monarch Sudoipha Parvatia Raja. According to the custom of the Ahom court, the Buragohain and other ministers had to kneel down and pay their respects to the Barkuanri along with the king. The Buragohain's daughter left her seat on the approach of her father. The king was annoyed at the premier's infringement of a time-honoured custom. An effective *ruse*, resembling a legal fiction, was then adopted: the queen sat with the sacred manuscript of *Ratnavali* placed on a tray; the Buragohain came and paid his homage to her. The daughter interpreted the obeisance as being paid to the sacred book; and she thereby eased her filial conscience: the king thought it to be the homage paid, as required by custom, to his queen.

The third lady Princess Jaimati has become a household word in Assam, and her sacrifice to protect the life of her husband Prince Gadapani has conferred on her an eminent position in the pantheon of Assam's noble and heroic women. Laluk considered Gadapani to be the most powerful opponent of his scheme of self-aggrandisement, and directed his emissaries to seize Gadapani and kill him. He fled from home, first took shelter in the Naga Hills and then wandered from place to place as a fugitive. Laluk's men inflicted on Jaimati the severest tortures to extract information from her about the whereabouts of her husband; but the bold princess remained adamantine in her refusal to give any clue whatsoever, and she died in consequence. Laluk was killed afterwards as a fitting sequel to his brutalities; Gadapani became king of Assam; and his son king Rudra Singha excavated a tank and erected a temple at the site of his mother's death. Princess Jaimati's memory is kept green by these two memorials of her martyrdom—Jaisagar and Jaidoul.

In addition to these three stars of the first magnitude, we come across a number of women whose actions and utterances have been recorded in the contemporary chronicles. Kusumi Barkuanri, the chief consort of King Jayadhwaj Singha was a patron of the leading Vaisnava monastery Bengena-ati Satra. Kusumi and her sister had to console their husband when he sobbed having had to abandon the capital Gargaon on the approach of the Moguls. The boldness with which they vindicated their own innocence at the trial of Khamun Rajmantri Phukan, and castigated the monarch Chakradhwaj Singha for having dishonoured them, have rendered their names memorable to posterity. Pakhari Gabharu, mother of Ramani Gabharu, had a series of changes in her matriomonial relations. After her husband Jayadhwaj Singha's death she became the chief consort of his successor Chakradhwaj Singha; but she taunted the king once having seen him flirting with a maid, in consequence of which she was deprived of the dignity of a Barkuanri. Debera's spies included a number of women in the employ of the king; and they reported to him daily about the developments at the palace. One Suhung Raja, a nominee of Debera, had three consorts selected by Debera himself. One of them was Pakhari Gabharu who was specially commissioned by Debera to educate the monarch in the formalities and manners of his exalted office. She explained to Suhung Raja the extent of Debera's villainy; she was in consequence killed, and her remains were interred in the grave of her first husband Jayadhwaj Singha. Arjun Raja's wife, in her desire to protect the interests of her four sons persuaded him to free himself from the overbearing influence of Atan Buragohain, and in the contest that followed the king lost his throne and his life. The last woman of any consequence was the wife of Bhotai Deka who was responsible for the murder of Laluk. Her husband was asked to surrender himself to the king which he avoided. It was through her persuasion that the daring gallant appeared before the monarch to ask pardon for having set up a parallel government of his own. Thus, in the chronicles which have come down to us, men and women are equally represented in the vast drama of national ups and downs.

An important feature of the period is the bestowal of royal patronage on the Assamese Vaisnava monasteries or Satras. The mission of Vaisnavism was in the beginning improperly understood by the Ahom court, and several pontiffs were executed in the reign of King Pratap Singha for alleged propagation of heterodox doctrines. But King Jayadhwaj Singha established two principal Satras, Auniati and Dakhinpat, and made endowments of extensive revenue-free lands. He took his initiation from Niranjan Pathak, the first Adhikar of Auniati Satra, and was greatly devoted to Banamali Gosain of Dakhinpat Satra. His successor Chakradhwaj Singha was also equally devoted to Banamali Gosain. Udayaditya Singha's attempt to undermine the influence of the Assamese Vaisnava Gosains resulted in his deposal and death. His successors were the disciples of one Vaisnava Gosain or the other. Lora

Raja was a disciple of Banamali Gosain who naturally desired the boy-king's continuance in power. But the last king of the age, Gadadhar Singha, was made of a different mould. He looked at the ascendancy of the Satridhakars from a political view-point, having seen their pomp and power during his wanderings as a fugitive. He looked at them at so many centres of political distraction, and attempted therefore to pull down the edifice of Vaisnava monasticism. He became a patron of Saktaism, though he was not a disciple of any Sakta Guru. His son King Rudra Singha's formal acceptance of Saktaism was not materialised owing to a sudden disinclination on his part on the arrival of the priest who had been invited to offer him initiation. Rudra Singha's son Siva Singha became a full-fledged Sakta, as well as his four successors, Pramatta Singha, Rajeswar Singha, Lakshmi Singha and Gaurinath Singha; and most of the nobles followed the faith chosen by the monarchs.

In spite of the deep engrossment of the Assamese people in resisting the imperialistic designs of the Moguls and in setting their own house in order, the progress of literature went on apace, though it received considerable set-back owing to the political upheavals. King Jayadhwaj Singha was himself a song-writer, but only one of his songs has come down to us, being preserved in an old anthology. The *Rag* used is Jayashri, and the song embodies Sri Krishna's desperate appeal to his beloved Radha to appease his passions "as his body is burning with the flame of love". The song is extremely sensuous as the lover's infatuation springs from the passion-provoking features of his beloved. It ends with the words,—"King Jayadhwaj Singha sings this song depicting the love of Radha and Govinda". It is possible that this song has received the reflection of the king's amours with the sister of his chief consort Kusumi Barkuanri, which were well-known at the time.[205]

205. *Gita-latika,* an old Assamese anthology of songs, manuscript in the library of the Department of Historical and Antiquarian

As far as is known at present, the only poet of note was Ram Misra Kavi, son of the famous ambassador Madhab Kandali Kataki. He lived in Dichoi village near the capital, under the patronage of Khamun Rajmantri Naobaicha Phukan, popularly known as Gargayan Rajasahur. The poet eulogises in his colophons his patron, his two daughters and their husband King Jayadhwaj Singha, and the patron's youngest son Bhadrasen. Ram Misra was the author of three poetical works,—*Bhisma-parva Mahabharat, Hitopadesa,* and *Putali-charitra,* though it is believed that he also wrote several other books which have not yet come to light.[206]

The Ahoms had their own code of political conduct preserved in their traditions and literary remains. But, having come under the influence of Hinduism, and having had to deal constantly with their Hindu subjects and neighbours, they thought it would be advantageous to know what Hindu classics had to teach in the matter. The three books of Ram Misra were no doubt compiled to satisfy this laudable craving for enlightenment.

The first book *Bhisma-parva,* like its Sanskrit original, describes the battle of Kurukshetra centering round the deeds of the great Kaurava hero Bhisma. It contains a vivid description of the war array of the two parties, the disposition of their camps, the formation of their phalanxes, and their respective ethics of warfare. The book thus offered a helpful guidance to the princes, nobles and captains of Assam to conduct their military operations against the Moguls which constituted the principal preoccupation of the age.

The second book *Hitopadesa* is an Assamese rendering of the immortal Sanskrit classic of the same name, compiled by Vishnu Sarma for the edification of the sons of a king. Ram Misra compares this book to 'a parijat flower the sweet-

Studies in Assam. The amours of King Jayadhwaj Singha with Kusumi Barkuanri's sister are described in MS. Assam Buranji No. 40. See also S. K. Bhuyan's *Ramani Gabharu,* pp. 5-6.

206. For Kavi Ram Mishra, see the articles by Sonaram Chaudhury in *Milan,* Vol. IV, Agrahayan 1847 *saka;* by Utsavananda Goswami in *Banhi,* Vol. XVI, Vaisakh 1848 *saka.*

ness of which is felt by a black-bee as soon as it drops on its pollens.' This book was compiled under the orders of Bhadrasen. There are several Assamese translations of *Hitopadesa,* made subsequently by different authors at different times, one of them being the version compiled by one Vagish Dwija, under the orders of Numali Rajmao, mother of King Kamaleswar Singha, 1795-1811.

Ram Misra's *Putali-charitra,* containing an Assamese version of the popular stories described as being told by the thirty-two images of the throne of King Vikramaditya, was compiled under a different patron, namely, the Barphukan, or Ahom viceroy of Lower Assam, belonging to the family of Tarun Duara. The book is thus introduced by the author,—"Listen, Oh, ye members of the congregation, to this picturesque poetical work *Putali-charitra,* written by Vararuchi. The Barphukan has ordered me to undertake the work with a view to see the stories in a poetical garb [in Assamese]. He belongs to the family of Tarun Duara, and he is cool and dignified in his mind and behaviour. The king refrains from setting aside his recommendations and orders, and he never speaks anything but truth; and his commands are obeyed by the Garos, the Bhutias and the Kacharis".

I shall conclude this chapter by a brief enumeration of the events and uterances which are likely to provide materials for inspiration and emulation in ages to come:

The alertness with which King Jayadhwaj Singha took advantage of the War of Succession to the Delhi throne, recovered Kamrup from the Moguls, and overran the territories up to the neighbourhood of Dacca;

The boldness with which the Assamese envoys Sanatan and Madhabcharan repudiated Nawab Shaista Khan's suggestion that Mir Jumla should be placated by the Assamese in all possible ways if they wanted to preserve their cows and Brahmans;

The organised manner in which the Assamese conducted their guerrilla campaign to harass the Moguls during their stay in Assam;

The sacrifice made by Jayadhwaj Singha by parting with his daughter Ramani Gabharu in order to preserve the integrity of his kingdom;

The measures of quick rehabilitation adopted by Jayadhwaj Singha after the ravages of Mir Jumla's invasion;

Jayadhwaj Singha's longing to have a last look at the capital Gargaon in spite of the prohibition of the ministers and priests and his own serious illness;

Jayadhwaj Singha's death-bed injunction to his nobles to emancipate Assam from the disgrace of virtual subordination to the Moguls;

King Chakradhwaj Singha's open declaration that death is preferable to a life of subordination to foreigners;

Atan Buragohain's bold warning that without a sufficient store of war-provisions, military operations are bound to end in failure;

Chakradhwaj Singha's personal supervision and direction in the matter of preparations for war;

Chakradhwaj Singha's indignation at the humiliating request made by the Mogul Fauzadar Nawab Firoz Khan to furnish him with damsels from Assam for his amusement and diversion;

The recovery of Gauhati and Kamrup after their occupation by the Moguls for a little more than four years;

Atan Buragohain's letter to Nawab Shaista Khan inviting the latter to sue for peace;

The construction of forts and ramparts on both banks of the Brahmaputra, with batteries mounted at intervals;

The allotment of suitable commanders and soldiers to cover specific portions of the entire ring of fortifications round Gauhati on both banks;

The warning sent to Raja Ram Singha by his mother and his wife against the consequences of disturbing the peace of the hallowed land of Assam, where there was universal *Namakirtana,* and where Vaisnavas, cows and Brahmans were living in happiness and security;

Lachit Barphukan's temporary dismay at the sight of the huge Mogul army under Raja Ram Singha encamped in the areas adjacent to the Gauhati fortifications, and his exclamation,—"It is a tragedy that my country has to face this dire catastrophe during my Phukanship! How will my king be saved? How will my people be saved? How will my posterity be saved?"

The determination of the Assamese commanders not to accommodate Ram Singha by acceding to his demand for the evacuation of Gauhati;

Lachit Barphukan's presentation to Ram Singha of a tube filled with sands with the remark,—"This is the characteristic of our soldiers";

Lachit Barphukan's stern orders that delinquency would be punished by instant decapitation;

Atan Buragohain's consolation offered to Lachit Barphukan to overcome the latter's depression on the loss of ten thousand stalwart Assamese soldiers in the battle of Alaboi;

Nara Hazarika's appeal to the retreating soldiers that they should not throw poison into a platter of gold;

Lachit Barphukan's rushing into the thick of the contest in spite of high fever, and his utterances to rouse the dormant patriotism of his soldiers;

The victory of the Assamese at the battle of Saraighat;

Raja Ram Singha's appreciation of the valour and organisation of the Assamese expressed at the time of his departure from Assam,—"Glory to the king! Glory to the counsellors! Glory to the commanders! Glory to the country! One single individual leads all the forces! Even I, Ram Singha, being personally on the spot, have not been able to find any loophole and opportunity! Every Assamese soldier is an expert in rowing boats, in shooting arrows, in digging trenches, and in wielding guns and cannon. I have not seen such specimens of versatility in any other part of India. One who comes to fight against Assam should be thrashed on the cheek by scavengers with their broomsticks".

Atan Buragohain's observations on the difficulties of an expedition against the border tribes living in inaccessible hills and forests,—"The Dufla miscreants can be captured only if an elephant can enter into a rat-hole".

Debera's championship of the cause of the Assamese Vaisnava Gosains against King Udayaditya's attempt to make them disciples of an unknown upcountry Sannyasi;

The one-mindedness with which the Gauhati commanders acted to terminate Debera's atrocities, and to restore peace and order;

Atan Buragohain's refusal to wear the kingly crown even though importuned by his colleagues on two occasions;

Atan Buragohain's conviction that rupture in the Assamese camp would encourage the Moguls in carrying out their hostile designs;

Princess Jaimati's determination, in spite of the severest tortures, not to give any information about her husband's possible whereabouts;

The deliberations of the Assamese nobles at Kaliabar to restore tranquillity and order by placing a powerful prince on the throne; and,

King Gadadhar Singha's expulsion of the Moguls from Gauhati, and recovery of Kamrup extending up to the Manaha river. This victory of the Ahoms marked the termination of the protracted Assam-Mogul conflicts of the seventeenth century.

APPENDICES

APPENDICES

A. A contemporary review of events, 1662-1682.

B. Atan Buragohain Rajmantri Dangaria, a brief sketch.

C. Observations in Atan Buragohain's chronicle.

D. Letters of Atan Buragohain.

E. Ramani Gabharu's letter to Laluk Barphukan.

F. List of Ahom kings of Assam.

G. Bibliography.

Index.

APPENDIX A.

A CONTEMPORARY REVIEW OF EVENTS, 1662-1682.

A summary of the events from the invasion of Assam by Nawab Mir Jumla in 1662--63, to the expulsion of Mansur Khan from Gauhati in 1682, is found in the old Assamese chronicle *Tripura Buranji,* compiled in 1724 by Ratna Kandali Sarma Kataki and Arjun Das Bairagi who had visited the Tripura court on three different occasions between the years 1710 and 1715, in connection with King Rudra Singha's attempt to harness the co-operation of the Hindu Rajas of India in furtherance of the plan formed by that Ahom monarch to invade Mogul India. The Assamese envoys were ushered into the presence of Raja Ratna Manikya of Tripura on the night of April 18, 1712, when they delivered the secret letter of King Rudra Singha addressed to the Tripura Raja.

During the course of the interview, the Dewan of Tripura asked Ratna Kandali and Arjun Das,—"Please tell us how Mazum Khan [Mir Jumla] overran your country, and how Mansur Khan occupied the fort of Gauhati".

A translation of the text containing the reply of the two envoys is given below:

"Then said our Katakis.—The grandfather [Jayadhwaj Singha] of our present monarch [Rudra Singha] was then on the throne. Baduli Phukan was appointed Sirdar and despatched to the battle. He fought against Mazum Khan at the fort of Gauhati for seven days. Our Maharaja then sent this message to Baduli Phukan,—"Nawabs like Mazum Khan with their twenty-two Omraos have been defeated by us on repeated occasions. I do not understand how the war is being conducted now though you are provided with so many men and such a large quantity of materials." Having thus expressed his indignation the king sent to Baduli Phukan the garments worn by women. Baduli being seized with extreme fear became friendly with the Moguls; and our soldiers and their camp-followers deserted the field of battle. Mazum Khan then reached the fort of Samdhara. Having heard this our Maharaja despatched a contingent of fighting men. The battle at Samdhara fort continued in various forms for twenty-two days. Mazum Khan having failed to occupy the fort, though he tried his utmost, established Thanas at that place. Then our men attacked his Thanas, and set obstacles to his communications. His soldiers suffered great hardships for want of food, being unable to make any purchases and sales. Mazum Khan then came down from Samdhara to Gauhati, which he left after having appointed Sayet Piroz and Sayet Sala as Subas. Then our forces attacked Gauhati, and brought Sayet Piroz and Sayet Sala as captives.

"Having heard this the Padshah [Emperor Aurangzeb] sent Raja Ram Singha. He tried hard in many ways, and fought for a long time, but having failed in his attempt he returned to Rangamati. The Padshah having received the report of Ram Singha's failure in the campaign recalled Nawab Shaista Khan from Dacca. Azamtara, son of the Padshah, was then appointed and sent as Suba of Bengal. He was charged with the execution of the order,—"You shall have to recover Gauhati". Ram Singha was then ordered to conduct the campaign in Ajmer. Having examined the situation Azamtara considered open warfare to be very hazardous. So he became friendly with the Barphukan, and said,—"Please allow me to occupy Gauhati for some time at least, and I shall return it afterwards. Let my prestige be thereby maintained before the Padshah for the present". He gave many presents to the Barphukan. The Barphukan then surrendered Gauhati of his own accord.

"Then Azamtara sent Mansur Khan, saying,—"Go and remain as Thanadar at Gauhati". Then Mansur Khan came and established a Thana at Gauhati and remained there. The father [Gadadhar Singha] of our Maharaja Swargadeo, after having ascended the throne, killed the Barphukan. There was an engagement with Mansur Khan, and he fled. Our forces captured a large number of his men as well as his provisions, and they occupied the fort of Gauhati.

"After our Katakis had given the account as above, the Dewan remarked,—"Oh, I see, it was for this reason that Baduli Phukan was living at Dacca" Our Katakis were then given leave, and they retired to their camp".

The above account of the two Assamese Katakis is accurate in substance. It is highly interesting as it reveals the manner in which the Assamese of those days desired the events of the period to be viewed in another country where they wanted to establish their reputation and prestige. And hence a slight tinge of publicity, if not of propaganda, is perceptible in the narrative. The omission of Mir Jumla's occupation of the Ahom capital Gargaon must have arisen from this attempt.

APPENDIX B.

ATAN BURAGOHAIN RAJMANTRI DANGARIA, A BRIEF SKETCH

Atan Buragohain Rajmantri Dangaria was one of those distinguished figures of Assam History whose names have now been consecrated to oblivion, but who piloted the affairs of the country in periods of storm and stress and left an indelible impression upon the hearts of their contemporaries. Had they been born in more fortunate surroundings a splendid array of literature would have sprung round their names; and historians, poets and dramatists would have vied with one another in portraying their achievements and triumphs, and setting them up as examples of statesmanship and unflinching devotion to their motherland.

Atan Buragohain flourished at a very critical juncture of his country's history. The imperialism of the Moguls could not tolerate the existence of a powerful independent territory on the eastern frontier of Hindusthan. The jat and sawar cavalry of the generals of the Timurid sovereigns were constantly knocking at the door of Assam threatening her peace and solidarity. When the tide of nationalism, evoked by the necessity to adopt concerted measures to resist the onrush of the invaders, had passed away owing to the forced withdrawal of the imperialistic menace, the country was swept by dissensions, internecine conflicts and ministerial usurpation of sovereign power.

Atan Buragohain, in his capacity as prime minister, was at the helm of affairs during the period from 1662 to 1679. Sober and steadfast in counsel, valiant and expeditious in battle, his political wisdom and foresight elicited unstinted praises from the lips of his adversaries, the Mogul generals; and made him, in the estimation of his countrymen their only regenerator and saviour. He refused the proffered crown not once but twice, and preferred to serve his country as a counsellor and adviser rather than as a sovereign. It may be added to his glory that he employed his unbounding power and influence for the good of his country, and never for the promotion of his selfish ends like the other potentates of the age.

His utterances, delivered on crucial occasions and interspersed in the pages of old Assamese chronicles, reveal his deep knowledge of human nature and the requirements of political expediency. They afforded ready solution of the complex problems of the state in times of peace and war, and gave a new turn to the course of his country's history. The Buragohain was also a military engineer of first-rate skill; and the forts and ramparts on both banks of the Brahmaputra at Gauhati, which were described as being "made by Viswakarma, and impenetrable even to the gods", were the handiwork of Atan Buragohain; as well as the Chintamani rampart constructed for guarding the environs of the Ahom capital Gargaon. To the qualities of a statesman, warrior and engineer, the Buragohain added the equipment of a trained historian as we know from the chronicle he compiled.

Atan came to prominence with his appointment as Buragohain in January 1662 on the sudden and unexpected demise of Lecham Buragohain. The additional dignity of Rajmantri which generally accompanied the office of Buragohain was enjoyed at that time by the king's father-in-law Khamun Naobaicha Phukan, and it was conferred on Atan after the execution of Khamun Phukan in 1664. Previously to this Atan had served as Khanikar Barua, or officer in charge of the guild of artisans and image-makers. Atan's father was at that time Neog Phukan-Gohain, in charge of the king's household troops.

Immediately after his appointment, the new Buragohain was placed in command of a division to resist the forces of Nawab Mir Jumla who were then marching towards Gargaon after the fall of Gauhati and Samdhara. There was hardly any well-equipped garrison or fortress in the districts between Samdhara and Gargaon, and the belated efforts of the Buragohain's forces to thwart the progress of the Mogul army met with reverses. Mir Jumla occupied Gargaon in March 1662, and appointed Thanadars in the newly erected Mogul outposts. A vigorous campaign of guerrilla attacks and ambushes was now instituted by the Ahoms under the direction of Atan Buragohain and Khamun Rajmantri Phukan. Ten months of unprecedented suffering in Assam, inflicted both by man and nature, made the Moguls anxious for withdrawal from that land; and the Assamese were equally eager to see their country emptied of the foreigners.

A treaty was concluded in January 1663 according to which the Ahoms had to part with Gauhati and Kamrup, pay a heavy war-indemnity and tribute in cash and elephants, and present a princess to the imperial harem. Ramani Gabharu, daughter of the reigning king Jayadhwaj Singha, was made over to Mir Jumla, and the first terms of the treaty were duly fulfilled for which the nobles and officers of Assam received praises from the Mogul general. Mir Jumla then left Assam wishing the monarch and the people prosperity and peace. The negotiations and parleys with the Mogul camp were conducted under the personal direction of Atan Buragohain who was one of the signatories to the treaty. After the departure of Mir Jumla, the first preoccupation of the Buragohain was to bring back the villagers who had fled to the hills and forests, and resettle them in their old homes and pursuits.

Embassies were now deputed to Cooch Behar, Jayantia and Cachar deploring the disasters of the previous year, and exploring possibilities of common action against the Mogul invaders. King Jayadhawaj Singha died soon after, his death being accelerated by continued repentance and remorse for having brought his kingdom to such a plight in consequence of which he had to part with his dear child, then only six years old.

His spirited successor Chakradhwaj Singha resolved to shake off his obligation to pay further instalments of the indemnity and tribute. He also gave vent to his determination to expel the Moguls from Gauhati. The king's impetuosity was checked by the Buragohain who pointed to the necessity of first collecting and storing sufficient provisions and war equipments before launching offensive measures. Early in November 1667, the Ahom forces reoccupied Gauhati and restored the old western limits of Assam at the Manaha river. Shivaji's initial successes against the Moguls in 1665, of which the Ahoms had received information in time, had spurred them to prompt and vigorous action.

Emperor Aurangzeb now deputed Raja Ram Singha, son of Mirza-Raja Jai Singha of Amber, charging him with the task of recovering Gauhati. The Ahoms replied to the Rajput Raja's persistent demands for the restoration of Gauhati with taunts and rebuffs like these: "God has given us Gauhati and Kamrup, and when He desires He will give them to our brother-sovereign the emperor of Delhi. Our sovereign the Swarga-Maharaja is the lord of the East, and the Padshah is the lord of the West: if they decide we can surrender our territory, and the Rajput Raja can also surrender Bengal. The Raja has been sent to win the glory of a victory, and his reputation for valour will receive a set-back if he returns from Assam empty-handed". Hints were also thrown in to show that the Raja was a mere servant of the Moguls, and that he had no umbrella over his head.

After a year of negotiations attended by abortive conflicts the Mogul forces led by the Raja were finally defeated in the naval battle of Saraighat near Gauhati. The victory of the Assamese was due to the intrepedity and leadership of the generalissimo Lachit Barphukan, and the sound direction and efficient organisation of the prime minister Atan Buragohain who had taken the field in person as commander of the division in the northern bank of the Brahmaputra.

Lachit Barphukan died soon after the battle of Saraighat, and was succeeded in the Barphukanship by his elder brother Laluk. Raja Ram Singha halted for five years at the frontier Mogul garrison of Rangmati hoping to reattack Assam when opportunities presented themselves. The Buragohain and the leading nobles had therefore to remain at Gauhati with a powerful army, ready to repulse any eventual attack by the imperialists.

The absence of the senior nobles and commanders at Gauhati encouraged the ambitious potentates at the capital to push forth their machinations and designs. Intrigues and conspiracies, attended by the murder of opposing nobles and the massacre of innocent princes became the order of the day; kings became puppets at the hands of unscrupulous ministers; life and property became insecure; and it seemed as if the whole country was going to be divested of the very essentials of peace and orderly government.

The atrocities at Gargaon having assumed intolerable dimensions, the stalwarts of Gauhati, with Atan Buragohain as their head, marched up to the capital, pursued and captured the leading miscreants, and brought them to condign punishment. Debera Barbarua, the arch-villain of the reign of terror, was executed after being subjected to severest tortures. During the course of his fateful trial Debera predicted a similar role on the part of his judge and accuser Laluk Barphukan.

Gobar Raja who had been placed on the throne by Debera was deposed and then killed. The nobles now asked the Buragohain to be the king, but he declined the honour, saying,—"I belong to a family of ministers, and as such I cannot wear the kingly crown. A member of the royal family should alone become a king. A shoulder-pole of reed cannot bear the weight of a bufallo-thigh, and a Sudra cannot wear the sacred thread of a Brahman". After a vigorous search for a suitable prince the Buragohain came upon Arjun Kowanr who was then living at Dihing. He was now placed on the throne, after which the Gauhati commanders returned to their respective charges leaving Atan Buragohain to manage the affairs of the capital. The country was now restored to tranquillity and peace which elicited the following observation from a contemporary chronicler,—"The people and the country became well settled, and the government began to function according to the usages of the past."

Troubles began to raise their head again when the week-kneed monarch Arjun Dihingia Raja gave his ears to the whispers of his seraglio and suspected the intentions of the

Buragohain and his friends; and in the struggle that ensued the king lost his throne as well as his life.

The Buragohain was now held in greater esteem as the benevolent dispenser of affairs, and the saviour of his country. On the death of Arjun Dihingia Raja, the crown was again offered to the Buragohain; it was pointed out that his refusal to do so on the previous occasion had led to the installation of a weakling on the throne who acted in defiance of his well-wishers and the best interests of the people. But, Atan Buragohain declined that honour on this second occasion also, saying,—"I thank you for your offer which however I cannot accept, as it is not proper for a minister to hold the office of a monarch. Kingship should go to the scion of a royal family, and saintship to the descendant of a saint." After a considerable search the Buragohain and his colleagues selected a prince who bore the marks of an able ruler. The new monarch came to be known as Parvatia Raja. Following the example of his predecessor, the new king conferred additional privileges and honours upon the Buragohain in appreciation of his refusal to wear the crown and of his services in elevating the prince to the throne. During the brief interregnum of three fortnights, between the deposal of Dihingia Raja and the succession of Parvatia Raja, the Buragohain had ruled the country with justice and firmness as the head of its government.

A Machiavelli now made his appearance in the arena of Assam politics in the person of Laluk Barphukan, the Ahom governor of Gauhati, who had under his command the well-equipped army posted at the viceregal capital. The Barphukan viewed with jealousy the growing power of the Buragohain, and his suspicions were fomented by the tell-tale favour-seekers of the viceroy and the interested opponents of the prime minister. Laluk had given evidence in the past of his adroitness and vigour by acting as a prosecutor in the trial of King Jayadhwaj Singha's father-in-law Khamun Naobaicha Phukan who had been accused of high treason. He also conducted in person the extirpation of that condemned potentate and his family. As a reward for these energetic services Laluk had himself been appointed to the vacant office of Naobaicha Phukan.

The Barphukan now resolved to make his position strong and invulnerable by an alliance with the Moguls. He made secret overtures to Emperor Aurangzeb's son Sultan Azamtara who was then seated on the musnad of Bengal. Laluk utilised in this connection the services of his uncle Baduli who had accompanied Mir Jumla to Bengal and had been living at Dacca as a protegé of the Moguls. The Barphukan sent a proposal to Dacca that he would evacuate Gauhati and Western Assam for being occupied by the agents of the Bengal Subedar, on condition that he would be given a cash reward of rupees four lacs, and that the Moguls would confer on him the rulership of the rest of Assam. Laluk had expected that his plans would also be promoted by his niece Ramani Gabharu, consort of Sultan Azamtara; but the patriotic Assamese princess characterised her uncle's proposal as unbecoming and reprehensible, which admonition however failed to deter the ambitious Barphukan from prosecuting his cherished designs.

Sultan Azamtara had himself demanded the restoration of Gauhati while he was encamping at Rajmahal on his way to Dacca to assume charge of his new office of Subedar of Bengal. To overawe the Assamese, the prince made mention of three hundred elephants and one lac horses as forming part of his war-equipment. Atan Buragohain's reply to Azamtara was of the same tenor as its forerunners to Raja Ram Singha. "The territories claimed by the Padshahzada", said the Buragohain, "are not his. He alone gets them on whom God is pleased to confer them. As to the information sent to us that he is accompanied by numerous elephants and horses, we would say that his horses, in our estimation, are as useless as deer, because horses can neither shoot an arrow nor fire a gun". Now, when Laluk Barphukan, the Ahom viceroy, offered to surrender Gauhati of his own accord, the Padshahzada acquiesced in the proposal with gratification and joy. He made preparations for despatching a force to Assam, and even asked the French and Dutch factories at Dacca to furnish European artillery-men to serve in the expedition.

Atan Buragohain who had been kept informed of the developments at Gauhati thought it prudent not to give prominence to the manoeuvres of Laluk Barphukan lest they gave an encouragement to the intriguing nobles to rally round the powerful viceroy for the accomplishment of their nefarious ends; and moreover, the Moguls who were intrenched at the frontier would rush into Assam the very moment they heard of any internal disorder. The Buragohain said,—"The enemy is lurking in our immediate neighbourhood; and hence it will be inadvisable to pursue the Barphukan and capture him, whatever may be the differences between ourselves. Such an action will give the enemy an additional incentive". He then constructed the Chintamani rampart as a bulwark of defence against the eventual entrance of the invaders into the environs of Gargaon. The Buragohain's hesitation to take timely action against the refractory Barphukan was not appreciated by his adherents and friends.

The Barphukan acted up to his promise; and by tacit support and connivance he made it easy for the Mogul forces to infiltrate into Kamrup and march gradually towards the fortifications of Gauhati. Towards the end of February 1679, the Barphukan evacuated Gauhati and sailed upstream to Kaliabar. Gauhati was occupied soon after by Azamtara's deputy Nawab Mansur Khan. This fact was proclaimed at Delhi as a great victory; and Emperor Aurangzeb paid handsome rewards to the messenger, and sent costly presents to his son Azamtara.

The Buragohain then sailed down to Kaliabar at the head of an army; but his forces were attacked on the way by the Barphukan and repulsed with heavy losses, whereupon the premier left the field in search of a refuge. He was hotly pursued by the emissaries of the Barphukan, and captured and imprisoned. Laluk Barphukan then marched up to Gargaon where he began to act in an independent manner, dismissing and appointing officers at his own sweet will in total disregard of the authority of the reigning sovereign Parvatia Raja. The king's attempt to suppress the Barphukan ended in his deposal and death.

Laluk then placed on the throne a stripling of fourteen, who is commonly known as Lora Raja. The Barphukan, now called Buraphukan, became the virtual dictator of affairs. He extorted from the monarch orders for the execution of Atan Buragohain and of his brother who was Naobaicha Phukan. The sentences were carried out at Kaliabar in November 1679 by executioners despatched from the metropolis. Thus died Atan Buragohain Rajmantri Dangaria, statesman, warrior and patriot; but Hamlet-like, cautious and reflective, and the excess of the deliberative temper brought him to retribution at the hands of his unrelenting and unobstructed foes.

Laluk Barphukan had persuaded Parvatia Raja to send an embassy to Dacca for the avowed purpose of offering felicitations to Sultan Azamtara as he was, by marriage, a kinsman of the Ahom Swargadeo. The Assamese envoys were entrusted by Laluk to carry his own secret communications to the Bengal Subedar. Meanwhile, Azamtara had left Dacca to meet Emperor Aurangzeb in Rajputana; and the letters and presents from Assam were delivered to the prince's successor Nawab Shaista Khan. The Nawab in reply sent a letter to Laluk Barphukan conferring on him the Rajaship of Assam. The embassy returned to Assam, accompanied by the Bengal envoy Govindaram, in the beginning of Lora Raja's reign. Laluk Buraphukan attached great importance to Shaista Khan's message, and he arranged to celebrate the occasion with due ceremony. He stole the regalia from the royal stores, and received Govindaram in the pomp and array of a crowned monarch.

Laluk then instituted a campaign of liquidating and mutilating the princes one by one as they were likely to contest the throne in future; and one of them, Prince Gadapani, son of a previous king Gobar Raja, saved his life by wandering from place to place. His wife Jaimati died in the midst of tortures inflicted on her by the agents of the Buraphukan in the course of their attempt to extract from her information about the movements of her fugitive husband. The murder of Princess Jaimati marked the climax of Laluk Buraphukan's orgies of massacre and treachery.

But, be it recorded to the eternal credit of the Assamese people that they refused to remain callous to the grave deterioration in their country's affairs brought to being by a succession of imbecile monarchs and self-seeking ministers. Laluk Buraphukan, the tyrant and imposter, was hated universally, though no one dared to attack him in person as he lived with the utmost vigilance. The distress of the people rose to such a pitch that the Ahom priests suggested the propitiation of the gods by offering human sacrifices at the Kachaikhati temple at Sadiya; and Bhotai Deka, a man of daring disposition and spotless body was chosen as a victim. Bhotai, in league with his friends, murdered Laluk Buraphukan one night while he was asleep in bed. The desperadoes were now acclaimed as benefactors of the country for having rid it of a common foe. Thus relieved of the Satanic regime of the Buraphukan, the people urged their leaders to meditate on appropriate measures for the restoration of peace and order, as well as for the revival of their perennial prestige of being successful resisters of Mogul imperialism. The nobles paid heed to their countrymen's demand, and on the plea of expelling the Moguls from Gauhati they sailed down to Kaliabar with a large and powerful force.

Here, in the new viceregal headquarters of Kaliabar, the nobles and officers of Assam deliberated coolly and dispassionately on the increasing tempo of inefficiency, intrigue and treason, and decided that the first step in the direction of improving the situation was the installation of a capable and vigorous ruler on the throne, for, said they,—"How can an incompetent monarch give protection to his people"? Prince Gadapani was selected for that exalted office in consideration of his manly physique and his forceful character, combined with the fact of his being the son of a previously reigning king. He was brought from his refuge, and declared king at Kaliabar. The nobles then sailed up to Gargaon, deposed the boy-king, and crowned Gadapani as the Swargadeo-Maharaja of Assam, whereupon he assumed the name Gadadhar Singha, August 1681.

The new monarch suppressed all existing and newly developed disorders, placed the administration on a vigorous and efficient basis, and after a year of preparations his forces expelled the Moguls from Gauhati, and restored the western limits of Assam at the Manaha river which remained undisturbed till the occupation of the country by the British in 1824-25.

Supported by the advantage of a stable government, and the warlike man-power and material wealth of Assam, and the active co-operation of its tribal allies and neighbours, King Gadadhar Singha's son Rudra Singha planned to unfurl the flag of victory in Mogul India. But the monarch's sudden death at Gauhati in September 1714 put an end to the prosecution of this ambitious project; and his successor, too pleasure-loving and refined, was incapable of executing the patriotic intentions of his illustrious sire.[207]

207. This sketch of Atan Buragohain was published in the Republic Day Number of *The Assam Tribune*, Gauhati, January 26, 1952.

APPENDIX C

OBSERVATIONS IN ATAN BURAGOHAIN'S CHRONICLE

The chronicle of Assam compiled by Atan Buragohain has been described in Chapter XVIII, *ante*. The Buragohain's views on a number of important subjects are to be found in his chronicle; they are now collected and reproduced in this Appendix.

The relevant passages give us an insight into the Buragohain's conception of good government; he also refers to the origin of several social, economic and political practices. He refers, in addition, to the existence of old chronicles for which he cut short his own description of certain events and situations.

As a record of the views of a great prime minister of Assam who was an acknowledged authority on the traditional lore of the country, these extracts, it is hoped, will be treasured by all who want to get a first-hand insight into the political ideology of the Assamese people long before the old order had yielded place to the new.

1. *Buranjis to be kept secretly*: This is an account of the family of Shri-shri Swarga-Maharaja. Bahgaria Buragohain, the prime minister of the Maharaja, has dictated it elaborating the details. It is to be kept secretly, and it should be shown only to a person if he is a friend, and if he is not of hostile disposition, as Pundits have prohibited the disclosure of the mysteries of princes.

2. *Love and brotherhood in the Satya-yuga*: At the end of the primordial deluge, Brahma made three attempts to create man. Having failed, he planted the sapling of a pumpkin. Men were begotten inside, and they came out bursting the pumpkin. But they did not know anything, and they resembled animals. Having seen this Indra sent one Brahman to live with men and impart knowledge to them.

From that time men began to derive knowledge from what they heard and saw. This was the *pralaya,* or cataclysm, mentioned in the scriptures. The Satya-yuga then passed in love and amity. Men used to take food in the same dish like sons of the same mother, and nobody entertained any jealousy or hatred towards any other person.

3. *Justice under Khunlung's descendants*: Khunlung, the grandson of Indra, returned to heaven in consequence of a quarrel, and his brother Khunlai remained in the earth, and his descendants reigned for many generations. At the end of thirteen generations, a Naga subject named Mene, expelled the king and himself became the monarch. In his reign the people became very miserable, and they suffered from all kinds of epidemics and maladies. Having seen their plight the Pundits examined the legs of fowls, and announced,—"A non-descript man has become the king." In pursuance of this verdict, the counsellors and ministers deliberated together, and killed Mene. After a search they came upon a descendant of Khunlung, and made him king. During his rule the sufferings of the people came to an end, and they became happy as before. He governed his subjects looking upon them as his own son. There was no taxation in his days. He lived in the ways of righteousness meeting out due punishment to every guilt, and bestowing reward and honour for virtue and ability. His descendants ruled for many generations.

4. *Chomdeo, the tutelary image of the Ahoms*: The king of Nara had two sisters; and Sukranpha was born of one sister, and Sukapha of the other. Sukapha was brought up by his grandmother. Their father died after some time, and also their maternal uncle. Sukranpha became king at that place [Nara]. In consultation with his grand-mother Sukapha said,—"Two tigers do not live in the same forest, and there cannot be two kings on the same throne". Having thus deliberated Sukapha said to his elder brother,—"I am going to the down country, and you will remain here as the king." To this Sukranpha replied,—"All right, brother, you may go, you will have to pay me a tribute annually." Then Sukran-

pha Raja and Sukapha's grand-mother gave Sukapha ornaments and decorations worthy of a prince. They also gave him the image of Cheng-Chom, having kept with them a replica of the stone of the same quality and pattern. This is the property of Chomdeo: kingship never descerts its owner, and Lakshmi, the goddess of prosperity, herself dwells in Chomdeo; there are besides many other miraculous virtues.

5. *Beginning of Ahom historiography*: Then Sukapha Raja moved about in many places, and subdued a large number of Nagas, and brought their villages under his sway. Those who were defeated in battle were cut to pieces, and the survivors were made to eat the flesh after it was boiled. Sukapha reached Khamjang after having crossed a river. He counted his followers, and he found that six were dead, and seven were missing. Then ordered King Sukapha,—"The Pundits should write down all particulars, whenever an incident takes place, when a person dies, and when we acquire new followers."

6. *Admixture of blood:* King Sukapha met people at different places, and they rendered him good services. He gave them new names according to the nature of the services they rendered. Sukapha met the Chutias, Barahis and Morans at different places, and their services to him were more endearing than those received from his own followers. Since that time there was an admixture of blood, and the children were of mixed origin, as the Ahoms had not brought their women with them when they first came from Nara, and as they accepted wives only when they came here.

7. *Original settlers and new-comers*: Sukapha Raja then sent the following invitation to the people of the country,—"You are invited to come to us so that we may see and know each other. We have come from the eastern region, and you are *sthana-giris*, or original settlers [literally, lords of the place], and we are guests, and you should therefore acquaint us with the villages and their inhabitants.

8. *Peerless Ahoms*: Then the Barahis and the Morans, after consulting between themselves, furnished to Sukapha

supplies of vegetables and fire-wood, and they remarked,—"These are not men of ordinary lineage: these are the Ahoms, famed as *Deo-manuh*, or god-men, and others are not *sama* or equal to them.

9. *Brahman princes*: At that time [A.D. 1380-1389], the country was governed without a sovereign. One Thao-mung Cheokham had gone to the north bank to buy cows, and he met Suhan and talked with him. Having recognised Suhan to be a prince of royal blood, Cheokham reported the matter to the Dangarias. They sent men to bring Suhan, but the prince said.—"I shall sit on the throne on condition that the Brahman boys with whom I have lived and played are also admitted to the royal rank." Seven Brahman boys were also brought with Suhan. They were given presents of elephants and horses, and the title of prince was conferred on them, and Suhan was made king. Bamun-kowanrs or Brahman princes came into existence since that occasion.

10. *The three pillars of state*: King Chao-Suhumpha [Dihingia Raja I, 1497-1539] said to the two Gohains [Buragohain and Bargohain] about his son Kancheng,—"I am a dịsh of gold, and you are two supports of silver, and a third support is needed. Kancheng is my flesh and blood. So please allot to him a contingent of retainers and servitors, and make him the third support [to constitute a regular ministerial tripod for conducting the administration of the state]."

11. *Inauguration of taxes in money*: In the reign of Burha Raja [King Pratap Singha, 1603-1641], the Moguls took Parikshit Narayan [Raja of Kuch Hajo] as a captive. The money to be contributed to Parikshit [for his release] was inadequate, and so monetary taxes were imposed on fisheries, fairs, ferries and trade centres. Taxes in money were introduced from that time. Parikshit died in the Mogul territories.

12. *Proper hour for attacking the Moguls*: Then said Akhek [an Ahom noble who had deserted to the Moguls],—"It is out of fear that I am living as a fugitive in the midst of the Bangals. I feel like going from here immediately if

I am given an assurance about the preservation of my life". The Gohains sent the reply,—"We are prepared to protect Akhek Gohain even by placing our own necks on the top of his neck". Hearing this Akhek Gohain became delighted. He sent information about the proper ways of attacking the Bangals.—"They keep awake in the early part of the night, and they are therefore to be attacked during the last part of the night". The Buragohain brought Akhek Gohain into his camp giving him assurances of protection. He passed one night inside the Buragohain's camp. [After some time, under the orders of the king] Akhek Gohain was flayed alive in the reverse manner [from the feet to the head].

13. *Salt-eating implies loyalty*: Satrajit [Mogul commander] being unsuccessful [in active warfare] sent a message to the Swargadeo trying to establish between them the relations of father and son. Satrajit wrote in his letter,—"I have become the son of the Maharaja. I shall remain as the son of the Swargadeo if he be pleased to call me as such, or as his servant as he may designate me." The king said in reply,—"A son should suck the breast of his mother. I send this water, and it should be considered as his mother's milk". The king also sent some salt and rice of superior quality, saying in explanation of the reason for sending them,—"Because, he who eats the salt and rice [of one country] should not think of evil to that country".

14. *References to other chronicles*: Our king Dihingia Raja went round the Chutia Raja's capital where he obtained a large quantity of goods and articles. They were loaded in boats and sent down to Dihing. Phachengmung Bargohain also came back in the company of the Swargadeo. I have written here a short description of the events of the [Chutia] campaign. I have not described them in detail, as they are already recorded in the war-papers or military despatches.

Having heard of Biswa Singha the Ahom forces pursued him, and Biswa Singha came of himself and offered his submission by presenting two pots of gold and silver. The Ahom commanders headed by the Bargohain said,—"The king of Gaur has presented to our monarch a beautiful princess, with a dowry of five villages, namely, Sherpur, Koroibari Daskaunia, Bahirband and Bhitarband. Now that you have submitted of your own accord, we make you the ruler of this place, and have thus settled and preserved you [*thapita-sanchita*]. You should send appropriate presents to the Swargadeo annually, and visit our place in a friendly manner. The Ahom commanders then returned to this country, *saka* 1427 [1505 A.D.]. The other events, in addition to the one described above, are to be found in other chronicles. Having killed the king [Dihingia Raja] his son the Gargayan Raja [1539-1552 A.D.] ascended the throne, and his history is narrated in other writings.

During the reign of Khora Raja, [1552-1603 A.D.] there was a war with the Koches: being unable to resist, the Ahoms secured the retirement of the Koches by some means or other. The Koches came again, and chased the Ahom king, compelling him to take shelter in Choraikhorong, and they were sent back only by giving hostages. These facts are narrated in other writings, and I have therefore made a brief mention of the events.

Khora Raja's son Burha Raja [King Pratap Singha] became king. I shall omit the other details of his reign, and I shall give an account of his conflicts with the Bangals.[208]

208. These statements are taken from the chronicle of Atan Buragohain, inserted in S. K. Bhuyan's *Deodhai Asam Buranji*, pp. 88-117.

APPENDIX D

LETTERS OF ATAN BURAGOHAIN

Fifteen letters written by Atan Buragohain Dangaria are inserted in this Appendix, and these are all that we could presently glean from the contemporary chronicles. Seven of the epistles were addressed to Nawab Rashid Khan, the Mogul Fauzadar of Gauhati, 1663-1667; one, to Nawab Shaista Khan, Subedar of Bengal; one, to Raja Prananarayan of Cooch Behar; and six, to the two Rajas of Jayantia, Jasamatta Rai and his successor Lakshmi Singha. In the letters to the Mogul Fauzadar, the Assam premier dealt generally with the delay in the payment of the war indemnity; in one of them he repudiated the accusation of the Moguls that some of their subjects were killed by the Assamese. The letter to Shaista Khan narrated the circumstances leading to the resumption of hostilities in 1667, the most provoking being the request for Assamese damsels made by Nawab Syed Firoz Khan, the successor of Rashid Khan at Gauhati. The letter to Raja Prananarayan reiterated the friendly relations existing between Assam and Cooch Behar for ages past. The letters to the Jayantia Raja dealt with the age-old friendship between the two states, and the epistles also disclaimed any territorial obligation on the part of Assam.[209]

The full implications of the letters written by Atan Buragohain can be understood only by a study of the originating epistles, and they have been adequately drawn upon in the narratives of this history. They have been omitted here as

209. Letters Nos. 1, 4-8, and 10-11, addressed to Rashid Khan and Shaista Khan are translated from the originals in MS. Assam Buranji No. 41; letters Nos. 2, 9, 12-15, addressed to the Jayantia Raja, from S. K. Bhuyan's *Jayantia Buranji*, 1937, pp. 28-52; and letter No. 3, addressed to Raja Prananarayan of Cooch Behar, from the original in MS. Assam Buranji Nos. 3 and 8.

they will increase the size of the book a great deal. We however consider it proper to reproduce below the letter of Nawab Shaista Khan written to the Buragohain who received the same in September 1664, as being illustrative of the tone and temper of the Moguls in their relations with Assam in the post-Mirjumla period.

"We are all well here", wrote Shaista Khan to Atan Buragohain, "and you should delight us by writing about your happiness and prosperity there. You had sent your two Ukils Sanatan and Chandra Kandali, for an audience with the emperor of Delhi, and I also wrote in your favour to the Umara [Jafar Khan Dewan?]. Out of love and cordiality towards your Raja, the Umara arranged the presentation of your envoys to the emperor. The extent of the emperor's affection towards your Raja will be known to you from the lips of your two envoys. This happy result has been achieved through your loyal exertions. Our Umara also, out of his abundant love for your Swargadeo, has sent his trusted emissary Punditrai with a pair of *Jamdar* and a *sirpao*. I request you particularly to act in a manner which will please the Umara, and you should send back Punditrai quickly. It is through your good fortune that God has sent such a Brahman and a Pundit to your place. He is well inclined towards you. So please give him full satisfaction; it will lead to your well-being and prosperity, whereby the purposes of both *Dharma* and *Karma* will be served. About the balance of the indemnity, in elephants and money both, please send all of them quickly; besides, delay is not desirable. My heart is longing for your friendship and love, but I do not find similar sentiments in yours. I have come here a year and a half ago, but, how is it that you have not written any friendly note in recognition of my presence here? Nothing endures permanently in this world except love and amity, and we always desire for your good. I am giving this advice simply for your welfare. Your Swargadeo will see much happier days if he remains active in his exertions and services to the emperor. You know for yourself the kind of man the Padshah is. So please act accordingly, so that your men and women, and the cows and Brahmans may remain in peace and contentment. You will hear in detail the rest of the message from your Ukils Madhabcharan and Purnananda. What shall I write? You know everything. 1074 Hijira, dated 29, *saka* 1585."

The letters of Atan Buragohain reveal a combination of restraint and boldness. They decreased and increased respectively as Assam's war preparations gradually rose to the point of perfection, and the culmination was reached when Atan Buragohain, after the recovery of Gauhati, wrote to the Subedar of Bengal,—"Now, if you are desirous of friendly relations with us, please send for that purpose Ukils and epistles. If you have no such desire, well, it is your lookout. What shall I say more? You are all-knowing yourself."

Atan Buragohain's letters are reproduced below:

1. To Nawab Rashid Khan, Fauzadar of Gauhati, February 1664 A.D.—

   What you have written about elephants and money is not unreasonable. But, you have yourself seen the plight of our country; and it is for this reason that we have not been able to deliver the entire complement of elephants and money. Still then, we had made over at the beginning the sum of rupees 140,000 and 74 elephants, and we have now sent with Syed Kamal and Piroz Khan rupees 40,000 and 20 elephants. We shall send the remainder in due course. Do you think that we have wilfully refrained from delivering the remaining portion? Our four sons are with you, and the Nawab is aware of the affection which a father entertains towards his son. Please consider also the fact that elephants can be captured only during the winter season. If we succeed in catching a large number, we shall not only send the remaining elephants, we shall also send 50 elephants, small and large, in lieu of rupees 100,000.—Phalgun 9, 1585 *saka.*

2. To Raja Jasamattarai, Raja of Jayantia, April 1664.

   Your letter has given us great joy. Your solicitude for our success in our crisis has made us particularly happy. Besides, it is proper that you should express a desire for amicable relations with us. His Majesty the Swargadeo of Assam is living on friendly terms with the Rajas of Nara and Mantara and a host of other rulers; but that friendliness does not approach the intensity of the sentiments of friendliness towards you. Your Jayantipur has become Gargaon, and our Gargaon has become Jayantipur. Our friendship has progressed through the ages in an uninterrupted manner, and it can be preserved and maintained only by adherence to time-honoured practices. How can that friendship continue if we cease to remain steadfast in the observance of our old usages? —Baisakh 12, 1586 *saka.*

3. To Raja Prananarayan of Cooch Behar, June 1664.

Here, we are in the enjoyment of health and happiness, and we desire that you should be the same. It is reasonable that you should send a message of friendship through Ramcharan. We have also been greatly delighted on receiving this message. But this friendship is not of yesterday's growth; it has subsisted for a long time. We wish that this friendship will be progressively on the increase. You are yourself aware of the wholesome outcome of the friendship between Rajas. What shall I say more? The rest of the message you will learn from the lips of the Katakis.—Ashar 2, 1586 *saka.*

4. To Nawab Rashid Khan, Fauzadar of Gauhati, July 1665.

Since previous times, the Nawab stationed at Gauhati remains in charge of the transactions between the two countries, and we are in the habit of conducting our correspondence and negotiations with the Gauhati Nawab. Now, you are responsible for the work in that place as we are responsible for the work over here. You should therefore act in a manner which will be satisfactory to His Majesty the king of Assam. It cannot be presaged whether an innovation will lead to good results or untoward consequences. You will therefore concede that adherence to previous practices is the desirable course. It is meet and proper that you should ask for the delivery of the stipulated elephants and money. But you know very well that we have delivered a portion already; and what remains undelivered will be sent during the winter. You should not therefore entertain any anxiety or dissatisfaction on this account.—Sravan 2, 1587 *saka.*

5. To Nawab Rashid Khan, Fauzadar of Gauhati, September 1665.

Your request for five elephants has been forwarded to the two Phukans with instructions to deliver them to your agent Jalil. You should inform me if the Phukans have not yet supplied them. If they have acted up to my instructions I presume you have not been able to take the elephants to your place on account of the rains. I do not understand why you should repeat your request. You should take the animals when the season becomes dry. What you have said about elephants and money is not entirely baseless. Now, we have no money with us to be sent to you. We have already sent you five elephants, and we have now sent five more with Piroz Khan. Thus we have sent ten elephants altogether, both male and female, and also rupees 20,000. Please accept them, and make a note of what remains to be delivered. We shall send the remaining elephants in due time, and as many of them as may be necessary to make up the cash indemnity of rupees 100,000. Is it possible that we have refused to send them even if we could? You know full well that it is to our advantage if we could pay up all our dues. Delays for a few days are unavoidable under the circumstances, and you should not worry about them. —Bhadra 16, 1587 *saka.*

6. To Nawab Rashid Khan, Fauzadar of Gauhati, September 1665.

You have asked whether we intend to deliver the remaining portion of the indemnity. We have entered into a solemn agreement to deliver the stipulated quota of elephants and money. In fulfilment of our promise we have given what we could. Now, we have made over to Piroz Khan ten elephants in lieu of rupees 20,000. We admit there is a balance to be delivered. At the present moment, we have no money with us. We however promise to send some elephants during the ensuing dry season. If, as a reprisal for our delay, you propose to send our hostages to Dacca, the responsibility is entirely yours, as, on our side, we have strictly adhered to our promises. You have besides referred to the murder of some men. How is it possible for us to indulge in such wanton slaughter, and to what purpose, having kept our sons, two Ukils, and one Barmudoi [leading merchant] in your care and custody? I would ask you to overlook this incident. You have fixed your eastern boundary at the Bharari river, and the incident has thus taken place in your jurisdiction, and how shall we know who is murdered and who is the murderer? It is not proper that you should hold us responsible for murders occurring inside your territory? If it transpires that our subjects have perpetrated the crime we shall hand over the offenders to you, and you can cut off their heads. If the crime cannot be laid at the door of our subjects, then, what shall we do?—Bhadra 26, 1587 *saka*.

7. To Nawab Rashid Khan, Fauzadar of Gauhati, July 1666.

Your letter has reached this place. We have sent whatever money we could collect; and as regards elephants, we have sent a number of them as you will learn from Piroz Khan. We have already made a promise to give you the entire quantity as you are fully aware. You have besides referred to Punditrai's intercession on behalf of Baduli; but we are not going to do anything which savours of impropriety. You are however at liberty to plead for a cause though it appears to us untenable, because you are concerned with our mutual transactions. You have shown your knowledge of the Dimarua people, and if you ponder a little you will also know about the practices prevailing in higher society. The son-in-law of Dimarua Raja is reported to have come: do you know who this man is? He is a scion of the family of

Parikshit Raja, and you are not ignorant of this fact. What you know for yourself should not form the subject of a communication to us.—Ashar 27, 1588 *saka*.

8. To Nawab Rashid Khan, Fauzadar of Gauhati, August 1666.

With reference to your letter about elephants, we have already made over fifty of them in lieu of rupees 100,000. They have not yet reached your place possibly on account of the rains; you are sure to get them soon. You have asked us to depute a Kakati, or accountant, to prepare an inventory of the elephants and money already delivered and still to be delivered. We have maintained proper records of what we have sent, and you have done the same with regard to what you have received. What we have given to you in the shape of elephants and money is only because our sons are with you as hostages. Could you ever doubt that you will not get the balance? Your promises diminish in value in proportion to the loss of our sons; and hence you should send back our sons quickly.—Aswin 20, 1588 *saka*.

9. To Raja Jasamattarai of Jayantia, November 1666.

Your letter has reached this place in time, and we have noted its purport with joy. You have stated that we have deviated from the ways of amity. If that be the case, how would you explain our request for friendship communicated through your envoy Ramai? You should also note that we have not withdrawn our Barmudoi from your country. We have been exchanging messengers and epistles in remembrance of the fact that the pious do not become altered even after the cessation of affection. We have continued in the old ways of friendship. As your letter did not conform to the practices of old times [the letter concerned had only one *Shri* before the name of the Assam king] we declined to send envoys and epistles. As you consider Jayanti and Gargaon to be one and indivisible we also consider them to be as such. The party responsible for the despatch of an epistle improperly addressed has undoubtedly fallen from the path of truth. Attempts should therefore be made so that our relations of friendship may continue as before in an undisturbed manner.—Agrahayan 8, 1588 *saka.*

10. To Nawab Rashid Khan, Fauzadar of Gauhati, April 1667.

I have received your message embodied in your letter, and that communicated by Daud Khan and Kola Barua. You have expressed a desire to buy elephants. But elephants of the specification measured with your yardstick are not in our possession. If you had wanted elephants measured with our yardstick we could have supplied you some small ones.—*Baisakh* 16, 1589 *saka.*

11. To Nawab Shaista Khan, Subedar of Bengal, November 17, 1667.

All the prestige and honour of our country vanished when you devastated our territories. We then promised to give three lacs of rupees and ninety elephants. We made this promise only to preserve our boundaries as well as our integrity and honour. In pursuance of that promise, we have given to you elephants and money, and our sons are with you as surety for the balance of the indemnity. Still we have not got back our territories, nor our subjects who had gone over to your land. Rashid Khan Nawab inflicted severe insults on our envoys during the reception at Umananda; and our Barmudoi was also grossly abused. Besides, requests are made for the supply of damsels, and when they are sent they are returned back. His Majesty the Swarga-Maharaja of Assam became highly incensed on receiving reports of these affronts, and he commanded us to attack Gauhati; but we interceded at the feet of the monarch, and he condescended to withdraw his orders. After this, Syed Piroz, on assuming charge of his office [as Fauzadar of Gauhati] deputed Syed Jafar Ukil to our place. His Majesty came to know that Syed Piroz Nawab was a good man, and we also came to the same conclusion. We sent nine elephants to Gauhati during the stay of Syed Jafar Ukil at our place. We were then told that Syed Piroz Nawab had made a request for furnishing him some virgins. Having heard this, the Swargadeo was seized with indignation and wrath, and ordered an attack on Gauhati. [Gauhati was attacked and occupied by the Ahoms on November 4, 1667, thirteen days before the date of this letter]. Now, if you are desirous of friendly relations with us, please send for that purpose Ukils and epistles. If you have no such desire, well, it is you look-out. What shall I say more? You are all-knowing yourself.—Kartik 30, 1589 *saka*.

12. To Raja Jasamattarai of Jayantia, December 1668.

We have communicated to His Majesty your solicitude for friendship, and he was greatly pleased. His reply is embodied in his letter, and you will also hear about it from your Ukils. We also desire the continuity of this age-old friendship between us. You have yourself seen the consequences of a rupture with our monarch. You should therefore exert yourself to avert the violation of our friendly relations. As to your proposal to establish matrimonial relations with the Swargadeo, I would point out that such relations had been established in earlier times, and your desire to renew them has been timely and proper. But, it would have been befitting if you had offered your niece [sister's daughter] only in the event of your having no daughter of your own. Would you confess that your love for your niece is the same as that for your daughter? So you should give your own daughter in marriage to our sovereign. You have also expressed your joy on the recovery of our old territories. It is appopriate that you should give vent to such sentiments, as your joy is in consonance with our uninterrupted friendship. You have besides informed us that your forces are ready for marching through the Dimarua route, and that they are waiting for your signal to depart. You know full well that we have never acted in these matters by following a route suggested by others. Besides you have said,—"The Moguls are not only your enemies, they are also our enemies, and so we should help you with soldiers." We expect therefore that you should immediately despatch twenty or thirty thousand men to us. We shall bring them by whatever route is convenient and practicable to us. They will be able to help us in the erection of our forts and ramparts. These projects cannot be executed in a day as you know full well.—Poush 4, 1590 *saka*.

13. To Raja Lakshmi Singha of Jayantia, February 1673.

Here, we are all in good health and cheer, and we wish that you should be the same. We have received your message of indelible friendship and love with great satisfaction. We expect the Raja to continue in his present relations of friendliness. There will be diminution of love only when there will be deviation from old usages. And hence, old practices should be adhered to at all cost. We need not say more, as you are a knowing person. The rest of the message, if any, will be delivered by Baloram and Jaikrishna.—Magh 24, 1594 *saka*.

14. To Raja Lakshmi Singha of Jayantia, November 1675.

It was you who had mooted the idea of matrimonial relations, and in adherence to old practices we despatched ornaments for the princess in question. If you are not able to fulfil your promises then why did you broach the proposal through Ramai? You have also written about the principality of Dimarua. We have got possession of Darrang, Beltola and Dimarua after having vanquished and slain Syed Babakar [Abu Bakar] and his twenty-two Omraos. Just recently we have reacquired Dimarua after having defeated the Omraos including Syed Piroz. It is needless to describe the conflicts we have waged for the sake of Dimarua since the days of Raja Parikshit. We have acquired Dimarua after a great deal of trouble, and you should not say anything about it. Now that you have laid your claim on Dimarua, I would characterise your action as very improper. You have also said to Nirah and Birina [Jayantia envoys],—"If the Ahoms agree to return Dimarua, you should accept and bring it; and if they do not give Dimarua, the Ahoms should remain in their homes, and our Ukils should come back to theirs." The above instruction of yours is in abject violation of our old friendship; and it is for this reason that we did not despatch any messenger of ours. Still then, on the representation of your agents we have allowed the markets and fairs to continue as before. If you desire for peace, then please send envoys and epistles as before, and if you do not entertain any such desire then it is your look-out.—Kartik 18, 1597 *saka.*

15. To Raja Lakshmi Singha of Jayantia, November 1678.

Your letter has reached here in time, and we have received your message with great joy. We have entered into a solemn agreement that our mutual relations of friendship will not witness any diminution even if the sun rises in the west, the Lauhitya flows eastward, the crow becomes white and the heron turns black in hue, and we have continued in that path of friendship in a steadfast manner. You had refused to receive our Ukils, and we said that we would not despatch any messenger or epistle. Subuddhirai then submitted to us his prayer,—"Your refusal to send messengers and epistles is tantamount to the termination of our agreement for friendship. If you are not willing to send messengers you should at least send epistles." We then said,—"If we had deviated from the path of friendship we would have also refrained from sending letters in spite of your prayer. You will see that we have adhered to the path of friendship." We therefore despatched letters in a desire to maintain the thread of amity. You have refused to receive our Ukils in the face of our old agreement: all that has followed is the offshoot of this unusual situation which is absolutely your creation. Why do you lay the blame at our door? What should I say more, as you know everything. The remaining message will be delivered by Baloram and Jaikrishna.—Agrahayan 4, 1600 *saka.*

APPENDIX E

RAMANI GABHARU'S LETTER TO LALUK BARPHUKAN

The letter of Ramani Gabharu, or Rahmat Banu Begum, daughter of King Jayadhwaj Singha of Assam, and consort of Sultan Azamtara, son of Emperor Aurangzeb, is found in an old Assamese manuscript chronicle obtained by the Department of Historical and Antiquarian Studies in Assam from the family of the late Pundit Hemchandra Goswami.[210] It was addressed to her maternal uncle Laluk Barphukan, and was written at Bhati or Khizirpur, the naval sub-capital of Bengal. The letter bears the date 1599 *saka,* which year ended on April 13, 1678 A.D. The Persian text of the letter in Assamese script as well as a contemporary Assamese translation of the same are both preserved in the chronicle. A correct recension of the Persian text has been prepared for me by Maulvi Abul Fazl Sayed Ahmed, M.A., formerly Senior Professor of Persian and Arabic at Cotton College, Gauhati, Assam. An English translation of the letter is given below:

> May God in his infinite mercy shower blessings, as numerous as the hairs of your head, upon the glorious seat of your magnanimity, and may the longings of your auspicious heart be crowned with fulfilment and joy.
>
> I believe you have not forgotten me, a child of your family, living long in a distant land, and I hope also that you have not forgotten my name. I am longing to get messages of your welfare. This solicitude is accompanied by my recital of your virtues in a hundred thousand ways, and my salutation at your noble feet.
>
> My second message relates to the fact that we are all well in this place. I pray to the merciful God day and night for your welfare, and I desire that He may be propitiously disposed towards you.

210. MS. Assam Buranji No. 6.

This is what I have to say in particular.—I was wrested away from my parents at the age of six, and sent as a present to the Moguls. And now I am nineteen years old, and you have not made any enquiries about my miserable self at any time and on any occasion.

You know well what friends or relatives I have or have not in Hindusthan. I have continued to be a stranger to you all up to this age of nineteen. You, my uncle, used to convey to us your news through your messengers despatched to Hindusthan.

Be it what it may, we are grateful to the merciful God that we have now come to Bengal from Hindusthan, though I have not received any message from you till this day. Meanwhile two Katakis or envoys coming from your place have arrived at the Saheb's court. The articles of present you sent with those trusted emissaries reached our hands in a favourable moment; and they have greatly augmented our prestige and glory in the eye of the men of Hindusthan.

It is now a year since we arrived at Kisirabad [Khizirabad, Khizirpur] in Bengal. The four elephants, beautifully caparisoned and decorated, which you have sent as presents to me and the Begum have been duly received. Through your blessings, I am not short of any article at present. Still then, on account of the presents sent by you, your name and fame, as well as our prestige and honour are shining forth in greater brilliance. I am surprised to hear that the thing you sent with Madhabcharan Brahman and other Katakis has not reached my hands. This article was in addition to the presents despatched by you.

And so I implore you, if you have any affection for me, do please take Moina from here by any means. The Padshahzada in a fit of vexation had confined the Ukils sent by you. It was this very Moina who came to the inner apartments and reported the matter to me. I interceded with the Padshahzada, and succeeded in obtaining the release of the messengers. The Padshahzada was pleased with them, and I got two thanas allotted to the messengers by making a similar request to him.

I have thus informed you as to what a daughter of your family can do under the circumstances. I therefore pray that you should not do this unbecoming act till Moina reaches your place.

The entire message will be communicated to you by Madhab Brahman who has seen and heard many other things here.

You should arrange that I may be in constant receipt of news about your welfare and health. What more could I write?—Bhati, *san* 1599 [*saka*].[211]

211. *Riyazu-s-Salatin,* translated by Salam, p. 175, *f.n.* 2. Bhati was the name of the low-lying flood-exposed area of Bengal extending from Ghoraghat Pergana in Rungpore District to the Sunderbuns. Khizirpur, near Narayangunj, was the chief town of Bhati. It was the naval base, and also the sub-capital of the Bengal Subah. The town Khizirpur was also known as Bhati.

APPENDIX F

LIST OF AHOM KINGS OF ASSAM.

			A.D.
1.	Sukapha	..	1228-1268
2.	Suteupha	..	1268-1281
3.	Subinpha	..	1281-1293
4.	Sukhangpha	..	1293-1332
5.	Sukhrangpha	..	1332-1364
6.	Sutupha	..	1364-1376
	Interregnum	..	1376-1380
7.	Tyao Khamthi	..	1380-1389
	Interregnum	..	1389-1397
8.	Sudangpha, Bamuni-kowanr	..	1397-1407
9.	Sujangpha	..	1407-1422
10.	Suphakpha	..	1422-1439
11.	Susenpha	..	1439-1488
12.	Suhenpha	..	1488-1493
13.	Supimpha	..	1493-1497
14.	Suhungmung, Dihingia Raja]	..	1497-1539
15.	Suklenmung, Gargayan Raja	..	1539-1552
16.	Sukhampha, Khora Raja	..	1552-1603
17.	Susengpha, Pratap Singha, Buddhi-swarganarayan, Burha Raja	..	1603-1641
18.	Surampha, Bhaga Raja, Jayaditya Singha	..	1641-1644
19.	Sutyinpha, Naria Raja	..	1644-1648
20.	Sutamla, Jayadhwaj Singha	..	1648-1663
21.	Supungmung, Chakradhwaj Singha	..	1663-1670
22.	Sunyatpha, Udayaditya Singha	..	1670-1672
23.	Suklampha, Ramadhwaj Singha	..	1672-1674
24.	Suhung, Samaguria Raja, also known as Khamjangia Raja, for 20 days only	..	1674-1675
25.	Gobar Raja, for 20 days only	..	1675

26.	Sujinpha, Arjun, Dihingia Raja II	..	1675-1677
27.	Sudoipha, Parvatia Raja	..	1677-1679
28.	Sulikpha, Ratnadhwaj Singha, Lora Raja	..	1679-1681
29.	Supatpha, Gadadhar Singha	..	1681-1696
30.	Sukhrungpha, Rudra Singha	..	1696-1714
31.	Sutanpha, Siva Singha	..	1714-1744
32.	Sunenpha, Pramatta Singha	..	1744-1751
33.	Surampha, Rajeswar Singha	..	1751-1769
34.	Sunyeopha, Lakshmi Singha	..	1769-1780
35.	Suhitpangpha, Gaurinath Singha	..	1780-1795
36.	Suklingpha, Kamaleswar Singha	..	1795-1811
37.	Sudingpha, Chandrakanta Singha, first time	..	1811-1818
38.	Purandar Singha	..	1818-1819
39.	Chandrakanta Singha, second time	..	1819-1821

1821-1824, Burmese rule, with the puppet Ahom monarch Jogeswar Singha on the throne.

1824. British conquest of Lower Assam.

1825. British conquest of Upper Assam.

1826, February 24, Treaty of Yandabo, by which the king of Burma ceded Assam to the British.

1833, April, Raja Purandar Singha installed as tributary ruler of Upper Assam.

1838, October, resumption of the territories of Raja Purandar Singha by the East India Company.

APPENDIX G

BIBLIOGRAPHY

ENGLISH :

BATAVIA DAGH REGISTER, ANNO 1663, compiled by J. A. van der Chijs, 1891. Dutch merchants' interest in Mir Jumla's return from Assam.

BERNIER, FRANCOIS. *Travels in the Mogul Empire,* edited by Archibald Constable. Second edition, Oxford University Press. London, 1916.

BEVERIDGE, H., AND BAINI PRASHAD. English translation of *Maasir-ul-Umara* of Shah Nawaj Khan and Abdul Hayy. Vol. I, Asiatic Society of Bengal. Calcutta, 1911-1941, Vol. II, 1952.

BHUYAN, SURYYA KUMAR. *Lachit Barphukan and His Times,* or a history of the Assam-Mogul conflicts of 1667-1671. Gauhati, 1947.

— *Annals of the Delhi Badshahate,* being an English translation of an old Assamese chronicle *Padshah-Buranji* with Introduction and Notes. Gauhati, 1947.

— *Anglo-Assamese Relations,* 1771-1826. Gauhati, 1949-50.

— *Mir Jumla and Ram Singha in Assam.* Journal of Indian History, Madras, December 1926.

— *New Lights on Mogul India from Assamese Sources,* and *Annals of the Delhi Badshahate.* Published as serials in Islamic Culture, Hyderabad, Deccan, in 1928-29 and 1933-34 respectively. Incorporated in *Annals of the Delhi Badshahate,* Gauhati, 1947.

— *Assam in the Eighteenth Century,* being Dr. J. P. Wade's *Geographical Sketch of Assam,* compiled in 1792-1800; edited from a manuscript in the India Office Library, London. Published as a serial in *Assam Review,* Silchar, 1928-29.

— *Shivaji Maharaja from Assamese sources,* in Shivaji Nivandhavali, Part II. Siva-charitra Karyyalaya, Poona.

— *Atan Buragohain Rajmantri Dangaria.* Cotton College Magazine, Gauhati, Vol. IX, Part 3, and Vol. X, Part I, March and September 1931.

— *Lachit Barphukan*, being a summary of the paper read at the first session of the All-India Modern History Congress held at Poona in June 1935. Proceedings of the session, published in October 1938 by Prof. Datta Vaman Potdar, Poona.

— *Account of Assam,* compiled in 1807-1814 by Dr. Francis Hamilton, formerly Buchanan, edited from a copy in the India Office Library, London, Gauhati, 1940.

BHATTACHARYYA, S. N. *A History of Mogul North--East Frontier Policy.* Calcutta, 1929.

BLOCHMANN, HENRY. *Kuch Bihar and Assam*, with translations of portions of the *Fathiyya-i-Ibriyya* and other Persian chronicles. Journal of the Asiatic Society of Bengal, 1872, Part I, No. 1.

BORA, M. I. *Baharistan-i-Ghaybi*, or a history of the Mogul wars in Assam, Cooch Behar, Bengal and Orissa, by Mirza Nathan. Translated from the original Persian. In two volumes. Gauhati, 1936.

BURN, SIR RICHARD, editor. *The Cambridge History of India,* Volume IV, Mughal Period. London, 1937.

CUNNINGHAM, J. D. *A History of the Sikhs.* Edited by H. O. L. Garrett, Oxford University Press. London, 1918.

DESHPANDE, BABA SAHEB. *The Deliverance and Escape of Shivaji the Great from Agra,* Poona, 1929.

GAIT, SIR EDWARD. *A History of Assam,* Calcutta, 1906, 1926.

— *Koch kings of Kamarupa.* J.A.S.B., 1893, Part I, No. 1.

— *Report on the Progress of Historical Research in Assam,* Shillong, 1897.

GLANIUS. *A Relation of an Unfortunate Voyage to the Kingdom of Bengala,* London, 1682.

GRANT-DUFF, JAMES. *A History of the Mahrattas,* in three volumes, Calcutta, 1912.

HODIVALA, S. H. *Studies in Indo-Muslim History,* Bombay, 1939.

IRVINE, WILLIAM. *Later Moguls,* 1707-1739. In two volumes, Calcutta, 1922.

KINCAID, C. A. and PARASNIS, D. B. *A History of the Mahratta People,* Vol. I, Oxford University Press, 1918.

MACAULIFFE, MAX ARTHUR. *The Sikh Religion.* In six vols. Oxford, 1909. Volume IV contains the life of Guru Teg Bahadur.

MANUCCI, NICCOLAO. *Storia do Mogor,* translated by William Irvine. In four volumes. London, 1907.

SARKAR, JADUNATH. *Assam and the Ahoms in* 1660. Translation of a part of *Fathiyya-i-Ibriyya.* Journal of the

Bihar and Orissa Research Society, Patna, Vol. I, Part II, December, 1915.

— *Mir Jumla's invasion of Assam*, being the relevant portion of Glanius's Dutch chronicle. *Bengal: Past and Present*, Calcutta, Vol. XXIX, Part I, January-March, 1925.

— *History of Aurangzib*, Vol. III, Calcutta, 1916.

— *Shivaji and His Times*, Calcutta, 1919.

— *Fall of the Mughal Empire*, 1739-1803. In four volumes, Calcuta, 1922-54.

— *Short History of Aurangzib*, Calcutta, 1930, 1954.

— Edited by, *History of Bengal*, Vol. II, Muslim Period, Dacca University, 1948.

SARKAR, JAGADISH NARAYAN. *Life of Nawab Mir Jumla*, Calcutta, 1951.

SEN, SURENDRA NATH. *Siva Chhatrapati*, being a translation of Sabhasad Bakhar, etc., Calcutta, 1920.

SHIHABUDDIN TALISH. *Fathiyya-i-Ibriyya*, or victories that give warning. An official diary of Mir Jumla's invasion of Cooch Behar and Assam, 1661-1663. See under Henry Blochmann and Jadunath Sarkar.

SHARMA, SRIRAM. *The Religious Policy of the Moguls*. Oxford University Press, London and Calcutta, 1940.

— *Maharana Pratap*. D. A. V. College Historical Monographs, No. I, Lahore.

— *Bibliography of Mughal India*, Lahore, 1939.

SINGH, ARJUN. *Relations of the Sikh Community with Assam*. Gauhati, 1946.

SINHA, H. N. *Rise of the Peshwas*, Allahabad, 1931.

SMITH, SIR V. *Akbar, the Great Mogul*, Oxford, 1926.

STEWART, CHARLES. *The History of Bengal*, Calcutta, 1910.

TAVERNIER, JEAN-BAPTISTE. *Travels in India*, edited by V. Ball. In two volumes, Oxford University Press, 1925.

TOD, LT.-COL. JAMES. *The Annals and Antiquities of Rajasthan*. Madras, 1880, Vol. II deals with Amber.

TAKAKHAV, N. S., and KELUSKAR, K. A. *The Life of Shivaji Maharaj*, Bombay, 1921.

VAIDYA, C. V. *Shivaji, the Founder of Maratha Swaraj*, Poona, 1931.

VALENTYN, FRANCOIS. *Oud en Nieuv Oost-Indien*. In five volumes, Amsterdam, 1726. Volume V contains a map of Hindustan, prepared by Matthew van der Brouke, showing 'Azo' and 'Chamdhara' in Assam.

VANSITTART, HENRY. *A Description of Assam from the Alamgirnama of Muhammad Kazim*. Asiatick Researches, Vol. II, London, 1807.

ASSAMESE:

BARDOLOI, KIRTINATH. *Sandipika*. Jorhat, 1933.

BARGOHAIN, KHETRADHAR. *Lachitar Kahini*. Avahan, Calcutta, Vol. V.

BARUA, INDIBAR. *Jivanadarsa*. Sibsagar, 1889.

BARUA, KESABKANTA. *Baniya-Kakatir Vamsavali-sar*, Part I, Sibsagar, 1913.

BARUA, SARVESWAR. *Lachit Barphukan*, inserted in Srijut Padmanath Gohain-Barua's *Jivani-samgraha*, Part I, Tezpur, 1946.

BHUYAN, SURYYA KUMAR. *Mir Jumlar Assam akraman*. Gauhati, 1956.

— *Ramani Gabharu*, a sketch of Rahmat Banu Begum, consort of Sultan Azamtara, son of Emperor Aurangzeb. Gauhati, 1951.

— *Buranjir Vani*, containing sixteen historical articles. Gauhati, 1951, 1955, 1956.

— Presidential speech at the anniversary of Lachit Barphukan held at Jhanji on February 26, 1956.

— *Saraighatar subachani*, or notable sayings and observations of Assamese leaders during the conflicts with the Moguls, 1663-1671. Ready for the press.

— *History of King Rajeswar Singha*. Banhi, Gauhati, Vols. XV and XVI. Enlarged version ready for the press.

CHAUDHURY, SONARAM. *Kanai-barasi-boa-silar phali*. Alochani, Dibrugarh, Vol. VIII.

GOSWAMI, HEMCHANDRA. *Saraighatar yuddha*. Usha, Tezpur, Vol. I; and also in Alochani, Dibrugarh, Vol. VIII.

— *Barphukanar jayastambha*. Alochani, Dibrugarh, Vol. VIII.

— *Kanai-barasi-boa-silar gadya*. Alochani, Dibrugarh, Vol. VIII.

GOSWAMI, SARATCHANDRA, editor. *Niti-latankur*, an old Assamese treatise on warfare. Gauhati, 1940.

LEKHARU, UPENDRA CHANDRA. A list of the military outposts and fortifications of Assam, compiled about 1681 A.D., Avahan, Calcutta, Vol. II.

SAIKIA, BHRAMAR CHANDRA. *Buranji-kanika*, or historical tit-bits. Banhi, Gauhati, Vols. XIII and XIV.

SHARMA, BENUDHAR. *Bangamua apadiya nau-yatra*, being a translation of Glanius's Dutch chronicle. Gauhati, 1956.

— *Phul-chandan*. Milan, Calcutta, Vol. V, Sarat number, Bhadra, 1849 *saka*.

BENGALI:

AMANATULLA AHMED, KHAN CHAUDHURY. *A History of Cooch Behar*, Vol. I, Cooch Behar, 1936.

BHUYAN, SURYYA KUMAR. A Review of Haliram Dhekial Phukan's *Asam Deser Itihas*, in the Journal of the Bangiya Sahitya Parishat, Calcutta, Vol. XXXIII, No. I, B.S. 1333.

PHUKAN, HALIRAM DHEKIAL. *Asam Deser Itihas*. Samachar Chandrika Yantra, Calcutta, 1829.

ASSAM BURANJIS

The Buranjis are contemporary Assamese chronicles compiled under the supervision of state officials from records deposited in the government archives. The Buranjis, even when they cover the same periods or events, are not mere replicas of one another, and each Buranji contains fresh materials not recorded elsewhere. For further information, the reader may refer to Dr. S. K. Bhuyan's paper *Assamese Historical Literature*, published in *The Indian Historical Quarterly*, Calcutta, for September 1929, and incorporated in his *Studies in the Literature of Assam*, 1956.

PUBLISHED ASSAM BURANJIS

(i) *English translations*:

BARUA, RAI SAHIB GOLAP CHANDRA,—*Ahom Buranji*, from the earliest times to the British occupation of Assam. Ahom text in Ahom script with parallel English translation. Shillong, 1930.

BHUYAN, S. K.,—*Tungkhungia Buranji*, from 1681 to 1826, being a translation of Srinath Duara Barbarua's chronicle, with prefatory and supplementary chapters, Glossary, Genealogical Tables, Index, etc. Oxford University Press, for D.H.A.S., 1933.

—— *Annals of the Delhi Badshahate*, being a translation of the Assamese chronicle *Padshah-Buranji*. Published as a serial in Islamic Culture, Hyderabad, Deccan, from July 1933 to July 1934. Since published in book-form by the D.H.A.S., 1947.

WADE, DR. JOHN, PETER, — *Account of Assam,* being mainly a translation of a Buranji in Ahom and of another in Assamese. Compiled in 1792-1800. Edited by Srijut Benudhar Sharma, Sibsagar, 1927.

(ii) ***Assamese texts, with Prefaces and Introductions in English*** :

EDITED BY S. K. BHUYAN,—*Assam Buranji,* from 1228 to 1826 A.D. An enlarged version of the chronicle by Radhanath Barbarua and Kasinath Tamuli Phukan, by Harakanta Barua Sadar-Amin. D.H.A.S., Gauhati, 1930.

Kamrupar Buranji, dealing with Assam-Mogul conflicts with chapters on ancient Kamarupa, and 18 diplomatic epistles. D.H.A.S., Gauhati, 1930.

Deodhai Assam Buranji, a collection of old chronicles dealing with earlier Ahom history, neighbouring tribes, Ahom customs, etc. D.H.A.S., Gauhati, 1932.

Asamar Padya-Buranji, two metrical chronicles of Assam, 1679-1819, by Dutiram Hazarika and Bisweswar Vaidyadhipa respectively. D.H.A.S., Gauhati, 1932.

Tungkhungia Buranji, 1681 to 1806, by Srinath Duara Barbarua, D.H.A.S., Gauhati, 1932.

Kachari Buranji, a chronicle of Cachar from the earliest times to 1714. D.H.A.S., Gauhati, 1936, 1951.

Jayantia Buranji, a chronicle of Jayantia from the earliest times to 1744. D.H.A.S., Gauhati, 1937.

Tripura Buranji, or *Tripura Desar Katha,* an account of Tripura with special reference to the events of 1710-1715, by Ratna Kandali and Arjun Das Bairagi, the two ambassadors of King Rudra Singha to the Tripura court. From the original manuscript in the British Museum, London. D.H.A.S., Gauhati, 1938.

Assam Buranji, from the earliest times to 1694, from a manuscript obtained from the family of Sukumar Mahanta. D.H.A.S., Gauhati, 1945.

Padshah-Buranji, a chronicle of the Muslim rulers of Delhi, from the establishment of Muslim supremacy to Maharaja Jai Singha II of Jaipur. Kamarupa Anusandhan Samiti, Gauhati, 1935.

EDITED BY SARAT KUMAR DUTTA,—*Assam Buranji*, from Swargadeo Jayadhwaj Singha to the accession of Swargadeo Gadadhar Singha, 1648-1681. D.H.A.S., Gauhati, 1938.

EDITED BY HEMCHANDRA GOSWAMI,—*Purani Assam Buranji*, from the earliest times to Swargadeo Gadadhar Singha. Kamarupa Anusandhan Samiti, Gauhati, 1922.

MANUSCRIPT ASSAM BURANJIS

A complete list of the manuscript Assam Buranjis, used in the compilation of *Atan Buragohain and His Times*, is given below. Some of these Buranjis have been published, while others are still unpublished. The original manuscripts are mostly deposited in the library of the Department of Historical and Antiquarian Studies in Assam. The serial numberings of the Buranjis have been followed in the footnotes of this book:—

1. Buranji-viveka-ratna, Part II, or Assam Buranji by Maniram Datta Dewan Barbhandar Barua, political, administrative and ecclesiastical. MS. obtained from Shrishri Troilokyasobhan Chandra Goswami, Sarujana Dihing Satradhikar, North Gauhati.

2. Assam Buranji by Padmeswar Singh Naobaicha Phukan, from the earliest times to the advent of the British, with chapters on Ahom institutions and customs. MS. obtained from Shri Chandreswar Singha Naobaicha Phukan, Sibsagar.

3. A collection of 192 diplomatic epistles exchanged between the Ahom court and the courts of Delhi, Dacca, Cooch Behar, Jayantia and Cachar, compiled from contemporary Assamese chronicles. Transcript obtained from the office of the Commissioner, Assam Valley Division, Gauhati.

4. List of the fortifications, ramparts and outposts on both banks of Gauhati, and other places of military importance in Assam, compiled in the 17th century. MS. obtained from Shri Upendra Chandra Lekharu, North Gauhati.

5. From the accession of Pratap Singha in 1603, to the nomination of Prince Gadapani to the throne at Kaliabar in 1681. MS. obtained from the family of Pundit Hemchandra Goswami, Gauhati.

6. Historical letters between the Ahom and Mogul courts, with narrative interludes, from the treaty of 1639 to

the reception of Mogul Ukils from the Thanadar of Rangamati in 1739. MS. obtained from the family of Pundit Hemchandra Goswami, Gauhati.

7. From the earliest times to the expulsion of the Moguls from Gauhati in 1682, with miscellaneous accounts, and diplomatic epistles. MS. obtained from the family of Pundit Hemchandra Goswami, Gauhati.

8. From the earliest times to King Chakradhwaj Singha, with diplomatic letters exchanged between the Ahom and Cooch Behar courts. MS. obtained from the family of Pundit Hemchandra Goswami, Gauhati.

9. Miscellaneous events and episodes, *e.g.*, origin of Kacharis, Jayantias, Naras and Chutias; early Ahom kings; rulers of Cooch Behar; letters between Assam and Cooch Behar; together with a chapter on the foundation of Muslim supremacy in India, and a list of the rulers of Delhi, from Yudhisthira to Alamgirshah Padshah. MS. obtained from Ahom Juvak Sanmilon.

10. Reigns of Jayadhwaj Singha and Chakradhwaj Singha. Transcript obtained from Shri Umanath Gohain, Jorhat.

11. Legendary kings of Kamarupa; Cooch Behar princes; Ahom kings from Khunlung-Khunlai to Rudra Singha; and a list of the Hindu kings of Delhi from Yudhisthira to Hari Singha, *saka* 537. MS. obtained from India Office Library, London.

12. Ram Singhar Yuddhar Katha, or an eye-witness's account of the war with the Mogul general Raja Ram Singha. MS. obtained from Shri Nagendra Nath Gogoi, Cherekapar, Sibsagar.

13. Account of different Ahom *phoids* or clans, with lists of officers and royal matrimonial alliances in the respective reigns of Ahom sovereigns. MS. obtained from Shri Ripunath Buragohain, Dilihial Gohaingaon, Sibsagar.

14. From the creation of Brahman Katakis in Pratap Singha's reign to the nomination of Prince Gadapani to the throne at Kaliabar in 1681. MS. obtained from Shri Ratneswar Phukan, Cinnamara, Jorhat.

15. From Suhungmung Dihingia Raja to King Pramatta Singha, 1497-1751 A.D. MS. obtained from Shri-shri Satradhikar Goswami of Bengena-ati Satra, Majuli.

16. From the reign of Jayadhwaj Singha to Rudra Singha's Kachari campaign. MS. obtained from American Baptist Mission, Gauhati.

17. Lai-lit Buranji, being a translation of an Ahom chronicle, dealing with later Ahom rule. MS. obtained from late Shri Nandanath Deodhai Phukan, Akhoya-Deodhaigaon, Sibsagar.

18. Belimarar Buranji, or a metrical chronicle of the conflicts with the Moamarias and the Burmese, by Visweswar Vaidyadhipa. MS. obtained from Shri Anandiram Gohain, Morigaon, Nowgong.

19. Rajniti, being a manual of the functions, insignias, and precedence of the officers and nobles of the Ahom government. MS. obtained from Shri Anandiram Gohain, Morigaon, Nowgong.

20. From the earliest monarch Swarga-narayan-deva to King Gadadhar Singha, with supplementary matters, *e.g.*, principal Ahom clans; origin of the Naras, Mantaras, Kacharis, Jayantias and Chutias; and the sacred hills and shrines at Gauhati and its neighbourhood. MS. obtained from the family of Sukumar Mahanta, North Gauhati.

21. Assam-Koch relations from Biswa Singha, and Assam-Mogul conflicts upto the final expulsion of the Moguls from Gauhati in 1682. Manuscript obtained from American Baptist Mission, Gauhati.

22. From Khunlung and Khunlai to the death of Naria Raja in 1648 A.D., dates mentioned according to Ahom Taosingas and Laklis. MS. obtained from American Baptist Mission, Gauhati.

23. From the end of Rajeswar Singha's reign to the first few years of Lakshmi Singha's reign. MS. obtained from American Baptist Mission, Gauhati.

24. Lailik Buranji, a fragment describing Ahom reaction to King Rudra Singha's acceptance of Saktaism. Transcript obtained from Shri Umanath Gohain, Jorhat.

25. Kalibharat Buranji, or a metrical chronicle of Assam by Dutiram Hazarika, from Lora Raja to the execution of Maniram Dewan, 1677-1858. MS. obtained from Asam Sahitya Sabha, Jorhat.

26. Assam Buranji by Radhanath Barbarua and Kashinath Tamuli Phukan, enlarged version by Harakanta Barua Sadar-Amin. MS. obtained from late Promodkanta Barua, North Gauhati.

27. Datiyalia Buranji. Assam's relations with vassal chiefs of the plains frontier, Sat-rajias and Panch-rajias. MS. obtained from Shri Mohar Singh Deka, Barkolagaon, Nowgong.

28. Account of the well-known Assamese Daivajna family, Sonamua Mayur Mazumdarar Ghar, by Harakanta Barua Sadar-Amin. MS. obtained from late Promodkanta Barua, North Gauhati.

29. Relations between Assam and Cooch Behar, with diplomatic letters, and Ahom-Kachari and Ahom-Jayantia relations upto King Rudra Singha's reign. MS. obtained from the family of Pundit Hemchandra Goswami, Gauhati.

30. Jayantia Buranji, from the legendary origin of the Jayantia Rajas to Assam-Jayantia relations of King Rudra Singha's reign. MS. obtained from the family of Pundit Hemchandra Goswami, Gauhati.

31. From Khora Raja to King Rudra Singha, with accounts of the relations of Assam with Cooch Behar, Jayantia, Cachar and Mogul India. MS. obtained from the family of Pundit Hemchandra Goswami, Gauhati.

32. Buranji by Atan Buragohain Rajmantri Dangaria, from the earliest Ahom rulers to King Pratap Singha. MS. obtained from the family of Pundit Hemchandra Goswami, Gauhati.

33. Tungkhungia Buranji by Srinath Duara Barbarua, from King Rajeswar Singha to the first nine years of Kamaleswar Singha's reign. MS. obtained from the family of Pundit Hemchandra Goswami, Gauhati.

34. Abstract of the events of the reign of Suhungmung Dihingia Raja to that of King Rudra Singha, with copious dates. MS. obtained from Shri Chidananda Bezbarua, Nazira.

35. Changrung Phukanar Buranji, or a manual of construction, relating to royal camps, materials necessary, landmarks, *viz.*, Alikekuri Pukhuri, Jaisagar Pukhuri, Madhava temple at Hajo; Umananda temple, and Aswakranta temple at Gauhati. MS. obtained from Shri Nagendra Nath Gogoi, Cherekapar, Sibsagar.

36. List of Ahom kings, and their respective Patramantris, *viz.*, Buragohain, Bargohain, Barpatra Gohain, Barbarua and Barphukan. MS. obtained from Shri Nagendra Nath Gogoi, Cherekapar, Sibsagar.

37. Relations of Assam with the Koches, Kacharis and the Jayantias. MS. obtained from Shri Upendra Chandra Lekharu, North Gauhati.

38. Tripura Buranji. Account of Assam's diplomatic missions to Tripura in King Rudra Singha's reign. Compiled by two Assamese ambassadors Ratna Kandali Sarma Kataki

and Arjundas Bairagi. Photostat copy obtained from British Museum, London.

39. From Suhungmung Dihingia Raja to King Gaurinath Singha, 1497-1795 A.D. MS. obtained from Srimati Jayantipriya Devi Medhiani, Barpeta.

40. Miscellaneous events, *viz.*, early history of Kamrupa; early Ahom rulers; Cooch Behar princes, Assam-Mogul wars, conflicts with the Naras, Chutias, Barahis, Morans, Bhuyans, and Koches. MS. obtained from the family of Kaviraj Krishnakanta Adhikari, Gauhati.

41. Diplomatic epistles of the reign of Jayadhwaj Singha and Chakradhwaj Singha, with narrative interludes. MS. obtained from Shri Benudhar Sharma, Charing, Sibsagar.

42. From the earliest Ahom rulers to Mir Jumla's invasion of Assam. MS. obtained from Shri-shri Dakshinpat Satradhikar Goswami, Majuli.

43. From the first monarch born of Indra, to the first stage of Mir Jumla's invasion of Assam. MS. obtained from Shri Benudhar Sharma, Charing, Sibsagar.

44. Dihing Satrar Buranji, in verse, by Dutiram Hazarika, from Gopaldeva to Brindaban Chandra Deva and Ballabh Chandra Deva, Satradhikars of the Satra. Transcript obtained from Shri-shri Troilokyasobhan Chandra Goswami, Sarujana Dihing Satradhikar, North Gauhati.

45. Brief account from Vasistha's penances to the Assam-Kachari conflicts in the reign of Suhungmung Dihingia Raja. Transcript obtained from Shri Bhadra Kanta Gogoi, Golaghat.

46. Reigns of Kamaleswar Singha, Chandrakanta Singha and Purandar Singha upto the resumption of Upper Assam by the British in 1838. Translated by Dr. S. K. Bhuyan, from the English version of an Ahom Puthi. Transcript in English obtained from Shri Umanath Gohain, Jorhat.

47. Account of the four principal Satras of Assam, *viz.*, Auniati, Dakshinpat, Garamur and Kuruavahi, compiled in 1904 by the respective Satradhikar Goswamis. Transcript obtained from Shri Umanath Gohain, Jorhat.

48. Tuklai Buranji. Translation of an Ahom Buranji from King Rajeswar Singha to Prince Brajanath Singha. MS. obtained from Shri Nandanath Deodhai Phukan, Akhoya-Deodhaigaon, Sibsagar.

49. Assam Buranji from Jayadhwaj Singha to the first eight years of King Rudra Singha's reign. Transcript obtained from Shri Anandiram Gohain, Morigaon, Nowgong.

50. Reception of Bhutia and Jayantia envoys at the court of King Kamaleswar Singha, on Choitra 26, 1723 *saka*, and Aswin 10, 1725 *saka*, respectively. MS. obtained from Shri Anandiram Gohain, Morigaon, Nowgong.

51. Reception of Khyrim envoys at the court of Sandikoi Gogoi Barphukan at Gauhati, on Friday, Baisakh 4, 1708 *saka*, from *Assam-Bandhu*, edited by Gunabhiram Barua, Vol. I, No. 9, Aswin, 1807 *saka*.

52. Raja-vamsavali, metrical chronicle of the Koch rulers from legendary times to Harindra Narayan Raja of Darrang, by Ratikanta Dwija. Transcript obtained from Kamarupa Anusandhan Samiti, Gauhati.

53. Darrang-raj-vamsavali, metrical chronicle of the Koch rulers from legendary times to Balinarayan, *alias* Dharmanarayan, Raja of Darrang. MS. obtained from Kumar Bhupendra Narayan Deb, Darrang Raj family, Howli-Mohanpur, Mangaldoi. Illustrated.

54. Heramba-rajamala, or a list of the kings of Heramba or Cachar, from Bhimasena to Janardan Chandra Narayan. Transcript obtained from late Shri Kaliram Medhi, Gauhati.

55. Description of the king's palace at the Ahom capital Rangpur. Transcript obtained from Shri Benudhar Sharma, Charing, Sibsagar.

56. Descent of Khunlung and Khunlai, grandsons of Indra, upon this earth, and names of prominent members of the Bailung *phoid*. Transcript obtained from late Shri Anandiram Gohain, Morigaon, Nowgong.

57. List of the kings of Delhi during Kali-yuga, from Yudhisthira to Alamgirshah Badshah. Transcript obtained from Shri Krishnanath Barua, Chamata, Kamrup.

58. Mussalman Rajar Katha, or *Padshah Buranji*. An account of the Muslim rulers of Delhi. MS. obtained from Shri Benudhar Sharma, Charing, Sibsagar.

59. From Khunlung and Khunlai to the accession of Jayadhwaj Singha in 1648 A.D. MS. obtained from Shri Anandiram Gogoi, North Gauhati.

60. Datiyalia Buranji. Assam's relations with vassal chiefs of the plains frontier, Sat-rajias and Panch-rajias. MS. obtained from Shri Bhumidhar Kakati of Baligaon, Nowgong.

INDEX

THE END

ERRATA

Page	*Line*	*For*	*Please read*
55	23	nor	or
56	11	Purananda	Purnananda
112	12	younger	elder
133	4	Kharangia	Khowangia